Responses to
Self Harm

Responses to Self Harm

*An Historical Analysis of
Medical, Religious, Military
and Psychological Perspectives*

LEIGH DALE

McFarland & Company, Inc., Publishers
Jefferson, North Carolina

Library of Congress Cataloguing-in-Publication Data

Dale, Leigh.
    Responses to self harm : an historical analysis of medical, religious, military and psychological perspectives / Leigh Dale.
        p.   cm.
    Includes bibliographical references and index.

    ISBN 978-0-7864-9675-4 (softcover : acid free paper) ∞
    ISBN 978-1-4766-1925-5 (ebook)

    1. Self-mutilation—History.   I. Title.
RC552.S4D35 2015
362.2'7—dc23   2015008758

British Library cataloguing data are available

Front cover © 2015 Shutterstock

Printed in the United States of America

McFarland & Company, Inc., Publishers
  Box 611, Jefferson, North Carolina 28640
    www.mcfarlandpub.com

For Sarah Ferber

Contents

Acknowledgments

I thank the Australian Research Council (ARC) and its Discovery Grant Program for funding the project "Alien Selves" (2004–2006; DP0449594); Veronica Kelly for invaluable advice in preparing the successful application; Robyn Dale (Italian), Helen Ferber (German), Helen Bode (Spanish) and Sarah Ferber (French and Russian) for their assistance with translations and transliteration; and Helen Bode and Amanda Lynch for exemplary research assistance. I owe a debt to colleagues in libraries and archives I have been privileged to work in, including public libraries in Chicago, and London. The American University and Georgetown Universities in Washington, the University of Illinois at Chicago, and the University of Texas at Austin had unexpectedly rich caches of resources, as did the Austin City Library, the Bodleian Library, the British Library, and the Library of Congress. Colleagues in Interlibrary Loans at the University of Queensland and at the University of Wollongong have been efficient and skillful. Thanks to Andrew Clark for permission to quote from his letter to the *British Medical Journal* 30 March 2002.

I need to thank the very large number of students, colleagues, friends, family and strangers who have made essential contributions to this research by drawing countless works on self harm to my attention. They have also discussed self harm as they have experienced it directly, or via personal and professional relationships with those who self harm. I am grateful to the members of the Moggies, a medical humanities discussion group at the University of Queensland convened by Dr. Sally Wilde, for cheerily scathing responses to drafts of chapters, and to Jennifer McDonell, for snapping at my heels when completion seemed a long way off. I thank my colleagues at the University of Queensland and at the University of Wollongong for their intellectual generosity. Thanks in particular to Tim Chandler, Guy Davidson, Sarah Ferber, Jo Robertson and Ika Willis, who read chapters at a late stage, and Greg Ratcliffe and Chris Tiffin for a very careful read. Thanks also to Chris for the index. Special thanks to Jo Robertson, for illuminating views on the ways medical knowledge moves between popular, scholarly, and historical domains, and Samantha Allender for discussion of her research. Louise Wilson, my (medical) doctor, has been kind enough to show interest in this project in its various forms, has generously answered many questions, and provided one of the more unusual referrals in medical practice. I also want to thank, in particular, those writers who have experienced self harm and who have written autobiographical and academic studies, many of whose work is cited herein.

Almost every writing project has an interlocutor, a person with whom ideas are tested, developed, challenged and winnowed. Such a role involves maintaining faith in the idea and the author. I thank Sarah Ferber for her support for this long-running project, for the example of her scholarship on the history of religion and on medicine, and for her own research which enabled me to spend additional time on the project in Austin and in Oxford. Her academic standards and her companionship have influenced this book at every stage. I can never thank her sufficiently for spotting the career-ending typographical error.

Notwithstanding this array of support, I take responsibility for all remaining errors, as well as the sometimes polemical lines of interpretation offered here.

Preface

When the American Psychiatric Association (APA) released the fifth edition of its *Diagnostic and Statistical Manual of Mental Disorders* in May 2013, the *DSM V*—a globally influential reference work for those working in mental health—it included for the first time what it termed "non-suicidal self injury" (NSSI). This inclusion was preceded by a brief debate about whether or not self harm was associated with postmodern Western societies, or whether it was an historical phenomenon (Gilman). Debate about self harm is centuries old, but it began to take its modern shape in the second half of the twentieth century, when writers in various medical fields began to claim to have identified distinctive syndromes.[1] This book contributes to that debate, as a study of narratives about extreme forms of physical self harm, in particular amputations of limbs or genitalia, or removal of the eye(s). As a history and historiography of representations of self harm, it is a critical study of the ways representations of self harm have circulated in academic cultures. Its focus is not the causes of self harm, nor the stories of those who engage in it, but the ways in which professional cultures of different kinds represent self harm in their scholarly literatures. From the analyses of those sources, and in opposition to the claims of the *DSM V*, it comes to the conclusion that self harm is not a specific form of illness, nor is it "a behavior that typifies a specific diagnosis" (Lang and Sharma-Patel 23).

My research began in 1997. It was prompted by reading a novel by David Foster, *The Glade Within the Grove*, which had just won Australia's most prestigious literary prize, the Miles Franklin Award. The centerpiece of the story is when the quasi-mythical protagonist, Attis MacAnaspie, cuts off his penis. I drew my own conclusions, expressed in a review of the book, but Foster's centralizing of emasculation stayed in my mind. The following year, due to a late switch in teaching duties, I had to teach another contemporary Australian novel, *The Jesus Man* by Christos Tsiolkas, in which the same thing happened:

1

a young man cut off his penis and died as a consequence. If the recurrence struck me as unusual, it also seemed odd that two writers seeking to take a position in contemporary cultural debates about the status of masculinity would use the same plot device (removal of the penis) and theme (the destruction of masculinity) to opposing political ends (see Dale). Both novels are part of a trend that Katherine Bode identifies as a crisis of the male body in Australian culture. Tsiolkas, working from a Marxist perspective, finds male decline a consequence of industrial change and the paring back of opportunities for working-class men. Foster, socially conservative, identifies the causes of debilitation as feminism and cultural pluralism. Tsiolkas, too, sees loss, but for him cultural pluralism and feminism are sources of hope and energy; the debilitation comes from the changing structure of the labor market. All this seems rather obvious, as a collision between right- and left-wing politics. But at the time it also seemed implausible, at some level, for one man (let alone two) to commit suicide this way—even in fiction. And as it turns out, men do *not* usually die if they cut off their penis.[2]

In my efforts to understand the self harm that is the heart of these novels, I looked for scholarship in my own field and the adjacent ones to which literary scholars routinely turn: cultural studies, history and sociology. There was a small amount of material in sociology and in cultural studies, but it did not deal with cases as severe as these; the focus was on practices termed "body modification" which seemed to be working to quite different ends (Sullivan). The reading snowballed: I soon found myself sitting in medical libraries reading hundreds of the many thousand case reports of patients who had inflicted the same or equally serious injuries. And talking to friends and colleagues, I began to hear stories which suggested that many incidents never make it into writing. For example, one friend told me of a case involving a child, under the age of ten, who was admitted to a hospital in which she had worked, after he had cut off his penis. This kind of anecdote resonated with case reports from a century ago which describe young boys inflicting horrible injuries on their own genitalia (Kellock). The many published studies of self harm which implied or suggested that it was a practice specific to the second half of the twentieth century, and one dominated by women, came into question early on.

Self harm was not then very common in fiction and related forms such as drama and poetry, but there are now dozens of texts, particularly teen fiction, in which it is the centerpiece. In fact the two novels with which I began were part of a wave of fiction, film, and television programs in which the plot centered on self injury. But having realized that the novels I had reviewed and taught were merely amplifying a known phenomenon, I found that the scholarly literature from medicine did not provide the kind of insights that would allow me to discuss the representation of self harm in fiction. Reports by doctors of specific instances tended to offer only brief or implausible speculations on how self harm might be interpreted. My search for an "analytical" literature—large-scale studies or extended discussions of individual or groups of cases—led to disciplines like criminology, psychiatry and psychology. Bibliography, identifying and obtaining source materials, became a bit of an obsession. Developing discipline-specific genealogies of understandings of self harm entailed tracking down hundreds of articles and monographs that had dropped out of sight, albeit now often available on the web.

Psychoanalysis seemed to offer the most promising leads in relation to interpretation, but I was also drawn into reading in medical fields in which there was strong interest in self harm, such as dermatology, as well as topics in medical history, notably the First World War. This reading revealed such an astonishing degree of differences in approach and argument that those differences started to become a point of interest. This interest in differences of approach and understanding increased as I began to hit literatures which offered mechanistic or one-dimensional accounts of the phenomenon. Occasionally, writers within these fields tried to swim against the tide of incomprehension and disapproval routinely proffered in their professional literature; more often, they worked without reference to fields of knowledge that would have been useful. Over time, then, the differences of perspective and the attitudes of writers themselves became part of the problem of researching self harm. Restoring visibility to some key early works also meant trying to show how academic knowledges work within and against each other.

A key argument made here is that the widely varying contexts in which self harm is encountered have led to a fragmentation of academic knowledge, mainly but not only along disciplinary lines. Competing arguments are difficult to see not only because disciplines have their own publishing venues and their own authorities, but their own conceptual tools. As far as current research of self harm goes, it seems clear to me that levels of usage of these conceptual tools better reflects disciplinary convention than it does the efficacy of specific approaches for understanding self harm. Academic institutions build lenses through which cultural practices and illness itself are seen. The study of self harm reveals what some researchers have called the "narrowness of disciplinary fields of vision" (Chandler *et al.* 108).[3]

This book is a kind of "map" for those trying to make sense of categorical but contradictory claims about how to understand those who injure themselves; it is also a map for those who wish to identify the histories of ways of thinking in their own and adjacent academic disciplines. By understanding something of the context in which debates about self harm emerge, and the context in which contributors to those debates have been praised or ignored,

I hope to enable researchers to make more productive use of their time, understanding the positioning taken in key sources. The task I have set myself is to understand the assumptions underpinning the stories doctors and others who observe self harm tell themselves in order to rationalize the patient's behaviors and their own response. Because of the historical impulse there is an emphasis on bibliography, with footnotes used to identify sources used by the writer being quoted, as well as complementary accounts.

Because of the historical and bibliographical focus, emphasis has been put on recovering a "lost" literature of self harm from the nineteenth and early twentieth centuries, and works which for reasons of disciplinary protocols or prejudice have been less visible or seen as less valuable than they might. Numerous works published between 1840 and 1940 address self harm exclusively and at length. However, the conventional view of the history of self harm is that "The first major advance in the modern understanding of self-injury was made by Karl Menninger" in 1938, who argued in his book *Man Against Himself*, "Self-injury represented a sacrifice of one part of the body for the sake of the whole" (Strong 31, 32).[4] Menninger terms this "focal suicide." Another favored approach is to spend a page or two recounting "the history of self-mutilation" in terms provided by Armando Favazza and Barbara Favazza in their field-defining book *Bodies Under Siege* (1987). This, coupled with reference to occasional historical, religious, cross-cultural, and animal studies (e.g., Karpinski 12; Newman 27–29; Mesirow 9; Merenova 5–7; Schmieder 22–23) serves as sufficient introduction before moving on to the "main business" of the research, the present. However, by restoring the early studies to view, we can see that key contributions like *Man Against Himself* and *Bodies Under Siege* in fact continue rather than inaugurate the study of self harm.

The lack of awareness of history shapes the medical and social sense of what self harm is, which is to say, scholars' assumptions about who is likely to harm themselves and the explanations that might be offered. In the most extreme case, it can lead to the assertion that self harm "was virtually unreported until the 1960s" (Bierdrager 1), or that "male genital mutilation has been found in the literature for 20 years, [but] no cases of genital self-injury by females appeared until the last decade" (Cynthia Anne Simpson 18). The loss of history is significant in particular because it is in the second half of the twentieth century that the practice has been associated with women. Thus Adler and Adler claim in their recent monograph, "The past several centuries saw this behavior regarded as a form of psychological pathology, practiced mainly by people, especially young, white, middle-class women, who suffered from mental illness" (*The Tender Cut* 2). As Chandler *et al.* note, the prevalent view "that the typical self-injurer is female (Favazza and Conterio;

Schoppman *et al.*) ... is then reproduced in review articles" (Chandler *et al.* 101). Those review articles do not simply describe fields; in describing, they help to shape them. In historical terms, what such statements allow us to track is the structure of research on self harm, not its practice.

Each of the four chapters of this book focuses on a particular disciplinary mode or set of disciplines. The first chapter, on religious stories of self harm, unplaits the layers of source and commentary on the ancient accounts of self harm cited by (mainly) twentieth-century writers. It is essential to understand the cultural contexts and contested provenance of these ancient stories if we are to understand the significance of the ways in which their re-use can make fixed what was once disputed. Put simply: there are always centripetal and centrifugal forces, the former simplifying and solidifying stories, the latter distributing them, multiplying and reforming them. This has implications for the way we understand some of the most resonant stories of self harm from ancient cultures which are continually retold in modern medical writing. The second chapter analyzes case reports: descriptions by doctors of their work in responding to extreme forms of self harm. It focuses on opening out the differences between doctors in the extent to which their responses to self harm understand volition, the patient's capacity to choose. In essence, this can become a question about how moral judgments interweave with medical ones.

Chapter three extends the focus on these problems of volition and morality in focusing on criminology and military history. It also considers the paradigms of fraud and deception that are also often present in medical discussions of self harm. It shows decisively that self harm has been present in Western cultures for at least the last two centuries. However, under the heading of "malingering," and isolated in overlapping literatures of criminology and military medicine, it has been of little interest to researchers over the last few decades. The final "discipline-based" chapter considers dominant paradigms of self harm in psychiatry and psychology. It examines the ways in which these approaches facilitate the development of more sophisticated models of self harm, but also the ways in which these disciplines can resort to the same uses of generic social categories and stereotypes. While these chapters consider the ways in which the disciplines of the psyche sought to gain control of the terrain of self harm, and the ways in which institutions like the army and the law fought to retain control of those they termed "malingerers" or criminals, when read in conjunction these two chapters show the breadth of the gaps between different forms of expertise.

Increasing contestation within and between the emerging sciences of psychology, psychiatry, and neurology in the late nineteenth and early twentieth centuries, as well as the debates about human behavior they were able to generate, occurred in the context of the spread of specialization in medical treatment, as well as cataclysmic events in Europe in the world wars. The development of belief in the concept of the unconscious (in its various forms) had opened up the possibility that some instances of self injury could be understood as involuntary, a point always in tension with the predominant view that self harm is done for gain. Although few health professionals would now dispute the notion that extreme forms of physical self harm can usefully be thought of in relation to mental illness, this is not always the case, and was unlikely throughout most of the nineteenth century. Thus this book is an analysis of the ways in which forms of medical knowledge are created and affirmed, *as well as* the ways in which they can be discredited and sidelined. This, in turn, suggests a more complex genealogy of concepts of self harm than has so far been offered (Gilman; Millard).

The tools used in this research to produce the analyses of writing about self harm come from literary criticism. Criticism does not rely on using fixed schema to identify elements of a text in the way that content analysis, commonly used in social sciences, does. Content analysis focuses on identifying the frequency and significance of specific elements of language (Hill and Dallos). The data tends to use samples of the same kinds of language as it is used by different speakers or writers. Literary critics, in contrast, tend to focus on texts regarded as unique and complex. Methodologically, criticism works on the very different assumption that we cannot know the best questions to ask of any text(s)—what will generate the most robust and culturally insightful interpretation—until we are familiar with them. There is, therefore, a recursive relationship between the formulation of research questions, and reading itself. Reading—the work of literary criticism—entails determining the meaning of narrative, with reference to its form and its cultural context.

To explain this methodology in its simplest form: literary critics pay attention to what are termed "paratexts" (the surrounding material of a text such as covers and title pages); context (the situations in which texts are written, published, and circulated); narrative form (the structure of a text—its temporal, spatial and characterological arrangement); narrative voice and the distribution of agency (who speaks, about whom, with what knowledge); what kind of language is used (tone, audience, formality); and tropes (such as metaphor, simile, or metonym). Most literary critics would resist the schematizing of their work in this fashion. It is also worth noting that most people use similar skills when they encounter a story, whether it is told by a family member or a famous author—they just do not use this kind of vocabulary to describe what they are doing, and they do not do it in such a systematic and structured way. In discussion with a student who is a medical health professional, we agreed on the similarities between reading and the work of diagnosis and monitoring that accompanies expert care. In her words, it is not (just) the numbers on the chart but the signs of the body and the patient's story that are useful—even smell might be important to getting a sense of what is going on.

No health professional listens to a patient without "reading," or making an interpretation, of the patient's speech as well as their body: are the symbols or signs offered by the body confirmed or contradicted by the patient's speech and behavior? Does the patient seem credible? What view do they have of their illness? What is their capacity to be a "reliable witness" to their symptoms? Are they likely to be exaggerating, forgetting, understating, or foregrounding something irrelevant? Might they simply forget, or want to hide, some key detail? And might they use figurative language—irony, metaphor, metonym, simile—that demands interpretation? Analogously, the work of the literary critic is *interpretation*; we are trained readers. Our scholarship focuses on understanding and elucidating the significance of specific elements of a story; to do it well we need to understand not only the language of the story, but the cultures in which that story is conceived, produced, circulated and responded to. Just because we might disagree on which of these elements are significant or useful does not mean that interpretation is "subjective": the credibility of a reading, like the credibility of a diagnosis, hinges on the extent to which it adequately explains the phenomenon we are describing. Notwithstanding this analogy, it is clear that this method does not entail discussions with patients and/or doctors, let alone responding to people who have harmed themselves in a professional capacity. My respect for both groups has grown as the research has extended. I make these arguments, in spite of that distance, because I believe that specialist reading enables us to have insights that we would not otherwise have had—insights into texts, and insights into cultures in which they have been produced or are now read.

It is true that what we foreground in our reading often reflects our own experiences, training, and intellectual influences. Just as with diagnosis, if we fabricate, misread, or ascribe disproportionate weight to insignificant elements of a text, our reading is likely to be discounted. All readings are contestable. All readings are contestations. There are more and less astute readings, more and less convincing ones. The aim of most forms of interpretation is, in the end, not so much to determine truth or fiction (for all literature is fiction, or so we say) as it is to determine the *basis of authority* and *patterns* which signal the main concerns of the text. When taking a very large body of texts as its subject, as this book does (body, of course, is a metaphor), there is a further challenge. That challenge is to identify the patterns which connect and make sense of the content of and relationships between different kinds of texts. This research, then, is a search for patterns in accounts of self harm written by writers who have seen themselves equipped (or ill-equipped) by specialist knowledge to deal with those who have deliberately injured their own body. In the process of developing an understanding of those narratives and their patterns, I have developed my own views on the ways in which stories of self harm function, and identified some recurrent tropes in these literatures. These speculations are set out in the conclusion.

Sources

Every recent writer on self harm is indebted to Armando and Barbara Favazza, whose study *Bodies Under Siege: Self-Mutilation in Culture and Psychiatry* was published in 1987. The second edition of *Bodies Under Siege*, published in 1996 under the sole authorship of Armando Favazza, is much more widely held in U.S. and other countries' libraries than the first, and is the most cited version of the book. The revisions to the book include a small but suggestive change to the subtitle: *Self-Mutilation and Body Modification in Culture and Psychiatry*. The addition of the term "body modification" shows the influence of research in sociology and cultural studies which aimed to regard self harm positively, particularly when experienced in religious or ritual contexts. A third edition was published in 2011, again with a minor modification to the subtitle, the addition of "Nonsuicidal self-injury," that signalled the consolidation of this shift. In the third edition, "self-mutilation" is frequently replaced with "self-injury" and Fakir Musafar, who contributes the Epilogue to the second and third editions, is praised for being part of "a universally noble tradition in which spirituality is gained by taming the bonds of the flesh": "By conquering pain and transforming his body, he walks on the path to enlightenment" (2011: x).

The source base for this book is the some 5,000 case reports identified by the Medline database, and around 1,500 further references located outside of Medline, many of which were first brought to my attention by *Bodies Under Siege*. I have located additional material through searches of catalogues and visits to libraries in North America and the UK, supplemented by searches of catalogues of European and Pacific rim libraries, and checking the bibliographies of theses on self harm. A very useful set of news and medical clippings on self harm (broadly conceived), particularly covering the first decades of the twentieth century, is in the papers of F. Parkes Weber (1863–1962) held at London's Wellcome Library. Most of these clippings have a hand-written reference; where possible I have verified this. I sought information from federated catalogue systems including Libraries Australia (which links university, state and municipal libraries in Australia); Melvyl, which links the University of California library systems; ILCSO, which links libraries in the state of Illinois; and COPAC (which links UK research libraries), as well as WorldCat and OLIS. To a lesser extent I made use of Aladdin (Washington, D.C., area libraries), BOBcat (downtown Manhattan—NYU, New School, etc.) and the CUNY library system. Many universities and systems require searches of individual libraries, or did at the time when the bibliography was being compiled. Thus, while nearly a hundred theses had been identified via theses catalogues, a further thirty or more, several of them central to the topic, along with a dozen or so crucial and little-known historical studies from the early twentieth century, were identified via smaller library catalogues. This list of references is available from the author upon request.

Introduction

For the purposes of this book, self harm is usually defined as self-inflicted physical injury which prompts medical intervention. Paradigmatic and common forms include amputation of a limb or the genitals, or removal of an eye. Other relatively common forms include severe scarification or abrasion (often with chemicals or fire), and ingestion of dangerous objects (such as needles). These forms of self-injury are significantly less common than the kinds of self harm which have captured the attention of researchers (outside fields like surgery) over the last two decades. This focus means that deliberate injuries to the body are differentiated from other forms of self-abuse—alcoholism, bulimia, anorexia, for example—on the perhaps tenuous basis that the intention to harm the body is more directly experienced. More problematically, particularly for recent commentators like Favazza (1996; 2011), the nature of my source base means that I can be seen as presuming the pathological nature of self harm, although the literatures considered in chapter one do not work this way. The book also includes discussion of a small number of incidents or cases in which "self" harm is inflicted by a third party (e.g., through amputation). These cases are compelling for the ways in which doctors describe their realization that the serious injuries they are treating have been self-inflicted.

The most commonly used term in the nineteenth and twentieth centuries (thence in catalogues and databases) in English has not been self harm but "self-mutilation." And for most of this period the term "malingering" and formulations of "factitious disorders" can encompass deliberate self harm. The shift from "self-mutilation" to "self harm," a less pejorative term, was identified and driven by Favazza's *Bodies Under Siege* (1987; 1996; 2011). Just as the increased visibility of self harm over the last decade seems to have prompted the proliferation of large-scale studies determined to establish prevalence, so the change in terminology has shifted the shape of research: over the last two decades, more physically damaging forms of self harm have been pushed back into the case study literature, as disciplines like psychology focus on the practice of cutting and a wide range of practices are subsumed under increasingly capacious definitions of self-destructive behavior. There has been a further, recent change: in medical writing of the last couple of years the preferred term is "nonsuicidal self-injury" (NSSI), a term now sanctioned by the *DSM V*.[1] Any term which presumes the nature of the relationship of self harm to suicide is problematic.

As the specialist reader will have realized, the definition of self harm used here is therefore simultaneously strict and capacious, having been shaped through interaction with the collections of texts described in the Preface. One of the *aims* of this book is to investigate the contestation of definitions (especially in chapters two and three), and by foregrounding that contestation, show that there are competing understandings of who is ill, and how they should be responded to. Always at issue in discussions of self harm is the question of motivation. As an indication of the degree of difference, in times of war self harm can be seen as a criminal act deserving of the death penalty or as indicative of serious illness demanding hospitalization. In a high school, on the other hand, individual acts might be seen as part of a fad, or indicative of serious mental illness. The difficult work of making judgments about specific individuals—which often hinge, in a sense, on that discernment of "motive" and thence of the level of volition—falls to doctors and others who might be as influenced by their own cultural values (their views, for example, of patriotism, or of teenagers) as they are by medical science. And the medical professional or lay person—prison guard, teacher, military officer—who *misjudges* the situation risks disaster.

Common sense notions about the universality and strength of "instincts" for "self-preservation" might lead lay persons *and* doctors to presume psychosis after the fact of serious self injury. However, one Australian study published in 2012 found that of 41 survivors of self-inflicted stab wounds (selected from 2,119 patients who had been assessed as inflicting deliberate self harm), only 15 were diagnosed with psychotic illness (Gerard *et al.*). On close inspection, many claims that an act of very violent self harm was carried out in a psychotic state turn out to be retrospective, and therefore in some sense speculative. Certainly some studies note the lack of evidence of or uncertainty about psychosis or use of drugs (e.g. Coons *et al.*; Monasterio and Prince; Sinani *et al.*); Greilsheimer and Groves, in a much cited study from 1979, concur. But some writers on self harm are unequivocally of the opposite view. Marc Feldman, for example, who later produced a monograph on the subject, asserts that people "who engage in bizarre, grotesque, or very severe mutilation, such as eye removal or self-castration ... can be assumed to be psychotic, and probably schizophrenic" ("The Challenge" 253). There is little proof for this claim, and in fact there are numerous case reports which contradict such assertions (e.g., Shimizu and Mizuta 188; Wan *et al.*, 287). The latter authors even conclude that their patient's "genital self-mutilation might be considered to have occurred in an appropriate context" (287), seeing logic in the cultural and emotional reasons proffered by their patient.

How common is self harm? Answering such a question opens up the difficulties intrinsic to the definition and reporting of instances. One large-scale study of a non-clinical population in the United States published in 2003 gave self-reported levels of 4 percent (Klonsky *et al.*), whereas a 2007 study of nearly 26,000 people admitted to hospitals in Ireland gave the incidence as closer to 2 percent (Corcoran *et al.*). The latter findings accord more closely with a 2013 study in Australia which found that 2.8 percent of patients admitted to a major hospital for burns had injured themselves deliberately (Henderson *et al.*). Lower rates were found in another, much larger Australian study from 2010 which reported levels of 1.1 percent for self injury among 12,000 participants interviewed by telephone (Martin *et al.*). Some researchers argue that the rates are much higher: a 2012 study claims that "one in twelve teenagers" in Australia harms themselves (Moran *et al.*), and a 2011 study by British and American authors that "rates of [deliberate self harm] among various nonclinical young adult populations rang[e] from 17 percent to 41 percent."[2] Claims such as this, or that "Recent studies of high school populations in the U.S. and Canada reliably show a 13–24 percent prevalence rate" (Brown and Kimball 195), are now routine.[3]

The rates proposed by modern researchers, which push towards 30 or 40 percent of the general population, seem extremely high. They prompt questions about what definition is being used, questions which recur in psychological research, and about whether there is a relationship between the proliferation of mega projects aimed at identifying self harm and its increased visibility in the medical and social policy literature. And the number and size of such studies might even raise the question (as one article title puts it), "Does Screening High School Students for Psychological Distress, Deliberate Self-Harm, or Suicidal Ideation Cause Distress—And Is It Acceptable?" (Robinson *et al.*). (Predictably, albeit against a tidal wave of evidence which links self harm to contagion, these authors find the answer to their second question is "no.") Another large-scale project, the Child and Adolescent Self-harm in Europe Study (CASE) from 2011, surveyed more than 30,000 high school students in Australia, Belgium, England, Hungary, Ireland, the Netherlands, and Norway (see Madge *et al.*). The design and execution of such research signifies the bringing together of new forms of capacity: increased logistical power to collect and analyze large volumes of data; the provision of large amounts of funding for researchers of self harm; and incentives given to international collaboration. The conduct of such studies signals to researchers, policy makers and patients that the identification and management of self harm now has a significant place on the public health agenda.

There is a concurrent trend in patients' rights literature and in sociological and cultural studies to represent self harm as a self-regulatory, therapeutic, or empowering experience.[4] This "new orthodoxy" has influenced policy, medical training, fiction, film and the media, but has not gone uncontested. Newspapers responded quickly and skeptically to the information, for example, that a conference of nurses in the UK in 2006 was holding a session about teaching patients to cut themselves safely, although more balanced writers noted there was debate within medical professions about the best way to respond to self harm (Frith). Taking up the debate, one recent article asks "Can Supervising Self-harm Be Part of Ethical Nursing Practice?" (Edwards and Hewitt). Given the proliferation of stories of self harm in film, fiction and current affairs (including on *Oprah Winfrey*), it is likely that students will have encountered instances or representations of self harm before they enter formal training, and a possibility that these representations or encounters will influence their views.

For professionals working in a range of contexts, self harm at once simplifies and complicates questions of aetiology (causality), diagnosis (discernment of the nature of the illness), and treatment. For example, something might be seen by the patient as sufficient reason for their self harm—cutting off one's penis in order to stop masturbating, for example, or to avoid marriage and fathering children as in cases described by Milne (1914) and Jiménez-Cruz (1995) respectively. However the order of diagnosis and treatment is reversed. The initial crisis of the body, stark in its urgency, must be dealt with first—in the case reported by Milne, when a relative arrives at the hospital carrying a severed organ. In such circumstances, discerning the reasons for self harm might never become part of the medical agenda. And while in some instances it is clear that an injury has been self-inflicted, this might not be the case; the work of discussing the possibility of self harm might be fraught. Thus in many instances, self harm disturbs the sequence of diagnosis and treatment, as well as the relations of power between patient and professional. To seek medical assistance is implicitly or usually to put one's self in the hands of others. But to injure one's body is potentially to know some thing(s) about that injury that professional providers of care might not. The process of discovering or disclosing self harm can be complicated diagnostically and *socially*: it is played out in an uneven, unpredictable, unsettling of the (power) relationship between medical professional and patient. Self harm implicitly prompts the question, who is an expert on discernment of the causes of this injury?

The simplest and least sympathetic interpretation of self harm is that it is self-serving: motivated by the desire for gain in forms that might include attention and sympathy from family or doctors; relief from incarceration or military service; or financial reward, including compensation. Self harm can be seen as something approaching a fashion, proliferating and intensifying in institutions like hospitals, prisons, schools and military units, or as something radically intractable, at the limits of efficacy for almost any form of treatment (see Sanislow *et al.*). One rare longitudinal study of self harm which followed teenagers into adulthood from 1992 to 2008 found that "Most self-harming behavior in adolescents resolves spontaneously" (Moran *et al.*)—which is to say, without intervention. Something similar is implied by a very brief account of an "outbreak" of self harm in a U.S. school which found that the majority of those involved "did not demonstrate any severe overt psychopathology" (Fennig *et al.* 403). These are unpopular views. Christopher Bollas writes of a psychiatric hospital in which an "outbreak" entailed escalating physical damage: "the women have opened a competition, daring each other on, cutting deeper, spreading the wound to the body politic" (137–38). It is necessary to keep in mind that almost opposite things can be true of different cases of self harm and of its proliferation.

Self harm comes to the attention of a range of medical specialists, notably emergency department workers, psychiatrists and psychologists, and surgeons. It is also dealt with by counselors, general practitioners, and nurses in a variety of wards and contexts. Within and between these fields of expertise there are debates about the best way to understand self harm. This debate has been given ethical charge by the fact that patients who injure themselves often provoke a negative reaction in medical and paramedical professionals,[5] and by the fact that patients themselves have widely differing views of their actions. The term "self" harm implies volition. Some and perhaps many medical professionals see those patients as "Neither Ill, Nor Victim," as the title of Rosana Machin's 2009 study of the emergency department of a public hospital in São Paulo puts it. At the very least, many who encounter those who self harm or stories about them are puzzled: graduate researcher Lynnette Whitney writes in 2004, "Self-mutilation is a confounding issue. It is difficult to understand why someone would turn against him/herself and purposely cause pain and injury to his/her own body" (20). Admission to a hospital can present practical difficulties related to categorization and treatment, and leave medical staff feeling unprepared, or believing that other patients are more deserving of priority (Hopkins, writing in 2002). So, too, can friends and family feel out of their depth (Oldershaw *et al.*, from 2008).

As Lois Arnold and Anne Magill comment in their sensible and sensitive handbook *Working with Self-injury* (1996), for any given patient (let alone in any profession or region), "There may be sharply conflicting views within and between groups of professionals as to what approach should be taken" (12). This can imply pressure to produce more severe forms of injury to ensure that the patient's illness is "taken seriously":

> Linked to the lack of understanding [and sympathy in the mental health field] was a sense in which self-harming behavior was sometimes judged as superficial, with workers becoming de-sensitised to the pain and the hurt.... The perverse, no doubt, unintended message that is also being sent to people who cut their arms is that to warrant attention, they will need to harm themselves more dramatically [Chantler *et al.* 70].

These words come from a report on south Asian women in northern England published in 2001. Across the Atlantic, around the same time, an American graduate researcher quoted one of her subjects who justified having resorted to extreme physical self harm after being told she would be returned to her abusive family: "'It got people to listen to me.'" As the researcher points out, her teenage subject "has learned to speak the language of violence that 'they' listen to," but because she has done so knowingly, "it leads Abby to be labelled as 'calculating,' 'manipulative,' 'controlling,' and 'trying to get attention'" (Machoian 70). Many accounts see self harm as an emotionally sophisticated strategy, evidence of "cunning" and control; even self harm by the intellectually disabled can be labelled "attention seeking" (Kirman 1085).

Self harm is not the only form of patient behavior that can prompt a lack of sympathy. One writer recounts the disturbance caused in a set of aligned medical institutions by a patient who had requested surgery for gender reassignment in terms that are similar to patient accounts of being treated after their self harm:

> During presentation of this case to the panel of urologists, there was a tense and somewhat hostile atmosphere.... One of the participants in this discussion, who was actually in favor of surgery, described in detail his feelings of repulsion upon rectally examining another transsexual (after surgical sex reassignment) and finding a prostate in this individual.
>
> On the day of the patient's operation, the procedure was cancelled due to a protest by the head nurse. This resulted in a refusal to perform surgery for administrative reasons. The patient's transfer to another hospital was arranged.
>
> At this other facility, the director of surgery refused to allow the procedure because of a lack of precedence. The decision was left up to municipal authorities and this time permission was granted....
>
> Resistance on the part of medical personnel to the patient's sex reassignment was widespread. Here again, a female nurse contemptuously disclosed the patient's illness to other patients, and refused to provide analgesic medication on the night after surgery.... The nurses who acted out their hostility refused to talk to the author. The majority of those who agreed to discuss the issue expressed feelings that could be summarized as follows: "How does he

dare to be a woman? I have ovaries. I am a woman and he never will be" [Jonas 17].[6]

There is a clear link between disapproval, and the refusal to provide pain relief: pain is seen as an appropriate punishment for wanting to have one's genitalia removed. The question of the patient who is deserving of sympathy and care is discussed in chapter two, but for the moment what I want to note is the anxiety generated by damage or transformation of the body, especially genitalia.

Hostility to those with different sexualities or gender identities—or even just women—is another common element of the literature of self harm. The literature of self harm examined in chapter three, focussing on men in the military and in prison, demonstrates the tendency to react with hostility to men who fail to live up to expectations about masculine behavior or even masculine bodies. Conversely, women who self harm can be derided for behaving in ways seen either as stereotypically feminine (manipulative) or troublingly dissident ("treatment resistant").[7] Some research, especially that by graduate students in the humanities and social sciences, has been underpinned by the desire to challenge stereotypes about female weakness and/or duplicity. For as Barbara Jane Brickman succinctly explained in 2004, "despite recent efforts to change the nature of research on self-mutilation, the model developed by psychiatric studies decades ago ... that pathologizes the female body continues to work in both scientific and popular discourses today" (88). Views about how men and women should behave inform the schadenfreude evident in the story of responses to gender reassignment, as they do in a casual 1969 account of the effect of a lobotomy on a patient that is dropped into a formal academic reply to three essays on self harm. Robert C. Burnham's anecdote begins by describing a group of patients whom he says were "celebrated for years as cutters and swallowers," one of whom "finally provoked a frontal lobotomy" after which she "busied herself with cutting out paper dolls" (224). Burnham does not see this as a new form of cutting, one which eerily re-enacts both the surgery and the "behavior" said to have "provoked" it.

Views about gender-appropriate behavior remain central to debates about self harm and responses to self harm. It is not necessarily "pathologising the female body" or even women's minds to speak about self harm among women. On the other hand, scholars *are* pathologizing women if we assume that there are weaknesses which make women physiologically vulnerable to certain kinds of mental illness, or naturally inclined to self-destructive behavior. Chapter two and chapter four will show such assumptions are prevalent, notwithstanding research like the 1974 study by Evenson *et al.* of more than five thousand reports of "disturbing behaviour," which found that men were four or five times more likely to engage in self-injury than women (271).[8] In this context, it is significant that self harm was long been thought of as a *male* phenomenon, its social epicenters the army and the prison.

The first chapter considers accounts of self harm that can be called "literary," while the second chapter foregrounds a very different genre: the case report. The third chapter shifts to monographs, along with memoir, newspaper stories and case reports, which set out the problems and practices of doctors dealing with self harm in prisons and in wartime. The "battle for the psyche" evident in some of the literature on self harm in the First and Second World Wars becomes the subject of the fourth chapter, which examines historical debates in psychoanalysis which underpin twentieth-century interpretations of self harm. The "founding narratives" of self harm in Western cultures are the religious, poetic and dramatic stories on which nineteenth- and twentieth-century medical authors draw in making sense of their patients. These stories show self harm as being distributed among men and women, and often reify it as a practice associated with the glories of asceticism and the tragedies of alienation. It is to those religious stories that we now turn.

1

Classical and Christian Stories of Self Harm

The key documents in classical and Christian literature pertaining to self harm, and the cultural and religious groups said to be influenced by them, are discussed because they are invoked by patients, and because they inform the medical literature.[1] A third reason is more complex. Self harm seems to have a relationship to metaphor, to be in some sense metaphorical (where A stands in for B) or perhaps synecdochically (where the part stands in for the whole).This kind of understanding is implied in Susan Scheftel's explanation of the actions of the patient Mr. G, who traumatizes an entire hospital (the focus of Sheftel's dissertation). In an evocative description which is the closest Scheftel comes for giving a "reason" for his actions, she writes: "Mr. G's destruction ... can be seen as a kind of symbolic switching point, where dominant life-historical themes emerge" (3). I think what Scheftel means by this is that experiences from Mr. G's childhood and adolescence were replayed, re-formed, and even (paradoxically) controlled, in actions that could be read as catharsis, erasure, re-enactment, and substitution. That these actions then had a devastating effect on the staff of the hospital shows the complex ways in which self harm can reverberate, become its own wave of story *within* in medical cultures. The way in which stories and images are split and reconfigured by the psyche, thereby demanding interpretation, offers a useful metaphor for the ways in which a set of foundational stories about self harm circulate in Western cultures.

As Scheftel's use of the phrase "symbolic switching point" implies, the particular form taken by Mr. G's self harm can be read in terms of condensation and displacement, the transformations of objects, experiences and people into images and events which Sigmund Freud argues are characteristic of meaning-making through dreams.[2] This is part of Freud's larger argument that the unconscious can only be known through proxy. In his essay "The Dream-Work," Freud suggests that the psyche compacts images and experience, leaving a remnant—the dream. Each element of the dream draws upon and signifies multiple elements of the emotional response to experience. Condensation entails repetition, "the formation of new unities (composite persons, mixed images), and the production of common means" (Freud, "Dream-Work"). There is a volatile relationship between elements of the dream and the thoughts to which they refer. The order of importance of these elements can be shuffled, or displaced: "the dream may reject ... intensely emphasized and extensively reinforced elements, and may take up into its contents other elements" (Freud, "Dream-Work"). More crucially perhaps, for considering self harm, "Displacement usually occurs in such a way that a colourless and abstract expression of the dream-thought is exchanged for one that is pictorial and concrete"—in Freud's view, then, our "processing" of emotional reactions at the level of *representation* entails a search for tangible forms.

There are three reasons for introducing Freud's arguments here. The first is to prefigure the reading of self harm that will be proffered in the conclusion. The second is to suggest that literal reading practices are not an adequate scholarly basis for the interpretation of modern stories about self harm (regardless of whether they are "fictional" or "true"). The third suggests that literal reading of mythological accounts of self harm risk, in George Bush's evocative term, "misunderestimating" the complexity of those stories.

Many approaches to self harm are implicitly functionalist, using a basis for interpretation very different to that used by Freud. An example of functionalist thinking might lie in contending, for example, that the proliferation of piercing and tattooing reflects the desire to "return to a primitive way of life" (Grognard). Notwithstanding the claims to more complex modes of interpretation implied by his title, Alan Dundes works in this mode in his book *Bloody Mary in the Mirror: Essays in Psychoanalytic Folkloristics* when he proffers the following account of self harm:

> Though typically adjudged to be bizarre behavior, the various forms of religious self-mutilation represent a perfectly logical thought process, albeit unconscious, manifested in a series of actions designed to attract the favorable notice of a deity which in effect compel him or her to pay attention to the supplicant. Without psychoanalytic theory, these seemingly excessive masochistic practices must remain aberrant behavior apparently totally irrational in nature [11–12].

In Dundes' view, self harm is seen by practitioners as a means of attention seeking, not of families, or doctors, but the gods. This is the deeper meaning of practices that on the surface seem "totally irrational."

Such interpretations establish strict polarities between rational and irrational, conformist and aberrant, benign and malignant forms of divine power and human behavior; they attribute an ultimate logic not to the unconscious but to religious beliefs. The difficulty lies in the presumed separation of religious belief and irrationality; as will be seen, this is problematized in many individual cases of self harm. Functionalist assumptions, and specifically the methodology of "structuralist functionalism," is associated with research into indigenous cultures by an early generation of professional anthropologists including Bronislaw Malinovski and A.R. Radcliffe-Brown, and often retains the traces of ethnographic stereotyping. For functionalist accounts often implicitly position the author as a rational modern observer who is able to discern the "true" reason for self harm as it is practised by primitive or ignorant peoples who lack the observer's capacity for sophisticated thought. This does not explain the continued use of stories from ancient cultures as points of reference in case reports of patients who self harm.

Ethnographies of the Galli

The best-known and most influential story of self harm in ancient Mediterranean cultures, one which circulates frequently in medical literatures, is that of Attis. Attis is said to have been a beautiful young man who castrated himself in order to serve the cult of Cybele, also called Mater or Mater Magna, the great mother. Attis is taken as the prototype for male self castration, a form of self harm that has received extensive attention in medical literatures— rather more, in fact, than it has in classical studies. In the ancient world Attis was identified in particular with the Galli, a priestly caste, who in turn were associated with the ancient Turkish regions of Lydia and Phrygia.

The region called Phrygia lay in the central region of what is modern Turkey. Lydia was to the west and included much of what is now the western half of Turkey. The "high water mark" of Lydian culture, with its famed king Croesus, was the sixth century B.C.E. But Attis and the Galli are more often identified as Phrygian, an even more ancient culture associated with central Anatolia and an equally famed ruler, Midas. In Graeco-Roman culture, Phrygia connoted antiquity (Rives), just as Graeco-Roman culture now does in the West. There are limits, however, to the usefulness of this nomenclature. Phrygia and Lydia can each be taken as referring to a culture, a place and an historical epoch, but these cultures overlap historically and geographically (see Strabo). Given the cultural and historical overlap between Greece and Rome, much scholarly debate about the ancient religions with which Attis and the Galli were identified focuses on trying to understand the extent to which specific figures or practices can be identified with any time or place. Three studies of Attis and the Galli by Hugo Hepding (in German, 1903), Henri Graillot (French, 1912) and James Frazer (English, 1914), have set the terms for interpretation of the ancient sources by modern commentators.[3] The accounts by these three early twentieth-century scholars often displace the stories produced in Greek or Latin, with one crucial exception. Catullus' poem 63, about Attis, has gained most attention from writers on self harm and it will be discussed in the next section.

Because we cannot be sure about the provenance of the Attis stories, thus their relationship to the meanings given to religious practices, so the apparent continuity in the name "Attis" is potentially deceptive. And part of the contestation over the meanings given to Attis and the Galli arise from disagreement about the status of the goddess to whom he is said to have sacrificed his genitals, Cybele. Cybele is identified as a Phrygian goddess, but it is accepted that she was formally installed in the Roman pantheon in a major ceremony in 204 B.C.E. (Roscoe 200–01). There was a pragmatism involved in this adopting of a foreign deity: it had been prophesied by the oracles at Delphi that welcoming Cybele to Rome would ensure victory over the Carthaginian invader Hannibal. The delegation who heard the prophecy duly journeyed to Phrygia, receiving at Pessinus a sacred stone from the king. This account, given in Livy's *History of Rome* (29.14), rather disapprovingly notes, "According to traditional account her reputation had previously been doubtful," but on her entrance to Rome "the Mother Goddess" was welcomed by the great and good of the city. Nevertheless her status was contested, as Roman citizens were forbidden to participate in her worship. Commensurately, the status of the Galli at this time is unclear, notwithstanding Will Roscoe's assertion that the priests were "part of an official Roman state religion with manifestations in every part of the Greco-Roman world and at every level of society" for nearly six centuries (196). In the long period during which Cybele was officially honored but her priests were *persona non grata*, it is difficult to know what was made of Attis. But an important change occurred in the reign of the Emperor Claudius (C.E. 41 to 54), when "rites honouring Attis, in which the Galli were prominent became part of official observances" (Roscoe 201).

The most extensive descriptions of the Galli are in the second book of the long poem *On the Nature of Things*, a discourse in Latin on material form and its origins by Titus Lucretius Carus (c.99–c.55 B.C.E.). Lucretius depicts the worshippers of Cybele as outcasts, yet he implies that they were significant players in the celebrations which honor spring and harvest, food and fertility. Of Cybele and the Galli, he writes,

> Now, adorned
> With that same token, to-day is carried forth,
> With solemn awe through many a mighty land,

The image of that mother, the divine.
Her the wide nations, after antique rite,
Do name Idaean Mother, giving her
Escort of Phrygian bands, since first, they say,
From out those regions 'twas that grain began
Through all the world. To her do they assign
The Galli, the emasculate, since thus
They wish to show that men who violate
The majesty of the mother and have proved
Ingrate to parents are to be adjudged
Unfit to give unto the shores of light
A living progeny. The Galli come:
And hollow cymbals, tight-skinned tambourines
Resound around to bangings of their hands;
The fierce horns threaten with a raucous bray;
The tubed pipe excites their maddened minds
In Phrygian measures; they bear before them knives,
Wild emblems of their frenzy, which have power
The rabble's ingrate heads and impious hearts
To panic with terror of the goddess' might [Lucretius].

The picture is one of wild celebration: cymbals, pipes, tambourines, horns, along with singing, signify an ebullient mood, "maddened minds." This frenzy or excess is explicitly identified as "Phrygian": eastern, chaotic and threatening, yet *also* the "source" of that grain or harvest which is being celebrated (this part of the poem deals with seeds and particles). Lucretius has nothing to say about why or how those who lead the worship have been castrated; what his description does show is the contradiction evident in the representation of the place called Phrygia. It is the "ingrates," "Unfit to give unto the shores of light / A living progeny" who have the leading place in the rituals which honor the goddess.

A similar description is presented by Apuleius (c. 125–c. 180 C.E.), also writing in Latin. In his *Metamorphoses*, sometimes referred to as "The Golden Ass," the narrator describes other forms of self-inflicted injury carried out by the priestly caste. (At this point the narrator has been turned into an ass, making his reliability difficult to assess.) The worshippers of Cybele are described as cutting their arms with the two-edged axe called the "labrys" (typically identified as Lydian), and whipping themselves (Apuleius 139). The distaste—coupled with fascination—is explicit in the translation used by Roscoe, which describes the participants as "hideously made up, their faces crazy with muddy paints and their eyes artfully lined":

Then, from among them, one of those pouring forth in raving pretended to be stricken with madness [*vecordiam*] and affected repeated gasps from the depths of his breast, as if filled with the power of a divine spirit—as if, in other words, the presence of a god were not accustomed to make men better but weaker and ill! ... You could see, by the cutting of the swords and the blows of the whips, the soil become wet with the filthy blood of the effeminates [qtd. in Roscoe 202, interpolation and ellipses in original; see also Apuleius 138, 139].

The narrator presents the religiosity and the physical performance as fraudulent, a performance which betrays its falsity through effeminacy. The account goes on to explain that the Galli extract food and other gifts from the local populace, their celebrations culminating in the sacrifice of "a very fat ram" to "the Syrian Goddess" and the pack rape of a robust young man (Apuleius 139). Apuleius describes the priests' hedonism and their attacks on their own bodies, "wantonly tossing their pendulous hair in a circular motion and sometimes biting their muscles" (Apuleius 138).

A third source on Attis is an essay often attributed to Lucian (Λουκιανὸς ὁ Σαμοσατεύς, said to be an exact contemporary of Apuleius, and possibly Assyrian). The reference to the Galli comes in an essay called "De Dea Syria" ("[On] The Syrian Goddess"), and is introduced as a "sacred story which I had from the lips of a wise man" to explain a shrine he has seen in Phœnicia, on the eastern shore of the Mediterranean. But the narrator then explains that this informant is wrong, and that in fact

the goddess was Rhea, and the shrine the work of Attes. Now this Attes was by nation a Lydian, and he first taught the sacred mysteries of Rhea. The ritual of the Phrygians and the Lydians and the Samothracians was entirely learnt from Attes. For when Rhea deprived him of his powers, he put off his manly garb and assumed the appearance of a woman and her dress, and roaming over the whole earth he performed his mysterious rites, narrating his suffering and chanting the praises of Rhea.... He also affirmed that the Galli who are in the temple in no case castrate themselves in honour of Juno, but of Rhea, and this in imitation of Attes. All this seems to me more specious than true, for I have heard a different and more credible reason given for their castration [Lucian, *The Syrian Goddess*].

Twice, then, readers are warned that there are contradictory explanations of the places and practices associated with Attis. But Lucian concurs with Lucretius in asserting that the castrations take place as part of the celebrations of spring, the largest festival to which "a great multitude flocks from Syria and all the regions around."

The act of castration and its aftermath are described in detail in *The Syrian Goddess*, and imply the popularity of the rite:

On certain days a multitude flocks into the temple, and the Galli in great numbers, sacred as they are, perform the ceremonies of the men and gash their arms and turn their backs to be lashed. Many bystanders play on the pipes while many beat drums; others sing divine and sacred songs. All this performance takes place outside the temple, and those engaged in the ceremony enter not into the temple. During these days they are made Galli. As the Galli sing and celebrate their orgies, frenzy falls on them and many who had come as mere spectators afterwards are found to have committed the great act. I will narrate what they do. Any young man who has resolved on this action, strips off his clothes, and with a loud shout bursts into the midst of the crowd, and picks up a sword from a number of swords which I suppose have been kept for many years for this purpose. He takes it and castrates himself and then runs wild through the city, bearing in his hands what he has cut off. He casts it into any house at will, and from this house he receives women's raiment and ornaments. Thus they act during their ceremonies of castration [Lucian, *The Syrian Goddess*].

There are some points to note about this description: that the celebrations involve large numbers of people, whether Galli or onlookers; that they take place *outside* the temple; that many who attend become caught up in them, even if they had not intended to; and that being "made Galli" does not seem to entail self castration in the first instance. The latter point leaves open the possibility that self castration was not limited to the Galli and perhaps that not all Galli castrated themselves. That the young men after the ritual are able to run through the city suggests this; that they exchange their genitals for the clothing of women implies that their gender identities are now changed. Taken together these suggest the contested status of the rites and their practitioners: excluded from the temple, yet intruding in homes in a most intimate way; demanding of support (the supply of clothes); able to seduce onlookers with the intensity of their celebration.

This story also encourages us to take up the question of what it is the young men remove: penis; scrotum; all?[4] None of the sources, or at least, none of the translations, specify this. Classicists—i.e. readers of the original texts, not the translations used here, which might be expected to euphemize—also seem stumped. Roscoe, for example, is uncertain about how to interpret Pliny's observation, in his *Natural History*, that the Galli "practiced emasculation ['amputantibus' vol. 3: 596] 'within the limits of injury'" in ways designed to avoid "dangerous results" (see Pliny, vol. 3: 597; vol. 9: 383)[5] and Augustine's that "'neither is he changed into a woman, nor does he remain a man'" (Roscoe 203). Here, Gary Taylor's reminder that self castration could mean not simply removal of the penis but removal of the testicles works within the limits of possibility set by these two sources. Given that the young men run through the town after performing the amputation, removal of the scrotum, being less damaging, would seem more likely. If done this way, the practice would align with those used for domestic and working animals. And it is worth remembering that castration and its consequences would be familiar to most members of society.

That the actions of the Galli were meant as *celebrations* of fertility and reproduction, and that the audience understood this, is hinted at by another story told by the narrator of Lucian's *The Syrian Goddess*. He says that as a young man, he had cut off his first growth of facial hair and dedicated it to the gods, leaving the vessel containing the hair in the temple, marked with his name. Claiming to have left his name in the temple, and telling the story, suggest that he does not see any negative associations in sacrifice of body parts. He wishes to signify his own dedication, but the version of the ritual he describes uses hair as proxy.

Another ancient source, rarely used, is the first-century doctor Aretaeus. In *The Causes and Symptoms of Chronic Disease*, Aretaeus describes a mania in which

> Some cut their limbs in holy phantasy, as if thereby propitiating peculiar divinities. This is a madness of the apprehension solely; for in other respects they are the same. They are roused by the flute, and mirth, or by drinking, or by the admonition of those around them. This madness is of divine origin, and if they recover from madness, they are cheerful and free of care, as if initiated to the god; but yet they are paled and attenuated, and long remain weak from the pains of the wounds [Book one, Chapter six, 59 of 253 (304)].

The comment is glossed by the nineteenth-century translator—himself a physician—as "evidently refer[ring] to the worship of Cybele, on which see in particular, the *Atys* of Catullus" (Aretaeus 59 of 253). This account suggests greater physical damage but what is significant is the statement that "in other respects they are the same."

Analysing the suspicion towards the Galli (and other groups who disrupted notions of gender in the ancient world), Roscoe uses Plato's argument that the intended beneficiaries of the rituals were not the gods but those who participated in and observed these rites. Perhaps unconsciously adapting theories of the effect of tragedy (outlined in Aristotle's *Poetics*), but citing Plato, Roscoe suggests that such rituals were intended "to restore peace of mind to individuals suffering from psychological distress by inducing a temporary, healing form of madness or loss of consciousness," and thence that the "intended effect" was "a collective catharsis on the part of onlookers" (202; 203). The Galli are associated with "orgiastic and unrestrained religious behaviour"; the stigma associated with self castration "often merged with the charge of cowardice into a general reputation for effeminacy" (Rives 239).

The association between despotism, castration, feminization and invasion of the West by the East exemplified by the Galli leaves its shadow over texts ancient and modern, creative and scholarly. For example, Euripides' play *The Bacchae* has Dionysus declare, in the scene-setting opening, that he has spread his orgiastic cult in Lydia and Phrygia. These associations are amplified in early modern dramatic literature, texts in which eunuchs (the castrated) are

associated with "an 'Eastern' rather than a 'Western' culture" (Taylor 77). Lynne
Roller suggests that there has been a desire to believe that the existence of a
cult of self castration in ancient cultures can be explained in terms of the corrupting influence of "the effeminate east" on an otherwise "civilised" Mediterranean. In evidence she quotes one scholar (publishing in 1984) who remains
puzzled by how "a *barbarian* deity, whose worship consisted of mystery and
orgy" could "suddenly became a *civilized*, Roman deity" (23; emphasis added).[6]

Between the four descriptions of the Galli by Apuleius, Aretaeus, Lucian
and Lucretius, the level of fear or distaste varies considerably. Lucian and Aretaeus are relatively matter-of-fact, suggesting that in ancient times the rites of
the Galli were not always regarded as especially peculiar or threatening. This
view is emphasized by the mention of sizeable crowds from the city and surrounding regions. Although we are told by Lucian that the festival he describes
is well attended and eclectic—many bring their gods and icons—the actions
of the Galli seem to be a kind of centerpiece; at the same time, the exclusion
from the temple hints at competing views of the legitimacy of self castration.
What is debated is whether these acts were understood as the high points of
priestly devotion; as cultish barbarity; as neither of these things, or both at
once. And in considering the readings of these sources made by commentators,
we should note the proximity of the divine to the human, the mythological
to the realistic, even the literary to the literal. In the description of the Galli
in Lucian's *The Syrian Goddess*, for example, or in Lucretius' *On the Nature of
Things*, we cannot deduce whether the narrative mode is ethnographic or
mythological.

Because we do not know the exact religious or cultural provenance of
these stories, we cannot understand in fine-grained detail the historical or
imaginative relationship between the various versions of the myth and social
conditions in which they were produced and circulated. We cannot even say
for sure that "the priests of the cult of Attis scandalized the Romans" (Favazza,
1996: 39)—we have only a handful of stories to work with. Some of these
indicate that the Galli were outcasts, others imply that their rituals were among
the most popular and significant of the religious year. And the status of Cybele
herself was contested. For example, Pliny claims that a fabulously valuable
painting of a priest of Cybele by Parrhasius was kept by the emperor Tiberius
(vol. 9: 313; book 35, section 36), but this anecdote might be included to denigrate Tiberius for debauchery. The most extensive of the sources on the Galli
suggest they were both revered and feared. The evidence leads historian of
classical religion Philippe Borgeaud to almost the opposite conclusion to
Favazza: in his view, the priests were "saintly characters who were far from
being marginal" (37).

What is implied in both the sources and scholarly readings is the normality or normativity of Graeco-Roman cultures, in which the rituals or deities of the East are not merely intrusive but corrupting. In this sense, the representation of the Galli conforms to that form of scholarly vision Edward W. Said has called "orientalism." In Said's view, Western scholarship has helped to disseminate (in seeming to discern) an Islam which "symbolize[d] terror, devastation, the demonic, hordes of hated barbarians" (59). What the sources and commentary together show is that the troping of "the East" this way actually pre-dates the emergence of Islam. The materials also show that representations of the people of Europe's "East" are structured by anxieties around gender identities, which inform related assumptions about barbarism, despotism, and irrationality. These qualities are thereby identified as alien even when they occur in the heart of Rome. Such views reverberate in the accounts of the Galli, remembering that what is used here are largely nineteenth-century or early twentieth-century translations. All writers seem fascinated by, while recoiling from, rituals represented as explosive, chaotic and dangerous because seductive or spectacular, rituals in which devotees publicly and irrevocably announce their dedication to the mother goddess of the East.

Discussion of these stories by medical writers, especially in psychoanalysis, tends to offer a selective recycling of the brief mentions of the Galli by Pliny the Elder and Lucretius, as well as the slightly longer description of their rituals from *The Syrian Goddess*, the essay attributed to Lucian.[7] Read within the context of elevated respect for the ancient cultures of the Mediterranean and their literatures this apparently describes an alien or improbable practice. And it seems significant that for the doctor translating Aretaeus, the poet Catullus is a source of equal authority on the practice. However, if we "resituate" these stories within the context of the literatures of self harm, in which religious belief is a recurring element, the accounts suggest a historical practice. If readers leave open the possibility that the accounts are based on actual events, then nothing in these sources contradicts the possibilities left open by modern medicine, a point discussed in the next section. But for the moment we can note that even Apuleius—or at least, his ass narrator—is sceptical, but that skepticism is focused on the motives of the practitioners, rather than the existence of the rituals.

Mythographies of Attis

Situated across the cultures of ancient Greece, Rome and the eastern Mediterranean, "Attis" is, in various sources, of Phrygia, journeying to Phrygia, or associated with Phrygia; is Greek or Roman; a man or a god; priestly or noble; effeminate or rampantly masculine; or in painful transition between these identities. There is disagreement about whether the name "Attis" refers to an individual (and if an individual, mythological or actual), or whether it refers to a priestly caste, called the Galli. The distinction between Attis as an individual and Attis as a generic term for those with priestly roles is one Philippe Borgeaud is at pains to argue for; more typical is Guila Sfameni Gasparro, for whom Attis is simply "the prototype of the Gallus ... the worshipper who celebrates the mystic-orgiastic cult of Cybele and, in a fit of total devotion to the goddess, under the influence of the mania, dedicates his own virility to her" (26).[8]

For Borgeaud, the first reference to Attis in classical literature is in fragment 27 by Theopompus, in Greek; in Borgeaud's view, this text "can be dated between 410 and 370 B.C.E." (34). In the "Lydian tradition" (on which he cites Hepding), Attis is killed by a boar. However Latin writers on Attis draw from what are termed "Phrygian" stories, these tending to emphasize the protagonist's self-castration. Borgeaud argues that the stories of Attis spread more widely at the end of the third century B.C.E. (35). The later commentators on Attis are Diodorus Siculus (c.90–c.30 B.C.E.), Porphyry (c.234–c.305), Julian (c.331–363), Sallustius (4th century) in *On the Gods and the Cosmos*, and Marinus of Neapolis (c.450–c.500). The most extensive source is Pausanias, writing in the second century of the Christian era, while the most influential of the "historical" accounts is by Arnobius of Sicca. The sources discussed here are from Diodorus Siculus, Pausanias, and Arnobius of Sicca, and then "Poem 63" by Catullus.

Diodorus, whom Borgeaud suggests takes his information on Attis from Dionysos Skytobrachion,[9] reports two versions of the story of Attis, neither of which mentions castration. In one brief mention Atys, son of Croesus— and therefore Lydian—is killed while out hunting (*Diodorus of Sicily* vol. 4: 39). The other, much longer story is identified as a Phrygian tale. In it, Attis is killed by the father of Cybele, who is enraged because the young man has made his daughter pregnant (vol. 2: 273–77). After the murder Phrygia is cursed by "pestilence" (vol. 2: 277), because Attis's body has not been buried:

> Consequently the Phrygians, since the body had disappeared in the course of time, made an image of the youth, before which they sang dirges and by means of honours in keeping with his suffering propitiated the wrath of him who had been wronged; and these rites they continue to perform down to our own lifetime [*Diodorus of Sicily* vol. 2: 277].

Borgeaud notes that this story is taken up by Ovid, who retells it in *Fasti* (4.223–44). Ovid's account in turn informs another version of the myth, by Pausanias. James Frazer, who translated both Pausanias' *Description of Greece* and *Fasti* by Ovid, shifts his interpretation of the Attis stories between the publication of the second and third editions of *The Golden Bough*. In the earlier editions he argues that the "rudeness and savagery" (131) of the story are the signature of its antiquity, a view commensurate with his evolutionary model of religion. In the extended revisions Frazer pays much more attention to Attis's self-castration, something he had barely mentioned, and shifts away from the interpretation which emphasizes fertility and harvest. This later view underpins the English-language literature which associates Attis not with reproduction and celebration, but with paternity, loss and sorrow. This is the mood, too, of Catullus' poem.

Both Pausanias and Arnobius of Sicca write in the Christian era. Pausanias' second-century work *Description of Greece* (also translated as *Guide to Greece*) and Arnobius' *Arnobius Adversus Gentes*, also called *The Case Against the Pagans*, from early in the fourth century (Bland) both associate Attis with Pessinos, a city on the Anatolian plateau. In the two versions of the Attis legend told by Pausanias, there is emphasis on the proximity and connection between the human, the divine, and what might crudely be called the agricultural realms. The first story Pausanias tells comes from Hermesianax of Colophon, a city in Ionia (now the west coast of Turkey). This version, from Greek, has Attis born in Phrygia and moving to Lydia in adulthood. There he participates in the celebratory rites for the Mother goddess "and came to be so honoured by her that Zeus was angry and sent a wild boar to the Lydian farm-land" (Pausanias, *Guide to Greece* 271). The apparent spread of this myth to Gaul is said to explain the prohibition there against eating swine.

Pausanias notes, however, that the Gallic version of the legend of Attis is rather different. In James Frazer's translation,

> Zeus in his sleep let fall seed on the ground, and in course of time the earth produced a demon with two genital organs, one of a man and one of a woman; and this demon they name Agdistis. But the gods feared Agdistis, and cut off his male organ of generation. From it sprang an almond tree with ripe fruit, and they say that a daughter of the river Sangarius took of the fruit and put it in her bosom. The fruit immediately vanished and she conceived. The male child whom she bore was exposed, but a he-goat tended him. As the boy grew in stature his beauty was more than human, and Agdistis loved him. But when Attis was grown to man's estate, his relations sent him to Pessinus to wed the king's daughter. As the wedding song was being sung, Agdistis appeared, and Attis in a fit of madness mutilated himself, and so did his father-in-law. But Agdistis repented of what he had done to Attis, and he got Zeus to grant that no part of Attis's body should moulder or decay. These are the best-known stories about Attis [*Pausanias's Description of Greece*, vol. 1, 353].[10]

In terms of the representation of masculine reproduction it is worth noting that the patriarch of this story is not Phrygian at all: he is the greatest of the Greek gods, Zeus, ruler of Olympus. But there are unexpected "infiltrations" or transformations of his lineage which arise from carelessness, cowardice or malice: the earth produces a demon; a severed penis produces an almond tree; fruit brings forth a human child; the child is reared by a goat. This is the interconnectedness of animal, vegetable, and divine noted above. There are two acts of castration, both associated with vengeance. In fact, both Agdistis and Attis are punished twice, Agdistis by castration then grief, Attis by abandonment then self castration. Implicitly, the trouble is started by Zeus when he fathers the bisexual demon who must have his masculine organs removed. Throughout the story it is "carelessness" about paternity or reproduction that is punished, but Attis is rewarded—or punished—by eternal life, effecting thereby a strange preservation of Zeus's lineage. But we can note the Christian thematics emerging here, of eternal life and "wasted" seed.[11]

This version of the story seems recognizable in the account given by Arnobius (227–31). Arnobius, however, says that he takes his story from Timotheus (227). In his version, the story of Attis begins with Jupiter [Zeus] failing in an attempt to rape "the Great Mother." In frustration, Jupiter "spen[ds] his lust on the stone" and so Acdestis [sic] is born, his mother the rocks of "unheard of wildness in every respect" (Arnobius 227).[12] Acdestis is a violent and lustful creature, said to have "regarded not gods or men," and to have "scattered destruction" (228). In an effort to curb Acdestis, Liber sets a trap by filling a spring with wine; when Acdestis falls into a drunken sleep, Liber ties Acdestis' genitals to his own foot so that they are torn off when he awakens (228). The resulting flow of blood carries the severed parts into the earth. A fully loaded pomegranate tree springs up at this place (again, we have parentage of god and earth). Nata (or Nana), daughter of the river god Sangarius, gathers this fruit and places it "in her bosom," thereby becoming pregnant (228). Her father imprisons and starves her as punishment for the pregnancy and when the child is born he is exposed. But the baby is found by Phorbus, who rears the boy on goat's milk and names him Attis, "as handsome fellows are so named in Lydia, or because the Phrygians in their own way of speaking call their goats *attagi*" (229).

Acdestis (his grandfather) gives the young man gifts of wild animals so as to act in "wicked compliance with his lust" (Arnobius 229). The young man boasts that he has killed the beasts, but when drunk, admits that they are gifts from Acdestis. Midas, the king, resolves to "save" Attis from this liaison by marrying the young man to his own daughter. The gates of the city are closed for the wedding ceremony but the mother of the gods knows that Attis can only be safe while he is not married to a mortal. She enters the city to rescue him, her head becoming crowned with towers (229–30). Acdestis bursts in through the now broken walls and induces frenzy among the Phrygians.

A daughter of adulterous Gallus cuts off her breasts; Attis snatches the pipe borne by him who was goading them to frenzy; and he, too, now filled with furious passion, raving frantically [and] tossed about, throws himself down at last, and under a pine tree mutilates himself, saying, *Take these, Acdestis, for which you have stirred up so great and terribly perilous commotions* [Arnobius 230; interpolation in translation].

The bride, Ia, cradles Attis and then kills herself; her blood is changed to violets (230–31). The mother of the gods gathers up the severed parts of Attis and buries them, then carries back to her cave the pine tree under which Attis castrated himself (231). Acdestis begs Jupiter to restore Attis to life. He refuses (231), but does allow that "his hairs should always grow ... the least of his fingers should live, and should be kept ever in motion" (231). Acdestis consecrates the body in Pessinus, where it is honored with "yearly rites and priestly services" (231).[13]

In the commentary that follows, which is about twice the length of the story itself (231–41), Arnobius draws out, as his late nineteenth-century translator says, what he believes to be the "absurdity, indecency, and silliness" (221) of stories which, he complains, appear in "grave, serious, and careful histories" (222). He casts doubt on the divinity of the Mother Goddess, and condemns Jupiter for being "prepared to attempt a filthy contest," the rape of his mother (233). In relation to Attis, he is appalled in particular by the claim he was raised by a goat: "Oh story ever opposed and inimical to the male sex, in which not only do men lay aside their virile powers, but beast even which were males become mothers!" (236–37). In making these criticisms Arnobius runs two contradictory arguments: that the events are implausible (for example, it is not possible for rock and man to produce offspring); also, that they are blasphemous (gods would not behave this way). His focus is on immorality, asking rhetorically, "of what had Gallus been guilty, and his concubine's daughter, that he should rob himself of his manhood, she herself of her breasts?" (237). His challenge is explicit: "What say you, O races and nations, given up to such beliefs? When these things are brought forward, are you not ashamed and confounded to say things so indecent," "the cutting off of breasts, the lopping off of men's members" (237). For Arnobius, making his "case," it is clear that the story of the gods on which religious practices are based must surely be "false, and wholly untrue" (238).

Ironically, then, perhaps the best evidence that there is historical truth in the stories of the Galli and the rituals associated with the worship of Attis comes from Arnobius. For after offering these criticisms of the plausibility and morality of the stories of Attis, he concedes their influence—indeed, this influence is what he writes against. He explains, for example, that when "on fixed days" the people bring pine to the temple, they recall and reverence Attis' self castration by re-enacting Cybele's journey bearing the pine under which he removed his genitals. "Is it not in imitation of that tree, beneath which the raging and ill-fated youth laid hands upon himself" (239). Arnobius's criticisms of the Galli are based on their imitation of Attis:

What [mean] the *Galli* with dishevelled hair beating their breasts with their palms? Do they not recall to memory those lamentations with which the tower-bearing Mother, along with the weeping Acdestis, wailing aloud, followed the boy? ...

Or if the things which we say are not so, declare, say yourselves—those effeminate and delicate [men] whom we see among you in the sacred rites of this deity—what business, [what] care, [what] concern have they there; and why do they like mourners wound their arms and breasts, and act as those dolefully circumstanced? ... For either this is the cause which we have found in your writings and treatises.... For who would believe that there is any honour in that which the worthless *Galli* begin, effeminate debauchees complete? [240–41].

For Borgeaud, the background of each of Pausanias and Arnobius is significant. "Everything about him leads us to believe that Pausanias was originally from western Anatolia, and more precisely from the region of Mount Sipylos or Pergamon, where the memory of ancient Phrygian stories remained intact" (43). Arnobius was a Christian theologian, writing from the northern coast of Africa. Pausanias because of his own travels and cultural background supplies a version of the story of Attis which "refreshes" its Phrygian elements, or perhaps more accurately, is comfortable giving positive connotations to the Phrygian identity, whereas Arnobius is shaped by and is helping to shape an opposing interpretive tradition which aimed to discredit the Graeco-Roman pantheon.[14]

It is impossible to know how widespread the practices of the Galli were. While it is in Arnobius' interests to imply that their rituals were more prevalent, more violent and, in particular, more highly sexualized than they might actually have been, the sources together have sufficient breadth and detail to suggest they have some connection to practice. For example, we can note the detail of the still growing hair in Arnobius' version of Attis, and the claim in *The Syrian Goddess* that the speaker had placed his hair in a jar and placed it in a temple (Lucian). And Borgeaud asks his readers to consider a time and place in which rituals of self castration characterized a group who were active participants in the religious life of ancient Rome. For him, the stories of Attis, and specifically of castration, illustrate the relationship between religious ecstasy, male sexuality, and political authority in a parable which opposes "the savage and the civilised ... hunting and marriage": "this Hellenistic version of the story not only makes an inventory of the deviances in terms of which a Greek order is defined but also signal the insufficiencies through which this apparently dominant order would be subverted from within" (Borgeaud 56). This reading, which emphasizes self harm as an allegory for the destruction of the state from within, brings us close to Clifford Ronan's interpretation of Shakespeare's *Julius Caesar*, a play which he argues is "full of voluntary wounds" (218). What is crucial, says Ronan, is that "the civil wound[] is deeper than any foreigner could make" (219), leading Shakespeare, for example, to represent civil war as a kind of self mutilation, not only in *Caesar* but also in the endings of *Titus Andronicus*, *King John*, and *Richard III* (220).[15]

The most influential version of the story of Attis since the nineteenth century has been a literary one, Poem 63 of Catullus, which "has had a decisive impact on virtually everyone, scholar or layperson" who has considered Attis (Roller xvi). Gaius Valerius Catullus, thought to have lived in the first half of the century before the Christian era (and therefore a contemporary of Lucretius), individualizes Attis. Catullus removes any reference to procreation, lineage and inheritance, making the drama a psychological and sexual one. In these ways the story is more recognizable to modern readers, better schooled in the drama of the individual than the dynamics of gods, mortals, and features of the natural world like rocks and trees. Catullus draws upon stories of Attis but invents some distinctive elements, intensifying the focus on gender transformation and on punishment. In particular, he shows in powerful terms the ensuing sorrow and regret felt by Attis after self castration. The only source to attend in more than a half sentence to the self castration, the poem has also been read as proof of the psychological consequences of this act.

Catullus' intense and astonishing poem begins with a description of Attis arriving in Phrygia from Greece, cutting off his genitals in the pine grove of Cybele, encouraging his fellow worshipers to ecstasy.[16] Unlike any other writer whose work is extant, Catullus focuses on the *aftermath* of castration, troping it as catastrophe. Thus the ending has Attis awakening as a woman, "in rage and remorse returning to the shore / and staring, streaming-eyed at the sterile sea" (Catullus, 1969: 127). Sharpened by regret, now spoken of with feminine pronouns, Attis asks the goddess whether she now must "Be a maenad, a moiety of myself, a man-corpse?" (129). Peter Green's 2005 translation of the poem renders these key moments—Attis's arrival and castration, her awakening and regret, this way:

> Over deep seas Attis, carried on a rapid catamaran,
> eagerly with hurrying footsteps sought that forest in Phrygia
> penetrated the tree-thick coverts, the goddess' shadowy habitat,
> and there, by furious madness driven, wits adrift in insanity,
> seized a keen flint, slashed away the weight of his groin's double complement...
>
> So after slumber, now abandoned by her frenzied paroxysm,
> Attis reflected on the deed that she herself had initiated,
> saw where she was, what things she'd lost, mind purged to diaphanous clarity.
> Back to the shore she forced her footsteps, heart full of simmering bitterness,
> and there, as she gazed with tear-filled eyes at the ocean's lonely immensity,
> thus she addressed her distant homeland, in saddest accents and piteously
> [129, 131].

The poem ends with Cybele punishing Attis for her apostasy—her lament at having made the "sacrifice"—by sending a lion to terrorize her. The last three lines have Attis pleading to the goddess that the furies and ecstasies be visited on others.

The changes Catullus made from versions of the stories circulating in the ancient world are noteworthy: his Attis is Greek, not Phrygian. He is thereby a representative of "civilisation," as opposed to "barbarism." Catullus' Attis arrives in Phrygia from the sea and goes to the grove of Cybele, where he castrates and thereby "feminises" himself, not as part of a celebratory crowd but as an outcast, alone; he is mortal, not a god. Attis laments her exile in terms that equate loss of culture with the loss of the male genitals. And the poem ends not with her death, but with Attis driven back into Cybele's grove by one of the goddess's lions, forever enslaved, forever female, forever prey to an aggressive and punitive "nature."[17] This is, then, a poem about the terrors of migration and nativization, processes which are represented as a kind of castration, equated to an "irreparable" feminization that is a radical diminution of the capacity to live, to be part of society. As Green points out, Attis has "severed himself (in every sense) from his own country and society, as well as from the masculine status that defined his existence" (Catullus, 2005: 237). Migration, worship, ecstasy, and femaleness are all reasons for regret; her apostasy makes Attis the object of Cybele's punitive fury.

There is a complicated geography as well as an equally complicated textual history to the circulation of the stories of Attis. Borgeaud begins his discussion of the origins of the cult of the goddess he calls Cybele [the Latin name], and thence of Attis (for Herodotus [485–425 B.C.E.], Atys) by noting that the stories, while "on the face of it entirely Greek," are identified with journeys to and from Greek lands in Asia, "the extreme frontiers of Hellenism" (32).[18] The similarity of Borgeaud's formulation of Greek understandings of self castration (as a "foreign" practice) to those many hundreds of medical accounts which represent it as something culturally or historically distant, a response to peculiar local conditions, might suggest that one of the ways to manage the narrative relationship to extreme physical self harm—thence, perhaps, the intellectual and emotional one—is to position it as a practice beyond the horizon of the writer's own time and place. The practice among men of removing their genitals threatens the notion of the polity and of the self so decisively as to make it literally unrecognizable *except* as the act of a foreigner, someone who stands outside the systems of value and meaning which regulate behaviors. Yet that said, what is notable about the tone of a key source like *The Syrian Goddess* is the equanimity with which the events are related: there is neither the distaste nor the disapproval that so often characterizes accounts of self harm.

Of the known story-tellers it is Catullus who has the most resounding voice; he and the obviously fictional *Metamorphoses* of Apuleius have done much to shape the modern sense of ancient views of self harm. Frazer, for example, speculates, "When the tumult of emotion had subsided, and the man had come to himself again, the irrevocable sacrifice must often have been followed by passionate sorrow and lifelong regret. This revulsion of natural feeling after the frenzies of a fanatical religion is powerfully depicted by Catullus" (270). But just as we do not take *King Lear* as an account of British history in the period of Midas, nor should we take Catullus' poem as "true" in the ethnographic sense. Catullus, a poet, is not "recording" the story of Attis; he is positioning his reader to be appalled by the story of the man who "gives his masculinity" to Asia, perhaps, like Arnobius, seeking to contest the status and practices of the Galli. We can therefore read the poem as an index of the author's response to practices he may have found repulsive not least *because* popular and tolerated by Roman officialdom.

The debate about whether "Attis" refers not to an individual or to a god or to a priestly class, and the evidence about the widespread nature of the practice of self castration, suggests that we can understand the removal of the male genitalia as an actual practice; as part of a major annual ritual; as something which generated debate as to its origin and value; and as something which exerted influence among those who were or wished to be identified as worshippers of Cybele. It can be seen as a social practice with specific (Phrygian) cultural associations and considerable religious importance, while also being deeply threatening to some observers and writers because of the renunciation of male sexual capacity.

But the conventional view of nineteenth- and twentieth-century writers is to emphasize the marginality of the Galli and the revulsion they incited, as Catullus and Apuleius do. This approach leaves the Graeco-Roman edifice and its more revered forms of masculinity in some sense "intact." Two things drop out of sight in the citation of the poem by Catullus in medical writing. The first is that it is a *poem*, which is to say, an imaginative representation of self castration. The second is cultural context. What is now called Poem 63 was produced in a culture in which the rituals of self castration were a part of official religion *and* associated with a "foreign" priesthood condemned for their alien and alienating desire to renounce the male power of procreation. But even this is contestable: for if the accounts of the spontaneous participation of on-lookers are correct, then some of the Galli were Romans, made "foreign" not by their ancestry but by their actions. Either way, because the nature of its truth is complex, in reading it we must try and do two things at once: refuse to read the poem literally (as a documentary about a young man which proves that self castration leads to horrible remorse), and at the same time, insist that it is a testament to powerful if competing streams of value in Roman culture.[19]

Psychoanalysis and the Uses of Attis

The reason for unplaiting the strands of the Attis story is to emphasize the complexity of the literary and religious examples provided by classical sources and commentary on them. In so doing, a second aim is to provide a foundation for querying the uses made of these stories in medicine. There is an important example of this in Menninger's *Man Against Himself*, a book rarely neglected by a thesis writer considering self harm: along with Favazza's *Bodies Under Siege*, it is essentially definitive of the field (although see chapter four). Menninger makes considerable use of the Attis stories, basing his assertions on an essay by Bernice Engle, "Attis: A Study of Castration" (1936). Engle's discussion of Attis, at that stage an unpublished paper, is first cited by Menninger in his 1936 essay "A Psychoanalytic Study of the Significance of Self-Mutilation" (423). In *Man Against Himself*, published two years later, Menninger cites Engle's now published essay in a voluminous footnote (249).[20] Thus Engle's history and interpretation of the stories of Attis are literally foundational, occupying a position in English-language commentary which the more erudite essay by Edith Weigert-Vowinkel on the same topic, published two years later in a new American journal, was unable to challenge or change.

There is no basis for Engle's claim that "the cult of Cybele and Attis originated in Phrygia after the sixth century B.C." (363). While there is general agreement that the Phrygian mother of the gods was worshipped earlier, Roller and Borgeaud assert that there is no good evidence that Attis as a singular figure (as opposed to a priestly type) had an existence in Phrygia at all. The implication of their assertion is that Attis is the creation of Graeco-Roman legend, given Phrygian characteristics to signify his alien and feminine status within "civilised" culture. He is also a kind of metonym of the Galli, the individual signifying the group. Engle's claim that the earliest legend is told by Pausanias in "about 340 B.C." (363) is some 500 years wide of the mark: Pausanias is thought to have been writing around 174 C.E. The fragment from that time cited by Borgeaud (above) as the earliest reference to Attis is from Theopompus, a historian at the centre of Greek culture (a student of the philosopher/teacher Isocrates), not the traveller from the east that Pausanias was. In claiming that the Christian theologian Arnobius tells "a similar story" to that presented by Pausanias, a reader might well miss the point that Arnobius's version of the legend is part of his argument against pagan religion. Losing the distinction between the stories, Engle contends that "Agdistis and Cybele are the same person," in order to claim that the stories are structurally similar.[21] This misses the key point that a figure of destruction who frightens even the gods, Cybele, the "Great Mother," is associated with harvest and regeneration.

More of a problem than these historical errors (easily made by the non-specialist) is the fact that Engle misrepresents the scholarly debate of her own and earlier periods, particularly in the claim that "by the fourth century" the legends of Attis "had assumed definite shape" (363). As we have seen, no such "definite shape" exists, unless we assume that a later source is somehow more authoritative than any earlier one. And the contestation is evident from Engle's own canvassing of the multiple versions of the Attis stories; the variations are discussed at length by one of her main sources, Frazer, whose own account is also richly footnoted. As shown above, the sources available consist mainly of brief mentions about which it is difficult to be conclusive; the difficulties are compounded as the classical writers often claim to be working from hearsay, or themselves note competing views. Nevertheless, a newly singular and simplified version of the Attis story becomes the basis for Engle's theorizing of male self castration. Engle relies on the most obviously partisan account of Attis in the historiographic sources, Arnobius of Sicca's version in *The Case Against the Pagans*. Contrastingly Hepding, perhaps the most comprehensive student of the Attis stories, concludes it is impossible to offer a definitive interpretation of the legend of Attis because of the thin and contradictory archive (Weigert-Vowinkel 258).

Engle summarizes the stories, and notes the agreement between pscho-analysts Menninger, Karin Stephen and Ernest Jones that

> Self-castration impulses exist in the unconscious of normal people; that it has for its psychological mechanism a fourfold base: a sense of guilt, self-punishment, misdirected aggression, and an erotic goal. These may appear singly or in combination in the individual case. In addition, there is bound up with this mechanism the feeling that castration or its less severe substitutes may through punishment for a feeling of guilt serve as a vicarious offering of the giving up of life itself.
> Religious fanatics, whom Dr. Menninger ranks with psychotics, usually satisfy their guilty feelings of sex by direct action, that is, by self castration [Engle 364].

But as we have seen, the sources on the Galli do not necessarily support the equating of self castration with religious fanaticism, nor that "fanaticism" with psychosis—although the poem by Catullus could be read that way.[22]

Engle's discussion of self castration suggests that it relieves fear of death, and "helps to solve the Oedipus complex and the problem of the man who has guilty homosexual feelings" through punishment and instant feminization (364–65). The theory Engle proposes is then extended, buttressed by reference to classical stories which function as a kind of precedent: "clearly the deeper meaning of these myths is that Attis wishes to commit incest and in remorse emasculates himself" (365). Yet even the story from Arnobius of Sicca does not support this interpretation. Jupiter has tried to rape his mother Cybele but does not emasculate himself; Acdestis becomes the lover of his grandson and his genitals are torn off by his own actions, but only as the result of a trick played by his fellow gods. There is neither guilt nor repentance in either instance. Attis and his bride are punished more than Acdestis—which is to say, the mixing of god and mortal, in an implicitly monogamous heterosexual union, is prevented. In ending the chaos which ensues from the appearance of the gods at the wedding ceremony, Attis's self-castration is represented as a kind of propitiation of Acdestis, who has induced frenzy among the Phrygians who begin to self-mutilate. When Attis snatches Acdestis' "frenzy inducing pipe" he enacts a kind of castration. The sexual dynamics of the story are intense but they are also dramatically volatile; insisting that any one of these actions or characters is central is a path to misreading. For example, Engle argues that there is obvious phallic symbolism in the still growing hair and the still moving little finger (365) but Borgeaud sees these elements as incongruous attempts to incorporate a quasi–Christian element of resurrection. For him, "Far from proving the permanence here of a system of thought or behavior," they are proof only of "direct contact and borrowing" (47), here, with Christianity.

A different approach, one which engages with the specifics of self castration, is taken by Edith Weigert-Vowinkel in her 1938 essay which proposes a psychoanalytic reading of the legends of Attis. Whereas most commentators concentrate on the masculine elements, for Weigert-Vowinkel the proper focus of such inquiry must be consideration of the maternal, given the position of Cybele as the supreme deity. Given the association between Cybele and nature, fertility and harvest, she asks, what are the consequences for the way in which authority is experienced by the Galli? In answer, she proposes that "the worshipper's masochistic acts" arise from "a desire for expiation and reconciliation": "Attis and his followers cast away the organ of procreation, they sacrifice it to the mother, as though that were her command ... in order that they may possess the mother forever in passive dependence" (372). Whereas Borgeaud finds the signs of resurrection incongruous interpolations, Weigert-Vowinkel argues that they are symbolic of the psychic effectiveness of amputation, for they signify that "the castration is rescinded" (372). In this sense the process is "artistic," "the beginning of resurrection in their satisfaction of the artistic sense," giving expression to "creative liberation" (Weigert-Vowinkel 371). In symbolic and psychological ways, then, the self harm provides or proves a conduit to the maternal, the reproductive, the resurrected, and the reconciled. In her reading, the self castration of the Galli is a vehicle, ecstatic and theatrical, for religious power and transformation.

Self Harm and Religious Expression

Daniel F. Caner, in an essay exploring the practice of self castration in the ancient world, implies that even those not regarded as followers of Cybele might have chosen this form of religious expression. What more powerful signifier of the capacity for devotion, of the certainty of the renunciation of the world and its pleasures, could a male priest make? And provocatively, Edith Weigert-Vowinkel asserts that the trace of the Attis rituals remain in modern Christianity in symbolic form, "the tendency of believers towards self castration and femininity" being demonstrated by the demand for "celibacy and in the special clothing of priests" (348).

Caner argues that self castration became a point of debate in the emerging Christian church. Much of the focus of the historical and theological discussion is on the fourth-century priest and theologian Origen, who was "accused" by Eusebius of Caesarea, one of the key sources on Origen, of having castrated himself. Origen and Eusebius are in turn central to debates within and about the Christian church about how widespread self castration was. Working to dispute the claims of those who see self castration as a marginal or even heretical activity (397), Caner suggests that it "should be viewed more generally as a practice of early Christians who, prompted by their understanding of Matthew 19:12 and other influences (not necessarily by alliance to a heretical group), embraced radical corporeal asceticism as a fundamental part of Christian devotion" (397–98).

Origen considers self castration in his commentaries on the gospel of Matthew, commentaries in which he warns on the dangers of reading literally. For some, these serve as evidence that he did not actually castrate himself. For those who believe that he did, the motives and meanings of his action are likewise contested. The most obvious explanation might be that he borrowed or was inspired by a religious practice visible in the Roman Empire. Caner suggests that Christian arguments about the merits of the practice served wider agendas, allowing followers to associate themselves with self-control and piety. Contrastingly, opponents of self castration and of the Galli could characterize both as barbaric corruptions of the Orient. But the coupling of the Origen question—did he or didn't he?—with Origen's own claims about the necessity of reading *metaphorically* the injunctions of the gospel of Matthew prove a flashpoint for debates about the prevalence and significance of male self castration in religious life in the ancient world. In the case of Origen, the desire to differentiate Christianity from the religions of Rome, and equally, to separate Christian "morality" from "pagan" dissipation, personified in the Galli and expressed in its most dangerous form through the cult of Attis, allowed the strengthening of opinion against self castration in the early church. Caner concludes, "A figure that once was used to signify the virtuous alterity of Christian communities to non–Christians became a figure of suspicious alterity within the orthodox church" (415).

Gary Taylor, in his book *Castration: An Abbreviated History of Western Manhood*, argues that early theologians such as Augustine moved to differentiate Christianity from paganism by condemning male self castration. However, this maneuver was problematic because it necessitated reading allegorically the passages in Matthew which ask devotees of Christ to consider the possibility of self mutilation (69). Taylor also suggests that in making arguments about Christian doctrine, Augustine "was actually targeting intellectual opponents much closer to home": "a particular Christian heresy [which] had collapsed the distinction between Jesus and Attis by interpreting the castration of Attis allegorically" (72). The basis of Taylor's argument is in part the claim that "Similarities between Attis and Christ had become increasingly prominent in the ritual celebrations of Attis in Rome" (72). Taylor is not alone here: Roscoe contends that after the middle of the third century "the Phrygian cult began to compete directly with Christianity in the dissemination of resurrection and salvation themes" (205–06). Likewise, Borgeaud suggests that the Attis who finds an "echo in old Anatolian stories of the second millennium B.C.E. concerning heavenly royalty" who then appears as the lover of Cybele "finally emerges as a pagan response to Christian apologetics" (39). This Christian interpretation or inflection of the story takes precedence in influential accounts. For example, Favazza summarizes the myth like this: "Priests devoted to the great mother goddess Cybele castrated themselves to demonstrate their mourning and identification with Attis, who had castrated himself, died, and was resurrected" (1996: 227).[23]

The proposition that male self castration was accommodated as an early form of Christian asceticism is contentious, although some suggest that medical staff can admire actions seen this way (see Scheftel 46, citing Podvoll 219). But as Taylor suggests, "Such developments obviously made [some] orthodox Christians uncomfortable, and Augustine was not the only Christian writer intent upon differentiating Christ from Attis, a crucifixion that meant something from a castration that meant nothing" (72). And so, as Caner also argues, the practice and the meaning of self castration were points of contention in the struggle between those affiliated to a Christian god, and defenders of the established religions of Rome and their deities. Perhaps it was also that these proponents were unhappy with the commixtion of apparently separate religious traditions (indicated by the adopting of Cybele). Either way,

> the relationship between Christianity and the Cybele religion in late antiquity is more complex than one of simple antagonism, although there was plenty of that.... In some areas, interesting syncretisms appeared. The Roman bishop

Hippolytus, writing in the first half of the third century, described at length the cult of the Naasenes, in which the worship of Attis and Jesus were thoroughly merged [Roscoe 205; 206].

But Roscoe also notes the preoccupation with differentiation: "Time and again, Christian apologists cited the Galli as representative of all they abhorred in pagan culture and religion" (196). As some groups embraced self castration, others wrote to accuse them of blasphemy, corrupting or misunderstanding the meaning of Christian practices. But self castration was increasingly marginalized and vilified: the Council of Nicaea in 325 and the slightly later *Apostolic Constitutions* banned anyone who had castrated himself from becoming a member of the Christian clergy (Caner 407, 413).

Another key element in the debate about castration is the (reading of) the Gospel of Matthew. Although it is given as an analogy, Matthew 19:12 has been taken as an injunction to self castration:

> For there are some eunuchs, which were so born from their mother's womb: and there are some eunuchs, which were made eunuchs of men: and there be eunuchs, which have made themselves eunuchs for the kingdom of heaven's sake. He that is able to receive it, let him receive it [Matthew 19:12, King James version].[24]

The question regarding the Bible is the same as that which we have for Catullus, and even Lucretius: how should the text be read? What rhetorical relationship does it have to its own culture? What does it amplify, repress, condense, displace or reproduce (to use the terms of Freud's dream analysis)? In particular, the mention that some had *made* themselves eunuchs poses a question of *how to read*: does this mean that some had castrated themselves? Or, does it just mean that some men had elected to remain celibate (Taylor 69)? Does the ambiguous last sentence of the verse serve as an encouragement or a warning, and if so, is it made to those who would become a eunuch, or to those who would condemn them?

Earlier in this gospel, a warning against sin is even more explicit and a range of savage forms of self harm is described:

> Woe unto the world because of offences! for it must needs be that offences come; but woe to that man by whom the offence cometh! Wherefore if thy hand or thy foot offend thee, cut them off, and cast them from thee; it is better for thee to enter into life halt or maimed, rather than having two hands or two feet to be cast into everlasting fire. And if thine eye offend thee, pluck it out, and cast it from thee: it is better for thee to enter into life with one eye, rather than having two eyes to be cast into hell fire [Matthew 18:7–9, King James version].

These verses are repeatedly cited by patients who have removed eye, hand or genitals, as they are also cited by doctors either in confirming the patient's own "version" of the reason for the self harm or in establishing a kind of "precedent." These uses will be discussed in greater detail in the following section, but for the moment what needs to be noted is that these describe very specific acts. More generally, inflicting physical punishment is associated with a range of religious practices where mortification of the flesh is seen as proof of various kinds.

Debates about self harm have recently been re-energized by popular accounts of the influential lay Catholic organization Opus Dei, which is said to encourage its members to practice mortification of the flesh (in medical contexts called self harm). There is a long tradition which links mysticism and mortification, exemplified in a figure like the Dominican friar Heinrich Seuse, who describes in his autobiography the fearsome forms of self punishment he devised (37–47). Among the best-known of the groups taken to be influenced by injunctions to physical atonement for sin are the Penitentes of the south-western United States, who include savage self-flagellation in their Easter rituals.

The best study of the Penitentes is by Michael P. Carroll; behind his work lies a rich archive of sensationalist stories which often implicitly secularize and sexualize the Penitente rituals. Alberto López Pulido's account, published in 2000, emphasizes the hysteria generated by press coverage of the murder of writer Carl Taylor in New Mexico in February 1936 (25). Although the murder was fairly quickly attributed to an employee, Taylor's associates who knew that he working on an article on the Penitentes preferred to blame the brotherhood for his death (see Meléndez 58–62). Coverage of the murder in newspapers across the United States, discussed by Pulido (25–29), was fuelled by the release of the film *Lash of the Penitentes* which ends, in Pulido's account, with this warning: "Here in our own country, we can see the very heart of Africa pounding against the ribs of the Rockies" (30). Through such rhetoric self harm is sensationalized as primitivism.

The accounts of travellers to New Mexico such as Earle R. Forrest's *Missions and Pueblos of the Old Southwest* (1929) and Alice Corbin Henderson's *Brothers of Light: The Penitentes of the Southwest* (1937, 1998) helped to bring the Penitentes to a broad or popular audience. These built on earlier accounts by Josiah Gregg (1844) and Charles Lummis (1889) (see Pulido 32–35). Forrest sets the tone of sensationalism, warning readers that he will tell "a fearful tale of self-inflicted torture" (200). He begins by claiming there are "hundreds" of crosses which mark the graves of those who have succumbed to the rituals: "Each one of those white crosses, bathed in the life-blood of some human being unable to survive the most fearful and agonizing suffering since the days of the Spanish Inquisition, marks the spot where his soul has found a refuge and rest from religious fanaticism" (195). Forrest goes on to describe in detail the Easter procession in which selected members of the group lash themselves, and the even worse punishment meted out to those who "fail": "If one of the brothers should falter, or cringe before the torturous lash he is brought back to his self-inflicting punishment by the Guide who cuts into the quivering flesh with a black-snake whip" (200). It is a tale Pulido repeats, twice.[25] Mark Thompson's description of the Penitentes in *American Character* (2001) is similar in emphasizing the coercive quality of the rites, those who falter being whipped. This goes hand-in-hand with ascribing the intensity of the rituals to the primitive cruelty of participants. In the tradition set by nineteenth- and early twentieth-century writers, Thompson describes the Penitentes as a "Catholic cult with mysterious roots, possibly reaching back to Spain in the Dark Ages" (102).

For Forrest, the origin of these practices is European: the Penitentes are "descended from the Flagellantes that swept Europe in the Middle Ages," "mutating" into a more savage version after the Mexican War of Independence, when the Penitentes were left "without regular government" (205). The implication is that without the restraint of the clergy, the uneducated laity increased the intensity of practices "alien" to the established church. Henderson's account is less sensationalist and more sympathetic, although she too understands the practices as "a genuine Old-World survival" of Spanish Catholicism (7). Warren A. Beck likewise asserts that "the Penitentes of New Mexico are a true representation of Spanish religious thought and Spanish culture in general" (172), but sees them as "representatives of the fusion of Moorish and Judaic traditions in Hispanic civilization" (176). For Beck, the most powerful and distinctive aspect of Spanish Catholicism is its sense of proximity to death (173). Beck cites a leading Spanish intellectual authority in support of his view that some element of extreme physical suffering is at the heart of what Beck understands not as a particular form of religious expression but as "the Spanish character," a phrase he uses several times.[26]

Alice Corbin Henderson, who unlike Forrest seems to have seen the rituals at issue, interrogates practices she found admirable but troubling. Seeking to identify their beginnings, she cites a 1598 source: Canto 11 of Captain Gaspar Pérez de Villagrá's *Historia de la Nueva Mexico*. The history describes the brutal Easter rituals of the party of Don Juan de Oñate: soldiers beat themselves "until the camp ran crimson with their blood," while the Franciscan friars chant their penance, "clothed in cruel thorny girdles" (Pérez de Villagrá 110). The leader secludes and scourges himself; the punishment of all continues throughout the night (110). She tells an anecdote which features a doubter, "'an Indian Wizard'" who was

> much angered [by the rituals] and said at the top of his voice: "You Spaniards and Christians, how crazy you are! And you live like crazy folks! ..." I asked

him wherein we were crazy. And he must have seen some procession during Holy Week in some Pueblo of Christians, and so he said: "You Christians are so crazy that you go all together, flogging yourselves like crazy people in the streets, shedding your blood..." and with this, greatly angered and yelling ... he went forth from the pueblo, saying that *he* did not wish to be crazy. Over which matter we were left laughing, and I much more, since I recognized and was persuaded it was the Demon, who thus went fleeing confounded by the virtues of the Divine Word [Henderson 5].

Henderson sees the communities which the Penitentes belong to as growing from "an arid soil dependent upon wind and chance" (22), and the rituals themselves as demonstrating "the heart of the Middle Ages" (30). Yet even as she condescends, she is prepared to claim some kind of connection or understanding: "all this has an inescapable emotional effect upon us, even though the faith that is moving these simple, impassioned people out of a bygone century is buried deep down in some remote fiber of our own race memory" (10).

There are two strands of interpretation of the rituals of the Penitentes. The first sees the self flagellation as a residue of Spanish Catholicism; the second sees the flagellation as a *corruption* of that religion. Either way, what every history searches for is a "savage ancestor." Those who argue for continuity claim the continued influence of "strains" of Judaism, "Moorishness" or Hellenism. Such thinking allows Beck, for example, to ask, "is not the Penitente in his quest for communion with God through his rites being the man of the Old Testament who is still seeking for something?" (173). In the case of those who see the Penitentes as having strayed from the path of a true Christianity, it is their isolation, their ignorance, and their literalness that have seen them embrace self flagellation with inappropriate fervor. In either instance, we can see the Penitentes being represented as people out of time: Forrest, writing in 1929, remarks, "It is impossible to believe that such things still exist in the United States at the present time unless you have been in the land of the Penitentes" (195).

Whether writers represent the ritual practices of the Penitentes as heroic or bizarre, whether they attribute these rites to the purity and intensity of Spanish religious culture or to its corruption, to the inherent cruelty and primitiveness of the native Americans of this region or to the brutality of their colonizers, they have in common the assumption that the self harm and its display are collective, that they derive from authentic local religious beliefs, and that they "make sense" with the community. They might be alienating for the outsider but they are not pathological. Embedded in recognizably Christian frameworks of belief, self flagellation among the Penitentes, however brutal, acquires dignity and persuasiveness. In that respect, there are instructive similarities between the accounts of the Galli and the stories of the Penitentes: the mix of revulsion, bewilderment and fascination that marks the descriptive accounts by writers positioned outside the framework of belief that sanctifies the self harm. In both instances, writers less accepting of the religious framework attribute the self harm to the influence of foreign cultures and ancient times, seen as cruel and labelled primitive. Here it is worth noting that the source material comes from the same historical period and similar genres: nineteenth- and early twentieth-century translations of works which hover between travelogue, ethnography, and literature. And in both cases, the voices of those who participate in the rituals are unheard.

While the self harm of the Penitentes is seen as reinforcing the social architecture provided by religious belief and that of the Galli as eroding it, another group who engaged in self harm motivated by religious precepts became official enemies of the state. The Russian Skoptsy, active from the early 1770s until the 1930s and perhaps longer, were persecuted by the Tsarist secret police and under the Soviet state. Apart from ecstatic worship and public social conformity, the practices of the Skoptsy include removal of the scrotum, removal of the scrotum and penis, and for women, removal of nipples, of breasts, and of the labia (Engelstein 5 and *passim*). Laura Engelstein's 1999 book *Castration and the Heavenly Kingdom* argues that the Skoptsy did not mutilate because they believed literally in the gospel of Matthew, as is often claimed in citations recorded in medical literature. Engelstein suggests that the Skoptsy saw removing parts of their body as a way to express an ecstatic spirituality:

> The confusion of literal and symbolic enacted in narrative terms was a central component of the faith. The confusion worked in both directions. In reading holy Scripture, the Skoptsy rendered metaphor—or what church doctrine construed as metaphoric—concrete. In representing their faith, they operated in reverse, draping the substantial in allusive figures of speech [Engelstein 33].

In the context of the religious diversity and long histories of practices of self harm, I am not quite convinced by Engelstein's attributing of "confusion." I would see this *exchange* between the literal and the metaphoric as a specific mode of religiosity, one in which the refusal to distinguish between the physical and the metaphysical produces the body as a mechanism through which faith can be attested to, and made manifest. For believers, the body is at once literal, in the sense of being "concrete," and symbolic, in the sense of being able to be used to represent something else, here, faith in God. On this basis, we might say that the mutilated body becomes proof of the existence of God. Thus it becomes possible to understand the self harm as a way of reconciling the demand for proof of the existence of God with an equally powerfully felt demand to express the truth of one's faith through a somatic language. In that sense, it is not uncertainty but its opposite, an *excess* of certainty, more usually called fanaticism—from the Latin *fānāticus*, belonging to a temple, perhaps derived from the rituals of the Galli (see Weigert-Vowinkel 353)—that enables self harm in this case.

This interpretation is congruent with what Engelstein has to say elsewhere: as she describes it, for the Skoptsy, removal of the genitals was used to fortify faith and community by exploiting the emotional power of persecution and suffering. As she puts it, "Having interpreted the original crucifixion as Christ's castration, [the Skoptsy] re-enacted the tragedy of social annihilation and moral abasement as the triumphant drama of salvation. They were taking agony into their own hands" (36). In his participant-observer ethnography of snake-handling Christians of the Appalachia, Dennis Covington describes the people of Sand Mountain in terms which likewise structure religious practice and identity through the coalescing of conviction, physical pain and marginality. As Covington describes it, the view of the members of this group is that "this is warfare, spiritual warfare. The tragedy is not the death of a particular snake handler, but the failure of the world to accept the gospel that the handler risked his life to confirm. Or, at least, this is how the handlers seem to see it" (Covington 184–85).

In each case—the Galli, the Penitentes, the Skoptsy, and the snake handlers of Appalachia—the body is an instrument for the expression of faith, and simultaneously, risk or ensuing damage entailed in the ritual practice becomes a lasting image of that faith for the community. At the same time, the diversity—flagellation, self castration, removal of the genitals by men and women, handling poisonous snakes—shows the specificity of actual or potential forms of self harm. The importance of cultural specificity and local influence in religious traditions is reinforced by the enduring influence of the story of the Bodhisattva Loveliness in cultures where there are followers of Buddhism. This story represents self-immolation as the ultimate form of expression of devotion to the Buddha (see Benn).[27]

"The Story of the Bodhisattva Medicine King" from the Lotus Sutra, contemporary with the plays of classical Greece, describes a monk who spends 12,000 years travelling and meditating on the Buddha, "after which he attained the contemplation of revelation of all forms," then disintegrated and rained from the sky as dust and flowers (Katō *et al.* 304). Concluding that his homage to the Buddha has been insufficient, because supernatural, the monk decides to offer his body, which he anoints with oils and incense and then sets alight. The flame illuminates the world and burns for a further 1,200 years, causing the buddhas (or "enlightened ones") of the Ganges to applaud the monk's fervor. His sacrifice "is called the supreme gift, the most honored and sublime of gifts" (Katō *et al.* 305). The monk is reborn as the Bodhisattva Loveliness and ascends to behold the Buddha himself, who on his ascension is able to prepare himself for parinirvāṇa or "perfect quietude, when all illusion is destroyed" (Katō *et al.*

308). We might characterize this as reading perfected: there is no act of mediation, only pure apprehension.

After this, the Bodhisattva Loveliness gathers his relics and makes 84,000 stupas (or pagodas) and adorns them, but again feels his devotions have been inadequate and declares to the gathered gods and attendants that he plans to pay further homage. He burns his arms for 72,000 years, and they disappear. His deformity is lamented and his arms are restored, "through the excellence of this bodhisattva's felicitous virtue and wisdom" (Katō *et al.* 307). The Buddha then asserts that

> If anyone with his mind set on and aiming at Perfect enlightenment is able to burn the fingers of his hand or even a toe of his foot in homage to a buddha's stupa he will surpass him who pays homage with domains, cities, wives, children, and his three-thousand-great-thousandfold land with its mountains, forests, rivers, pools and all its precious things [Katō *et al.* 307].

After these devotions are recounted, much of the rest of the parable claims the pre-eminence of this above all other sutras, or teachings, of the Buddha. Two doctors report on cases of self immolation which reference this story (see Budny *et al.* 336), while the political uses of self immolation are well documented (see Benn). These practices are often received in the West as heroic demonstrations of resistance to political expression rather than as the kind of abhorrent or even barbaric practices Said's *Orientalism* might encourage us to expect they would be. But such examples might, at the same time, be understood as expressions of political protest, of religious devotion, or even of the outcome of suggestion or coercion implied by sympathetic acceptance in the world's media. What is significant is that the practice is identified with *some* cultures in which Buddhism is a major religion but not all.

At the same time, claiming that a practice now seen as alien is "normal" in other times, places, or subcultures has a double blinding effect: it becomes more difficult to see the ways in which rituals which demand the experience of severe pain, even death, can be normalized, particularly within "microclimates" like institutions or peer groups; such claims make it more difficult to see that "rituals" might be one of several reasons for self harm, not all of them related to religious faith. For example, Geoffrey Oddie argues that a primary motivation for the practice of hook swinging, in which hooks are passed through the skin and the participants are suspended from poles, lies in compulsion. Oddie argues that in Bengal, the rituals could involve "individuals who were drawn from the lowest ranks of society being pressed into service and compelled to swing for landlords and others who had much to gain from the patronage and perpetuation of hook-swinging exhibitions" (33). Oddie adds, "The poor, unemployed and needy adopted the practice as one way of gaining an income" (33). Nevertheless, local religious frameworks represent hook-swinging as a kind of spiritual "resource," one which "could make a difference between life and death, rains and drought, health and sickness or fertility and infertility" (Oddie 41). What Oddie demonstrates here is that it is not just anthropologists who attribute meaning and causality to such rituals; within the society itself, the severity of pain seems to affirm the spiritual or practical efficacy of the outcome. The intensity of such rituals demands and thereby perhaps encourages intense devotion, as it also encourages contestation of these meanings within such societies, by scholars, and by writers populist and literary.

Modern Medicine and the Uses of Myth

Apart from the greater emphasis on the moral elements of medical decision-making, one notable characteristic of case reports of self harm is the recurrence of references to the kinds of stories of self harm, particularly classical and religious ones, canvassed in this chapter so far. Patients can cite religious stories as a kind of narrative backdrop against which their own actions can be described and interpreted; so too do doctors invoke literary and religious precedents (in particular) of radical self harm. While Attis is the point of reference for male self castration, for self enucleation the examples are proto–Christian: St. Lucia, patron saint of Syracuse; St. Triduan of Scotland; and St. Medana of Ireland—the latter almost mythical figure proclaimed by one writer as the patron saint of British ophthalmology. All three female saints are said to have removed their eyes, and references to them and to Sophocles' *Oedipus Rex* are routine in accounts of patients who have removed their own eyes, in such a way as to blur the meaning of the term "literature."[28] For example, reporting on a case of self-enucleation in 1985, Jemshed A. Khan and colleagues observe, "Self-enucleation first appeared in the literature of Greek mythology.... The legends of patron saints who punished themselves in a similar manner reflect the classic theme of self-enucleation as a noble act of penance and self-sacrifice" (Khan *et al.* 388–89), the article going on to offer a précis of the story of St. Lucia. Brown *et al.* recount the legend of "Saint Lucia" and "St. Triduna and St. Medana" (496), also noting the stories of Oedipus, Odin and Marco Polo.

That doctors in Los Angeles in 1984, Liverpool in 1991, Singapore in 1996, and Spain in 2003 should use these narratives of saints and heroes from Odin to Oedipus signals that medical writers in a range of cultures believe that ancient stories provide meaningful points of reference for writers and readers working in modern scientific contexts.[29] None of these articles suggests that the relationship between such stories and an individual's actions is well understood, but there seems general acceptance of views like this, from a 1978 essay on "Religious Delusions and Self-mutilation": "Delusional systems involving religious, mystical, or supernatural beliefs have been associated with mental illness throughout recorded history" (Goldenberg and Sata 2). Such statements prompt questions, including how a particular belief and its associated practice is or is not delusional. We might, for example, disagree on whether it is always safer to bring a box of rattle-snakes when travelling in a car, as some members of the community described by Dennis Covington believe, or indeed on whether the eye is the signifier of sin, the latter belief being associated not only with the gospel of Matthew but with psychoanalytic theory.

When a medical writer discards the patient's own account, which often is linked to a profession of religiosity, they can be forced to the conclusion that a patient with no apparent history of mental illness was temporarily in a delusional state when they injured themselves but has entirely recovered by the time they are interviewed. Typical is this 1981 report from Washington, D.C., which presents four patients. The first is a woman who removed her own eye, citing the gospel of Matthew, but "In the hospital she showed no signs of hallucinations or delusions" (Arons 551). While she is greatly concerned with right and wrong, especially her desire to murder her parents, "She spoke of her self-mutilation with a calm, detached, intellectual approach" (Arons 552). The second patient injured both his eyes; he had murdered his mother when he was a child, and consequently was in a mental institution between the ages of twelve and fourteen. On the day of his injuries, he is said to have reported an earlier injury to his wrist, in a calm, unemotional fashion. The third patient, who amputated his hand with a saw, was likewise able to speak of his injury in terms which presented it as "a necessary act" (Arons 554).

All of these patients have traumatic life stories and appear to be suffering severe mental illness: two of four are diagnosed as having schizophrenia, a third has some symptoms. But the evidence that the terrible injuries were inflicted while in the grip of psychosis is weaker. Three of the four patients cite the gospel of Matthew; for the other (patient no. 2 in the report), there is no record of his explanation for his injuries. The patients describe the ways in which they persuade themselves of the moral or spiritual "need" for self harm. The discussion does not attempt to reflect in detail on the relationship between religious belief, (possible) delusion, and self harm, nor to consider the ways in which the patient's reading of the religious story or their understanding of its meaning might become a template through which they explain their actions *before* and after they occur.

W.J. Bishop's survey of accounts of self harm presented to the Scottish Society of the History of Medicine in March 1961 refers to reports as early as 1797, in England, of self-castration by a young man who "'in a fit of religious enthusiasm made an incision into his scrotum and removed both testicles"' (Bishop 23).[30] Examples proliferate: Origen is discussed under the heading "psychotics and sexual perverts" (23) as is a bricklayer from 1797, although no evidence is given that suggests either person fits either term in the heading. It is proposed that those under the influence of delirium tremens belong also in this category, which serves as a means of introducing the story of a man who in 1885 severed his right foot. Another "category," of "Feeble minded or extremely ignorant persons" is used for a Czechoslovakian patient who removed his eye (Bishop 23). Immediately after the author moves to "prehistoric cave paintings in France and Spain which depict fingerless hands," which it is said "some authorities regard ... as examples of ritual mutilation" (Bishop 24). In such accounts we see the kinds of uses to which cultural analogy, however weak, can be put. The "explanations" of self harm which they imply are not based in medical practice, but in cultural convention, especially stereotype.

Yet patients can also confound these categories. A simpler, briefer 1987 report on a patient—himself a doctor—who had removed his genitals and his tongue, injuring also his ear drums and his eyelids, notes that the man "felt that he had made his peace with the Almighty" (Culliford). Likewise a patient to whom psychosis was attributed is described in a 2012 letter as "calm ... with clear consciousness and without any obvious distress or regret about his act" (Omidvar and Sharifi). Kimber and Pridmore's 2009 case of a woman in florid psychosis who removed her eye noted the patient's claim, made several days before, that she had removed her penis. As with the other cases, delusion is, like the biblical stories, made to signify causality through proximity—"surely the patient was mad" is unsaid, but becomes an inescapable conclusion.

One of the more troubling examples of the use of ancient story in modern medical writing occurs in a 1999 case report of a woman who injured her genitals. The authors present the following account of the patient and their understanding of her actions:

> Patients with genital mutilation tend to fall into four distinct subtypes: psychotic patients with delusions regarding their genitalia, patients with severe personality disorder, transsexuals with self-sexual reassignment, and people whose mutilation reflects religious or cultural beliefs (for example, female circumcision among Moslems [sic] and in certain Australian and African tribes [sic]. [The reference given is Favazza, *Bodies under Siege*, 1996.] ...
>
> The name Caenis syndrome has been suggested for the triad of genital self-mutilation, hysterical personality disorder, and eating disorder [citing Goldney and Simpson]. Neptune, the god of the sea, raped Caenis, a lovely girl in Thessaly. Neptune subsequently granted her a wish that her genitalia be ablated so that she might never again be sexually violated. Our patient repeatedly inserted a razor blade into her vagina but denied sexual gratification or psychotic symptoms [Alao, Yolles and Huslander 971].

The juxtaposition of the two-sentence précis of the classical story with the description of the patient's actions implies that the woman's insertion of razor blades (so deep they had to be surgically removed) is the equivalent of the removal of Caenis's genitalia by the god of the sea.

Even if we are to take the reported actions of gods as paradigms, it is still the case that Caenis does not remove her genitals; in this version, her rapist does.[31] A brief anecdote is lacquered with the authority of classical story, the patient paralleled to "a lovely girl in Thessaly." Yet the three doctors involved in the case surely agreed that the report was worth publishing, and the essay passed the refereeing and editorial processes of the journal in which it appeared (*Psychiatric Services*, a publication of the American Psychiatric Association). There is consensus, then, that this is a "scholarly" account. The article was contested by a letter, but what that writer objected to was the "omission of patients with dissociative disorders" (see Waugaman), not the terms of reporting.

The 1975 essay by Goldney and Simpson which proposes the terminology "Caenis Syndrome" itself bears scrutiny. The focus is on a woman who is said to have rejected her femininity. She is described as having "sharp features," "plain clothes," "hirsute legs" and "short dark hair," "brushed back and parted in a manly manner." These characteristics, and her habit of wearing her husband's socks, are adduced as evidence of her failure to value the feminine role and commensurately her "difficulty in dealing with her sexuality" (436). The case is serious: the woman is repeatedly hospitalized, not only for extensive vaginal bleeding but for complications relating to pregnancies and then a hysterectomy. The other two women these authors describe were diagnosed with anorexia nervosa; both had shaved their pubic hair. In order to fit the latter two patients into the proposed template, and as with the reading of Lucian proffered above, the hair is interpreted as a substitute. However, in the medical essay the shaving is subsumed under the heading of "self mutilation"—that is, it is no longer read *as* a substitution, thus these two women can be described in terms of the proposed "Caenis syndrome." Goldney and Simpson read Ovid's myth as a parable about refusing femininity, then lay that reading over their patients' behavior to make sense of it. In this very specific sense, we can say that the woman who inserted razorblades into her vagina is made sense of within a framework of myth. The authority of this account of a woman in the city of Adelaide in 1975, made newly legible by the work of a Roman poet, is consolidated by its location in the definitive handbook of self harm, Favazza's *Bodies Under Siege* (1996: 198).

Goldney and Simpson admit their concerns about naming a syndrome on the basis of such a small sample, but they propose that this kind of "shorthand" "often enable[s] isolated symptoms to be more easily incorporated into one's *gestalt* of illness" (440). In other words, literary and mythological terms are a kind of mnemonic, one which the writers say facilitated "the recall of two previous patients who in retrospect appear to fulfil these criteria" (440). The honesty of these writers points to a significant issue in medical education and practice: *how to remember*, in particular, how to remember *collections* of apparently disparate signs, how to read volatile or contradictory or hidden or paradoxical symptoms. The etymology of the Greek term "diagnosis" is not simply "recognition" or "knowing" (associated with gignōskein), but "dia," apart, thus the term builds in the notion of *discernment*. It is not so much a *thing* as a set of (potentially competing) patterns that the medical professional must identify. In that particular sense the essay, through its frank explanation of the benefits of using the term "Caenis syndrome," provides us with another way of understanding the appeal of using literary sources in medical literatures: they provide a more memorable and more easily recognized set of conditions or constellation of symptoms (when seen *again*) than any individual patient can. The *use* of this repertoire of mnemonics from high culture has a secondary effect. It positions the doctor as a member of the *cultural* class who "knows," who recognizes, stories or symbols from literature, opera, painting, film or sculpture.

These stories or symbols often provide a kind of entrée or "frame" for the "scientific" ones (being cited in the opening paragraphs), but the more powerful narrative shape of the former—by which I mean simply that they are more persuasive, more famous, and are more memorable—is used to impose form on doctors' accounts of their patient's actions in ways that allow the cultural authority of medicine and literature to split and overlap. We can see this process operating in another "foundational" case report for medical writers on self harm, the 1993 essay "Genital Self-Mutilation" by Aboseif, Gomez and McCanich, writing from the San Francisco General Hospital and the University of California Medical School. It begins by noting that self mutilation is extremely rare, then cites five case reports before also suggesting that "Since ancient times, self-mutilation has been performed willingly" as part of religious rites (1143). Aboseif *et al.* claim that the first "scientific" report is from 1901, then note Nolan D.C. Lewis's use of "the Phoenician belief that Eshmun, the beautiful god of spring" castrated himself to avoid the sexual advances of the mother Goddess (1143). The first paragraph concludes by noting that "Menninger in 1938 cited numerous other examples in ancient religion." Then: "Since these early reports, more than 70 cases of intentional self-mutilation of male genitals have been cited in the literature" (1143). But by no stretch of the imagination can this collection of writing on self castration be characterized as "early reports." Lewis and Menninger are medical writers (see chapter four), but they too make reference to mythic sources. Here, the lines between myth and medicine seem to blur.

Doctors clearly struggle in coming to terms with what can be their patients' own literal interpretation of texts which induce or imply approval of radical acts of self harm, such as those of Attis. Literature also seems to function as a kind of "transporter device" which shifts an encounter out of its hospital setting into a literary realm that can be entered by colleagues. And by such means, writers can attempt to inject humor into even the most horrific stories. This capacity of story, to mediate the horror of actual cases, is typified by Ward A. Holden's discussion of "An Ancient Saint [St. Lucia] and a Modern Sinner," the latter a prisoner who had devised an elaborate device which would, after drugging him, cause catastrophic and permanent injury to his eyeballs. In the case of Lucia, enraged by her virtue, or perhaps by her claim that while he could torture her body he could not claim her mind, the Governor of Sicily ordered her burned alive; according to some stories, she had plucked out her eyes earlier in life. Holden writes,

> The avulsion legend has numerous versions, but *the one that pleases me most* came in a letter from an artist with whom previously I had talked of these pictures. "As I remember it," he wrote, "a would-be husband spoke his admiration of the lady's beautiful eyes. Being as ignorant as fair, unaware of the use of beauty and its meaning, she said in effect: 'If you like them, take them'; and, so to speak, forked them over" [Holden 56; emphasis added].

There is a similar story of sexual sacrifice told by Georges Bataille, who purports to retell a story from Michel de Montaigne's *Essays* of a man who surrendered his genitals to the woman to whom he had been unfaithful: "Mortified by an amorous adventure in which he behaved foolishly, a gentleman 'mutilated himself' and sent his mistress the organs that had disobeyed him in his desires, as a kind of *bloody victim* capable of *expiating* the offense he believed he had committed against her'" (Bataille 71 note 8, in which he also cites Aretaeus). But Montaigne's account is slightly different: whereas Bataille cites infidelity as the "cause," Montaigne is explicit that the young man's humiliation and his chosen form of atonement arise not from promiscuity but almost its opposite. In the translation by Charles Cotton, the story is told like this: "having by his perseverance at last mollified the heart of a fair mistress enraged, that upon the point of fruition he found himself unable to perform" (Montaigne). The presentation of the genitals is made by way of recompense.[32] In each instance, self harm is seen as risible.

While stories are used, recycled, revived and re-presented in different ways, it is clear that there is an assumption that patients and doctors have very different relationships to them, even when (as in some reports) doctors themselves become patients. What, then, is the effect of citing biblical or classical literature, or more precisely, of making what we might reasonably call the diagnostic short cut of "literal reading," shown for example in the essay by

Goldenberg and Sata on religious delusion which claims that four patients have tried to cut off their hands "because the *Bible* tells them so"? Ascribing "madness" short-circuits the investigation of how religious belief functions in the psyche. For religious belief is not (generally) regarded as madness, but literal reading of the Bible is, in this case, equated with madness. By such a move, the edifice of religiosity can remain intact, not only for the patient but for the doctor. Yet the story is also told in such a way as to distance the patient from the sphere in which medicine operates: the modern, the secular, the rational; above all, the use of classical sources differentiates the writer from their subject in terms of cultural authority. There is a world of difference between behaving like a character in Greek tragedy or classical myth or the Bible (as the patients seem to do), and knowing these stories *as* stories (as doctors do).

Medical accounts are also likely to imply that violent rituals or credulity are the province of the ignorant, those who seek to placate or approach a divine being by replicating the bodily sufferings of his mortal representative. Thus Bernice Engle describes Attis's self castration in ways that equate the "primitive" with "the psychotic": using the "direct logic characteristic of psychotic and primitive people he identifies his sexual sin with his genitals and by personification lays the blame wholly upon them" (366).[33] Similar assumptions about literal reading and susceptibility to self harm inflect medical reports throughout the twentieth century and after. For example, a 1996 case report of a 22-year-old man in the United States who severed his penis with an electric chainsaw identifies the patient's actions with a story he had seen on television earlier that day: Lorena Bobbitt's attack on her husband, John, during which she severed his penis with a knife. The patient himself, denying any hallucination, drug use, or prior thought about self harm, reported that he had experienced an overwhelming desire "'to become a girl'" and that he had cut off his penis "'because of the stuff on tv'" (Catalano *et al.* 40).

Catalano *et al.* note that two current affairs programs which had included segments on the Bobbitt case had concluded at 7:30 p.m., the time the patient said he had experienced his desire to become female. They ask whether, in the light of the patient's relatively poor mental functioning, he might have been particularly vulnerable to suggestion (43). They propose that it is "the young, the mentally ill, and the intellectually impaired" who are impressionable. Likewise, interviewees reported in a more recent study: one says that she began cutting the day after reading about the practice in a teen magazine; another after learning about the practice in a health class; another from "'a cool guy'" (Adler and Adler, "The Demedicalization" 551). Three cases of self-amputation of the ear—a highly unusual form of physical self harm—were reported in an Australian prison, the second patient claiming (like the first) that his action was caused by the refusal of prison authorities to allow him to attend a relative's funeral (Alroe and Gunda 509). In two other cases noted by these authors, the prisoners claimed to have been reading the autobiography of a noted criminal who engaged in self harm (511).[34]

But it might be worth questioning the assertion that it is "the young, the mentally ill, and the intellectually impaired" who are influenced by stories in coming to acts of self harm, or more generally, that religious belief is the province of the "uneducated or the socially marginal" (Ferber, *Demonic* 2). Some writers claim that public expressions of penance such as those practised by the Penitentes, for example, were the preserve of the social elite, not of the poor or unlettered. Henderson notes a claim that the Franciscan Third Order (a forerunner of the Penitentes) includes "nearly every leading citizen" of New Mexico; likewise she quotes [Frank Brangwyn and] Hugh Stokes' *Belgium* on a French visitor's impression of Brussels, the streets "crowded by penitents of the nobler classes": "Many of them, covered by a rough cloak, carried a heavy cross on their shoulders. Others, half-clothed, flagellated their body, or whipped themselves with chains. Mingling the profane with the sacred, they displayed their wounds to the ladies who flocked to admire their divine ardor" (Henderson 100). Weigert-Vowinkel, citing Hugo Hepding, asserts that it was "the Roman aristocracy who begged in the service of the Great Mother" (351).

The classical, mythological and religious stories of self harm used by patients and by doctors are *culturally* authoritative, and they are *diagnostically* flexible. By this I mean that they have a "substance" which is used to give meaning to the medical report, while they retain an "openness" that allows the doctor/author to connect the story to their own experience and observations. I suggest, though, that they serve a third function: they allow the reporting doctors to tell the story of their *own* trauma in ways which accrue a kind of intellectual seriousness. The irony here is that medical writers' use of these stories replicates that literal reading that they often accuse their patient of making. In fact, that reading error is central to what we might call the economy of delusion, the circuitry of story, belief and obedience which underpins so many accounts of self harm. This makes sense of the fact that a case report like Goldenberg and Sata's on a young man's self-castration is driven not so much by the search for an understanding of the relationship between religious belief and delusion—this is quickly encapsulated as "obedience" and is not investigated—as it is a search for a "cause" in terms of "affiliation or association with countercultures and obedience to religious dogma" (5). Thus Goldenberg and Sata write that the young man "said that religious preoccupations gradually were dominating his life" but their argument leaves some key elements of belief intact, while terming others, such as homosexuality, pathological.

The flexibility and reach of the authority of these sources is demonstrated in those reports which purport to analyze self harm in other cultures. Beilin and Grueneberg's 1948 essay "Genital Self Mutilation by Mental Patients" resorts to fantastical ethnographies to explain the actions of patients: self harm is said to be a manifestation of "autoalgolania," desires embracing pleasure and pain, and has been observed "among some primitive peoples" who practice "genital self-mutilation ... as a ritual or magico-religious rite, or as therapeutic measure in the effort to remove bad blood or evil humours" (635). Recounting five cases of severe genital self harm by men, they conclude by gesturing to "unconscious homosexual tendencies" and "the persistence of infantile sexuality patterns" as further contributory causes (640), although their accounts concentrate on the details of surgical treatment and offer little in the way of history or psychological assessment. At the same time, the references to "unconscious ... tendencies" and "infantile sexuality" indicate that these authors used Freudian concepts in what might almost be termed a "common sense" or non-specialist way. Their report demonstrates that those who *did* take up psychoanalytic theory, and therefore (hypothetically) had access to a way of understanding the symbolic significance of self harm, could remain unable or unwilling to apply this knowledge.

Spectre and Spectacle: Self Harm as Performance

> Many provinces [in the Philippines] ... have crucifixion ceremonies during Easter, or "holy week" as they refer to it. But only one, in Gua Gua, Pampanga, less than two hours north of Manila, features such a real life re-enactment.... It's great sightseeing and one of the best photo opportunities. One of the best travel photos I've ever taken was shot from crawling on my stomach amongst a dozen others where I was able to capture the silhouette of the nail punctured left hand on the cross....
> ... The best [crucifixion] is outside of Gua Gua, Pampanga, because the "Christ's" hands are pierced with spikes after being tied to the wood cross.
> ... Three crosses are hoisted up for a few minutes. As the "Christ," is being prepared there's a eery humming chant that allows the "Christ" to reach a trance like state so I doubt he feels much pain. It's a mystical experience for all who witness the event.[35]

This description of crucifixion re-enactment ceremonies in the Philippines reveals the mix of fascination and separation that inheres in watching self harm. That this may have an erotic element is suggested by the participation in 1996 of Japanese national Kaneko Shinichiro, whose request was granted on compassionate grounds (given that he was not a Christian) after he claimed that his younger brother was terminally ill. But "months later it was discovered that Kaneko was actually a pornographic actor specializing in sado-masochistic roles whose crucifixion was filmed for video-release in sex-shops in Japan" (Baker). Such examples are not so much proof of the bizarre as indications of the contemporary popularity of sadistic rites that have been given the gloss of religious ceremony, and the potential for those rites to be redeployed in a range of contexts.

Art itself can draw attention to the nature of symbol and the practice of interpretation in contexts which deploy the affective power of self harm. A surrealist performance held in the Paris flat of Joyce Mansour in 1959 dedicated to the Marquis de Sade, who gave his name to sadism, built to a charged climax in which self harm was first performed and then "replayed" by a member of the audience. *The Execution of the Testament of the Marquis de Sade* entailed a strip-tease by performance artist Jean Benoît. The concurrent narration explained the symbolism of each element of the costume Benoît removed piece by piece. He

> finished the performance by raising a hot branding iron to his chest and burning the word "Sade" onto his bare flesh, making a sacrifice of himself as a finale to his Sadean testimony. No sooner had Benoît removed the iron from his burnt flesh than the surrealist artist Roberto Matta spontaneously stepped forward, moved by the intensity of the performance, and thrust the hot iron at his chest too [Mahon 285].

Matta inserted himself by way of echo or encore that was homage to the emotional impact of the performance. In so doing, in the eyes of the movement's nominal leader André Breton, he became an authentic member of the surrealist group (Mahon 325).

It is impossible to recreate the dynamics of self-conscious avant-gardism and eroticism which charged an event conceived as a kind of burial service for Sade. But the account—which *includes* Matta's response to Benoît, then Breton's response to Matta—shows the flexibility in the meanings attributed to self harm. While nominally either pathological or highly ritualized—and it requires careful cultural work to ensure that the same actions are differentiated in terms of circumstances and the credentials of the performer—in the heady mix of the surrealist avante-garde, self harm becomes a vehicle for the illustration of ideas thought dangerous to social order. The literal branding is made a powerful signifier of the intensity and integrity of the commitment of artist *and* audience to somatic experimentation. Precisely that contagion noted by Lucian ("many who had come as mere spectators afterwards are found to have committed the great act") and implied by Lucretius is in evidence in Matta's response to this performance, which became participation in it. And in this "echo" we see an extravagant example of the seduction of self harm, whether the austere preserve of that artistic elite, or overtly and commercially sexualized as part of what could be termed popular culture, as in the example of Kaneko.

Among the best-known of those working in a tradition of sado-masochistic performance art was Ron Athey, who suffered from cystic fibrosis. In his essay "Ron Athey: Self-Mutilation as Religious Experience," theatre scholar Theodore Shank describes one such event:

> Athey enacts an intravenous drug-user in withdrawal convulsions. He inserts about twenty hypodermic syringes into his arm and sticks other needles into his scalp, which causes blood to trickle down his face. In the final scene Athey officiates at a wedding ceremony. The three brides are naked except for loincloths, and dozens of bells have been attached to their bodies—chests, breasts, backs, legs—by needles. Athey talks of having grown up with sounds of people speaking in tongues and fits of religious ecstasy. He tells of having renounced his religious heritage, of his heroin addiction, and of his salvation in a metaphorical church of self-flagellation. To the beat of drums played by the men, the women dance wildly until exhausted as the bells bounce up and down and from side to side, making their bodies bleed. From time to time they and the men scream. Athey says, "there are so many ways to say Hallelujah" [Shank 223–24].

The performance, according to Athey, "explores the role personal fetishism plays in our sanity.... And further, acknowledging the role of self-destruction ... I think there's something inherently spiritual in what I do that makes it a ritual. It's like a public sacrifice I think. It is really parallel to doing penance" (Shank 224). Acts of self harm which are congruent with religious belief seem to be attempts to demonstrate both subjection to belief (obedience) and the operation of free will (choice). This is a situation that performance artists like Athey seek to expose, and to parody, but also, at the same time, one senses, in a particular way, to honor. And it brings us close to Weigert-Vowinkel's interpretation of stories of Attis and the Galli, specifically, in her reading of the celebration as evidence of that "passive dependence" which accompanies the renunciation of male power.

While both Athey's and Benoît's performances are positioned as avant garde, at least one set of late nineteenth- and early twentieth-century performances of self harm were unashamedly populist. Advertisements for a self harm extravaganza which toured Europe and Britain show that mix of disdain for and fascination with the East that marks the orientalist:

> Inexplicable riddles of / Piercing, / Cutting, / Beating / of any part of the body, NOT ONLY by the Fakirs themselves, but / BY ANY MEMBERS / OF THE AUDIENCE / WITHOUT PAIN ! ! ! WITHOUT BLOOD ! ! ! / Programme / In the presence of the Medical Profession, of the absolutely unique and astonishing mysterious Séance and Experiments by the Indian Fakirs—Saadi Djebarri and Soliman Ben Said & Sons / Part I. / Experiments of the Indian Fakirs: / Incredible experiments on their own bodies—Piercing of Cheeks, Arms and Neck by Soliman Ben Said and Saadi Djebarri. / Piercing of the Muscles of Hands of Ben Said with needles by volunteers from the audience. / Experi-

ments on his own body—Driving a Sword through his own Abdomen by Ben Said. / 15 minutes pause / Part II. / Producing of Apples and Sabres / The severing of an Apple wrapped in a handkerchief without injury to the latter. / Experiments, Dancing, etc., on broken glass. / Experiments from the realm of Psychological Manifestations—Thoughtreading [Soliman].

The point is not whether this was self harm or conjuring, but that the audience is lured with the promise of "incredible experiments," including the opportunity to pierce the bodies of the performers and witness them dancing on broken glass. And if such prose seems antiquated we can note its resemblance to an advertisement for a documentary film, "Cut Up Kids," the promotional prose for which cultivates fear of contagion and contamination: "An unspoken, terrifying cult is sweeping through young people. Largely unreported, self-harm is turning into an epidemic with around 500 young people ending up in casualty each week in the UK alone" ("Cut up Kids"). This terminology clearly recalls descriptions of the Penitentes.

As these examples suggest, extreme forms of physical self harm can be positioned quite differently within the apparently separate but sometimes overlapping domains of medicine, high art, religious ritual and popular culture. And when a ritual like hook swinging is migrated from its Bengali contexts into an academic monograph by self harm's most influential scholarly writer, published by the world's leading medical university press Johns Hopkins (see Musafar), even the same *form* of self harm can take on quite different meanings. My point is neither to demean Musafar nor to press the case for the seriousness of the documentary (or the "Inexplicable Riddles"), but to note the mobility of self harm, and the proliferation of meanings associated with it. In the examples discussed in this chapter, self harm is situated in the theatre, the street, the temple, the hospital, the private residence and the music hall. Commensurately it is understood as anything from private penance to public performance, from the meaningless act of a psychotic individual to a profound evocation of the most intense and inspiring forms of devotion to a deity, collectively performed and collectively acclaimed.

The prevalence of religiosity, but also stories from popular culture, in accounts of radical self harm leads one to speculate on the ways in which certain kinds of narratives are selected, retained and redeployed as part of one's *own* life story. But how to understand the processes by which individuals deploy stories of others in their own lives, using them to structure and justify our behavior? Might this process resemble the academic "citation" made conventional not only by scholarship, but institutions like law and medicine, in which authority hinges on precedent? For stories of all kinds, from great myths of antiquity to fleeting news reports, can be used in all kinds of ways. Like stories from soap operas, sporting events or gossip columns, they become a kind of currency and a means of generating recognition for the tale being told. In a 1999 case report, the authors describe a patient who had inserted forty or fifty stainless steel needles into his limbs to strengthen them: "P had seen the movie [*Terminator*] 10 times and believed that the steel in his body would make him powerful as the terminator" (Bharath, Neupane and Chatterjee 184). Psychoanalysis in particular turns to literary narratives, notably classical drama, as a template for some its most powerful explanatory parables. Sophocles' play *Oedipus Rex* is a reference point for the Oedipus complex, for example. Debate about psychoanalytic concepts can proceed via debate over the interpretation of literary texts. So prevalent is this use of literature that leading early practitioner Sándor Ferenczi suggests that "for any useful writings on individual-psychology we have to go not to scientific literature, but to belles-lettres" ("Psychosexual Impotence" 18).

While it is a commonplace of modern cultural studies of medicine to observe that the narratives and tropes of popular culture influence "scientific" ways of speaking, and it is even more commonplace for doctors to use narratives from literary or popular culture as a template or backing beat for their discussion, the processes by which individuals might bend elements of popular story into the narrative of their own life, and thence structure their behavior around them, is not yet the subject of serious study in either medicine or literature.[36] This might seem a frivolous or even derogatory analogy, but it is not intended to be. It is a way of trying to understand why narratives with little obvious explanatory power proliferate in case reports, as they are mentioned by patients themselves and by doctors. This produces an effect whereby a single story (that of the patient) becomes overlaid and intercut with a series of *other* stories (about other patients, about religious figures, about mythical figures). One aspect of this social function is that myth has a ready-made credibility not available to the patient, which is perhaps why some reports work overtime to consolidate the authority of stories from classical, Christian or ethnographic sources.

2

Delicate Structures?
Case Studies of Self Harm

[H]ow can a distinction be made between a wise act carried out by a madman, and a senseless act of folly carried out by a man usually in full possession of his wits?—Foucault, *History of Madness* 33

You can't diagnose it unless you think of it. Once considered, "look with new eyes" at the entire case and the medical record.—Bryk and Siegel 6, emphasis in original

Foucault's *History of Madness* concentrates on the dialectic between philosophy (reason) and madness, arguing that this dichotomy underwrites understandings of "civilisation" in Western Europe and the United Kingdom. Threaded through his study is a set of questions about the relationship between the will and mental illness which boil down to this: in what sense can someone who is thought to be mentally ill be held responsible for their actions?

Foucault explores the question of will and responsibility through reference to early modern textbooks of the law, part of his larger project of critiquing the philosophical and religious foundations of Western institutions like medicine, the law and the family. He quotes one such textbook: "Madness or eccentricity is an alienation of the spirit, an unhinging of reason which prevents us from being able to distinguish between the true and the false, and which by its continual agitation of the spirit *removes the subject's power of assent*" (qtd. in Foucault, *History* 137; emphasis added). In Foucault's view, by emphasizing the responsibilities and capacities of the mind, the new rationalism associated with the Enlightenment "shaped a *moral* experience of unreason" (*History* 106; emphasis added). In its simplest terms: if a human being possesses the capacity for reason, they must be responsible for their actions. The residue of this assumption, as far as Foucault is concerned, is that the starting point for understandings of mental illness in the West is moral condemnation (106).

What is the value of Foucault's claims for conceptualizing self harm? They allow us to see that there is a double trap for those who injure themselves, in terms of how doctors might respond. If the doctor understands the self harm as somehow involuntary, then arguably there can be no effective treatment. But if self harm can be held to be "deliberate," it might not necessarily be an illness. Holding the patient responsible for their actions honors the modern faith in the capacities of the individual, but such approaches are also often caught up in scientifically dubious and culturally inflexible assumptions about "character." The questions about self harm (say, of the last two centuries) which thereby arise are these: how likely is it that a patient seeking medical assistance for extreme forms of physical self injury will be held responsible for their actions? How do medical professionals understand "the will" in their responses to patients who self harm? If patients *are* held responsible, what are the consequences for modes of treatment? Or do responses to patients who self harm confirm Foucault's claim that "Unintentional madness or the intention to appear insane *are treated in the same fashion*, perhaps because they are dimly perceived as having a common root in evil, or at least in a *perversion of the will*" (Foucault, *History* 136; emphasis added). It is competing ideas of what Foucault refers to in passing as "the delicate structures of responsibility" of the patient that are the focus of this chapter.

The case reports which are the "raw material" or archive for this discussion belong to a genre which usually presents the encounter(s) between a specific doctor or doctors, and specific individuals. The case report develops medical knowledge at the micro level, through accumulation of precedents. Every case report is in one sense a description of the interaction between doctor and patient and in that respect, case reports taken together offer by far the largest single archive of responses to self harm. They are used in this chapter to show that every case of self harm potentially re-opens, *in a new way*, that question about responsibility and volition just discussed. For in some instances, even the apparently simple line between the expert surgeon and the patient in dire emergency is blurred. Here, it is also necessary to acknowledge the conceptual limitations of the genre: the demand for brevity means there is little time to explore the social conditions or the patient's background, or even the patient's actions. The setting out of precedents is necessarily cursory; the conclusions are usually limited to the final paragraph of the discussion.

A small and interesting minority of writers wrestle with the moral, intellectual and medical consequences of finding their most trusted conceptual tools unusable. What is also evident is the struggle between the medical convention which demands diagnosis and prognosis,[1] and the search for a helpful and reasonable response to actions that are unpredictable in outcome. Taken together, they show the frequency with which self harm raises what Amer Chaikhouni compellingly describes as "the agony of making the proper decision," "not in the clear zones of medical science but in that gray aspect of the art of medicine where the practicing physician is alone" (248). And to speak again in terms of genre, the case report always walks a line between conformity and innovation. Fitting the patient to a category or offering a new category is a key element of the structure, as we have seen with the discussion of the coining of the term "Caenis syndrome" in the previous chapter. The most prevalent forms of extreme physical self harm documented in case reports are amputation of some body part, usually the eye or genitals, severe abrasion, and the ingesting of dangerous objects.

Self Enucleation and Ingestion of Needles

Like amputation of the hand and penis, cases of self-enucleation have been linked by patients to religious belief.[2] For example, James C. Howden, writing in 1882, notes that a patient of his "thought that God had ordered her to burn herself in order to purify her soul" (50), inflicting severe injuries on her tongue, eyes, arms and vagina. (In terms of the ways in which stories circulate and intensify within specific contexts noted at the end of the previous chapter, it is noticeable that the patient's brother had, like his sister, removed his eyes.) Perhaps because of the Christian and classical references to self-enucleation in the gospel of Matthew and the story of Oedipus, doctors confronted with individual cases have been far more ready to turn to symbolism and literature in order to find meaning and motive. That said, there are case reports which emphasize the neurological and physiological background of the patient and give almost no attention to psychological factors. For example, although reporting on a girl who explained the fact that her right eye was missing by saying it had "fallen out," and the next day that her left had done the same (following repeated self-extraction of teeth), Goodhart and Savitsky give minute attention only to physical detail. Indeed, they remark, "Careful psychologic probing was avoided because such attempts usually precipitated periods of marked dejection and apparently interfered with her progress" (677). Although claiming there is no evidence of trauma, they admit "We have not probed much beyond the surface" (677). By way of contrast, the authors of a much earlier account of a similar case of self-enucleation and auto-extraction of teeth, Cortyl and Martinenq, assert that "no physiological reaction is not the result of trauma" ("Aucune réaction physiologique n'est le résultat de ce traumatisme"; 429).

A report from the United States published in the *Lancet* in 1908—not long after X-ray machines were introduced to hospitals—cited a case of a female patient who had experienced multiple surgeries, investigation with the new technology having revealed needles distributed throughout her digestive system (Nicoll 773–74). The woman said she had swallowed the needles all at once 18 months before. Those found during the first operation had been in the body for some time, although subsequent interventions produced "bright shiny" ones (774). The account describes the woman's personality at length, not necessarily in pejorative terms—indeed, although there is some bafflement, the tone at times verges on admiring (776). There are similar, more recent cases: Barker and Lucas report in 1965 on a patient who ingested safety pins on numerous occasions and injured herself in other ways, but their focus is on demonstrating the value of hypnosis as a mode of treatment. Two cases were reported late in the twentieth century by James and Allen-Mersh: young men who ingested needles and pins respectively, as well as razor blades and a kitchen knife (107).[3] Several of the female patients described in Al-Qattan's 2001 study from Saudi Arabia had inserted needles in their hands or arms while Badano *et al.* in 2010 reported a woman with diagnosed mental illness who swallowed sewing needles (see also Moon *et al.*) The focus of these accounts tends to be on the surgical response. The issues of diagnosis, or treatment of the underlying issues which see the patients swallowing needles or inserting them into their flesh, are often not mentioned, or discussed only briefly if they are.

Such cases present doctors with a quite specific dilemma, outlined in a 1972 report on a woman who claimed to have inserted needles into her arm: "If the complaint were a somatic delusion, she might require increased antipsychotic medication. If her complaint were actual, the best management would be medication for pain and surgical referral" (Kraft and Babigian 128). As it turned out, both possibilities applied: the woman claimed to be experiencing pain in both arms, but X-rays showed needles in one arm. The main aim of the report is to show the limitations in diagnosis and treatment available in the emergency context, something also taken up by Rashid and Gosai in their 2011 account of a young woman with more than 150 admissions to accident and emergency for the ingestion of items including knives, razors and large needles. The sheer scale of this case, when set against the kinds of limits in capacity discussed by Kraft and Babigian, points to a central issue in the response to self harm: that experience of acute cases of physical injury occurs in contexts in which nuanced interpretation, preceded by carefully sequenced diagnosis, is all but impossible. The very notion of emergency implies trauma and, by implication, a medical issue well beyond the patient's control. That emergency rooms are both the literal front line of treatment, but perhaps not well equipped to deal with cases which require ongoing treatment and/or referral, is only highlighted by those reports which show a general practitioner or psychiatrist with the resources—not the least of which are usually time and prior knowledge of the patient to deal effectively with self harm.

In the most troubling of these cases of needle swallowing, reported by Judson B. Andrews in 1872, the author reported the extraction of around three hundred needles, their insertion having been "prolonged and distributed" (17). Of the needles removed during the patient's lifetime and after her death, exactly half were taken from the right breast; other areas of concentration were the left breast, genitals, abdomen, thighs and legs, and back. "The patient repeatedly and insistently denied any knowledge of having induced them" (19); she was treated as a morphine addict, severely afflicted by mental and various physical illnesses. Andrews concludes that the needles were introduced while "under the influence of morphia ... and while suffering from hysteria" (19). However, no background is presented on the patient: she is introduced simply as "thirty years of age, single, seamstress ... of a highly nervous and excitable organization, emotional and irregular in feeling; at times buoyant and lively, and then gloomy and depressed" (13). Andrews implicitly understands there to be some relationship between the woman's self harm and the (mal)functioning of her reproductive system, but this is not explored in detail; nor is any connection made between her occupation and the form of self harm. A 2012 report of a case in India written 130 years later mimics this lack of interest in background or the possibility of mental illness, the authors associating their patient's insertion of needles into various parts of her body with "command hallucinations" but not reporting on any discussion of circumstances beyond the fact that the commands were given by her sister-in-law and the symptoms commenced one week after her marriage (Sarkar and Balhara E10). In this and other cases, the needles were inserted directly into the body (as other objects can be—see for example Mario and Tare).

An overview and an attempt to provide typology of the ingestion of dangerous objects is given by Poynter et al., who begin in part by noting the "relative paucity of literature regarding efficacious long-term psychiatric and psychological management of these patients" (518). They observe that most information about the condition derives from the accumulation of case reports (519; see also Cormia "Basic Concepts I"). On the basis of their reading of the literature the authors offer four categories of patients who swallow dangerous objects: psychosis, personality disorders or suicide attempts, OCD and malingering. But perhaps the most important contribution lies in their observation, "The consulting psychiatrist should be aware of the necessity to address the frustrations of the medical or surgical team ... managing colleagues' countertransference is an integral part of the consultation request" (Poynter et al. 519).[4] They observe,

Psychiatric inpatient admission, by itself, *has not been shown to be effective in preventing future DFBI* [deliberate foreign body ingestion] and *may even foster regression* that leads to escalating swallowing behavior. When there is no other indication for acute psychiatric inpatient treatment, this likely negative outcome has to be explained and discussed with the ED or medical/surgical teams, as nonadmission to psychiatry can be construed (again, *in the midst of a countertransference storm*) as inadequate care of the patient or a dismissal of the profound impact these patients often have on the nonpsychiatric services, in terms of their efforts, emotions and expense [520; emphasis added].

These comments suggest that identification of the desire to self harm is in some senses a *social* judgment, "social" in the sense of demanding a relationship with the patient and with colleagues. The resulting difficulties are suggested by David L. Calof's assertion, made in 1995 to readers of a journal for those responding to survivors of sexual abuse, "Many clinicians are reluctant to address self-injury directly with their clients because of panic, uncertainty, or incompetency," or believe that by discussing self harm they will exacerbate it (11).

Malingering Versus Mental Illness: Respecting Patients?

In 1910 the *Lancet* published a report from 5 May 1832, in its "Looking Back" column (Seymour). Prefaced by Sydenham's contention that "one half of the disease of females are dependent upon hysteria," Seymour cites two cases: the first of a young woman who claimed she passed no urine (having drunk it), the second of a young woman who claimed to have passed gravel (found to be sea sand). Seymour, delivering a clinical lecture at St. George's Hospital, declared to his listeners, "The above cases are of downright imposition, and in all such cases as *these*, I would advise you to let the patient and her friends know that you are fully aware that her disease is all imposture, and you will generally find this remark sufficient to cure the worst symptoms." But whether it was intended that readers should interpret the story as a cautionary one about women, or an example of outmoded attitudes and therefore just funny, is not clear. What is interesting is that Seymour's key point—that the crucial work of the doctor is to "distinguish real cases [of hysteria] from feigned ones" is glossed over in the implied charge that all cases are in some sense fraudulent ("St. George's" 134).

For William White Cooper, publishing in 1859 on the general topic of the eye, what he termed "malingering" is simply and firmly attributed to "Evil design or hysterical monomania" (290), designations which recall Foucault's claims about the residue of moral values in modern medicine. He describes the case of a young girl whom he discovered was causing severe irritation by placing a piece of wood in her eye, the wood being discovered during an impromptu examination conducted after Cooper met his patient in the street (291). Such an intrusion was, he felt, justified by the outcome. This instance demonstrates the social power of the doctor, although it also implies the limits of such power: it is difficult to imagine the doctor making the same demand of a privileged patient, or of that patient yielding to it if he did. Warming to his theme of fraud, Cooper recounts cases reported by colleagues, mostly in the military (290–95). The final case described (via Lopez) is of a patient from whose eyes Lopez removed "between forty and fifty spiders, of three different species" (295). The two cases of what are termed "hysterical young women" bookend a discussion of self harm otherwise dominated by descriptions of self-induced injuries by men.

However the essay by Lopez offers a more troubled account of the patient than Cooper implies. In a case report published in 1843, describing events which unfolded over the course of 1840 in the city of Charleston in South Carolina, Lopez describes his daily visits to a young woman from whose left eye he removed numerous spiders, thence from both eyes, thence again from one eye only. He notes with distaste different kinds of responses to this case: sensationalizing press coverage (76); the tendency of some to attribute the appearance of the spiders to divine forces (which he clearly regards as superstition); and the contempt for his own skills evident among those who presume he has been deceived (79). After having considered cases in which animals (usually insects) were produced by the human body, and after carefully refuting a hypothesis about the possible procreation of the spiders in the body, Lopez comes to the conclusion that in his patient,

> there existed a want of nervous integrity, so operating upon the mind as to produce the form of disease which I have distinguished in my text as *Hysteric Monomania*; and I am induced to think that the various types of mental irregularities, which an unbalanced nervous system is so familiarly known to produce, sustains the belief [80].

He insists several times on the integrity of the young woman, notwithstanding that he knew she was placing the spiders in her eyes (76–77; 77). His emphasis is on the mysteries of the mind and he concludes that the events are "rather as a melancholy, though interesting feature of *disease*, than a subject of levity to be classed among the nine-day wonders of everyday report" (77).[5]

What is distinctive about Lopez's article is not just that the author embraces the complexities involved in discerning the patient's level of control over their condition, but that he does so after giving serious consideration to organic causes and to malingering, offering reasons to reject each. As far as

Lopez is concerned, all possibilities in relation to the dynamic between the will and illness are in play. His conclusion is that the ingestion of needles or the insertion of spiders occurs "under a state of mind beyond the patient's control" (78); the case is one of illness, but Lopez does not presume to understand its nature. Yet as we have seen, the case can be taken up and simplified by a later writer (Cooper), keen to find evidence for his views on the prevalence of duplicity.

The urge to simplify and to generalize is marked nicely by the different attention to quantity: Ballingall, occupant of a prestigious academic post, masses 300 and more second-hand cases under one rubric. He quotes Scott, Forbes and Marshall's account (in their *Cyclopædia of Practical Medicine*) of 300 soldiers who had eye problems as evidence for the scale and scandal of self-inflicted injury. Of the 300 cases, 250 were cured when the irritant was discovered in their hospital beds (*Outlines of Military Surgery* 1855: 610). Ballingall notes with satisfaction that searches began after the men were marched naked from their beds at midnight (610). In a similar vein W.J. O'Donovan considers "a class of young females who produce lesions that are very terrible, and whose mental state is a provoking problem" (12). There is a defensive edge in his claim that "the physician who tells his students that these are suffering from a self-produced disease may be described by the patient as an 'old fool'" (25) and his proposed response decidedly punitive: "Such patients must be admitted naked from the bath room to a bed in the nursing home; ... their belongings must be searched daily while they are being bathed" (28). The stripping and marching procedure might well have been taken from Ballingall, whose work was generally well known, he in turn having borrowed from earlier writers. The offenses committed by apparently duplicitous young women are not against military discipline, but against the dignity and professionalism of the doctor, whose goodwill and expertise are abused.

Lopez, a physician in a small city, insists on the specificity of his patient and the complexity of her circumstances. George Ballingall, occupying the prestigious post of Regius Professor of Military Surgery at Edinburgh from 1825 to 1855, differs in presuming that all self harm is transparently instrumental, that is, transparent *because* instrumental. While at one level it might seem that this is simply a difference of tone, in fact Lopez is just as unequivocal as Ballingall—it is just that he is unequivocal that his patient could not fully be understood. In that sense, a preparedness to countenance the possibility that illness has a mental or emotional element implies *a commensurate belief in the limits of medical capacity*. However, this is relatively unusual.

Bishop's 1961 discussion "Some Historical Cases of Auto-surgery" proffers an early history of self harm. Noting the problem that many cases "are reported only in newspapers" or under inappropriate subheadings, the author notes (but gives no details) of surveys from 1900, 1902, 1933 and 1936. The précis of his paper offers some dozen or more accounts of surgeons and those with no medical training operating upon themselves (with, it must be said, a high success rate). This lack of documentation raises the question of the writer's aim: since the article does not allow a reader to retrace its steps, it is working to a different purpose, which seems to be to verify the inexplicability of the past and of patient behavior. Like many published medical papers from mid nineteenth to the mid twentieth centuries, it began life as a spoken address to a meeting of colleagues. The tone (lofty) and speaking position (speculative observer) indicate the desire to cultivate the pleasures of professionalism. Here, the structures for the transmission of medical knowledge are relevant: annual congresses of specialist associations and regular meetings of local doctors, followed by publication in an association or general journal. The relationship of speech to writing, and of speaker/writer to audience, is critical here: as Foucault remarks, "A way of teaching and *saying* becomes a way of learning and *seeing*" (*Birth of the Clinic* 64). In this case, the talk and the essay demonstrate that "being a surgeon" is distant from, and different from, the ways of being a patient. As medical history, this essay works as enculturation, aimed at validating the social norms of the profession.

It is this tone and positioning that make Bishop's subsequent discussion of instances in which patients are judged to have "succeeded" in self harm so interesting. He considers cases of "Auto-surgery," a category which he further divides into "Auto-Operations by Medical Men" and those by "Normal Individuals for the Relief of Pain or in the Absence of Medical Aid." At this point the patients are no longer objects of pity or disdain, but people of "extraordinary fortitude and resolution" (32). Bishop's paper "sorts" cases into the heroic and the risible, the marker of heroism being not suffering, but the sufficiency of the motive of cure and the level of professional competence. This finding about self harm is not unique to Bishop. Something of the same respectful, if puzzled, tone is evident in Davidson's 1884 report of amputations of the penis in India by locals, which healed well, while the amputation he had performed upon a soldier killed his patient.[6] In the same mode but writing a century later, Kalin applauds the "impressive" degree of medical knowledge shown by a patient who performed two operations on himself: "the amount of preparation and necessary skill used in his surgery seems profound" (2189). Essays like these by Bishop, by Davidson and by Kalin implicitly establish norms not about *how* surgery is performed, but about *why* it is performed. And when patients act like surgeons—working from the same motives, and with a degree of "success"—their actions are regarded not merely as justifiable, but laudable.

These are by no means the only instances in which published reports of self harm show respect for patients, although in these other instances it is the extent of the injury that seems to inspire a kind of respect. In the example of a man treated twice in 24 hours for delirium tremens, the doctor was subsequently sent for at two a.m., to find a bedroom "deluged with blood." Francis and Grant, writing in 1870, describe the scene in detail:

> On the table lay the penis, the whole of the scrotum, and one testicle. When the patient had sufficiently recovered to be able to speak, which was not for two or three hours, he was questioned as to the fate of the other testis; he at once composedly replied, "Oh, I have chewed it!" and one of the neighbours stated that he had it in his mouth when he arrived. The whole of this formidable operation was completed with a blunt rusty pair of scissors, which were used instead of snuffers in the candlestick, the blades of which are not more than three inches in length. He stated that he did it under the effect of a vision, in which the mutilation was made a condition to his entry into heaven, and as a compensation for errors committed through the medium of these organs in earlier life.... Since then, the wound has gone on uninterruptedly well, notwithstanding being subject to pretty severe tension in some fits of delirium he has had since—one undoubtedly induced by a person very injuriously endeavouring to show the errors of Roman Catholicism; and another by entering into a conversation about his wife, from whom he is separated.... The patient still is liable to fits of excitement and aberration of intellect, in consequence of which we have thought it most prudent to place him in an asylum ["Amputation of the Whole"].

This example is quoted at length because of the non-judgmental tone (notwithstanding the two a.m. callout). There are, of course, elements of the report which indicate causality, here religious delusion, and some which imply a certain level of disapproval. However the patient's character is not dwelt on, and the act itself is characterized, rather ambiguously, as a "formidable operation." The report is useful, then, in demonstrating that in 1870, it was possible for doctors to report on a case of savage self injury in a way that was reasonably respectful to their patient, notwithstanding the distress the injuries might have caused not only the patient but also the treating doctors, and those neighbors and friends who had been charged with caring for the man ("Amputation of the Whole").[7]

Marcus Whiting's 1884 case of a marble cutter who attempted to castrate himself more clearly demonstrates sympathy for the patient (297–300). Decried by his wife because of his sexual demands, the man had attempted to remove a remaining testicle, the other having been damaged when he was a young man.[8] The account expresses no particular disapproval of the patient or his actions. Indeed, the response to being woken at two a.m. (like the doctors in the previous case), following the patient to surgery after being given the injunction "Do not say anything about this, I've *cut* myself," seems to demonstrate something like solidarity. Whiting's report is unusual for its equal attention to contextual and surgical factors—the patient's circumstances and his reasons for acting (his wife had left him because of his "brutishness"), the damage done, and the response to it first by the patient and then by the doctor. There is a similarly matter-of-fact tone in Daniel Stroch's "Self-Castration" (1901), a report which describes a man successfully removing both testicles in the hope of relieving pain in them and in his back. "He further said that he had for years meditated on the desirability of removing the testicles in certain individuals, to prevent the transmission of undesirable traits to posterity" (1901). The doctor also questioned him about sexual function, since the patient reported that he had never had sexual intercourse nor any "strong desire" for it. But the doctor's interest in the sexual elements are emphasized by his reporting of the patient's erotic dreams and nocturnal emission, and the careful examination of the patient's bed sheets and the severed testicles (the former under microscope). Yet this fascination does not develop into revulsion.

The same element, fascination, marks James Adam's "Cases of Self-Mutilation by the Insane" presented in the "Clinical Notes and Cases" section of the *Journal of Mental Science* in 1883. Adam asserts that self harm was prevalent, although he also takes the view that "instances of wilful self-mutilation, for its own sake, are much more rare" than those associated with attempted suicide (213). Citing the lack of information arising from difficulties in establishing the circumstances leading up to, during, and immediately following self harm, as well as the bafflement arising from "obstinate and persistent taciturnity, or by stupor," he argues for the value of those talkative patients who are able to explain the "hallucination or delusion" which led them to harm themselves (213). Adam presents two reports but perhaps more significantly, he precedes them with an anecdote of a man trained as a surgeon, subject to "occasional maniacal attacks" (214), who claimed to have suffered numerous broken bones and a wound to an artery. This doctor, an acquaintance of Adam's, bandaged the wounds himself. When these bandages were removed, it was clear that none of the injuries had actually occurred. Situating this anecdote in a report about two patients who inflicted serious physical injuries on themselves gives it an ambiguous quality: is the doctor who feigns illness a curiosity, a potential patient with serious illness, or a fellow doctor whose behavior demands collegiality? And by being used as a kind of framing device, the story *encourages* a mood or mode of puzzlement, not to mention implying sympathy for the two other patients: the first, a woman who, "an hour and a half after admission [to an asylum], gouged out her right eye, which now presents a horrible wreck" (Adam 215); the second, a young Presbyterian man who cut off his penis, and like the woman claimed he was "following out the Scriptural injunction" (218). The implication is that the doctor accepts the "rational" explanation of religious delusion, prompting interest in these patients and their claims, not condemnation.

Noting the immense difficulty of obtaining reliable information from patients as to their state of mind "before, at the time of, and immediately subsequent to, its infliction," Adam suggests that those patients in whom "we find the mutilative act the direct result of hallucination or delusion" are easier to investigate (213). This raises, of course, another possibility. One of the aspects of self harm which most frequently confounds is the prevalence of reports by patients of experiencing relief and gratification from their actions. So conventional has this observation become that one popularizing account of self harm contends, "Cutters are using the body's natural 'drug' of endorphins to alter their mood" (Rebman 67). Case reports and patient accounts offered in theses and other in-depth studies rarely mention pain, or shame; if they do, these negative reactions are often said to come later, not so much as part of reflecting on the act itself, but as a consequence of imagining how the self harm might be perceived by family, friends, teachers or workmates. It might be, though, that these versions of the experience of self harm are overrepresented because they are proposed by that group of patients able to give information in a sufficiently credible form for it to be recorded by the medical professional publishing on the case. Other stories might just be rejected. This is what Leon M. Beilin and Julius Grueneberg do in their 1948 essay in the *Journal of Urology*, when they remark, "The histories as given by the patients themselves may seem bizarre, vague, silly or humorous, but they are always unreliable" (635).

The Deserving Patient

In medical institutions often pressed for time and resources, we can anticipate that many and perhaps most are likely to respond in accordance with their assessment of the patient's "deservedness." Thinking about my teaching, perhaps many of us working in educational institutions do a similar thing, spending more time on or regarding more favorably students who we feel are "working hard," are attentive to what we say, and do what we ask them to do. This might have little or nothing to do with the degree to which those students "deserve" good teaching—if the reasons for being "deserving" could ever really be justified, let alone acted on, with integrity. But the tone of writing about patients who are known to have inflicted sometimes savage wounds on their own body suggests that these patients are likely to be late in the queue for attention, particularly in a larger institution like a hospital or prison.

One of the ways in which doctors and other writers have sought to respond to self harm is by differentiating between what they understand to be "false" and "genuine" instances, thereby anticipating or resolving the conceptual and moral problem set out at the beginning of this chapter. In some instances, "genuine" cases of self harm are understood as having an organic cause; some but by no means all writers consider the possibility of psychological causes. But the practical or clinical difficulties of discerning the difference between "fraud" and what might be termed hysterical or neurotic patients is hinted at in Ernest B. Emerson's discussion, recorded in 1917, of "Mental States Responsible for Malingering." Emerson argues that typical malingerers are those seeking to avoid criminal responsibility or gaol; the person trying to obtain compensation; and "the hysterical girl" who "simulates to attract attention and to gain sympathy" (434). He goes on to recount details of four patients whose illnesses he understands as simulation of insanity and concludes that

> in all instances of doubt, commitment to a hospital for the determination of the insanity, as provided for by statute, is most essential, not only for the protection of those truly insane, but for the elimination, if possible, of the malingerer, and incidentally for a study of the defect which is the fundamental basis of the deception. The latter may be of sufficient degree to absolve even the malingerer from being stigmatised a criminal [Emerson 436].

A discussion in London held around the same time ran into the same problem of distinguishing between true and false cases of self harm, raising the further question of whether or not it was best to tell the patient of the doctor's suspicions. Dr. Pernet presented two examples of patients with what he termed "dermatitis artefacta" to an audience at the Royal Society of Medicine. In discussion, Dr. Samuel sought to distinguish between the "true malingerer" and the "hysteric" (Pernet 90). After explaining Freud's theory of hysteria (in general terms, through repression), Samuel says the person should not be accused of injuring themselves deliberately: "One should never ridicule these poor sufferers or regard their symptoms as trivial" (91). But Graham Little "did not agree" that patients shouldn't be confronted. F. Parkes Weber, who had a particular fascination with self harm and simulation,

> thought that of all disease related to disorders of the psychical system, artificial eruptions in young women most deserved study from the psychical point of view, and it would have been a great advantage if Freud's teaching had concentrated upon this subject much of their psycho-analytic investigations. It would be a great gain to be able to clear up *the mysterious mental element* in these cases [Pernet 91; emphasis added].

In conclusion, Pernet gives further evidence of the early infiltration of psychoanalytic theories into mainstream clinical medicine in the twentieth century, agreeing to some extent with Samuel but disputing his definition of hysteria through reference to Janet (91). The diversion into theoretical questions about the function of the mind shows the difficulty in making such distinctions between "false" and "true" illness.

Broader political agendas could be in play in separating those whose self harm was in some way valid from those who were merely attention-seeking. Weber's own *Possible Pitfalls in Life Assurance Examination, and Remarks on Malingering* noted that

> Most of us recently have had to pay attention to the question of various forms of simulation in men. Amongst prisoners of war simulation of disease for purposes of repatriation tends, of course, to be regarded as fair play and as rather creditable than discreditable, if it is successful. In such persons, however, as in accident insurance cases and "traumatic neurasthenia," there may be a real functional nervous element combined with the simulation of disease [8–9].[9]

Weber, whose family was German and who worked at the German hospital, was unusual in suggesting that "simulation of disease for purposes of repatriation" during the First World War could be "fair play"—although an account of a scam by British soldiers who feigned madness successfully in order to accelerate their repatriation from Turkey was very well received by readers.[10] The key point of Weber's argument, though, is not the existence of dissimulation per se, but his contention that physical illness, illicit motive, and psychological disturbance could co-exist in a single patient—indeed, that they quite often did so.

The complexity of individual patients can mean that a doctor takes a considerable risk with reputation and social relations in coming to the view, or even raising the possibility, that an injury could be self-inflicted. The account by R.O. Adamson of "A Case of Dermatitis Artefacta, and its Sequel" in the *British Medical Journal* in 1910 involves dogged detective work, careful isolation of the patient, and eventual discovery of the fragment of a pumice stone which had been used to abrade the skin. In a sequel the patient claimed total constipation, an illness likewise resolved after being placed in care, and under constant observation. But the doctor rejected the notion of a disabling mental illness, asserting (as in the instance described in "Religious Monomania") that "In other respects this patient is a bright and pleasant girl, and no-one would, I think, suspect her of these 'hysterical' tendencies" (Adamson 15). On the other hand, the failure to raise the possibility of self-inflicted wounds could itself have catastrophic consequences. David Forsyth, writing in the *Proceedings of the Royal Society of Medicine* in 1932—and seeking, it is true, to score points in the argument with those who rejected psychiatry—recounts the story of a patient, "a young married woman with pronounced neurotic symptoms [who] had undergone eighteen operations, including two laparotomies" (36) without any physical illness being diagnosed.

In the light of this complexity, one appealing model is the spectrum, which sees fraud at one end and psychosis at the other, the doctor's difficult task being to determine where along that line an individual case lies. Thus Myriam van Moffaert, writing in 2003: "the spectrum of self-induced dermatological conditions is very extended. Self-mutilative and self-destructive psychological tendencies tend to express themselves in a continuum of behaviors motivated by a myriad of causes" (169). The advantage of this model is that it opens up a space for what is experienced as professional judgment, although that judgment might be shaped by the degree to which the patient is seen as tractable or deserving. As Farquhar Buzzard expresses it, commenting on a colleague's case report,

> While it was true that all these cases demanded not only their interest but their sympathy, and that in the large majority the application of the term "malingering" was grossly unjust, from a scientific point of view there was no hard-and-fast line between cases of pure hysteria on the one hand and ... malingering on the other, if they regarded the former as at one end of a scale and the latter at the other end, and realised that they met with cases showing all the intermediate stages between the two extremes [Buzzard (Comment)].[11]

While apparently leaving room for psychological factors, responses to patients who harm themselves can be shaped by the medical practitioner's emotions.[12] At the same time, that response is translated into a "professional" register, in which emotional reactions of the treating doctor are reconfigured as characteristics of the patient's personality or condition. The remarks also represent certain kinds of illnesses as being able to be judged morally as much as medically (or morally, and thus medically), in terms of the level of responsibility. Crucially, the underlying assumption is that any form of self-injury is necessarily the product either of (acute) mental illness, or of moral deviancy.

In some instances the apparent acceptance by the patient of their wounding, even their passivity, seems to inspire sympathy. Weber's file (Folder 3) includes notes of conversations with colleagues on this phenomenon. One note, dated 1929 and headed "A Self-mutilating Woman," recounts an instance in which the patient had injected herself with pus and then had to have an amputation. Another discusses "a really good woman," a nursing sister "who had done wonderfully good work for 15 years and then developed intermittent or remittent 'hysterical' paralysis in [her] legs for several years. It is often really good women who suffer in this way—teachers, nurses, &c.,—who have devoted their lives largely to altruistic ideals" (underlining in original). The qualification of hysterical with inverted commas and the underlined suggestion that it is "really good women" who injure themselves is evidence that Weber was sceptical about being able to determine the degree of volition in such instances.

More broadly, the capacity to engender sympathy is a significant element in the ways that doctors respond, with some reports—a minority, it is true—constructing a "deserving" patient.

One key instance of the "deserving patient" is the frequently cited "Case of Helen Miller" by Walter Channing, reported in the *American Journal of Insanity* of 1878. Channing offers a brief history of a woman whom he describes as "an intelligent German Jewess," and quotes a previous physician who attested to her good character ("I never saw the slightest evidence of her having led a fast life") while also noting her conviction on charges of theft and her addiction to opium (369). Miller's story is distinctive in that the wounds Miller made to her arms, generally inflicted by shards of glass, were exacerbated by her habit of inserting shards of glass and other items into them. Nearly a hundred such pieces were subsequently removed under ether but most were removed without. On one occasion an unhealed wound was so severe that a tracheotomy had to be performed to allow Helen Miller to breathe.

The response of both Miller and those charged with treating her shows the "splitting" which Edward M. Podvoll (1969) and Susan Scheftel (1995) suggest is characteristic of the response to patients who self harm (discussed at greater length below), as hospital staff, the patients themselves, and even physical objects shift from being "good" to "bad":

> Her happiest periods were when the wounds were healing, and she was the object of surgical interest. She took a special pride in having the attention of the physicians directed towards her.... [Her] remissions would last only a short time, to be succeeded by doubts, suspicion, jealousy of all about her, and final despondency, in which state she was constantly angry with the other patients ... and in utter hopelessness and despair as to her herself [Channing 375].

Although there is a general sense of sympathy towards the patient, and some brief attempt to consider causality, ultimately Channing asserts that his patient presents "only an example of the wonderful mystery of insanity" (376). His compelling observation that "She was evidently struggling with all her might to control her actions with the slightest amount of will remaining" in periods of greater lucidity and calm is not really investigated, nor is there reflection on the dynamics within the hospital although they are described in some detail. In these circumstances, we can only wonder about the extent to which Channing's claim that Miller greatly enjoyed the attention of doctors (375), and "apparently experienced actual erotic pleasure from the probings she was subjected to" (374), reflected the patient's, or the doctor's, experience.

Jacob A. Conn's less renowned but more psychologically compelling report (1932) notes that his patient was "at her worst" after a clinical demonstration (354).[13] Conn's discussion of his patient, a Boston telephonist who broke her own fingers and thumbs, includes the assertion that the woman "relieved the pains [in her back, neck, hands and head] by this procedure, and experienced very little discomfort": "When her mother entered her room at 8 a.m. the patient showed her malformed, bleeding hands 'in a happy way'; her mother fainted" (252). The young woman subsequently inflicted wounds on her hands and her right ear, including removing several fingernails (Conn 252). Admitted to a hospital, she showed little change, but after four months was discharged and eventually took up work in a factory. Eight years later the patient was readmitted, during her second pregnancy; she had resumed her work as a telephonist for two years immediately prior to this admission (254). Her reported comments capture the distinctive combination of dissociation and relief that characterizes many more recent accounts of the moment of self harm, and which is so unexpected by lay and medical readers alike:

> When ... asked what was in her mind when she was pulling her fingers, she said, "About going out of your mind. I had to see blood. I wanted to see blood come out. I wanted to keep the blood from reaching my head so I wouldn't go out of my mind, as I hadn't menstruated." But when asked why she dislocated her thumbs the next night she replied, "because the rest of my hands were broken," and she could not give any reason for twisting and fracturing the left little toe [255].

Conn proposes and discounts a series of hypotheses about the aetiology of the self harm, among which is the injunction from the verses of Matthew. Rather than causality, his main concern is with the social, sexual and familial circumstances of the patient, including masturbation and guilt about masturbation present from Miller's mid teens until the time of hospitalization. Yet after proposing this "punitive" motive, Conn suggests that "we must not be carried away by the general well fitting of the puzzle pattern," particularly given the "anomaly" of the woman's injury to her toe (259). After surveying relevant literature, Conn concludes that the illness is one "of the acute descending radicular type of encephalitis described by Pardee in 1920" which "removes the 'lid,' paralyzes protective inhibitory factors and permits the autoerotic conflicts to come to the surface" (262). This, says Conn, explains the relief and triumph which the woman appeared to demonstrate not simply when she had injured herself but after she had "displayed" her mutilated fingers to friends and family. Although he does not say it so bluntly, and notwithstanding his insistence on organic disease, Conn clearly understands this action as the young woman's subconscious attempt to "prove" that she has conquered her "deforming" habit of masturbation. Conn does not include references to thinkers from psychoanalysis, citing only neurologists, but this is a rare and significant example of a writer who brings *together* psychological and physiological factors; that he should consider his patient's condition in terms of their *interaction* is almost unique in the literature of self harm.

The Undeserving Patient

By way of contrast with Conn's brilliant account, a report from just a year later points to the flatness that can characterize accounts in this and indeed any period. For the purpose of demonstrating the "thinness" of explanations which can be offered in those instances in which the obvious sexual elements provoke revulsion, I want to quote the entire report made by John M. Bradley in 1933 of "A Case of a Self Made Eunuch":

> This case report is of a man sixty-one years old who has been a sexual pervert all his life. He was born and reared on a farm in Kentucky. He had his first sexual intercourse when he was nine years old and was always hyperactive sexually. On the farm he had intercourse with cattle, sheep and hogs. He was a chronic masturbator even when married.
>
> He was married three times. After his second marriage he became remorseful about his perversions. He went to the barn, sharpened his knife and cut out both his testicles. He did a good job and made a good recovery. He was forty years old at this time.
>
> Two or three years later he was still troubled with hypersexual activity, and he married a third time. He was still able to have intercourse after having his testicles cut out, though of course he had no discharge. After his third marriage, he contracted gonorrhea. Brooding over this and his continued hypersexual condition he got out his pocket knife and cut off half his penis.
>
> In Turkey and other Oriental countries it is a common practice to take boys eight or ten years old and castrate them. They are then trained to become servants in the harem. They are supposed to be impotent so that the master of the harem when away from home may feel that his wives are reasonably safe from democracy [sic].
>
> This case is unusual because: First, self inflicted eunuchism. Second, able to have intercourse after castration. Third, development of feministic characteristics at the age of forty.
>
> Unfortunately, I am unable to show the patient tonight. He is a prisoner, charged with attempting to rape a girl ten years old. When I asked him why he did such a thing and stated it would have done him no good, he said he thought it might do the little girl some good.
>
> After cutting out his testicles he developed feminine characteristics. These and the mutilations are shown in the lantern slides [133–34].

What I want to draw attention to is the rhetorical effect of placing contextual details against what are read not so much as symptoms but as the product of the patient's background. For example, because Bradley has placed these details in the same paragraph, readers are meant to infer that the man concerned had sexual intercourse at the age of nine, and subsequently with various animals, *because* he "was born and reared on a farm in Kentucky." Readers are inclined to resist the non-sequitur; if the information is not explanatory, why include it? The anecdotal paragraph about the making of eunuchs demonstrates the way in which the practice of castration can be relocated to another culture (implicitly a barbarous one, ruled by irrationally jealous men) and another historical period; at the same time, this barbarism is naturalized (in that culture) by the assertion that this is "common practice" (these people are barbarians). In invoking a decadent East, with which this patient is then associated, the writer implies without ever naming what is normative about American culture: heterosexual sex between consenting adult members of different sexes, both of whom belong to the human species.

As a story, this account does not so much illustrate the ways of eunuchs or despots or residents of harems as it does the author's positioning in relation to the practices he describes. Again, what is being constructed, here, is a normative authorial persona, one entitled to express revulsion at an "undeserving" patient from whom there is a demand for intimate medical services. It is not surprising that the counter to what is represented as social degeneracy—the report is written at a time when debates about eugenics were in the medical news—is a new technology, here, the slide, which records the damage in visual detail for colleagues. At this moment, American society is poised between the fate of the Kentucky farmer captured by bestiality, and the impulsive power of modern medicine which will rescue it from that fate. The interest in social differentiation, framed as professional curiosity, emerges not only in relation to patients but to medical tools and technologies. That is, forms of medical knowledge and sophisticated medical technologies themselves become levers by which doctor and patient are separated, in the sense that medical technologies become mechanisms through which patients can be distanced and objectified. This is evident in Douglas J.A. Kerr's assertion, made in a 1927 report, that "though cases of self-mutilation occasionally occur, chiefly in asylums, the accompanying illustrations are probably unique in the annals of forensic medicine."[14] The new technology is used to reinforce to colleagues the patient's debasement: a feature of Kerr's report is the close-up shot of two severely lacerated hands, the throat (which had been cut), and a longer shot of the body from the thighs up.

The unnamed man who was reported on by Kerr was of sufficient interest for the author or another to count the scars of "over four hundred and forty different cuts," most superficial but some deep enough to sever muscle. Although Kerr was at pains to stress the uniqueness of the patient's actions in his opening paragraph, his subsequent description hints at familiarity with similar cases: "Of special interest are the cuts on the palmar aspect of both hands. This is a most unusual place for self-inflicted injuries." Whether Kerr's experience lay in medical literature, his own work, or a combination of these is not clear, but in the three paragraphs of comment it is noticeable that the framing offered in the opening words of the article shifts: the patient is not unusual *because* his wounds are self-inflicted, but because of the deviation from known patterns of self harm. One could speculate that the former claim has appeal to a wider spectrum of readers, particularly in a general publication—here, the *British Medical Journal*—and a commensurate reluctance to construct an audience of specialists in self harm. There is little or no discussion of the man's state of mind, but what there is is fascinating in terms of the authority given to sources. Kerr's report notes the opinion of the deceased man's landlady, that she had "noticed that he was becoming strange in his manner." Kerr then asserts that "he appeared to be depressed, and was under the delusion that he had killed his sister." But the patient, who was found in a field, was "too weak to talk" on admission. It is not clear, therefore, whether the attributing of depression and delusion is a lay judgment made by the man's landlady; a professional judgment, made on the basis of the man's injuries, supplemented perhaps by an interview with the landlady; or, and perhaps this is the most likely, a medical diagnosis made on the basis of a report by a third party—the police?—to the doctor, of comments made by the landlady.

Other patients could be figured not only as undeserving but uninteresting—notwithstanding the publication of the case study. G.M. Jones introduced his 1857 example of "Extraordinary Self-mutilation" by noting that while most patients are reported as service to the profession, others "which come under the surgeon's notice are so disgusting in their details as happily to exclude the notion that anything similar is likely to be met with" (88). On the other hand, it is also clear that doctors have to negotiate patients whose injuries or illnesses they find not only professionally puzzling but emotionally shocking. Jones' "Extraordinary Self-mutilation" anticipates that desire for scandal said to motivate the populist writer who came to literary and journalistic prominence later in the nineteenth century; such writerly motives are perhaps made more difficult to see by the placement of the report in a professional journal. Although this claim about the ways in which certain professional discourses might have anticipated (and indeed, served as source material for) literary ones has not been much considered, the explicit discussion of physical detail and the uninhibited forays into psychological speculation available in medical literature may have provided rich inspiration for writers of "sensation" fiction. Expressing relief that the case "was unique," the author averred that "the same revolting process ... must be said to reduce man below the level of the brute" (G.M. Jones 88). The patient maintained a certain sang-froid in the face of what are reported as the doctor's "expressions of horror and disgust" at his "beastly propensities," a distaste exacerbated by resistance to the patient's expression of his motives: he is reported as justifying the act of incising his scrotum with a simple avowal of desire for sexual pleasure ("C'était pour mes petits plaisirs," G.M. Jones 89).

The account on the whole gives more emphasis to distaste than to treatment of a patient whose actions—removal of the scrotum—"must be said to reduce man below the level of the brute" (88). While the act of castration in its technical sense does invite the parallel with farm animals, it is worth noting Jones' remark that the man, a Frenchman and a gardener, aged 34, is quite articulate, "much better than many" of those "persons in his sphere of life" (89). This brief assuaging of disapproval is undone by the final sentence, in which Jones claims that "I have omitted to mention that the entire scrotum is completely filled with scars of different length" (89). But Jones *has* mentioned the scarring, when describing the difficulty encountered in suturing for "the edges of the wound were so cartilaginous (occasioned by numerous cicatrices) as to greatly impede the needle's progress" (88). Claiming to have neglected what he has described already, and is now reiterating, allows the author to highlight the most prurient elements of his patient's injuries.

A foreign patient who frankly admits that his injury has been self-inflicted for sexual gratification is framed very differently to the young woman who, in a case report published 6 years earlier, had inflicted savage damage—severing a hand, burning her other, and stabbing her eyes with a skewer—for reasons that are understood to pertain to "religious monomania": she had injured herself terribly because "God had told her to do so" (Lloyd). "When closely pressed as to how she knew she ought to commit such an act, she appears wrapped in her monomania, and merely answers, 'God knows'" (Lloyd). The diagnosis of monomania is emphasized on the basis that the young woman "gives very apposite and satisfactory answers respecting her age, state of health, family, and various other circumstances" (Lloyd). The tone of Lloyd's 1851 report is generally sympathetic, the last paragraph noting, "Although the poor girl has been very quiet since her admission, she is watched with great vigilance." Readers of the *Lancet* are assured, "We shall watch the progress of this case with painful interest, and acquaint our readers with its subsequent features" (Lloyd). From the beginning, for Lloyd, this patient "falls as much under the cognizance of the psychologist as the surgeon."

More generally, the patient who injures themselves can be positioned at times as having removed themselves from the social obligations binding patient and doctor. Haldin D. Davis, in a 1924 essay, proposes that self-inflicted wounds are "really the outward sign of an abnormal mentality, for it can safely be postulated that patients who intentionally produce skin eruptions must be possessed of minds perverted in one direction or another" (211). Writing in the wake of the First World War, Davis argues that all self harm is basically "malingering," performed to escape duty (military or work) on the part of men, or hysteria, to attract attention, on the part of women (211). "Those whose mentality is so perverted that such reasoned discipline [as that provided by a sympathetic and capable sister] has no beneficial effect, are not unlikely to become inmates of an institution for the mentally afflicted" (Davis 216). Davis's claims find echoes in post-war studies like that of Battle and Pollitt, who in 1964 declared of those who self harm that

> Many are social misfits, being unable to face up to problems in their lives and tending persistently to evade their commitments and to find the easiest and most pleasant path through life ... the malingerer is not concerned with pain but with the infliction of a wound sufficient to serve his purpose with least suffering to himself. He therefore selects insensitive sites for self-inflicted wounds.
>
> The psychopath can be recognised by his inadequacy at work, his unstable emotional life and the lack of personality traits usually associated with good citizenship.... His marital life is erratic or broken, often many times, and his friends are of the same personality type. He is unpredictable, unpunctual, irresponsible and unreliable, and he lacks moral sense.... Many criminals, deserters, tramps, layabouts, and prostitutes have this character, for which little can be done [Battle and Pollitt 403].

In categorizing all self-inflicted injury as malingering—that is, falsifying a medical condition rather than manifesting it—these authors remove the stages of investigation and assessment so essential to effective treatment. Thus their diagnosis is essentially one of social malfunction.

Assumptions about character and circumstance can inform the response to the patient who self harms: the moral weakness of women or yokels; the duplicity of foreigners or members of the lower classes. The frankly racist and entirely speculative account of amputations and self injury by professor of anatomy Roy L. Moodie (1920) becomes a catalogue of practices the author finds grotesque. Moodie sets the scene with his assertion that "The primitive mind worked in a curious manner" (1299) and admonishes the reader who might mistake the practices he discusses as curative in the medical sense: "That primitive men had any definite conception of what constituted surgery is absurd" (1301). Likewise R.A. Jamieson's account of purchasing the feet of a beggar who had used strictures to cut off circulation below the ankles sees the self harm as "throw[ing] a light on that singular mixture of courage, deceit, and sacrifice of almost anything to advance low enterprise, which characterise the lower orders in that country [China]" (398).[15]

Such assumptions are by no means exclusive to the nineteenth century. For example, reporting on patients who had inflicted eye injuries, Dutch authors writing in 1982 noted "such behaviour in foreign workers points to mental abnormality, although its purpose is comprehensible" (Kok-Van Alphen *et al.* 327).[16] Yet even in those instances of self harm in which an instrumental motive seems utterly clear and the social credentials of the patient strong, reports can leave traces of complexity. A 1990 account of a member of the U.S. navy notes his presentation at the medical department:

A corpsman told him the medical officer was seeing another patient and unless it was an emergency he could not be disturbed. The patient then pulled a razor blade from his pocket and began to make a series of cuts to his forearm and thenar eminence [the rise at the base of the thumb on the palm of the hand] saying, "I guess this makes it an emergency" [Wetsman 22].

While on the one hand the statement lays claim to a simple cause and effect—the cutting is done to obtain the attention of a doctor—it is not clear, given this seaman's complicated personal history and subsequent diagnosis (borderline personality disorder), in what sense his actions could be regarded as simply and only "attention seeking" or even "deliberate" in the sense implied by the terminology of *DSM V*.

Diagnosing and Disclosing Self Harm: Dermatology

Dermatology is one of the specialisms whose members are on the front line of dealing with self harm. There is a particularly rich literature of case reports in this field in which doctors often open up questions about motivation and state of mind, as well as monographs which attend to the relationship between skin and psyche. The scale of discussion and the sophistication of the understandings of the patients' circumstances often evident differentiates this scholarship from surgical accounts. This might be in part because surgical emergencies arising from the patient's self harm are such that circumstances might not allow for discussion with the patient, whereas an issue with the skin can generate multiple visits to general practitioners and specialists. On the other hand, we need to be cautious in presuming that the modes of response to patients inhere in the condition rather than the cultures of treatment in a particular specialism. Nevertheless, it is more common to argue in dermatology than in other fields that "in most patients with self-induced dermatoses, the frequency and severity of the self-injurious behaviours are directly related to acute or chronic problems with emotional regulation and dissociation" (Gupta, Abstract). Even this language—the use of terms like "emotional regulation" and "dissociation"—would be unusual in case reports from general practice, or from specialisms like surgery.

Self-inflicted abrasions, often caused or exacerbated by chemical means, can be so acute as to cause death, numerous reports showing the catastrophic effects of self-inflicted injuries of the skin (see, for example, Agris and Wilton Simmons). Yet the example of dermatology also shows clearly the diagnostic and social challenges that can be raised by patients who deliberately injure themselves. The answer to the question of volition posed by many cases of self harm is structured into the diagnosis of patients referred to dermatologists. In the language of that specialism, "dermatitis artefacta" signifies wounds which the patient does not admit their involvement in creating or exacerbating, "neurotic excoriations" those in which they do (e.g. Doran *et al.* 294–95; Gupta *et al.* 45, 47).[17] Two issues arise. The first is that the nature and seriousness of any underlying condition might not be related to the capacity or willingness to admit to self harm; the second, the distinction often cannot be made, particularly in the initial stages of treatment. Admissions might be partial, might be veiled, might be retracted, just as questions or accusations might be dismissed. The problem for the dermatologist, in terms of identifying the cause and then treatment, is that on occasions self harm can only be proven through intensive surveillance or even restraint, often of a patient deemed of exemplary character (see, for example, Walker, "A Lecture").

G. Norman Meachen reports on "a young lady, aged 23" who had an "an obstinately recurring eruption upon the face. In December 1912 she first noticed a burning and tingling upon the cheeks, and reddened spots would appear which did not, apparently, become blisters, but became 'dry and sore.'"

> On examination, there were several discrete, rather sharply defined reddish spots, the size of a sixpence, situated upon the cheeks and sides of the mouth.... She had been curetted twice, and she stated that the spots would be better for a time after the operations, and then they would reappear. The exhibitor suggested the possibility of a dermatitis artefacta, or of a very superficial type of lupus erythematosus, but he invited the opinions of the members of the Section. The general opinion expressed by the members was that it was a case of dermatitis artefacta.

While on the one hand readers might flinch at the use of the curette as treatment for a facial lesion, the patient's own report that the spots would be "better for a time" endorses the speculation that the treatment was in some sense effective.

Nothing demonstrates better the challenge of self-inflicted injury for medical professionals than R.M.B. MacKenna's essay "A Case of Extensive Self-Mutilation of the Scalp" (1930). MacKenna begins by noting that while self-inflicted wounds for which the patient denies any responsibility present difficulties, in the instance which he describes, he came to "doubt[] whether the patient [wa]s justified in his self-accusation" (313). It is the "confession" of self harm, *not* its concealment, which the practitioner comes to suspect. But the complexity of such cases is often hinted at in reports which mention but do not explore traumatic experience. A notable aspect of MacKenna's report is his passing remark that the patient, who is suffering from "acute alcoholism, delirium tremens and peripheral neuritis" had "never been out of England, except from 1914 to 1918, when he had served in France" (314). This reference to war is not taken up.

Writing around the same time, another British doctor ponders the fact that his teenage patient will allow him to "thrust" a pin through a fold of skin in her forearm, and includes the detail that "a week before [her] skin disease was noticed, on coming home from school [she] had found her mother burning fiercely behind the kitchen door" (O'Donovan, "The Psychological Factor" 51). It is not clear whether the "burning" was thought accidental or deliberate, and if the latter, self-inflicted or the result of an attack by another. MacKenna shows the way the experience of war was normalized; for O'Donovan the horrific accident or attack is recorded as an element of circumstance for his patient's condition but is not commented on. The following sentence simply records the treatment given, and the fact that it was effective.

William Pusey's paper, co-authored with Francis E. Sennear and delivered to the forty-second Annual Meeting of the American Dermatological Association in June 1919, takes up the question of self-inflicted or exacerbated skin conditions, firstly through the critique of existing classification and then through the presentation of three case studies. In each of the latter the damage was severe, one patient having spent up to five hours a day "digging at" the skin on his face and neck (274). Discussants tended to concur with the authors' nosology (classification) and with their focus on that aspect, but Dr. MacKee remarked, "The principal points were the diagnosis and recognition of a traumatic etiology" (Pusey and Sennear 277). All were in agreement that it was possible and necessary to distinguish between "feigned" injuries and those which were attributable—in a manner still unclear—to neurosis. MacKee had himself read a paper on the same kinds of patients at this conference, and there is considerable overlap between the two. He presents 14 cases, one of which is determined to be "malingering" in order to obtain insurance (267), but he concludes (somewhat abruptly) by pointing to the variety of injuries presented and the difficulty of diagnosis, including of wounds inflicted by those deemed "not neurotic" (269).

Several cases reported early in the twentieth century show the potentially catastrophic effects of the failure to realize that injuries to the skin were self-inflicted. One of these is described by Georges Dieulafoy (1908), in which a patient who had consulted 17 different doctors eventually had his arm amputated for what was later deduced to have been self-induced gangrene. Dieulafoy's case is often cited, but even more devastating is that reported by M.L. Heidingsfeld in 1915, which reverberated through the literature for several decades. Having described a set of patients who had injured themselves a decade earlier (those cases are summarized in his essay at 313–14), Heidingsfeld notes that his current case is "very unusual," having "escaped proper recognition and received misdirected surgical attention to the extent of removal of both breasts [and] amputation of the right arm with full consent of the patient" (311). Heidingsfeld's discussion is framed by a review of the ingredients of what he understands to be most often mere fraud: malingering and motives for it (311); means of self harm and clues for identifying the results (311–12); and tactics for engaging the patient (312). Unlike many of his colleagues he advocates dealing directly and only with the patient, the exclusion of relatives, friends or other staff being "for the personal interest and future welfare of the patient" (312). The strategy being confrontation, "It is highly essential, and important ... that the diagnosis be correctly drawn" (312).[18]

In the case under report, Heidingsfeld describes the process through which he addressed the issue. The woman's attendant was dismissed and then she was confronted by the dermatologist, a procedure which

> called forth a storm of resentment on the part of the patient and a threatened suit for damage to personal injury and reputation. Passion and resentment soon gave way to a flood of tears, and with the aid of expressions of sympathy for the patient's uncontrollable weakness and pledges not to reveal any proffered information to her attendant and personal friends, the patient finally admitted her guilt and acknowledged that the gangrenous ulcerations and bullous dermatitis were the result of lye poultices and caustic lye applications. Since the death of her husband she sought to make herself the subject of sympathy and interest and a charitable dependent, even at the cost of severe anguish and pain, and amputation of breasts and extremities [Heidingsfeld 313].

Crucially, after having agreed that yet another operation should be performed, the patient's doctor had sought a second opinion from Heidingsfeld. In the rooms of the dermatologist, a different diagnosis was reached: "A mere cursory examination revealed the true nature of the condition" (Heidingsfeld 313). The successful treatment is presented as an outcome of collaboration, with the grateful thanks of the referring physician recorded. Entirely contradicting the firm declarations of personality type offered earlier in the essay, Heidingsfeld observes that his patient is "a well preserved and well-developed individual, far above the average in intelligence and personal appearance, and showed no evidence of a weakened or impaired mentality" (313).

Such case reports become notorious. E.W. Prosser Thomas writing in 1937 (citing C. Augustus Simpson) and Simpson (1917) paraphrase Heidingsfeld but transform his "consent" into calm enjoyment: "a woman who had serenely witnessed the complete amputation of both breasts and one leg, and had given her consent to the amputation of one arm, before her condition was recognized" (Prosser Thomas 806; C. Augustus Simpson 493). Like Heidingsfeld, Simpson claims that "glaring artificiality" is evident to the "experienced eye" in "the majority of these cases" (494), a view implicitly supported by Prosser Thomas whose own patient began with a lesion on the finger which led to 33 operations (805). "The case presents the remarkable picture of a self-inflicted dermatosis maintained intermittently over a period of nine years, and achieving so successful a deception both in London and the provinces as to result in the piecemeal removal of an entire limb" (Prosser Thomas 805). Reports about patients who have such experiences function as parables of surgically induced harm: formidable *as* parables, they encourage the doubting physician to seek the view of a specialist so that no such incident will recur. In return, there is a courteous protection: the referring doctor in the Heidingsfeld report is identified only by one initial, for example.[19]

Dermatology and the *"mysterious mental element"*

H.F. Damon's *The Neuroses of the Skin* (1868) is one important early effort to consider the body, the psyche and self injury in relation to the skin. Damon claims that women are more susceptible to what we might now call mental illness while they are in "that period of life which is characterized by the greatest functional activity of the sexual system" (92). He quotes at length C. Hansfield Jones in *Clinical Observations on Functional Nervous Disorders*:

> "We shall always have much need to be on our guard against deception in the case of our meeting with the genuine hysteric; but, on the other hand, we have evidence enough, I think, that causes of exhaustion of nerve-power may generate all kinds of morbid phenomena.... Let us only think what must be the depressing effects of constant monotonous toil, scanty pay, poor food, bad air, and failing strength, especially when there is no bright ray of future happiness in a better state to light the gloom, and where, in the absence of healthful recreation, gin and prostitution are the Devil's substitutes, and then say if we can be surprised at any amount of physical nervous derangement" [Damon 93].

While Damon's excursions into questions of social conditions and mental illness more generally are quite limited, his raising of these environmental factors is of historical note. More generally, we can see in this field a willingness to draw on Norman Walker's assertion, in the seventh edition of his *Introduction to Dermatology* (1922), that "neither rank, education, intelligence, devotion to duty, nor the most exemplary character exclude the possibility of self infliction" (cited by Novak *et al.* 247; Sneddon 9; Doran *et al.* 295).

One writer in England remarked in 1914 that it is "to the French school of dermatology, as represented by Besnier, Hallopeau, Fournier and Brocq [that] we are indebted for the recognition and classification of the group of dermato-neuroses" (Sutton 2128).[20] Later writers were quick to integrate ideas from psychoanalysis into their thinking, and there was an efflorescence of work in the United States and France in the late 1920s and 1930s which brought together psychoanalysis and various specialisms. Writing in 1927 to challenge the purely physiological approach to diseases of the skin, W.J. O'Donovan aimed to "stress" "what appears to me incontrovertibly the fact—that psychic injury, emotional stresses, and nerve strain, anxiety, even greed, and laziness, may be the most potent factors in educing and continuing a cutaneous disorder" (10–11). This emphasis on the psychological elements by no means implies an interest in mental illness per se: O'Donovan's focus is on "the handling and reporting of cases that are concerned in the Workmen's Compensation Acts proceedings," the *Act* being known for "delaying the recovery of fractures and other illnesses" (11; 19). His point is that

> any patient who is the subject of a dermatitis should be examined to see whether there is not a powerful emotional history, whether there is, or is not, a history of mental injury, and whether or no there have been in operation such causes as are known to prolong invalidism after ordinary surgical accidents. For I wish to maintain that just as pains and disabilities may disappear marvellously after a County Court settlement, so too an application of "golden" ointment can work equal wonders in dermatology [12; similar at "The Psychological Factor" 50].

The argument is that the provision of compensation provides an irresistible incentive to self-inflicted injury.

Dermatology is structured by disagreement about the meaning of self harm, and disagreement about the extent to which psychological concepts should be used to understand those meanings. Writing in 1930, with the longer essay that is the signature of an attempt to intervene in the conceptual structuring of a field, John H. Stokes addresses what he sees as a determination among dermatologists to avoid psychology. He argues strongly that what he calls "the emotions of the skin," in which he includes self-inflicted injuries, must be considered in the context of sexual psychoses (803). Danish dermatologist Holger Haxthausen's "The Pathogenesis of Hysterical Skin-Affections" (1936) takes a similar line, the author referring to an extensive literature and asserting that "no doubt that by far the majority of hysterical lesions of the skin are of external traumatic origin and belong to the group appropriately labelled pathomimia" (563).[21] Haxthausen's view had support: the following year, W.N. Goldsmith's essays on "Pitfalls in Diagnosis" begins with a study of "Lesions of the Skin" (1937). Goldsmith divides patients into those with "malingering," "hysteria" and "compulsion-neuroses" (7). He discusses medical debate about whether or not hysteria could be induced by state of mind alone, before himself coming to this view (7–8).

Another of the more evocative pieces of writing pertaining to self harm published in this period is Paul Schilder's "Remarks on the Psychophysiology of the Skin," published in the *Psychoanalytic Review* in 1936. Schilder's essay speculates on what might be called a phenomenology of the skin, which is to say, the ways in which forms of knowing are developed through touch: "We acquire the knowledge concerning [our skin] by a continuous dynamic process by which we gain a definite borderline between ourselves and the outward world," a process in which "imaginations and representations" play a powerful part, "deeply modified and interwoven by the emotional attitudes and the problems of the individual" (275). Although Schilder is himself concerned with psychosomatic illness, his remarks have resonance for those interested in the psychological dimensions of self harm:

> Every perception of an organ of the body, and therefore also of the skin and its changes, is not merely a mechanical act but goes through the various symbolic stages by which it is brought in connection with the total experience of the individual. The self-perception of the body—I speak about the body image—is therefore a highly symbolic act, not less symbolic than the expression of the problems of the personality in functional and organic changes on the skin. Psychogenic manifestations on the skin have always a meaning [284].

Esther Bick's equally significant proposition that the development of an awareness of skin as a "container" for the self is foundational in the development of the self and its relationship to the world seems not to have been widely considered. Certainly these kinds of arguments rarely make their way into the self harm literature, despite their apparent potential.

Another dermatologist who took a sustained interest in self harm and its mental aspects was Henry MacCormac (1879–1950), whose publications make it clear that an interest in psychiatric and psychological literature was an important element of some dermatologists' thinking about the skin (against which, see Grant *et al.*). In one of two essays titled "Autophytic Dermatitis" (*BMJ* 1937) he reported that self injury was "far from uncommon, and ... therefore a subject worthy of discussion" (1153). Like many medical professionals, he drew a sharp line between those who belonged to "an entirely different category" from "malingerers and fraudulent individuals," being "hysterical subjects, invariably young women, who have no apparent motive for their action, and who may actually suffer material loss and become permanently disfigured by their act" ("Self-Inflicted Hysterical Lesions" 371). Perhaps this reflects the influence of the war years, in which "hysteria" and feigning injury were more likely to be attributed to men than to women, as men and their physical and psychological injuries came under unprecedented levels of medical and judicial scrutiny (see chapter three).

Given that most of these reports document periods of treatment of a few months, MacCormac's research, prompted by a student question which MacCormac said he felt unable to answer well, provides rare information about the long-term outcomes for those treated for self harm.[22] With data gathered from a survey sent to former patients of the Middlesex Hospital between 1913 and 1923, MacCormac offered some possible prognoses for those who had injured themselves and then set out to discover what had actually happened to those who had been treated for self harm. All the patients MacCormac was able to locate were unmarried and female, their ages ranging from 17 to 30. Only five of those contacted replied to his inquiries about their current circumstances—albeit a rate of return that would be seen as very good by modern standards, and perhaps indicative of the authority of formal communication from a doctor. Interestingly, two of those who replied did so in terms which effectively disputed the original diagnosis, although the grounds for this disputation are not made clear.

MacCormac remarks, "Those whose cases come under this heading are women of mature age, and they become or have been difficult and unreasonable. There is an attempt to evade unwelcome duties with simulation of illness to gather pity" (1154). Interested in "What happens to these patients?" he reports that

> All but one had ceased to inflict lesions on the skin, and the replies to my letters of inquiry received from some of the former patients reveal the curious fact that the knowledge of what they did had been forgotten or submerged. The foregoing is mainly concerned with the diagnosis, the signs by which self-inflicted lesions of the skin are recognized. That merely touches the fringe of the subject, for these eruptive processes are not skin diseases as ordinarily understood, except in the malingering class, but rather a reflection upon the skin of a disordered condition of the mind [MacCormac, "Autophytic Dermatitis" (*BMJ* 1937) 1155].

Perhaps the most poignant piece of evidence is MacCormac's final letter, relating to a woman who worked as a laboratory assistant and who suffered infected sores. MacCormac and a colleague had, at the time, disputed whether or not the infections were self-inflicted. He now reports, "The patient had come under the care of a surgeon, who found it necessary to perform an amputation of a finger. Thus mutilated she was apparently satisfied, and remained in good health until March, 1922" ("Self-Inflicted Hysterical Lesions" 375). F. Parkes Weber comments, on his clipping of this essay, "Some kind of double personality must, as Dr. MacCormac suggests, be the explanation of many remarkable cases of self-inflicted injuries."

By the early 1950s, in two essays on "Basic Concepts in the Production and Management of the Psychosomatic Dermoses," Frank E. Cormia was advising readers of the *British Journal of Dermatology* that observation and investigation were necessary to establish "the symbolic nature of the disorder" ("Basic Concepts I": 84). The emphasis is on the categorization of illness and the correlation of background factors. Although this is potentially restrictive, Cormia's general point that there is a psychological element to disorders of the skin is shown in various ways, as in his contention that the location of lesions is meaningful: "the nape of the neck was invariably associated with family troubles; on the face and front of the neck (blush area) with shame; on the knees, ankles and shoulders with excessive marital or family responsibility, and on the thighs or ano-genital region with sexual disorders" ("Basic Concepts II": 131). There is a kind of brisk common sense to Cormia's work, somewhat different to the more speculative, exploratory discussions by writers like Damon. This style is evident in a co-written case report which identifies severe neurotic excoriations as masturbatory and in turn attributes the patient's desire for masturbation in part to his wife's frigidity (Cormia and Slight). This "frigidity" is slightly reformulated as the woman's preference not only for clitoral orgasm but for a position astride her husband during intercourse: "It is worthy of note, as indicating the masochistic trends in the patient, that this form of coitus was particularly acceptable and desired by him" (528). Thus, although using more complex models of the relationship between body and mind, and of the mind itself, the explanation works within a highly restrictive framework of normative gender roles, a point discussed further in chapter four.

Maximilian E. Obermayer's *Psychocutaneous Medicine* (1955) constitutes a response to articles published in the 1920s and 1930s, as well as more extensive works examining the relationship between psychiatry and other branches of medicine.[23] Within this literature there is room for disagreement: Obermayer cites C.S. Wright as claiming that the majority of neurotic excoriations "probably are true psychoses" and H.E. Michelson's assertion that "a complex pattern of reactions underlies this symptom rather than a single neurosis or psychosis."[24] Some early writers took up evocative notions like Ingram's "personality of the skin" (889–92), or in Obermayer's words, "cutaneous personality" (34), discussed below. *Psychocutaneous Medicine* is the most comprehensive contribution to a literature that is both a response to, and participation in, debate in the middle decades of the twentieth century among dermatologists through which they sought to come to terms with their relationship with psychiatry, and to develop more sophisticated understandings of diseases of the skin and their relationship to emotional states.[25] What is significant about this debate for the history and historiography of self harm is that, just as they were among the most vigorous participants in discussions of the evils of deception, so dermatologists took a lead in discussions of self harm which moved away from criminal or deviance models.

Obermayer paid tribute in his opening pages to the work of Karl von Kreibich, whom he termed "The first author to recognize the serious import of emotional factors in the genesis of cutaneous disease" (5). Obermayer's own views are indicative of the scientific and moral ambiguity which self harm can generate even in those intent on showing openness to nuanced modes of diagnosis and treatment. At a key point in his discussion, Obermayer resorts to the most popular and least rigorous model for self harm, that which correlates the level of injury with the level of mental disturbance:

> The consequences of self-inflicted cutaneous injury vary widely, from aggravation of a pre-existing eruption by simple over-cleansing, to severe mutilation, such as the loss of a limb following continued self-production of deep ulcers. Correspondingly, the scope of emotional disturbance that constitutes the motivating, driving forces varies from mild neuroses to severe psychoses [118–19].

For Obermayer, there is no question that "Patients who damage themselves extensively are deeply disturbed" (119). He hypothesizes that self-inflicted injury is aggression which is, because of "fear and guilt," turned back onto one's own body, but is categorical in asserting that "deliberate self-injury ... does not occur in hysteria" (119). Such arguments represent an attempt to shift the terms of the debate from the literal to the symbolic, and reflect profound changes in thinking about the body and illness enabled by the infiltration of psychoanalytic theory into other branches of medicine.

The sophistication of some early work in dermatology has not permeated the field in an even way. One report from 1966, for example, identifies an association between self-inflicted injury and "the hysterical personality" and sets out the following identifying features for such patients:

> The hysterical personality is unreflective and flighty.... The person usually shows exaggerated interest in personal appearance and gives elaborate attention to physical fitness and personal grooming. The females often appear heavily made up, intricately coiffured, and overdressed.... Relevant to dermatology is the hysterical personality's fondness for display. This is most commonly manifested by histrionic speech and behavior which makes a dramatic production of the most commonplace situation [Ackerman *et al.* 736].

This report is neither the first nor the last to medicalize femininity or camp, but the simplifying of the diagnostic art is at odds with the careful work of previous generations. On the other hand, we find similar thinking in a 2010 case report of a patient who had claimed sexual assault and then admitted to self harm, including severe damage to his penis. The authors report that in previous cases of self harm, "changes in hair styles, flashy jewelry, or clothing styles" had been observed (Hendershot *et al.* 245).

Such "loss" of knowledge cannot really be explained by reference to differences in medical traditions. Rather, it points to the pressure to find a template for diagnostic procedure in the face of the challenges of self harm, as these Ackerman et al. themselves note: "Once the diagnosis is certain, the physician should not allow his resentment at having been duped to provoke him into angry accusation of the patient" (736). Yet these writers do suggest referral to a psychiatrist whereas colleagues writing around the same time suggest that "Detective work in medicine is challenging, and very rewarding when the 'how and why' of the well-concealed self-induced eruption that has baffled many is unraveled," making no reference to psychology in dealing with individual cases that show horrific self-induced lesions (S.A. Johnson 148; see photographs p. 142 and, esp., 143). While some dermatologists take the view that it is preferable for a patient to remain entirely under their care—even to the point of themselves prescribing psychotropic drugs (Crayton and Freedman 519)—the more prevalent view is that care requires some understanding of the mental elements of the patient, and that this care is best given by specialists in that field (Michelson 249; for successful treatment see Maio *et al.*).

Responding to Self Harm

The example of dermatology shows that the transmission of ideas about self harm within a specific specialization is an uncertain process: there is no inevitability in the outcomes of medical education or practice. Over the past century and a half there has been a struggle to reconcile what have been taken as common sense precepts about the desire of human beings to avoid pain, injury and illness, with the repeated presentation of evidence that the most horrific injuries can be self-inflicted. General practitioners and specialists wrestle with evidence that their patients are not necessarily psychotic (although they can be), nor overwhelmed by religious or other mania (although they can be), are not subjected in their lives to terrible trauma or threat of injury (although they can be), and are not involved in inflicting horrible wounds on their own body (although they can be). In short, taken *as a group*, case reports suggest that self-injury fails to follow any of the patterns which make for a correlation of symptom and treatment, whether of physical or psychological illness. This makes the convention of citation, generally found in the opening paragraphs of such essays, potentially counter-productive in establishing parameters through which the new patient is read. While such surveys often identify differences in *findings*, very rarely is their scope sufficient to allow the weighing up of different *approaches*. And in such circumstances—in which the patient's condition frustrates the intellectual and administrative processes through which the medical profession conducts its business of building and transmitting knowledge—patients are potentially vulnerable to the sensitivities and good will of the individual members of professions they encounter.

Among the few writers who examine the reactions of medical staff to patients who self harm themselves are Offer and Barglow (1960), Podvoll (1969) and Scheftel (1985), along with theses by French and by Madden. Podvoll and Scheftel use psychoanalytic concepts to explore the ways in which the patient recreates the psychic structures that underpin their own self harm in their relationships with hospital staff, "rewarding" those who perform roles concordant with that structure. Both conclude that the patient who self harms in some ways *recreates* with their carers the characteristics of relationships that they dread: abandonment, isolation, hostility. In that way, they exacerbate the destructive elements of the emotional environment associated with the self harm in the first place. These claims are supported by graduate researcher Katharine Oscroft, who remarks of the subject of her thesis that she had

> three strong hunches concerning her use of mutilation:
> (a) it served the purpose of facilitating a "traumatic bonding" between her and various professional helpers whom she desired a close relationship with;
> (b) she used it as a way of controlling an overwhelming amount of intrapsychic pain;
> (c) the act of self-injury re-enacted the victim/perpetrator dynamic of incest in a way which she could control [Oscroft 64–65].

This kind of dynamic is evident in Candyce N. Kuehn's "Management of a Self-Immolation Victim" (1994), which describes issues experienced by nursing staff during the five-month work of caring for a young man with burns to most of his body. After his girlfriend ended their relationship the young man had doused himself with petrol and set himself alight, in which state he drove towards her house, his body engulfed in flames (863):

> The nursing team faced many dilemmas during TJ's stay because establishment of a therapeutic psychosocial relationship with him was very challenging. Some staff members felt angry and raised ethical questions about all the energy that the team would expend on a person who "tried to kill himself." These conflicting feelings led to discomfort and discontent among the staff. Staff members were edgy and irritable, highlighting the need for psychologic and emotional support for the burn team as well as the patient...
> ... Both his [the patient's] communication and behavior were manipulative; he could push staff to their limits of patience and was masterful at staff-splitting....
> When TJ felt particularly powerless and was experiencing pain, he would often verbally fly out of control, becoming aggressive, threatening, loud, and vulgar. He continued to try and pit certain staff members against each other.... About 2 months into his hospital course, he became increasingly agitated and abusive, refused care, and started making inappropriate sexual comments. Nursing staff members were in conflict about his plan of care, and some nurses requested that they not be assigned to TJ [Kuehn 870].

In such circumstances, distanced self-restraint can become the default position, equivalent to hard-won professionalism. At the same time this distancing itself becomes part of the patient's environment and something they might challenge. Podvoll notes his patient's frustrated remark, "'If I came through your office door covered with blood and still bleeding, you'd probably just sit there and ask me what I was thinking about before I cut myself'" (215).

In an essay published in 1912, Hungarian psychoanalyst Sándor Ferenczi made the startling suggestion that every scientist should undergo analysis, because "the greatest resistances" to truth "are not of an intellectual, but of an affective nature" ("Symbolism" 256). The statement has profound implications for research into self harm, for ways of thinking about patients who have injured themselves, and for the way in which anyone involved in service provision interacts with those who seek their help. What is the impact, for example, of being confronted with symbolic self-castration by a patient who attributes their actions to religious belief or sexual self-control? How does a medical professional who shares those religious beliefs—or deplores them—draw conclusions about that rationale? What does a surgeon do—or more aptly, feel—when a patient has performed a major operation upon themselves? Scheftel even suggests that in responding to patients who self harm, "a cyclical process is set up [projective identification] in which the staff and patient mutually collude to perpetuate the symptom of self-mutilation" (43). If maturity, judiciousness and realism are characteristics of the professional self, it is not surprising that these should be assailed most effectively by those patients who proffer radical demonstrations of the failure to care for their own body.

Podvoll and Scheftel, both of whom have worked on the "front line" in responding to patients who injure themselves, and who are unusually reflexive about that work, speculate that the "recreation" of the psychic structures noted above occurs not only because of the difficulty for staff of coming to terms with the patient who has injured themselves, but because of the poor efficacy of treatment. This leads the hospital, in particular, to replicate and even reinforce destructive patterns.

> [O]ften a long line of failures precedes admission [to a mental hospital]; ... the family is in despair, therapists relinquish responsibility, special schools no longer accept them, and even previous hospitalizations have failed to deliver the expected results. As ordinary controls are given up, an air of increasing desperation on the part of the family leads to even more frantic attempts to subdue the patient. Electroshock, chemical convulsants, gas treatments, massive sedation, become assaults made in the name of treatment [Podvoll 215].

Podvoll argues that the crucial element of successful treatment is that patients are put in "a position to internalize the processes that lead to conflict resolution and the toleration of the profound ambivalence both in and around them"

(217)—that they are *participants* in medical decision-making, not merely its objects.

Podvoll's argument is that modeling more complex kinds of responses than "cut/don't cut" is part of constituting a more robust self, capable of nuance. In this way, treatment is no longer based on "a morality of acts," but a demand for reasoned thinking. Podvoll gives the example of a patient who in addition to cutting herself, began to starve herself (217). In response, the hospital administrator felt they had to make a decision about whether to allow the starvation, or to enforce feeding, and experienced this decision as a struggle of conscience. Podvoll suggests this situation could have been understood and responded to as a demand for conversation, one in which the patient would be asked to take some responsibility for the decision. What is crucial is that, in being asked to participate, the patient is thereby constituted (even partially or temporarily) as a person *capable* of making decisions. Such suggestions might seem idealistic or naïve, particularly when there is little reason to think that patients in poorly resourced institutions with little of stimulation or purpose, subject to peremptory and even coercive forms of treatment, do not find self harm an efficacious means of coping with trauma.

These claims, made in the late 1960s, were not taken up in any significant way in relation to self harm until the work of the Bristol Basement Project began to be published in the second half of the 1990s, including essays and books written by (among others) Diane Harrison, Maggy Ross, Louise Pembroke, Lois Arnold and Anne Magill. The work of all reflects the influence of Pembroke, and Harrison, in particular. Publications by the Project, which work across the boundaries that usually are understood as separating testimony from medical science, give a central place to voices of those who have harmed themselves.

Lois Arnold and Anne Magill suggest that the number of instances of self injury attributed to organic disease has been over-estimated. In their view, "most self-injury is a response to environmental factors" (*Working with Self-injury* 62). If they are correct, this has ramifications for thinking through the nature of response, and the ways in which self harm might be exacerbated by medical institutions. As these writers also suggest, responses to self harm are in part shaped by the gender of the patient, and it is not surprising that later twentieth-century debates are inflected by feminism, as well as by hostile responses to that movement. Throughout the nineteenth and twentieth centuries, medical reports are quick to label women hysterics and men malingerers. Such gender stereotypes are intensified and complicated given the pervasive association of nurturing with femininity. When those stereotypes are broken, the results can be dramatic, and in a sense the Bristol Basement Project can be seen as a very direct response to events in Britain earlier that decade which brought self harm to the front page of newspapers.

Demonizing Self Harm: Beverley Allitt and After

In 1993 British nurse Beverley Allitt was charged with four counts of murder and eleven counts of attempted murder. The charges arose from events which occurred when Allitt worked in the children's ward at Grantham and Kesteven District Hospital in Lincolnshire (Jonathan Foster; Katz; Askill and Sharpe). Because of Allitt's history of self harm, the report of the official government inquiry into these events recommended that anyone with a history of self harm, suicide or eating disorder must show that they had not sought help, and had been in full employment for two years prior to being appointed as a nurse (Great Britain).

For those who self harmed, or who were sympathetic to those who do, it was felt that the report (*The Allitt Inquiry*) did not acknowledge sufficiently "the factors that led to Beverley Allitt being able to commit such atrocities for so long" (Pembroke, "Louise" 52). Questions about the underfunding and mismanagement at the hospital which might have impeded the discovery of the murders and associated assaults were not responded to with the same level of regulatory change as those which applied to people who self harm (see Nick Davies). But in the aftermath of the findings, which implicitly associated self harm with the propensity to murder children, fear of and aggression towards those who self harm were ramped up. Louise Pembroke cites an instance of a nurse at Allitt's hospital being sacked after it was discovered that she had harmed herself; a (male) student nurse who sought help for self harm was dismissed from training (53).

The report of the inquiry and the prosecution of Beverley Allitt repositioned Allitt's self harm from the medical to the criminal realm, reversing a "migration" that had occurred over the course of the twentieth century (see next chapter). In explicit opposition to the report's recommendation, and the climate which Allitt's actions and the bureaucratic response to them had created, the National Self Harm Network campaigned against the stigmatizing of self harm (see Whittle), ensuring that this shift did not go uncontested in the medical or in the public sphere. In the wake of *The Allitt Inquiry* patients' rights movements have organized around resistance to moral condemnation of self harm, particularly as manifested in insensitive treatment or refusal to treat patients who have injured themselves, had challenged the assumptions underpinning the recommendations of the report. Pembroke, in particular, angrily casts doubt on the capacities of the medical profession, broadly conceived, to deal with those who self harm in a compassionate and productive way:

> Having worked in service provision with access to patient notes I am appalled at their inaccuracy and unreliability. The notes can appear like an exercise in

character assassination. The wrong questions are asked and the doctor writes down his own answers. Contact between psychiatrists and self harmers will continue to be fruitless or confrontational until psychiatry surrenders it's [sic] assumptions [(Pembroke, Louise Roxanne) 49].

A male writer has similar views: "given my experience and the experiences of others related to me, I fail to understand how any research based on Accident & Emergency records can ever give anything but a distorted view of the area" ([Smith] 18–19; see also [Helen]).

The guiding spirit of this kind of writing is flat rejection of the prerogative of moral judgment by medical staff. A secondary element, sometimes fragmentary or implicit but nevertheless vital, is the reconfiguring of self harm as a *therapeutic* practice, particularly for coping with unspeakable trauma. Something of the mood is captured in a description of her own self harm by Rosalind Caplin:

> I am beginning to make links between inner and outer reality—to ask this feeling what it is about—to try in whatever way I possibly can to divert the impulse, because I know, ultimately, for me, that is not what it is. I am angry, angry, angry yes—I am starting, tentatively perhaps, to own it, to see it as having a positive creativity, passion and clarity of vision. It need not be self-destructive and all-consuming but *contains within it also my will to live* [(Caplin) 29; see also (Smith, Andy)].

The strongest outline of this position comes in Louise Pembroke's final contribution to a collection of writing by those who self harm, an essay which amounts to a manifesto ([Pembroke, Louise Roxanne]). Pembroke's views, grounded in feminist thinking, have had an impact on fields like nursing, in particular. In terms of treatment, the argument is that by "taking control," for example, carrying a clean razor and bandages, those who practice self harm have been able to diminish the frequency and/or impact of their injuries. In an astonishing reversal of the climate created by the charging and conviction of Beverley Allitt, Britain's Royal College of Nursing held a session on "Safer Self Harm" at their 2006 annual conference (*Cutting the Risk* 9). Some presenters argued that teaching patients how to cut themselves safely was a valuable service which conformed to the ethics of care, an argument supported by at least one writer who says that by preparing to cope with his own self harm, by carrying a razor *and* first-aid kit (of his own construction), the effect "was to lessen the trauma of cutting to the point where I was able to cease" ([Smith] 19).[26] At least one British hospital has established a service to provide sterile equipment to those who have self harmed (Foss).

The session at the nurses' conference attracted media attention when it became known that delegates were debating the practice of instructing people in hygienic and safe methods of cutting themselves (see Triggle). But three years later, at the same conference, Susan Davies and colleagues presented a project from Wales in which the self-administration of acupuncture by patients who self harmed was being trialed (Davies *et al.*), suggesting a trend towards wider adoption. The debates and projects reflect the influence of "harm minimisation," a medical policy framework premised on the view that self-destructive behavior (notably the use of drugs) will be pursued regardless of prohibitions. In these circumstances, the optimal medical response is to find effective ways to reduce the impact of the behavior. An example of this kind of strategy would be provision of needles to drug addicts to prevent the spread of infectious disease. What is implicit is the belief that medical professionals should attempt to understand and work with self harm and therapy, such that treatment becomes a matter of augmentation of safety and alteration of patterns, rather than prohibition and punishment.

Opponents argue that such strategies are ultimately destructive because they seem like endorsement by the state of illegal or self-destructive practices. Miranda Frost, considering "self harm and the social work relationship," examines this complex issue, suggesting that "current social work response ... is demonstrated to collude with the promotion of self-harm, largely through its adherence to orthodox theory and practice, which aims to control, and, thus, disempowers service users" (1; see also Haughton). Frost argues that this "orthodox" model is

> broadly characterised by objectivist views regarding the nature of social reality, and by an emphasis on (objective) knowledge and a concern with regulation and maintenance; it is derived from a medical model of helping. People are regarded, and treated, as problems, and professional theories and assumptions inform practice. The second approach ... can be conceptualised as a bottom-up, user-informed approach [5].

Frost, who draws on the Bristol Basement Project writings, agrees with the notion that self harm is "a coping strategy" (10). But the question is then raised, by Frost, about the demands on providers this makes. She notes that staff of the counseling service in Bristol "take the view that if callers are going to injure themselves, it is better for them to cut when they are in contact with somebody (literally during the 'phone call) than to do it alone" but that this "demands a willingness by the workers to acknowledge and examine their own responses" (14).

The instance of self harm is particularly complex within the medical policy framework of harm minimization because of the structuring of the doctor-patient dynamic discussed above in relation to "good" and "bad" patients. In a 2004 essay on nursing cultures and responses to self harm, Estefan *et al.* argue that "psychiatric discourse ... constrained the ways nurses thought of their clients as 'manipulative attention seekers' who exhibited behaviours that are pathological" (43). In the same way, the *management* of an institution in and for itself shapes policy and practice, more particularly if money is short and aspiration or duty great. Understanding patients who self harm as disobedient or aggressive might not only be an effect of the psychological complex (see chapter four), but might also work best in terms of establishing clear and consistent practices for responding to instances of self harm. And nurses, like other professionals, "are pressured to conform to economic and organizational agendas" (Estefan *et al.* 31). The options can be particularly grim in places which house large numbers of patients whose illnesses are perceived as intractable. A 1987 British study found that two thirds of nearly 600 patients in one institution "were receiving psychotropic drugs, usually long term; many were also wearing protective devices" (Kirman 1086), to protect them from self injury. But the same problem can emerge in relation to individuals. In one case report from 1997, the patient had received 22 different medications in attempts to control what was diagnosed as bi-polar disorder (Khouzam and Donelly), in the attempt to control self harm. While these treatments can be read as sustained efforts at care, they also can be read as repeated failure, failure which reflects the limitations on financial, psychological and intellectual resources.

Throughout the nineteenth and twentieth century, the institutional and psychological issues posed by self harm remain remarkably similar, levels of sympathy and insight fluctuating through this period. One might presume that an interest in the psychological elements of a specific medical case is a modern phenomenon, but there is no evidence of a consistent trend in this direction to support such a claim. On the contrary, what is consistent is that whereas a small minority of doctors shows an interest in the mental element of their patients, the majority of those writing on self harm do not. A very small number of case reports demonstrate an interest in and respect for the patient on the patient's own terms: Conn is exemplary in this regard. Cortyl and Martinenq, too, writing in 1884, give attention to the psychological, the surgical and the physiological, not only in their concluding discussion but in the ten pages of the patient's history which precede it. The existence of such early, full accounts of patients who harm themselves suggests that interest in and a desire to understand self harm is by no means a new phenomenon. The evidence for an *increase* in knowledge about self harm over the period from the early nineteenth century or to the later part of the twentieth is thinner than one might expect.

Whether in a hospital, home or surgery, the patient is reduced to their illness, while those providing medical care are reduced—or inflated—to their professional competence. At the same time there is a sense in which the patient who has injured him or her self resists abstraction or reduction, *not* "the leg in bed seven" but the person who has injured their leg. In regard to self harm it is not the "owner" but the *creator* of [the condition of] the leg, the patient, who inserts him or her self into the story of symptomology and, even more threateningly, into the narrative of cure; indeed, what appears to be resisted and resented by those who write about their encounters with patients who have harmed themselves is that that person has usurped or undermined the power and obligation of medical staff to heal the sick. Susan Scheftel admits, on first encounter with the patient who is the subject of her thesis, "a stark failure of empathy" (7), so horrific was the destruction the young man had wrought on his own body. The difficulty arises when the determination to resist the institution and its treatments—a theme of Shelley Doctors' work, and that of others on "treatment resistant patients" (see introduction) becomes evidence not of illness, but of defects of character. The use of the "contract" between patient and carer, usually nurse, which does not permit self-harm, a development which on the one hand appears to empower the patient, at the same time implicitly understands self harm as "discretionary" and thereby reinscribes that question of will which Foucault identifies.[27]

In terms of the questions about volition with which this chapter opens, we can see ideas about the individual and their capacities being set aside in instances where a doctor believes that their patient is criminal or insane. These responses are underpinned by those "moral" elements which Foucault identifies. The authority of the medical practitioner over the patient who self harms is rarely questioned; that authority extends to the discernment, insistence on, or dismissal of the patient's capacity to take responsibility for their actions. Put another way, the emergence of the rational Western subject takes place in dialogue with the medical institution, whose prerogative it remains to attribute rationality. Unlike many other accounts of medical decision-making, quite a few writers of case reports on patients who self harm frankly describe the emotional elements of their own response, citing common sense and firm moral values as essential professional resources.

In the discussion of the Beverley Allitt trial and the ensuing patients' rights movement, it should be clear how large the range of responses to self harm can be. Particular attention has been given both to women as patients, and to case reports of men who have removed some or all of their genitals. This has entailed some preliminary discussions of the ways in which conventions about gender roles and sexuality shaped responses to patients, points which will be amplified in the following two chapters. In the next chapter, which deals mainly with self harm by men, the shift is away from individual patients and the responses of individual doctors, onto the institutional questions raised by self harm on a mass scale, particularly in prison and military contexts. The questions about morality, and in particular the relationship between gender and perceptions of moral behavior, raised in this chapter will be explored further.

3

Self Harm as Malingering: Criminology and Military Medicine

> Disease exists only in [the space of classificatory thought], since that space constitutes it as nature; and yet it always appears rather out of phase in relation to that space, because it is manifested in a real patient, beneath the observing eye of a forearmed doctor.—Foucault, *Birth* 9

> It is easy to believe that this new interest in the fate of the confined was the result of some generous liberal tenderness, and the greater probity in medical attentiveness could now see sickness where previously there had only been the punishment of faults. But in fact things did not come about in an atmosphere of well-meaning neutrality.—Foucault, *History of Madness* 358

In 1914 a war began in Europe that was to spread to the margins of the continent, and in the process destroy millions of human lives. A related set of conflicts broke out among doctors, debates which amplified and complicated the relationship between criminological, medical and military views of self harm. The outcomes of these debates, which played out in recruiting offices, field hospitals and military tribunals, had significant implications for combatants. In the process, self harm spread from these scholarly and institutionally specific contexts into the press and parliament. Doctors were divided on the issue of self harm in multiple ways. There were differences in the level of sympathy they were prepared to extend to patients; differences in their understanding of and even belief in what we would now call mental illness[1]; and differing levels of felt obligation to the military hierarchies within which medicine on the front line was forced to operate. In broad and simple terms, perhaps the

103

most important of these differences, as they affect the function of those services, was between those who believed that psychological illness is just that—an illness—and those who felt that maintaining a sound mind is a matter of will or character and commensurately, that some forms of illness reflect moral failing. Such writers often implied or asserted that "character" is unevenly distributed between those of different classes and cultures. This "sceptical" view of mental illness and associated prejudices about the perpetration of fraud was more likely to be held by those who were prepared to prioritize the interests of the army and the nation over those of individuals.[2] And those who believed that mental illness is either fraudulent, a failure of character or an effect of some organic fault or injury seem also to have been those more likely to express faith in the ease of separating right and wrong, strength from weakness, innocence from guilt.

Most doctors believed that they should enforce military discipline by detecting and reporting on what is presented as fraud through self injury, thereby protecting the reputation of the army or navy, and the values of society. Consequently, it is difficult if not impossible to conceive of much reported self harm outside of the framework set by a powerful notion of masculine character and an equally powerful counterweight of fear of fraud and evasion of duty. (Arguably, this is still true in many carceral contexts.) Yet, amidst such certainty, the publication of accounts which express sympathy for soldiers who have injured themselves alerts us to the longevity of debates about how to respond. As one dermatologist wrote in 1945, "The motive, to be sure, is intent to deceive, but the cause is only the desire to be sick ... in order to escape the misery of their lives and their inner conflicts" (Michelson 249).

What can broadly be termed the literature of fraud in studies of self harm has its parameters set by the desire to establish whether injury or illness is "truly" or "falsely" obtained. The criminalization of self harm implies that it is an act of will, and carried out for personal gain (in military contexts, the evasion of duty). Considered in this way, *all* self harm is a manifestation of criminality. "Guilt" entails loss of the moral right to treatment or sympathy. For many writers on the topic, particularly in the later part of the nineteenth century and the first part of the twentieth, their views about criminal behavior were framed by contemporary theorizing of human progress and decline, which understands criminality as a matter of biological destiny (Hahn Rafter). The paths of their life set by genetic inheritance, those of the lower classes are placed into social and diagnostic categories which pre-determine their guilt. Faux sciences like phrenology, which aimed to understand personality and behavior on the basis of the shape of the skull, have long been discredited; but other forms of inquiry which rely on similar *methodological* assumptions about the predictability of behavior on the basis of, for example, social categories like ethnicity, gender, or social class remain influential. Well into the late twentieth century, understandings of criminality have been entangled with prejudiced forms of psychologizing which relate disposition to cultural background. This is a characteristic of the scholarly literature, as well as public opinion and policy.

Commensurately, there is a large literature not normally addressed by scholars in the field of self harm because it is catalogued under the heading of "malingering" (see McMahon). This material aims to identify the defining characteristics of "the malingerer" for use by doctors or by military and prison authorities in preventing and responding to self harm. This "literature of malingering" might seem irrelevant, on the grounds that it belongs in the realm not of medicine but of the law. However, by excluding it, students of self harm miss the opportunity to try to understand what happens when contestations about medical categories migrate into adjacent institutional contexts (such as the army and the prison), and what happens when those contestations enter the public domain. Considering this body of work has the potential to enrich attempts to understand the ways in which the cultural and medical category of self harm has been constituted over the last 200 years: how it can be that a 1969 U.S. study could find that prison teaches its staff that inmates injure themselves "exclusively ... for secondary gain" (Elmer H. Johnson 38). In fact, in this literature, "malingering" is such a capacious and tenacious category that it can subsume even apparently clear-cut instances of mental illness, and self harm associated with them.[3]

This chapter examines the main lines of debate in overlapping literatures of self harm: a criminological literature, much of which attempts to provide a typology of forms of self harm; monographs published for the guidance of military medical officers particularly aimed at helping them to identify medical fraud; debates around self harm in military and prison contexts; and the proliferation of these debates before and during the First World War. Within the latter, there is a "debate within a debate" which impinges on self harm in specific ways. This is the collision between psychiatry and neurology, during and in the aftermath of the First and then the Second World Wars, in which some doctors attempted to argue for the existence of what would now be called mental illness and the relevance of that category to the treatment of soldiers incapacitated by combat. This debate is more difficult to track, being evident more in passing remarks and in creative texts than it is in the scholarly literature per se. The aim of the chapter is to challenge explicitly those modern scholars who take at face value the literature of malingering which criminalizes self harm (e.g., Anderson and Anderson). The further concern is to open up the literature of malingering by problematizing its placement of self harm in formal legal frameworks, thence within a moral economy which sharply differentiates evil from good. It should be noted that most of the material discussed in this chapter relates exclusively to men. The very existence of this literature allows us to call into question the view that self harm is typically a female behavior. That is not to say, however, that it does not occur at sites and in ways which reflect gendered identities.[4]

Militant Medicine: Self Harm as Crime

Laws in Britain and Europe which criminalize self harm have usually been enacted with the intention of deterring attempts to evade military service. Many studies report sharp increases in the number of instances of self harm during times of conscription, in heavy combat, in the aftermath of war, and in prison itself. Self harm in prison is often seen as a device that is frequently "used" by prisoners to avoid worse punishments, or to gain relief by being placed in medical care. Perhaps because of that frequency, understandings of self harm in carceral and military contexts often carry the association of criminality and weakness of character.

The first laws criminalizing self harm in Europe were passed in response to injuries inflicted to avoid sentences which entailed physical punishment, particularly rowing on a galley (a ship powered by oars):

> The attitudes of the convicts [who were galley slaves in the sixteenth and seventeenth century in France] is revealed by the frequency of self-mutilations inflicted for the purpose of avoiding the galleys. The practice became so extensive that a French decree of 1677 established the death penalty for it [Rusche and Kirchheimer 57].

The further logic used in the framing and application of such laws is that death is an appropriate punishment because military service entails a risk to life. It is commensurate that a soldier who shoots himself in the foot, or a civilian who makes themselves unavailable for service through self injury, should lose their life to the state, the fate matching that of honest contemporaries who do not avoid or even volunteer for participation in war.

Monographs which rely on this criminological framework were published in the nineteenth and early twentieth century. They set out a typology or classificatory system for forms of self harm, usually organized by body part or means of injury. The aim of most authors is to enable the military or prison doctor to swiftly and surely identify the counterfeiting of symptoms or injuries. Repeatedly, the expressed aim is to be "complete," thus the emphasis is on documenting as many forms of and subtleties in simulation as possible. These foundational works of military medicine—generally missing from the archive of discussions of self harm—are, in chronological order of publication, Hector Gavin's *On Feigned and Factitious Diseases, Chiefly of Soldiers and Seamen* (1843); Edmond Boisseau's *Des maladies simulées et des moyens de les reconnoitre* (simulated illness and means of detection, 1870; see also his earlier works); Roberts Bartholow's *Manual of Instructions for Enlisting and Discharging Soldiers* (1864); Wolfgang Derblich's *Die simulirton Krankheiten der Wehrpflichtigen* (simulation of illness among conscripts in Austria, 1878); E. Heller's *Simulationen und ihre Behandlung* (dissimulation and its treatment, 1882 and 1890); and A. Hutre's *Les maladies provoquées au pénitencier de la Nouvelle-Calédonie* (study of illness among convicts in New Caledonia, 1888).

Turn-of-the-century examples of the genre include J. Huguet's *Recherches sur les maladies simulées et mutilations volontaires* (research on simulated illness and self mutilation 1900); Georg Lelewer's *Die strafbaren Verletzungen der Wehrpflicht in rechtsvergleichender und rechtspolitischer Darstellung* (criminal injuries in conscription in comparative law and legal policy, 1907); Salvatore Salinari's *L'autolesionismo, nelle sue varie forme e nei suoi esiti* (self-mutilation, in all its forms, 1926); Hermann Stadelmann's, *Die strafbaren Fälle der Selbstverletzung nach schweitzerischem Recht* (punishable cases of self harm in Swiss law); Mario Pasini's dissertation, *L'autolesionismo nel diritto penale italiano* (on self-mutilation in Italian law, 1936); Fritz Böhni, *Richtlinien für die Beurteilung von Fingerverletzungen beim Holzspalten* (guidelines for the assessment of finger injuries in wood-chopping, 1949); Antonio Macià Borrell's, *La persona humana: derechos sobre su proprio cuerpo vivo y muerto; derechos sobre el cuerpo vivo y muerto de otros homres* (on law, suicide and self-mutilation in Spain, 1954) and Werner Zuppinger's, *Der Schutz gegen sich selbst im Polizeirecht* (protection against oneself in police law, 1956).

Several of these monographs are prize-winning essays, suggesting that self harm was of particular concern to military surgeons and that students who took an interest in it could be rewarded with academic distinction.[5] Hector Gavin's study was published at the University Press in Edinburgh in 1838 and in the intervening five years the author pursued his subject with enthusiasm, additions for his 1843 book running to some three hundred pages. Gavin states that the aim of the competition for which his essay was submitted was to produce, "besides a correct history of the modes of fraudulently simulating disease," "the formation of such a classification, as would enable the surgeon, *by it alone*, to form an idea, not only of the frequency and success of imposition in any particular disease, but also of adjudging to soldiers who were discharged with a pension, the rate of that pension" (Gavin, *On Feigned and Factitious Diseases* v, v–vi; emphasis added).

Identifying the fraud is the main concern, but protection of the physician is also high on the writer's agenda:

> Should the following essay serve, either to prevent the honourable physician
> from being made the dupe of the artful imposter, or guard him against judging
> too harshly in doubtful cases, and unjustly punishing the innocent; more espe-
> cially, from being himself the instrument of punishment in presumed cases of
> malingering, the object of its publication will have been attained [vii].

Citing sources from France, Gavin suggests that "a thousand reasons induced
the young men to feign disease to avoid conscription" (*On Feigned and Factitious
Diseases* ii). He returns to the time of Constantine, who ruled the Roman Empire
in the early fourth century, to cite instances in which laws were passed against
self harm, noting that soldiers who mutilated themselves were branded (v)—a
mark of criminality appropriated by Jean Benoît for his celebration of the outlaw
status of Sade. Considering laws which forbid self harm in Austria, in the
Netherlands, and in Britain (vi–vii), Gavin emphasizes the danger that attends
on collusion with or deception of medical officers. His taxonomy, outlined in
the opening pages, establishes four categories of feigned illness or injury: feigned
or purely factitious diseases, including pretended or simulated diseases (instances
in which the patient "fakes" the symptoms); exaggerated diseases; factitious diseases, i.e., those wholly produced by the patient, which differ from the first category in that the patient induces "genuine" symptoms; and aggravated diseases
(9–10). Elsewhere it is noted that the navy term for what the army calls a "malingerer" is "skulker," but that the colloquial term is "hospital bird" (13). What is
noticeable, then, is how *un*problematic Gavin feels his work to be: the challenge
lies in detection of *means* for inflicting injury, in contrast to the search for *motive*
which animates the mental sciences (see next chapter).

The use of the taxonomy, the identification of self harm with criminality,
and the affirming of the pejorative terms all work to simplify and solidify the
identification of the person who injures themselves. For such writers, if there
is a pathology or illness at work, it is a kind of *social* illness or deviance wherein
the person ignores normative judgments about right behavior. Not surprisingly,
those ideas about right behavior are identified with the writer's own culture
and social position. Gavin begins by taking the moral high ground in relation
to Britain, asserting that whereas the French and Prussian regulations focus
on the "simulation of defects" in order to escape compulsory military service,
the focus of British law is *dissimulation*, that is, the masking of conditions
which might make one ineligible for service (10). Nevertheless, he is able to
come up with a long list of those inclined to simulation of illnesses, who are
predominantly members of the lower classes: "sycophants," "Those who are
frequently termed fanatics, convulsionists, most probably all of those who
affirm themselves to be under the influence of animal magnetism" and those
who are "hysterical" (11). He also includes "Persons not at all in poverty, nor
living in a constrained position, who assume the semblance of disease from

some inexplicable causes: these are chiefly females," or "monomaniacs" (11). Gavin argues of monomania that "one or other mode of feigning is often resorted to in civilian life, especially among indulged females, in order to obtain compliance with their wishes, or to excite interest, or for the pleasure of deceiving; in such circumstances it is the practitioner who is in danger of being disdained by the patient for failing to detect fraud" (16). More generally, Gavin proceeds from the assumption that fraud is rife, citing as evidence the fact that the number of those receiving army pensions exceeds the number of those currently serving (14). Thus, while there is a brief nod to the dangers of incorrectly assuming ill will on the patient's part, the tone and the bulk of the content signify the assumption that most if not all instances of self harm entail patients knowingly pursuing personal gain.

All this said, Gavin's first example hints at the potentially greater complexity of specific instances. The example of self harm is taken from Henry Marshall's *Hints to Young Medical Officers on the Examination of Recruits, and Respecting the Feigned Disabilities of Soldiers* (1828). It describes a soldier "who divided the tendo–Achillis with a razor, and prevented as much as he possibly could its reunion, who bore an excellent character, had served twenty-six years, and might have been discharged with a good pension when he pleased" (17). Gavin goes on to muse that

> It is stated in the *Cyclopedia of Practical Medicine*, that there are cases which indubitably shew, that the simulation of disease has frequently been practised without the existence of any interested motive, indeed without motive of any kind; that there is, in short, a species of moral insanity of which this simulation is characteristic [17].

As in the introduction, the rhetorical maneuver is to introduce an exception in order to demonstrate judiciousness. But the conceptual issues raised by this patient are not taken up. In this sense, Gavin's work is crucial in alerting us to the prevalence of self harm and simulation, while his puzzlement at those patients in whom he can discern "no *interested* motive," thence none "of any kind," is indicative of a medical culture in which it was intellectually legitimate to presume fraud in all instances of self harm.

The same work of categorizing by body part, and categorizing the *population* by character and national identity, is evident in Roberts Bartholow's *Manual of Instructions for Enlisting and Discharging Soldiers, with Special Reference to the Medical Examination of Recruits, and the Detection of Disqualifying and Feigned Diseases* (1864), a work said by its author to be needed because of the particular circumstances of the United States (making dependence on foreign studies untenable). Before embarking on a delineation of those nationalities and personalities most inclined to fraud and simulation, Bartholow remarks that his own experience ... has given me a decided opinion on this point. I have very frequently observed, indeed, that the malingerers in our hospitals are not derived from the class of well-informed educated soldiers, of whom there are quite a large number in the ranks, but from the class of workmen, laborers, and uneducated men. The appearance of the former amongst a flock of "hospital birds" is an anomaly which attracts immediate attention [Bartholow 93].

Disputing Marshall's judgments on the Irish, the American author contends that it is the Germans who, for love of ease and money, are most often found among those feigning sickness (those of other nations being too few to mention) (94). Also inclined to simulation are older married men who, having enlisted in a fit of fantasy or to obtain a bounty, now find the call of home and family too strong to resist (94–95). Indeed, Bartholow goes so far as to offer a description of the typical malingerer: a man with "dark brown or hazel eyes, dark hair, and dark complexion; his face is stealthy, dogged, lowering" (96). While such a specific physical description is unusual (perhaps unique) in the literature of self harm, Bartholow's approach is distinctive in another way. He suggests that in the discernment of self harm, another important tool of the doctor is the co-operation of fellow patients. The malingerer's colleagues are, he suggests, willing to indict a patient whom they feel is "undeserving" of medical attention or even discharge, or whom they envy for his successful fraud (101). Here we see "duty" being leveraged in a particular way, as demanding or at least encouraging the monitoring and judgment of one's fellow soldiers.

More than eighty years after the publication of Gavin's treatise and sixty years after Bartholow's, we can observe a remarkably similar sense of the prevalence and danger presented by simulation and self harm in the work of Italian medical scholar Salvatore Salinari. Salinari, author of a number of works pertaining to war and injury, took as his starting point the claim that self harm is rife: his tone is one of crisis, that crisis being exacerbated by the failure of scholars to address what he presents as an overwhelming and urgent issue.[6] Salinari argues that injuring one's self within war time is pathological; in the context of the need for the maximizing of military resources, it is essential for scholars to get rid of "all that is false," to allow a more scientific approach to study of the practice (1). On this basis, he refuses the urge to summarize, for the practice is too widespread, in both civil and in military contexts, and summary risks being read as understatement (2). Salinari claims of self harm that "there is no more contagious thing than this" ("Che non vi la *lue* piu contagiosa di questa" 2). He also urges attention to cultural specificity, seeing that self harm flourishes more or less in particular times and places; the urgent question is therefore why people feel the need to resort to the practice in that time and place (8).

Salinari's views can be differentiated from those who regard self harm as pathological, or an expression of feeble-mindedness, as in the mode of Gavin. For the Italian author, the identification of self harm carries an import that is social, even national, and certainly moral, thereby making explicit what Gavin and many other British authors prefer to imply. Salinari's claim is that injuries began to proliferate because of conscription, reaching high levels during the Napoleonic wars in terms both of the number of instigators and the variety of forms (9). In the second half of the last century these began to diminish, considered not a collective evil but an individual phenomenon. Long periods of peace, progressive reduction in the size of armies and the length of service, as well as more relaxed discipline all contributed to diminished aversion to service in the military (9). In noting that the practice has spread from conscripts to the civilian population, particularly after the introduction of compensation for workplace injury (9), he shares some concerns of his British contemporaries. In contending that self harm also became rare in civil life because of the provision of health services and some welfare for the poor (9), Salinari proceeds from the assumption that all injuries are inflicted to gain sympathy, but he does not provide evidence. He concludes by expressing the view that prevention is undoubtedly better than oppression, an opinion borne out by his own results during the war (although he does not say what those "few simple preventive measures" were; 223).

Works like these have generally but not always been received with enthusiasm by reviewers. For example, the *Medical Echo* of October 1938 noted a new publication under the headline "Malingering":

> There are but few systematic treatises on this subject, so that a welcome will be extended to the recently published *Handbuch der Artefakte* (Gustav Fischer, Jena 1937) under the editorship of Dr. Julius Mayr of the University of Münster. This work is remarkably exhaustive and deals not only with those cases wherein a healthy person pretends to be ill, but also with those cases wherein an unhealthy person pretends to be well. The book ranges over the whole field of disease beginning with neurology and psychiatry, and ending with forensic and social medicine, embracing artefacts of the skin, nose and throat, disturbances of vision and hearing, surgical and gynæcological lesions ["Malingering" 54].

The reviewer was obviously comfortable with the associations which Mayr made between self harm and criminality, reporting Mayr's study of numerous patients with abscesses in a prison: "It was eventually discovered that this was managed by the smuggling into the prison of Record syringes placed in empty toothpaste tubes. The prisoners injected into themselves, benzene, paraffin, and even tuberculous sputum" (55). By foregrounding such comments in the review, the association between fraud and deliberate self injury is strengthened.

Self Harm in Prison

The prototypical understanding of self harm when it occurs in prisons focuses on affirming the criminality of the person who injures themselves. The tone and aims of prison itself and the research and reporting done about self harm are described effectively by John Joseph Gibbs. Gibbs interviewed four hundred people in prison in the course of his PhD research for the School of Criminal Justice in John Jay College in New York. The majority of these interviewees (333) had engaged in self harm. Gibbs' 1978 thesis is an unusual piece of scholarship, not simply for the extraordinary thoroughness of the primary research, but for the nuanced understanding of criminality and institutional processes it demonstrates. The author balances a range of competing perspectives, something in evidence in his overview of responses by prison authorities to inmates who injure themselves.

> The impression gathered from reading hundreds of institutional reports and interviewing approximately 50 staff members is that the predominate reaction to an incident of self-injury is an investigation similar in nature to queries made about any other events classified as "unusual incidents"—assaults, disturbances, injuries, etc. Investigations of self-destructive breakdowns and especially suicides appear to be geared to assigning blame or vindicating staff of responsibility [sic]. The goal of the inquiry is to demonstrate that the organization was not negligent. The obstensibly [sic] objective and detached flavor of these reports is not a cold-hearted response to human suffering, but a necessary and appropriate organizational response to potential law suits and head hunting by "watchdog" agencies. The prevalent premise is that inmate breakdowns are completely accounted for by personality. This suicidal act is evidence that the man is a "bug." "Bugs" are people who suffer from a variety of permanent personality defects such as "weak-mindedness," therefore, the only possible intervention is to watch them closely and/or "cool them out" with medication [Gibbs 244].

What Gibbs identifies here is the manner in which the institution structures and limits modes of response: in an environment that is primarily concerned with accountability, the focus is on demonstrating that all was done that could have been. Gibbs' account also suggests that within such environments, the use of pejorative terms for those who self harm becomes fulfilling, even tautological: just as the prison occupant's position (criminal) is proof of the essentially "fraudulent" (i.e. self-interested) nature of their self injury, so their use of such tactics (self harm) is proof of their criminality.

As Gibbs sees it, most studies of self harm in prisons assume that the self harm occurs because of the higher proportion of people with either serious mental health issues or dissident personalities. However, some writers suggest that conditions of incarceration can incubate self harm. For example, two scholars write in 1968 of one U.S. state prison system that the extremely poor conditions under which Texas inmates lived and worked [before 1948] proved to be time and again more than ample reason for the most violent and savage attacks upon self. As protests against the pervasive brutality, hands and feet were chopped off by desperate men. And, from sources now thoroughly concealed by the passing of time, inmates learned that slashing the Achilles' [sic] Tendon with always available razor blades, or any other sharp instrument at hand, was an effective means of winning sympathy and support for their immediate protest, which at various times was directed by groups or individuals against barbaric working conditions, putrid and tainted food, filthy and malodorous living conditions, etc. [Beto and Claghorn 25].

Beto, a sociologist and student of the prison system, and Claghorn, a psychiatrist, argue that in this world, self harm takes on new meanings:

not [being] used as a means of protest *per se*, but to attract attention, which is a manifestation of self-pity, to escape a situation they are unable to handle, or because they are very sick and hallucinating. The situational mutilator may be given cause to maim himself for the following reasons: fear of homosexual attack; death in the family and his inability to be there; fear of brutality from other inmates or guards; or a "Dear John" letter from his wife or girl friend [Beto and Claghorn 25].

They go on: "For the Latin-American, self-mutilation tends to serve as a means of proving oneself and establishing a type of individuality"; an African American man finds it "extremely easy to adjust to the pressure of a prison setting" because "He has always been part of a group" (26).

The aim, here, is neither to support nor to mock such claims, but to show the ways in which writing about prison populations seeks to identify the "type" as a means of managing behavior. This reflects the same logic of classification which underpins the early theses and handbooks of self harm, and which drives much psychological research: the belief, expressed in 1988, that "Eventually it will be possible to assemble [unclassified syndromes] in groups homogenous according to syndrome, and to compare each group with a comparison or control group" (Money 113–14).[7] The same impulse is evident in Favazza and Rosenthal's 1993 attempt to classify all instances of self harm under one of three headings, "major," "stereotypic" and "superficial or moderate," or in Cohen's 1969 attempt to find a classificatory system for what he terms "self assault." The larger context is the apparent need to find low-cost instruments with which non-specialist staff can predict, prevent and/or control self harm in large institutions. Such ambitions are predicated on a diagnostic model that presumes the stability of the identity or behavior—simply, that what has happened in the past is a reliable guide to what will happen in the future, or that the behavior of people with common characteristics such as gender, age, sexuality, mental health profile or—for Bartholow, hair color and facial expression—can be predicted.

The assumption that staff trained in prison operation and management can also be trained to recognize signs of potential self harm is in respect commensurate with a culture in which relations of power are tightly structured and authority is ceded to a single group. There is a sense not only in which judgments about the capacity of the authority group become unrealistic, but that their insensitivity to or even active maltreatment of inmates become intrinsic to that difference in status. Interestingly, one university experiment designed to explore this dynamic had to be halted prematurely after students became habituated to these differences of power. The 1988 experiment, in which participants simulated roles of prison inmates and prison guards, had been designed to run for two weeks but had to be halted after just six days. "Despite the artificiality of the situation ... the prisoners became passive and distressed and the guards became authoritarian and sadistic. The experimenters themselves began behaving irrationally" (Holley and Arboleda-Flórez 172–73). Nevertheless, criminological literature (broadly conceived) understands sites of injury as diagnostic categories. The desire to identify these sites or identities reflects not a theory of illness (why people self harm) but a theory of how truth is made (the means by which a doctor might recognize fraud; the means by which prison authorities might predict self harm). When they are used as part of manuals to identify forms of self harm, such studies prefabricate the criminality of the patient. In most instances, studies of self harm in prison or military contexts, although they base their narrative structure on the site of self harm (leg; eye; hand) or the means of effecting self harm (abrasion; ingestion; amputation), do not offer any theory of interpretation that makes either the site or method of injury meaningful.[8] Rare is the work in criminology which concedes that "we cannot escape the fact that treatment of malingering is, in the majority of cases, the treatment of psychopathology" (Biach 329).

Bryan Gandevia, an Australian physician, writes in the former vein when he records the stories of three convicts who had died after a doctor had judged them "malingerers" and they were therefore flogged (62). His 1978 essay quotes descriptions of prisoners who had resorted to

> driving a pick into the foot; applying leaves ... to their hands or feet for the night so as to produce a large blister ... and with this view I actually saw a man cut off the thumb and, if I mistake not, the forefinger of his left hand.
>
> The external application of poisonous matter was frequently resorted to produce sickness—and ... death in many cases ensued ... severe cuts were purposely inflicted with the hoe, intentional burning, scalds, forced dysentery, and tampering with the eyes to produce blind-ness, were common practice. So numerous were cases of this nature that in addition to a crowded Hospital there were daily from 80 to 100 ... in a room measuring 16 feet long by 12 feet wide a filthy and suffocating hole, and yet the greater number would prefer it

on bread and water to performing the labour which at that time was exacted from them. It was the last resort of a debilitated man worn down by hunger and fatigue [Gandevia 64].

Gandevia's tone is one of indulgent amusement. He does not consider the impact of circumstance, suggesting simply that "Successful suicides employing the traumatic methods available to the convicts appear less dependent on the social or physical environment, and probably reflect a psychotic personality trait" (80).

In René Belbenoît's autobiography *Dry Guillotine*, published in 1938, the author argues that injuring oneself is seen by prisoners themselves as an effect of imprisonment. The effort made to be sent to a hospital ward is at once logical, and symptomatic of the brutalization that is experienced. Belbenoît's account, which describes his experiences as a convict in French Guiana, foregrounds not deceit but desperation, not character but the consequences of self injury committed by those who are incarcerated. His autobiography presents quite a different view to that offered by scholars:

> Some find a way to wound themselves purposely, some smoke quinine to sham fever, some breathe sulphur to sham bronchitis or rub sperm into their eyes to induce a suppuration, others put castor beans in a cut so as to get a serious infection: they try everything. They impair their health, and often pay with a part of their bodies or with their lives [173].

Such accounts have rarely swayed public opinion, or the opinions of prison guards or administrators. But biography and autobiography, along with fiction, can contest the academic analyses of self harm which insist it is merely an extension of pre-existing criminality.

At the same time, autobiography itself can come to deploy the conceptual tools of scholarly literature, as successfully "recovered" patients use the terminology of their treatment to structure their understanding of their own self harm. Paul Marshall's *Scarred for Life* (2002) is one such criminal autobiography. Marshall, born in 1970, presents a textbook case of parental neglect and "juvenile delinquency." *Scarred for Life* describes his growing up and immersion in crime during the 1980s and 1990s, the first charges laid against him when he was ten years old. At one point, Marshall describes repeated acts of slashing his own arms, something done to prevent his transfer to another gaol. He explains it this way: "I hated using those measures where I've got to slash myself just to get a point across" (121), repeating similar remarks a few lines later.

At one level, Marshall's description of his reasons for injuring himself appears to be as clear an example of instrumental self harm, and of its relationship with criminality, as could be found. But this writer is also aware that his violence is horrifying to those who witness it—it is notable that Marshall's book is implicitly sanctioned by prison authorities, containing formal thanks to the Cooma Correctional Centre in the acknowledgments, as well as a fore- word by a professor of psychology, Alex Blaszczynski, and a preface by Kevin Waller, former chair of a committee advising on self harm in correctional institutions. While on the one hand the cover picture of a heavily tattooed and scarred author "authenticates" this book as a "raw, graphic and often shock- ing" account by a damaged and dangerous criminal, it is also a story of rescue and recovery. Authenticated by prison authorities, it is as close to a state- sanctioned account of self harm as one could get. Certified as a "true story" by its title and these paratextual elements, there is at the same time a curious opacity about self harm: readers are never told just *why* Marshall changes, nor do we know much about how; the "success story" is that the author has "gained a meaningful understanding of the futility of self harm" (xii).

Marshall works within a narrative frame that concedes that self harm can be traumatic to witnesses. For example, he notes that a psychologist who sees his cuts "freaked out" (121) and he recounts apologizing to other inmates in a truck before cutting himself again to prevent his transfer taking place: "'Sorry, fellas, but I have to do what I have to do'" (128). The cliché—"a man's gotta do..."—should not prevent us from noticing that the author is acknowl- edging (or hoping to be read as acknowledging) that self-injury is potentially traumatic even for other prisoners. In so doing, Marshall offers the suggestion that self harm is both less and more than a means of getting one's own way in institutions which deprive inmates of status or agency. Writing as a reformed member of society and a person who has ceased to self harm, Marshall rep- resents his actions as a means of expressing his distress and demanding change or relief. He says, still speaking of his attempts to avoid transfer, "Twice they stuck me on the truck and I slashed up. *You'd think someone would realise that there was something wrong if I was self-harming to get out of going to Goulburn*" (130; emphasis added). In his view, the self harm is less a mechanism of coer- cion than a medium of communication. That he should use this medium is a reflection of the strict limitations on expressivity that correlate with the adop- tion of the tough-guy role. This interpretation is buttressed by Blaszczynski's foreword; together, they present self harm in prisons as being instrumental in a slightly different sense from that which Gandevia and others would have it.

What is less obvious, here, is Marshall's demand that prison staff "read" his behavior. Specifically, he suggests that the warders should recognize his self injury as demanding interpretation. He condemns the literal reading, which is that self harm is a failed attempted at suicide. Marshall claims that the meaning which the guards should have deduced is that he would rather die than go to the jail at Goulburn, a "rational" action because he thinks he *will* be killed if he goes there. But in terms of establishing his authority over his own position and getting traction within the prison hierarchy, the acts of self harm are also part of a "status game" that one criminologist argues inheres in prison life:

> [J]uggling for dominance is more visible in the prison than in other social settings because the prison is blatantly status-depriving and thus creates a particularly acute need for indices of relative status.... The process can also be more obviously productive of trauma, since the losers of the game tend to be men who have lost other, similar games [Toch 64; see also Robert Johnson 480–81].

Elmer H. Johnson's 1969 study of the effect of prison in the United States likewise distinguishes between high and low status prisoners, groups whose self harm has different meanings. "High status" prisoners are seen as self harming in order to manipulate the system (94). On the other hand "low status prisoners," who are called "rats," victims of rape, injure themselves as an effect of their status (93). There is even a subgroup of low status prisoners, those who need to get themselves moved to a different place and self harm in order to do so (93–94).

Such claims open up the suggestion that incarceration in and of itself has the potential to create or exacerbate the potential for self harm. In the view of some doctors, some psychologists, some criminologists and some criminal autobiographies, prison seems to do this not merely by imposing restrictions and building frustration through physical restraint, but by reducing the media for expression and the means to influence the social and physical environment. These limitations are linked not only to the legal situation of inmates, but to stereotypes of identity. If this is true, the desire to identify and catalogue all forms of self harm and, more latterly, to design research that will develop predictive schema with which to identify those likely to self harm, takes no account of the fact that the environment might induce self harm or feed its proliferation. Given an instance from the 1970s—a time in which research into self harm in prisons was fairly active—an essay describing the presentation of 70 patients with lacerated tendons in 84 separate instances within one prison over a period of less than a year (see Grisolia *et al.* 206), it is not clear why the focus of researchers should be on the prediction of self harm. More prevalent and more pressing problems seem to lie in the induction and spread of self harm within prison environments.

Doctors Resisting?

If the military literature on self harm tends to inform the criminological literature, just as assumptions about criminality inform the handbooks for military medical officers in dealing with self harm, then some stories in which doctors *resist* the general mood of promoting participation in war are unusual.

That said, the popularity in the history of medicine of one account of resistance to the criminalization and punishment of soldiers hints that doctors can be interested in and even inspired by instances in which medical officers defy their political or military superiors. Dominique-Jean Larrey, revered for his surgical skill, logistical innovations, and the personal courage demonstrated in a long career in the French military, famously took a stand against Napoleon in 1813. After being told that nearly 3,000 soldiers had suffered injuries to their fingers and hands, Napoleon declared that a proportion of them should be shot since such wounds must have been self-inflicted. Larrey took the view that the soldiers had been accused by "certain persons who were accustomed to hide the truth" (qtd. in Dible 209), that is, who did not want Napoleon to know the true cost, in men wounded, of recently fought battles. The examinations of the soldiers, which lasted three days, showed that there was a strong likelihood of the injuries being the result of hard fighting or incompetence (Dible 210; Richardson 195–97).

Larrey's own account as presented in his memoirs emphasizes that often it is impossible for a doctor to discern whether or not a wound has been self-inflicted. Secondary sources emphasize Larrey's heroism in insisting that the matter be investigated, and his preparedness to certify that the wounds occurred in battle. What is also clear is that Napoleon's preparedness to accept Larrey's word depended in part on the reputation for expertise and integrity that his senior medical officer had established in an already distinguished career. That such a powerful parable about the duty of the medical professional to protect soldiers periodically recirculates in medical literatures, including in the First World War, is suggestive of the increased complexity and weight of the doctors' role (see for example "Self-Mutilation by Soldiers") and a commensurate eagerness to write and read of defiance of military or political pragmatism. Larrey is a key figure for surgeons in particular—his translated memoirs are published in the "Classics of Surgery Library" series. A modern note on Larrey declares his heroism: "He dared to oppose, single-handed, the Emperor, the highest military authorities and their concurring physicians and surgeons, armed only by his undisputed honesty, professional authority and exceptional reputation won over years of devotion to wounded soldiers" (Feinsod 408).

There is a greater significance of Larrey's actions, and the circulation of this story. While the moral of Larrey's stance tends to be seen in medical literature as lying in the demands on the character of the surgeon and the commensurate nobility of his response—it requires heroism to stand up to bureaucracy seeking a quick fix for a political or logistical problem—we can also see a *methodological* lesson. Larrey's conscientiousness and fortitude were demonstrated not simply by his querying of Napoleon's edict, but by his part in conducting more than two-and-a-half thousand examinations of individual patients over a period of just three days. While the speed of his work (particularly in performing amputations) is the stuff of legend, the *method* he insists on is the case study multiplied. The incident offers a demonstration of the belief that it is essential to examine each patient if the nature of their condition and its meaning are to be properly established. Even if he did not sleep for 72 hours, Larrey must still have spent much less than two minutes examining each soldier. Nevertheless, in insisting on this procedure, Larrey was rejecting the methods implied by those manuals of *Feigned and Factitious Injury* which see the character and motives of the soldier as fixed by their identity or as an effect of circumstances. We cannot pretend to think such examinations were thorough, but the approach is highly significant in implying a rejection of the principle of using category to arrive at a moral or medical judgment.

It can be difficult, though, for those with (only) medical authority to ask questions about the effect of incarceration on prisoners. Positioned as part of the hierarchies of prison itself, they may be regarded with suspicion by both inmates and prison administrators. A report by doctors working in Guantanamo Bay in the mid–1990s with would-be Cuban immigrants who harmed themselves noted that the authors "attempted to ... discuss the cause of the medical condition openly with the patients, and treat all but the most extreme cases locally" while conceding that "the effect on the physician–patient relationship" of the self harm "was profound: the care and trust that ideally characterize this relationship were supplanted by suspicion and deceit" (Andrews *et al.* 1253). The editor of the journal in which this essay appears notes that these doctors were "embedded in a system of military command that made it virtually impossible for them to attack the underlying disease: indefinite detention" (Eisenberg 1248). This detention came about because of a change in law. At the time of leaving Cuba, those able to reach the U.S. enclave of Guantanamo Bay were granted asylum in the United States. However the law had changed and they were placed in detention for an undetermined period on arrival in the U.S. The same circumstances, uncertainty in the period of detention coupled with the refusal to grant asylum, affects those seeking to come to Australia in the early twenty-first century, a situation that has seen self harm used as a method of protest. The *social* structures of the prison, particularly the disempowerment of inmates, leave self harm positioned (in the minds of some inmates at least) as a rational form of political self-expression.

The First World War

The looming war in Europe seems to have caused self harm to come onto the agenda of doctors in the second decade of the twentieth century. In 1913, in a "Discussion on Functional and Simulated Affections of the Auditory Apparatus," T. Mark Hovell asserted that self harm could be observed "most frequently ... in those individuals who wish to be exempted from military service, or who hope to obtain pecuniary advantage from the simulated disablement which is attributed to accident or other cause" (74). Entwined with ideas about the value of common sense based on visible reality—encapsulated in the nostrum "seeing is believing," and evident in the remark by Hovell—are beliefs about the dangers and indeed sheer waste of pursuing investigations into the non-physical aspects of the mind. Implicitly, all individuals are held responsible for their actions unless incapacitated by a physical illness. The desire is to shut down research into or discussion of psychological factors by invoking the value of manliness and the primacy of national interest.

Being determined to ignore the effects of war on participants meant avoiding questions about the justification of war itself. But there was not complete agreement on these matters: occasional queries, open dissent, and questioning of the import of self harm could emerge, from book reviews, diaries, professional discussion and even, in one notable example, the official national history of war. Accounts of professional meetings of doctors, books devoted to self harm and reviews of those books, and autobiographies and novels document, if in sometimes fragmented, allusive, or contradictory ways, the divisions among doctors and others on how to respond to perceived instances of self injury among soldiers.

These debates began before the formal outbreak of war, for they represented collisions between different approaches to medicine, and in particular the controversial status of the emerging science of psychiatry. A report in the *Lancet* for 26 November 1910 notes that Major C.E. Pollock read a paper on "malingering" which considered motives, means, and ways of evading military service in countries which at that point had conscription (that is, *outside* Britain). In the copy of this report preserved in the papers of F. Parkes Weber, Weber adds a hand-written note describing a case from Shattock, of self-induced "balls" floating in the bladder, which "they" think were induced to escape war service ("United Services Medical Society"). Weber's annotation—typically for him—seems on the one hand to accept and on the other to imply doubt about the neatly instrumental interpretation of the patient's situation.

A discussion on the same topic reported in the *Lancet* two years later was more explicitly controversial. The debate was introduced by the president of Edinburgh's Medico-Chirurgical [Surgical] Society, Byrom Bramwell. Bramwell stated that "the 'unconscious malingerer' could not exist, for there was no such condition" (Edinburgh 1653), an assertion that simply and emphatically precludes the notion of mental illness by declaring the absolute sovereignty of the will. As regards those who did injure themselves, "the largest number came from sailors, soldiers, prisoners, schoolboys, conscripts, hospital patients, hysterical young women ... and criminals," their numbers increasing since the passing of the *Workmen's Compensation Act* (Edinburgh 1653). The tone among those present seems to be indicated by several contributors who remark grumpily that fraud is rife and will cost the country a fortune. If some of this "professional concern" can be tagged Tory huff and bluster about the proliferation of mischief among the working classes, a mischief facilitated by ill-conceived government profligacy, there is almost an equal contempt for those with an interest in the mental aspects of illness.

But some present took issue with this view. Sir Thomas Clouston, a self-described "lunacy expert," said that in his experience it was

> often not easy to determine whether prisoners were malingering or not. Melancholic patients exaggerated their symptoms in order to appear more insane. Nervous patients might honestly simulate disease or exaggerate their symptoms, and, indeed, might really produce real nervous disease, and thus we might find them suffering from true organic disease [Edinburgh 1653].

Clouston makes a valiant attempt to problematize the question of what constitutes feigned illness, and to raise the possibility that self harm might have "genuine" medical causes. In short, his argument is that the induction of symptoms or wounds is indicative of a medical problem. He was supported by Edwin Bramwell, son of the President, who contested explicitly his father's claims by asserting that

> no definite distinction had been made between malingering and functional nervous disease, and many of the cases detailed by the speakers were really cases of hysteria.... Traumatic neurasthenia was a subconscious simulation very difficult to distinguish. Hysterical symptoms were frequently mistaken for malingering, and the hysterical patient had quite a right to compensation [Edinburgh 1654].

In his invoking of trauma, the subconscious and hysteria, which are presented not only as tangible medical concepts but as things worthy of investigation by the doctor, Edwin Bramwell seems to be distinguishing himself emotionally and methodologically from the earlier generation. Such terms were associated with the new sciences of the psyche, which were demanding but not always receiving recognition from medical practitioners and educators. While the lines of debate would shift slightly, the differences of view set out in this pre-war discussion held at the heart of the British and colonial medical establishment would remain germane to debates about how best to respond to soldiers with suspected or actual self harm on the home front and on the battlefield.

The First World War saw an escalation of self harm and increased attention to it among medical writers: specialist works were published, seminars and debates among doctors were held, and newspapers like London's *Times* reported on these occasions and on the general problem of what it termed malingering. An American doctor sent to research what he defined as "functional nervous conditions arising in soldiers" remarked that the conflict among and between neurologists, biologists, psychiatrists and the merely sceptical had produced "a large literature ... which must be rather chaotic for the average reader to whom it is accessible" (McCurdy 1, 3).[9] The war intensified pressures in debates about self harm in relation to civilian and military life. In interpreting the work of participants in these debates, it is worth remembering that the state has a financial and moral investment in disputing and ultimately refuting the claims of military personnel to be suffering any effects from combat. This is because of the drive to maximize the number of troops available for combat, to minimize the cost of pensions, and to deflate critics who draw attention to the debilitating effect of war on participants.

The strength of pressure to diminish the time and attention paid to mental illness in the combat zone is signalled in the Foreword to one study which commends a particular cure on the basis that once the treatment has begun, it must be completed in *one session* (Buzzard, Foreword vii). A British physician writing just after the war offers another example:

> In the most common type of case I believe that better results will be obtained by fresh air, sunlight, cheerful surroundings and light work, than by continuous searching for a hidden mental conflict. Of the value of psycho-analysis in certain intractable cases where there are reasons for suspecting a repressed memory or complex, I am not competent to express an opinion. Nor am I tempted to undertake the necessary investigations when I read that three years' study of the subject is essential, and that to unravel a complex, to trace some of its elements back, possibly to some incident in childhood, often a very muddy one, may occupy the constant attention of the psycho-analyst for at least several months, and sometimes for a year and even longer [Bury 68].

Modes of treatment, along with the framing and implementation of regulations in the military, were brought to bear on the same problem: maximizing the number of men eligible for front-line service, and maximizing the time they spent in combat while there.

One writer claims that "During the First World War veritable epidemics of self-inflicted injuries occurred. Entire hospital wards were filled with men who had been shot in one finger or one toe. No one will ever know fully how many of these were self-inflicted injuries, although medical officers then on duty believed the number would run into thousands" (Flicker, qtd. in Van Dyke 4). In considering the extent of self-inflicted injuries and feigned illness, the *Report of the War Office Committee of Enquiry into "Shell-Shock"* (1922) differentiates between "true malingering," which entails faking shell shock; partial malingering, defined as the exaggerating of symptoms; and quasi-malingering, not so much bothering to pretend debilitation as invoking shell-shock to escape the front line (Army). The report concludes that "If this breaking away of men in small and large numbers is to be classed as malingering, then it must be allowed that malingering occurred in unprecedented proportions" (Army 141). A precedent is cited in the British army's Caribbean campaign of 1794–96, during which troops ran amok and many died.

Responses to this proliferation took a range of forms. A report in London's *Times* newspaper on "Malingering and Self-maiming: Tricks to Evade Service" in September 1916 noted that a law had been passed making it an offense to feign disease or illness, or for a soldier or potential recruit to injure himself in a way "likely to render him, or to lead to the belief that he is, permanently or temporarily unfit for service, unless he proves that he did not so act with the intent of escaping service." Intriguingly, this framing leaves open the possibility that self harm might be committed for reasons *other* than escaping military service, even as the passing of the law hints at an increasing frequency of such instances. The wording suggests that the issues raised by criminalizing simulation were seen as less pressing than the need to formalize deterrents to deliberate physical self harm, in the manner of those laws against simulation which British authors had earlier derided.

The next year, 1917, the *Lancet* carried a report of an essay in the *Paris médical* which it praised as "an interesting attempt to clear the air and facilitate further investigation" on the subject of feigned injury ("Insincerity"). The two French authors whose work is described "are in charge of the centre, under the military government of Paris": their focus is said to be on "soldiers who, in the absence of evidence of organic disease, are suspected of 'ill-will'" ("Insincerity"). A later study by these French writers of simulation in war (*La simulation de l'aliéné devant la guerre*, 1918) was seen as identifying not "genuine" mental illness but the ironic "exaggeration of their mental troubles by avowed psychopaths" (Mourgue). The December no. of *Medical Science: Abstracts and Reviews* notes a paper in the *Münchner Medizinische Wochenschrift* "on malingering in Russia during the war. Mende, the writer of the article, claimed to have met with 1,200 patients with self-inflicted injuries in a little over two years. The most common problems were artificial swellings produced by the injection of liquid paraffin or paraffin mixed with Vaseline" ("Malingering and the Simulation of Disease"). The climate of discussion is significant: in Britain, doctors were clearly interested not only in the idea of fraud but in what was happening in military and civilian contexts in other countries.

One of the major players in the debate about self harm in Britain, Sir John Collie, had already written on the problem of "malingering" and updated his co-written book on the subject for a second edition published during the war. Collie saw himself as a proactive defender of the national interest, deploying his expertise to control the proliferation of behaviors (or diagnoses) that he saw as threatening the financial and military viability of the state.[10] Collie's take on mental illness is made clear in his assertion that "it is of paramount importance in the national interests that the great problem of obtaining the maximum of efficient work from all should be obtained" [sic] (Collie, "Prefatory Note" xv). Here he cites the work of André Léri, who had reported extraordinary success in returning 91 percent of soldiers (600) to the front line within days of being treated for "war neuroses"; the secret of success was said to be the Spartan conditions used by Léri, which included a prohibition on the provision of emotional or physical comfort (Rutkowski and Dembińska 386). In his own book, Collie notes the prevalence of malingering in army and navy, which he sees as having spread into the civilian population to such an extent that "it will be necessary for all medical men to look for the possibility of deceit or exaggeration in many cases that come before them" (Collie and Spicer 1).[11] Collie's book is unusual in that it shows no interest in detailing specific practices—the concern is *detection*, thence the legal contexts in which this occurs.

Collie's book, although nominally "medical" and written by a medical practitioner, belongs with those legal and military studies which begin from the premise that because much illness (mental or physical) is being feigned, the doctor's work is to detect. There can be some overly valiant argument entailed in supporting such a view. For example, Collie writes on hysteria that "broadly speaking, it may be said that the malingerer and the hysterical patient present symptoms which are so closely similar that a differentiation of the two may be difficult" *but* "Such a differentiation ... is perfectly possible ... and must, indeed, be made" (Collie and Spicer 83). Here it is worth noting that such approaches were not superseded over the course of the twentieth century: books are still being published which use the fraud model to offer a compendium of self harm, often with that introductory anecdote used to signify even-handedness (e.g. Rogers; Feldman, *Playing Sick?*).

A reviewer of Collie's later work, *Fraud in Medico-Legal Practice*, expressed revulsion for the approach taken: "Not the healing and comforting of the sick, but the almost hostile criticism and exposure of those poor unfortunates who come before him, for many long years, made up his daily work." Perhaps the crux of this reader's objection lies in the observation that "Doctors ... come out rather badly of these pages. They are pictured as not infrequently credulous, ignorant, prone to error, and venal" ("Doctor and Malingerer"). More subtly, Collie's *Malingering and Feigned Sickness* was castigated by the reviewer in the *British Medical Journal* (*BMJ*) for being insubstantial (Rev. of *Malingering, BMJ*). This led the editor of the *BMJ* to step into the debate in ways that naturalize malingering as something ancient and frequent, something indicative of a European disposition but alien to a British one:

> We publish this week two reviews of British works on malingering, and have brought together in the epitome a number of abstracts from articles in foreign medical journals which describe in detail some of the varied and devious ways of the malingerer in the Continental armies of to-day.[12] To malinger is defined by Murray as "to pretend illness, or to produce or to protract disease in order to escape duty." The term has been in military use in this country for several centuries, but shamming sickness or injury is as old as the human race, and has long been noted among domestic animals.... In the civil life of this country the Workmen's Compensation Act, and the legal liability of employers and railway companies for accidents, have elevated the feigning of injury and its consequences into a topic of special medical study; but until the second year of this war, when compulsory service was introduced, the military aspects of malingering received scanty notice. In countries, however, where a conscript army is an old institution, the simulation of disease, in order to evade military service or dangerous duty, has been closely studied for many years, and the war has only served to increase medical interest in the subject [Editorial].

The reviews of two British works on malingering—the very publication of which implies it is a topic du jour—are counterweighted by the inclusion of "a number of abstracts from articles in foreign journals," the reference to "the malingerer in the Continental armies of the day," and mention of those places in which "a conscript army is an old institution." Implicitly the rise of self harm is attributed to the provision of incentives for illness and injury, although this has benefits for the medical profession in making the topic a worthwhile area of study. Although the editorial purports to be even-handed, it is noticeable that there is no interest in either the impact of historical events on the medical profession or the interaction with patients, two things the reviewer of Collie's book highlights.

The *Lancet* reviewer of the "competing" volume, A. Bassett Jones and Llewellyn J. Llewellyn's *Malingering, or the Simulation of Disease*, complimented the authors on their apt and evocative use of literary quotation but chose not to mention the war, lamenting only that the nature of humankind was such that this kind of volume was necessary.[13] The reviewer acknowledged the difficulty of dealing with patients of whom self injury was suspected, but was almost laconic in commenting that the book's authors "demonstrate afresh the truth of the old dictum of the eighteenth-century Bath physician who declared it was more important to know what sort of patient had a disease than what sort of a disease a patient had" (Rev. of *Malingering, Lancet* 163). The sympathetic perspective on self harm is indicated by the satisfied note that, in dedicating the volume to liberal British politician Lloyd George, the authors were rejecting the view that the passing of legislation to provide workers' compensation and insurance—the *Workmen's Compensation Act* (1906) and *National Insurance Act* (1911)—had led to a proliferation of self-injury. That is, both authors and reviewer were disputing the claim by Collie and the editor of the *BMJ* that the introduction of these laws was the cause of an efflorescence of fraud.

The author of the *BMJ* review of Jones and Llewellyn's *Malingering* castigated Jones and Llewellyn for paying insufficient attention to the war. The review contests their views on the effect of paying compensation for injuries received at work, including in military service, in terms which imply that the book inappropriately plays down the significance of fraud:

> Not only is this subject of national importance in respect to recent legislative innovations, but even more so in connexion with exemption from military service and the granting of pensions for war disablement.
> We are rather surprised to note how little reference is made to the experiences gained in this war, in spite of the fact that the authors, on page 53, state that "our own experience of soldiers in the present war leads us to the conclusion that pure malingering is uncommon" [Rev. of *Malingering, BMJ*].

What is at stake is not only whether the ill soldier is returned to the front line, but whether or not he receives compensation after the war for disability. The conditions of the First World War made the situation more complicated than it had been. For example, the use of chemical warfare, which often entailed uncertainty about the boundaries of incidents, as well as medical uncertainty about how to determine and measure the long-term effects of twenty or more gases used by different armies, made it difficult to determine what proportion or kind of physical damage could be attributed directly to participation in combat. The number of war pensions came to be at issue in Australia, England, France and Italy.

Implicitly, through this focus on pensions and compensation, "malingering" was identified as something associated with poorer members of society, those most affected if they were unable to perform manual labor. What runs through the discussion is the presumption that the fragility of their work ethic inclines members of the working class to fraud and evasion, hence the exaggeration or invention of symptoms. When invalidism of soldiers reached high levels, critics of welfare and sceptics about the psychological impact of war saw the provision of medical pensions as working-class fraud committed on a mass scale. This element of class distinction underpins discussion of self harm in military contexts, not least because doctors were by definition officers, often superior in social as well as military rank to those whose health they were judging.[14] For example, Kloocke *et al.* note that in the German army the diagnosis of "neurasthenia" tended to be reserved for officers, whereas other ranks were said to have "hysterical reactions" (52). Neurasthenia was usually treated with rest and psychotherapy, whereas hysteria was generally dealt with by what was called "active treatment." The brutality of some medical treatment in the First World War was sufficient to attract the attention of political representatives (Kloocke *et al.* 48, 54), as well as a delighted London press. The author of "Hun Cruelty to Hun" (1914) records with satisfaction that patients in a German hospital had resorted to burning down wards in protest after their "nerve troubles" had been treated with electric shock.

The Secret Battle

In England, France and Germany, doctors were acutely aware of political pressures against invaliding men out of the fighting forces, and against the awarding of pensions to those said to have been permanently debilitated by war service; they also knew that if they made an accusation of self-inflicted injury known, their patient could be shot. Maxime Laignel-Lavastine and Paul Courbon's study of simulation of madness (*La simulation de l'aliéné devant la guerre*, 1918) was reviewed by R. Mourgue in *Paris médical* in 1918 in terms that reflected the increasing pressure experienced in times of war by doctors, who were aware of the high stakes now attendant differentiating simulated from "genuine" illness. Mourgue noted that the authors were concerned not with "genuine" mental illness but with "exaggeration of their mental troubles by avowed psychopaths," a practice they call "sursimulation." But this "pathology" is framed in terms of diminished love of nation. More bluntly, Kloocke and her colleagues conclude that in Germany, "The doctors' identification with the public interest was stronger than their sense of responsibility to the particular patient" (55).[15] The effort to keep in view at all times the possibilities and demands of simulation, pathology, and patriotism, and the admission that simulation could overlap with illness, is evident in the somewhat tortured logic.

Capital punishment for deliberate self harm dramatically raises the stakes for those whose job it is to arbitrate on the question of whether an injury has been self-inflicted. A paraphrased account from 1915 notes Paul Chavigny's view that

> there have been some undoubted cases of self-mutilation in the present war, and that several soldiers of the French army have been shot for this military crime. [Chavigny] hints, however, that in some cases the evidence has been insufficient to justify the penalty. The diagnosis is sometimes very difficult, and the trench fighting which has been going on has, owing to the nearness of the combatants to each other, created new conditions which make the problem more complex ["Self-Mutilation by Soldiers" 900].

The report goes on to describe in grim detail the laceration caused when a finger is placed directly over the barrel of the gun. Chavigny seems to have seen no clear line between injuries inflicted to escape military service altogether and those committed out of the terrors induced by experience or anticipation of combat. And one American writer in 1917 also takes this view, aware of the stigma of criminality attached to being branded a "malingerer."

> I feel that in all instances of doubt, commitment to a hospital for the determination of the insanity, as provided for by statute, is most essential, not only for the protection of those truly insane, but for the elimination, if possible, of the malingerer, and incidentally for a study of the defect which is the fundamental basis of the deception. The latter may be of sufficient degree to absolve even the malingerer from being stigmatised a criminal [Ernest B. Emerson 436].

However the author of the article on Chavigny's work published in the *BMJ* took a very different line:

> The possibility of the man being weak-minded or suffering from the mania of persecution, general paralysis, or other mental condition diminishing his responsibility must always be borne in mind. [But i]n the examination of men charged with self-mutilation, the medical officer should never forget that he is acting as an expert witness, not as an advocate. The decision must be left in the hands of the court ["Self-Mutilation of Soldiers" 900].

That the doctor is merely an "expert witness" is in one sense a quite disingenuous claim. The soldier will only be put on trial if the doctor's suspicion that he has wounded himself is made known. The use of the word "advocate" in this context is a kind of code. Readers—likely to be medical professionals—are implicitly being advised to avoid proffering an opinion on, for example, extenuating circumstances, including mental illness, that might exonerate the soldier.

Amidst these debates, one army offers a case study of different conditions. When shifted to the western front after the failed invasion of Turkey, Australian troops fought under the British *Army Act and King's Regulation*. These permitted Australian soldiers to be convicted and sentenced to death, however, that penalty could not be carried out without the permission of the Australian government. According to Colonel A.W. Butler, who served in the war and afterwards wrote the volumes of the official national history dealing with the medical forces, this permission was never given (Butler, vol. 3, 90). Structurally, other factors diminished the reporting of self harm in the Australian forces, particularly once the army had moved to the western front in 1916. Initial diagnosis was made by a Regimental Medical Officer, who did not keep records of cases or diagnoses (Butler, vol. 3, 91). It is this apparent absence of documentation that makes Butler's brief but explicit discussion of self harm so historically significant. What is also unusual is that Butler is equally explicit about the impossibility of making meaningful judgments about whether or not specific instances of injury constituted self harm.

For Butler and his fellow medical officers in the Australian army, the practical problem first arose in the confined battle space of the Gallipoli peninsular, following from the attempted British-led invasion of Turkey in April 1915. Geography and logistics—a cliff face, a narrow beach, supply lines under pressure—meant that soldiers were not evacuated unless they were adjudged completely unable to continue to perform their duties. As Butler points out, there were no resources or places or activities through which to gain respite. This produced "a large evacuation from psycho-physical and psycho-somatic breakdown," as well as physical disease or debilitation. The criteria for diagnosis and thence evacuation would seem clear cut, but as Butler argues, in field conditions "medical officers were brought abruptly face to face with the extraordinary moral and mental problems involved in the phenomena of the hysterical syndrome, in particular their relation to the conscious 'will'" (Butler, vol. 3, 79). In these conditions it is not surprising that an outbreak of self wounding should have occurred. What *is* surprising is that this outbreak is recorded in Butler's history, in an account all the more intriguing for its brevity.

In acknowledging that there were instances of self harm in a battle which looms much larger in their national history for Australian combatants than most others, Butler says only that there were "repeated short epidemics of self-inflicted wounds."[16] These he claims

> were not so much sophisticated and deliberate attempts to shirk, as a crude and instinctive reaction against a psychic impasse which in less determined and morally-poised men would manifest itself as hysteria—the "flight into disease." So far as records show, the outbreaks took the form entirely of personal maiming by rifle fire, or by exposure to enemy fire [Butler, vol. 3, 88].

For its own reasons at the time, the Australian Army Medical Services determined that self wounding was not a form of "Delinquent Conduct" (Butler, vol. 3, 88; note 49). What leads Butler to make this interpretation, I would argue, is not medical knowledge. In fact, he makes no effort to invoke or to dispute with the views about mental and physical illness that he has canvassed in detail, and which he says informed practice on the front. Rather, it is his determination to record, and his belief in, the "moral poise" of Australian soldiers that lead him to explain their actions as a coping strategy. Adopting this strategy is preferable to, *and different from*, that "flight into disease" he condemns. In this, Butler echoes Napoleon's surgeon-general Larrey, in working from the premise that the soldiers cannot be at fault and that it is the work of the medical officer to presume their dignity and find the best means for their preservation. While hysteria is framed as a retreat, self injury through rifle fire is represented by Butler as a heroic coping mechanism. It is heroic because it entails being wounded *as a soldier*, thence being treated and evacuated from the front line on that basis. Put bluntly, the means and motive of self harm presented here preserve the honor of both the soldier and the medical officer charged with his diagnosis and treatment.

Nevertheless, Butler is also of the view that there are serious practical and conceptual difficulties in identifying instances of self harm. He explains that while lawyers, doctors and military authorities wanted to draw clear lines between deliberate intention, actions affected by illness, and those committed in a state of delusion, in practice, these overlap, "at their clinical and administrative boundaries." Lamenting the fact that this view prevailed in those armies in which the death penalty was used, he writes:

> The importance of this overlap can hardly be too greatly stressed; we may recall that, *frequently enough to constitute a major tragedy*, the question whether a soldier should be "shot at dawn" as a military criminal, or be discharged as a battle casualty with a "wound stripe" and war-pension, was determined by the opinion of a medical officer as to which side of this clinical overlap the soldier's behaviour should consign him [Butler, vol. 3, 58; emphasis added].[17]

Whereas the reviewer of Chavigny's book implies that the moral and medical decisions in relation to self harm are relatively simple, not least because there is no overlap between the criminal offense of self harm and wounds received in combat, Butler suggests a more complicated situation. The question is not only clinical; it is also political, and it underpinned by culturally specific assumptions about honor and duty, brittle categories of behavior from which one lapse could be sufficient to bring about death by firing squad.

Butler's problematizing of the identification of self harm, which merges morality, forensic medicine and the emerging sciences of mental illness, is dramatized by A.P. Herbert in his novel *The Secret Battle*. As with the prison autobiographies, fiction allows the writer to make explicit what is often only implicit in academic literatures; in particular, those "grey areas" are opened out and explored, instead of being disputed or dismissed. *The Secret Battle* presents the story of a young English officer in the First World War, Harry Penrose, who voluntarily enlists, and voluntarily re-enters combat several times, but who is ultimately executed for cowardice. The author himself had served at Gallipoli and at the Somme. An officer, Oxford educated, he had nevertheless enlisted without a commission. There is no sense that the book is autobiographical, but there is a strong impression that the book is taking up a debate that Herbert had heard played out while at the front.

The basic thesis of the novel is that Harry Penrose is a brave soldier, his refusal to plead momentary breakdown confirmation of his courage and integrity. Herbert uses the device of a conversation among soldiers—by this stage, Harry is on trial for his life—to rehearse the range of opinions he implies were circulating among combatants about the delicate balancing of cowardice, self-preservation and military discipline in cases where deliberate self harm is suspected. The hard-line view is that Harry should be shot because this would protect the name of the regiment sullied by his actions. Others feel that any "suspect" event should be dealt with at the regimental level, not reported to more senior officers. The novel strongly suggests it is the conjunction of personalities in any given instance that determines whether a soldier's actions are ignored or condemned. The simplest example in *The Secret Battle* is that Harry is arraigned for bolting for cover under fire, whereas the man who had been hiding in the spot to which he retreats, an old enemy, successfully accuses Harry of cowardice. Harry's belligerent commanding officer is more than ready to hear the accusation.

The novel presents one example of those cases that Butler calls "a major tragedy": Harry Penrose is shot at dawn.[18] The problem explored in the book is how to determine the extent or the way an individual can be said to be in control of his [or her] actions if—and the "if" itself is in question—he is suffering from some form of mental or physical illness. Responding as Chavigny's reviewer would wish them to do, the military tribunal which considers Harry Penrose's charge is interested only in *whether* he was seen leaving the front line, not why. As one character remarks, "'they don't consider whether he was *capable* physically or mentally—*I don't know which it is*—of doing the right thing'" (Herbert 208; second emphasis added). The courtroom reduces the matter to the simple absolute of guilt or innocence. And medical authorities are complicit with this reductive approach: "the doctors don't seem to recognize—or else they aren't allowed to—any stage between absolute shell shock, with your legs flying in all directions, and just ordinary skrim-shanking'" (Herbert 210). There is no leeway in part because the assumption that it is possible to make such a judgment rests on the assumption that an individual is at all times in control of their actions; *implicitly*, the cultural belief is that such control is a matter not of illness or health, but moral fiber or "character." An officer who cannot maintain the appearance of character cannot be an officer. In a sense, then, these are not medical but cultural questions, returning us to the question of the will, as well as values. It is the cultural values which underpin the framing of the law, as much as it is the effects of the law, that come under scrutiny in *The Secret Battle*.

This question is also taken up by Butler, who avers that while the relationship between illness, free will and volition is undoubtedly a difficult one for "mental medicine," "it seems inevitable, as a practical basis for theories of pathogeny and principles of treatment, to postulate some degree of 'free will' as being the ultimate determinant in intelligent and 'normal' conduct" (vol. 3, 60). He writes not so much as one engaged by this intellectual dilemmas as one accustomed to having had to resolve it in circumstances where the demand for certitude outweighed the desire of the doctor or the need of the patient for the benefit of doubt. Butler is explicit in relating this approach to the larger fortunes of the army and, implicitly, the nation: character, which he distils as self-control, or "'captaincy of the soul,'" shapes not only "modern warfare" (vol. 3, 60) but, by implication, the nations which engage in that warfare. At the same time there is an obvious sympathy in his observation that "From fear, many men, not depraved or psychopathic, fled into disease, into wounds, even into death itself" (Butler, vol. 3, 92). In the face of diagnostic and ethical dilemmas, doctors were obliged to represent not only the army's interests but to maintain what some felt was a fiction of scientific certainty; for many, that certainty was experienced as fact.

The number of monographs on self-inflicted injuries, as well as the evident desire of authors to establish categories of injury, accurate modes of detection, and (implicitly) proper punishment, can be read as evidence not only of the prevalence of practices of self harm in military contexts—particularly in the phases of recruiting and heavy combat—but of the use of medical institutions and individuals as agencies through which the goals of military authorities and the state are reached. The assumption that doctors should enforce discipline by detecting and reporting on fraud and self-injury seems mostly to be taken for granted, at least as far as decision-making is recorded in published scholarly discussion. At the same time, the military situation—and this probably applies more to combat than to recruiting—encouraged some doctors to believe, and to work from the premises, that self harm was not always or not simply the reflection of a moral defect. Whether in situ or in retrospect, some writers attempt to argue that the traumas of war inflict psychological injuries. This makes the question of how to respond to any individual who seems deliberately to have injured themselves morally and medically complicated.

One of the key difficulties for Butler and his colleagues was that *physical* investigations into the brain had not yet offered insight into mental and moral disorders. There was skepticism about psychology in the Anglophone army medical units, and even stronger resistance to the work of Freud and his followers. Indeed the Australian Army did not establish facilities for treating psychological illness until early 1919 (Butler, vol. 2, 462), a lapse or lag that Butler attributes to the views of the surgeon-general. Likewise, Copp and McAndrew report an open contempt for psychiatry and, in particular, psychology in the Canadian armed forces at the same time (12–13).[19] Describing problems exacerbated by divisions within and between various specialisms, Butler quotes from *Instinct and the Unconscious* (1920) by his English colleague William Rivers:

Though the Russo-Japanese war [1904–05] might have led physicians to expect psycho-neurosis on an extensive scale, the medical administration of our own and other armies was wholly unprepared for the vast extent and varied forms in which modern warfare is able to upset the higher functions of the nervous system and the mental activity of those called upon to take part in it. Moreover, before the war, the psycho-neuroses had interested few practitioners of medicine. Common as these disorders are in civilian life, they are left almost without notice in medical education, while those who had paid special attention to the subject were torn asunder by fierce differences of opinion, not only concerning the nature of these disturbances of nervous and mental function, but also in regard to the practical measures by which they might be treated or prevented [qtd. in Butler, vol. 3, 73].

Butler outlines the logistical and intellectual forces which shaped debate about medical authority and, specifically, the relationship between "neurology, the medicine of the brain, and psychiatry, the medicine of the mind" (vol. 3, 93):

It was not the least significant element in the contest that the "rank and file" of medical (executive) officers understood little or nothing (and perhaps cared less) of the issues; but only that they had to "do something" and do it very urgently. Above it all, intellectually remote from the scientific and professional battle, loomed the Military Command and Medical Directorate, themselves at war for control of the same domain, but concerned with the urgent disciplinary problems involved in any failure of the soldier to face danger. The whole history of medical and military practice and policy in the matter of mental disorder on the Western Front reads indeed like the Battle of the Cards in *Alice in Wonderland* [Butler, vol. 3, 94].

While no discussion of these points can be found in the official history of the British Army Medical services, a point Butler notes (vol. 3, 94, note 58), we *can* see these debates occurring at meetings at which self harm and other problems were discussed before and during the war.

At the time the war commenced, neurology was proceeding along "physiological rather than psychological lines, and with a definite clinical and philosophic gap apparent between the specialities of *neurology* and *psychiatry*" (Butler, vol. 3, 68). In the Canadian army, as for the British, financial considerations impinged on discussions of psychological illnesses, and there was concern about how to diminish the number of those who might qualify for pensions. The Chief Neuropsychiatrist, Dr. J.B.S. Cathcart, was keen to help. He believed that all that was needed was a change of term, doing away with "shell shock": "As soon as the whole army learned that instead of being listed as shell shock these casualties were described [as] Below Standard, the flood would stop" (qtd. in Copp and McAndrew 13). While we might caricature these responses as reflecting habits of mind associated with national character, stereotypes of Britishness (not unknown in the Dominion armies, i.e., those of Canada and Australia), unquestionably these values *did* feed into discussion. Doctors no less than any other sector of society—perhaps more—experienced their own culture and their preferred contours of character as reference points against which illness could be diagnosed; unpredictable or unacceptable forms of "behavior" could be judged as that—behaviors, not illness.

Anthropologist and psychologist C.S. Myers claimed in 1940, "During the last twenty-five years, the position has now changed: the neurologist's methods of treating the psycho-neuroses have been very largely superseded by those of the psycho-therapist" (20), but this was an ambit claim. The supporters of arguments for physiological causes and treatment of mental illness more convincingly proclaimed their own victory, which rested on the assumption that mental illness had a physiological cause. Neurologist F.L. Golla, in the last of his four Croonian Lectures on the "Objective Study of Neurosis" delivered to the Royal College of Physicians of London in 1921 (reported in the *Lancet*) endorsed "the view that a neurosis is the expression of an organic disturbance" (377). The title of the lectures is revealing of Golla's implicit objection to psychology. His main opponent is neither Watson nor Pavlov, but the French neurologist Babinski, the main point of attack being Babinski's

> famous dictum—"Entre l'hystérie et la fraude il n'y a qu'une différence d'ordre morale." Hysteria, then, can only be distinguished from conscious simulation by a purely subjective criterion; it may appear to be a retrograde step to return to the old search for organic disturbance after our symptomatology has been carefully purged of the so-called stigmata. [sic] which have one after another been shown to be simply the response of the patient to auto- and hetero-suggestion [377].

Lest his audience mistake his mention of that "famous dictum" as praise, Golla reiterates his concern about the interest in the non-physical: "Great has been the work of Babinski and his school in demonstrating the mimetic nature of hysterical symptoms, it has been needlessly impaired by the criterion that they have adopted of what constitutes an hysterical symptom" (378). In his view, the war provided "irrefutable evidence" that an "organic disturbance or failure of organic equilibrium" always preceded "neurotic symptoms" (115).

If there was widespread resistance to arguments for the mental or non-volitional aspects of self harm, there was at the same time widespread interest in the new ideas of psychoanalysis and in continental medical education more generally. Many English-speaking doctors had a reading knowledge of at least one modern European language, usually German or French, often both. Many demonstrate familiarity with major themes in the work of Freud and others. But at the same time, many were sceptical of claims that severe forms of illness could be induced by psychological trauma, and even more sceptical of Freud's claims that these illness were grounded in failure to negotiate the control and expression of libidinous drives in forms commensurate with adulthood (e.g. Hart 166). As Butler argued, contra Freud, the war provided strong arguments for those who took the view that "the fundamental element in the motivation of war neurosis [is] the urge of self-preservation, as distinct from the other primal biological urge of race preservation, or sex" (vol. 3, 17)—although at this point Butler footnotes *Psycho-Analysis and the War Neuroses* by four of Freud's most distinguished students (Ferenczi *et al.*), commending its "admirably balanced and scientific presentation."

In commencing a lengthy chapter on "Mental and Moral Disorders" for the *Official History of the Australian Army Medical Service in the War of 1914–18*, Butler includes an intriguing survey and assessment of the state of medical knowledge at the time of the war's commencement. His argument pertains to the weak state of medical knowledge about what he understands as the less dramatic or less complex forms of mental illness. He contends that the sciences of physical medicine were relatively well advanced, and certainly that the study and treatment of mental illness had seen progress from the time "when Pinel, first of the clinical alienists, 'struck off the chains from insane patients at the Bicêtre'" during the French revolution (Butler, vol. 3, 71), that progress identified with the writing of Jean-Martin Charcot, Sigmund Freud and Pierre Janet. But there was a whole realm of illness which had, in his view, become the province of "quackery," being understood as psychological and not of sufficient seriousness to gain the attention of the great nineteenth-century doctors and their modern successors. The situation was exacerbated by suspicion of the idea of mental illness and of the unconscious mind in the wider medical profession, and flat hostility to it in the army. The work of Freud, of Janet, and even of some English psychiatrists "had not been accepted by the body of British medicine and was wholly alien and repugnant to the military mind" (Butler, vol. 3, 98).

Butler explains that, for the purposes of diagnosis and treatment, the key illness which came to be at issue in the Australian army was not the much debated shell shock but "D.A.H.," "disordered action of the heart," also called "soldier's heart" (Butler, vol. 2, 463; vol. 3, 59). He terms D.A.H. "one of the most clinically obscure among the 'medical' conditions causing disablement and one of the most difficult to treat" (vol. 2, 463); the condition affected slightly over one per cent of the Australian forces evacuated from the Gallipoli peninsula (vol. 3, 86). Butler ascribes the origin of this interest in the physiological basis of neurosis to the publication of Da Costa's account of "soldier's heart" arising from the Civil War, but F. Parkes Weber offers a quite different account. In notes on his copy of Charles Blondel's monograph, he attributes the discovery of the condition to a British colleague, and the popularization of the term to doctors in Italy:

> "Cardiopalmus" ... was, I think, first used for cardiac palpitation by Sir James Wylie, Bart M.D. (1768–1854), Imperial Court Physician in St. Petersburgh. (The Italian equivalent) "Cardiopalmio" was recognized by Italian physicians as exempting young men from military service. But during the Great War (1914–1918) it was artificially produced to obtain exemption from military service and it was discovered that some men chewed tobacco and took trinitrin to produce it. F.P.W.[20]

That such a condition was associated with fraud is attested to by this note by Weber; that it was widely known as such by doctors and the general public is signalled by a story in the *Times* about a doctor who had been distributing drugs which elevated the heart rate, thereby allowing men to evade conscription.[21]

In medical and ethical terms, this is difficult terrain. As Butler suggests, the problem is how to judge the extent of free will in any individual patient, something complicated by the fact that injuries might have occurred in circumstances which can only be guessed at or known through the patient's own account. Paradoxically, it might even be assumed that the patient's *incapacity* to give an account of their injury might count against a diagnosis of deliberate self harm. Oppositely, it is the co-operative patient who is likely to garner the doctor's sympathy. The précis of one such example offers insight into the ways in which medical staff in military contexts were, like their colleagues in general practice, prepared to accommodate some patients:

> A patient suffering from mutism after exposure to shell explosion at present under Dr. Buzzard's care was such a nice fellow that no one could call him anything but a case of functional or hysterical mutism. At the same time one had to admit that his only successful attempt to speak for some time after his admission to hospital was when he blurted out his conviction that he would rather be dumb for the rest of his life than return to the Front [Buzzard, (Comment) 66].[22]

Quite what the view of soldiers themselves was in such circumstances was we cannot be sure: the narrator of Herbert's novel shifts from admiration (Harry is "a marvel") to sympathy ("could not help feeling sorry") to condemnation ("made you sick ... that any man ... could be brought so low") in a few sentences, when discussing soldiers who shot themselves in the foot or hand, before concluding that "it was the uncertainty of their life that broke them" (157).

The general difficulty in thinking through the situation of military medicine is that much more was said and done by doctors than was ever written, and certainly more than was published. A passing remark in Myers' autobiographical *Shell Shock in France, 1914–18*, not published until 1940, gives a clue that explains the silence: authorities were concerned about the effect of discussing the fact of proliferating numbers of self-inflicted injuries in public (24–25). In general, the literature on hysteria and malingering does not consider physical self harm to any great extent: the essays in Miller's *The Neuroses in War*, for example, devote just a page to "self-inflicted wounds," which it is noted were accompanied by states of "great emotional tension" and "in a few cases," when "the man was in a state of pathological dissociation" (Miller *et al.* 80). But it is clear that debate about fraud is rarely far from the writer's mind when considering examples of patients presented *either* as malingering or as self injury, making it far more difficult to separate these literatures than is implied by their neglect in the scholarship of self harm.

Responses to self harm during the war were shaped by many things, not least of which was the diversity of views about the weight which should be given to the needs of the patient versus the demands of patriotism, the plausibility of mental illness as a category, and the credibility of those medical specialisms which claimed their capacity to treat it. For this reason we can observe fairly constant conflict between claims about the needs of wounded or traumatized participants in combat and demands to limit the flow of soldiers away from the front line. Almost no-one attempts to deny that combat takes a heavy psychological toll. If a clear line of difference does emerge, it is perhaps between the responses of participants not directly involved in front-line military medicine, who speak with open contempt for the malingerer, and the generally more sympathetic and more nuanced accounts of those writing during or after work as front-line army medical officers.

As we have seen with Myers and Butler, the advent of the Second World War provided a context in which reflection on the First was charged with greater meaning. Perhaps the context made these writers more determined to try to rectify what they saw as mistakes or injustices perpetrated by medical and military authorities during the 1914–1918 war. As both Myers and Butler would probably have predicted, the difficulty of drawing a line between self-harm, criminality, and psychological breakdown continued to be felt in the later conflict. As American psychiatrist William C. Menninger was to point out, "malingering" is a legal opinion, not a medical diagnosis. He remarks that "The motivation in this type of case was so uncertain, so lacking in proof, that further records were regarded as valueless" (215). More pertinently Menninger, some 150 years after Larrey, declares that "Medical officers were often not able to distinguish between malingering and valid psychiatric symptoms. This in part was due to ignorance and in part to prejudice against psychiatric problems" (211). Also at stake is national honor. A study of the Canadian First Division operating in the Second World War notes that within a three-month period, 67 soldiers were deemed to have inflicted wounds upon themselves in order to escape the front line while "an unknown number went undetected" (Copp and McAndrew 65). The report these authors cite claims 232 "*suspected self-inflicted wounds*" during 1944 (135), but figures for "accidental" injuries vary:

British 19.06, Canadian 64.80 and New Zealand 107.47 per thousand.[23] Copp and McAndrew note acerbically that "It would be interesting to determine why such widely varying rates were reported and why New Zealanders were so accident-prone" (206). In fact, such figures can be read as evidence of the willingness of medical staff to declare that specific injuries were the outcome of accidents—just as Larrey had, more than a century earlier.

Copp and McAndrew, in their history of Canadian involvement in the Second World War, describe an instance in which the senior doctor, Brigadier E.A. McCusker, "was caught uneasily between his medical and his soldierly convictions," although it was the latter which prevailed in determining his response to an officer who had broken down under shell fire (68), the example recalling the fictional story of Harry Penrose. Indicative of the culture of secrecy that prevailed even among the more severe of the medical staff, McCusker wrote privately to a fellow officer, "The pride that I have in our Canadian troops makes me hesitate to discuss openly such problems as the high incidences of SIW [self-inflicted wounds] and of neuro-psychiatric casualties during the past winter" (qtd. in Copp and McAndrew 68). But McCusker's commanding officer, Lieutenant-General Harry Crerar, felt that "While ... the real 'shell-shock' must be regarded and treated as a casualty, I consider it very important that the mesh of the administrative sieve should be so close that the fake exhaustion case should be detected and held ... suitably punished and not allowed to get away with it" (qtd. in Copp and McAndrew 69).

A U.S. account written soon after the end of the Second World War implicitly echoes Butler's interpretation of self wounding as a coping strategy, and differs from many writers on self harm in military contexts because of the obvious sympathy for combatants. R.F. Fidler's "Psychiatric Review of Fifty Cases of Gunshot Wound, Self-Inflicted" (1948) recorded cases three months after the Allied invasion of Normandy. Fidler argues that his findings are in "striking contrast to civilian experience of the gross degree of constitutional psychopathy in hysteric form that one usually associates with such lesions as dermatitis artefacta" (568). As far as he is concerned, the men he has examined "had coped with their innate handicap better and displayed greater stamina in that they faced the possibility of an immediately painful result of their acts more consciously than does the hysteric wanderer who is often near a fugue state at the time of desertion" (569). In his conclusions, Fidler asserts that most self-inflicted injuries "are early cases of exhaustion neuroses": "Few of them can be easily proven to be deliberate, and those that are so are drawn from similar psychiatric material compared with the variations one meets in unselected cases of battle neuroses; they were immature youngsters, genuinely exhausted" (571). The exercise of medical discretion in military contexts can sometimes be considerable: Garrard, reporting on what he claims is more than 300 patients with self-inflicted wounds at a hospital in France, notes that only 16 soldiers were "recommended for court martial," with no information given on the outcome (94).

Conclusions

The consideration of self harm in military contexts suggests that the actions of those who inflict severe self injury are demonized when it is in the interests of the state to criminalize such behaviors. Medical explanations for self harm could be offered, but sceptical and punitive responses seem to be more common. This approach usually but not always coincides with intellectual or institutional preferences for ready-made identification of malingerers, practices buttressed by a set of professional literatures ranging from studies of prisons to handbooks for military medical officers. Just as the passing of legislation which awarded compensation for injuries at work was greeted with concern that it would enable criminal exploitation, so a kind of professionally-authorized vigilance about "malingering" operated before and during the First World War. This vigilance was fuelled by stereotypes which war itself sharpened awareness of. Interestingly, neither the intensity of the scrutiny of soldiers nor levels of punishment for deliberate self injury seem to have gained momentum as the war went on. Perhaps greater experience of the effect of frontline combat tempered enthusiasm; perhaps there was greater sympathy for those seen to have escaped the front line.

There is evidence that self harm continues to be an issue in modern military forces, not simply as a means of evading combat or of ensuring repatriation, but as a response to stress. And the paradigm in which self harm is seen as instrumental, closely associated with criminality and manipulation of prison authorities, remains central for many authors on the phenomenon. Search "self-harm" in Medline, for example, and most of the examples which pertain to Germany will be linked to insurance fraud (see, for example, Bonte 70). A more recent account from Germany notes that claims to have suffered physical abuse by right-wing groups were exposed as fraudulent when two teenagers were found to have carved swastikas into their skin. For that scholar, if not psychotic (which they were not), such actions must be the newest manifestation of a well-known and frequently seen form of criminality:

> Self-induced bodily harm comprises the following main categories: simulation of a criminal offense (e.g. false rape allegation, feigned robbery), self-mutilation for the purpose of insurance fraud, voluntary self-mutilation and/or malingering among soldiers and prisoners, dermal artifacts and other

kinds of self damage in patients with personality disorders, suicidal gestures and (attempted) suicide. Medicolegal literature is abundant in systematic and casuistic studies of all the above-mentioned types of self injurious behavior [Faller-Marquardt 228].

But in those instances in which, for example, a leg or both legs are severed, limbs are shattered, or other terrible and irreversible injury is done, authorities can disagree on whether it is possible to decide that the motivation is greed. On the other hand, this might be a question of jurisdiction: Bonte recounts "the Marek case in 1926" in which "Vienna legal doctors considered it impossible that the engineer Marek, who was insured for high sums of money with several insurance companies, had had an accident at work" whereas "the court ... could not believe that someone would cut off his own leg with an ax" [sic] (71).

Just as it can be caught between medical and legal or military practice, self harm seems to open up or to slide into gaps between forms of medical knowledge. There is much less debate about the difference between self harm as conscious behavior—malingering—and self harm as symptom of a mental disorder than one might expect. While the social sciences, notably psychology and criminology, encourage the writer to consider social factors in analyzing instances of self harm, they have also encouraged that stereotyping and generalization that more sophisticated models warn against. There can also be a simple cross-disciplinary blindness. For example, Edward G. Carr's 1977 review of hypotheses on what he terms "self-injurious behavior" simply leaves out arguments proposed by psychiatrists, even Menninger. His typology of motives includes "positive reinforcement," "negative reinforcement," "self-stimulation," "organic" and "psychodynamic," the language indicating dependence on behaviorist models. Bennum's more methodologically inclusive review of 1984, written from the UK, suggests greater accommodation of the ideas of psychiatry and is more reflexive in categorizing models of self harm. Not surprisingly, given this inclusivity, Bennum concludes that "The problems faced by self-mutilating patients are so varied that no single form of treatment is likely to be universally appropriate. Regardless of the hypothesis or model adopted, treatment must be flexible" (183).

In regard to self harm, further complication lies in the relationship between body and mind: a physical injury is "proof" of a "genuine" condition, but how are we to understand "the cause" of an injury if there is suspicion it was inflicted by the patient? More problematically, how to prove that a physical injury is *not* the result of a genuine but *psychological* condition? This chapter has analyzed these problems in the context of the heightened concern about duty and patient morality which pertains in times of armed conflict. The discussion has shown that during the First World War, debates about self harm shifted from military medicine into the public and political spheres. In the process, the subsumption of self-inflicted injuries into the culturally powerful category of "malingering" could be questioned, but sceptics of mental illness and advocates of duty fought back, using "malingering" as a catch-all and pejorative term to designate the knowing evasion of duty through the feigning of illness or incapacity. The almost total dominance of the term in literature dealing with self harm in the period around the time of the First World War is a measure of the success of those who argued that the idea of psychological illness was itself a fabrication. Self harm continued to be read in military contexts most often as a form of cowardice; cowardice is criminal and warrants the death penalty. There is, commensurately, a strongly expressed hostility towards those suspected of inducing incapacity. "Malingering in the United States Troops Home Forces, 1917" from the Office of the Surgeon General captures the mood:

> The consensus of opinion has been that most of the malingerers had something the matter with them.... It was based in almost every instance on actual unstable or defective mental state.... Of the underlying causes, fear and timidity are unquestionably the most frequent and conspicuous and probably underlie all others.... Gross ignorance is responsible for much malingering.... The great body of malingerers who constitute problems for medical officers are simple credulous impressionable boys who exaggerate and invent without skill, or with no definitely conceived plan. Gunshot wounds have been more frequent than any other form of injury, after which came cutting injuries.... In a number of cases, amputation of fingers or toes has resulted from the soldier being caught under electric or steam cars.... In many instances the general attitude of the man had been one of dissatisfaction [qtd. in Van Dyke 4–5; ellipses in Van Dyke].

Some doctors sometimes found ways to exonerate or dismiss from service those soldiers whose illness or injury they found in some way convincing, and whose self harm was thereby given a certification of incapacity that was acceptable to military authorities.

F. Parkes Weber's hand-written notes in a London archive reveal that one of the more unusual responses to what was seen as feigned injury could be feigned treatment, problematizing even further the notion of genuine and fraudulent illness. Weber records that colleagues at Haslar Hospital, among others, sometimes used "fake operations" to cure what they saw as hysterical conditions.[24] The printed report on which Weber writes begins with an anecdote about a lance-corporal, made deaf by an exploding shell. He is cured when a loud noise is made during the operation, causing him to leap off the operating table. The authors conclude that the patient was not malingering but suffering from genuine, albeit non-organic, deafness. At the point at which doctors themselves are simulating a surgical cure for an injury which is at once "physical" and "psychological"—"genuine, albeit non-organic"—then the notion of the "spectrum," of a continuum between simulation and "genuine" injury, between physical and psychological illness, between volition and help-lessness, breaks down.[25]

Many doctors sympathetic to notions of self harm and sceptical of the power of the will relied on nineteenth-century formulations of "social disease," representing self harm as insidiously and incurably infecting the lower orders, destroying the moral economy and thus, just as surely, the monetary one. Even A.W. Butler's emphasis on the prevention of moral decay indicates his belief that mental illness is a degradation of character. In the meantime, the work of Sigmund Freud and his colleagues was beginning to influence the thinking of those who held to their belief in "non-organic" illness. Butler contends that "there is full evidence that before the end of the war the essential princi-ples and concepts of the Freudian system (of the 'unconscious' causes of behavior, the nature of hysteria, the place of 'anxiety,' 'conflict' and the gain motive) in the genesis of the war neuroses, were well recognised," indeed that they were "an essential part of the stock-in-trade of the officers who from early in 1917 were responsible for the treatment of the cases admitted to the special hospitals for psychiatric casualties—at the front, at the Bases in France, and in England" (Butler, vol. 3, 126).

4

The Alien Self:
Psychiatry and Psychology

Les automutilations sont notre pain quotidien. (Self mutilation is our daily bread.)—Troisier (1988) 767

The decision to discuss what might be called "the disciplines of the psyche" late in the book might be seen as implying that these offer a kind of "culmination" in modes of interpreting self harm. And in a way they do. They also tend to follow, historically, those other forms of representations of self harm discussed in other chapters—although the historical periods overlap, and the stories used by different disciplines, such as those of Attis, travel through time. The examination of the ways of representing self harm in the literatures of psychology and, in particular psychiatry, shows that these disciplines offer the most convincing ways of theorizing the function of self harm and its representation by patients. But they can also operate with restrictive or archaic cultural categories. The use of such categories limits the explanatory capacities of the many unsympathetic accounts of patients who have injured themselves.

The first section of this chapter briefly considers French monographs which aim to reconsider criminological debates on self harm in the light of then current research on what would now be called mental illness. After this, the focus is on a small collection of essays on self harm produced by followers of Sigmund Freud (1856–1939), among the most important of whom are Otto Fenichel and Karl Menninger. Other sections examine the writing of some of Freud's most articulate and powerful challengers, notably his French contemporary Pierre Janet (1859–1947), his one-time colleague and confidante Sándor Ferenczi, and feminist dissident Karen Horney who worked in New York. Janet's work differs from and pre-empts the Freudian model of the unconscious; his theories about the working and structure of self harm offer a way of thinking beyond the "fraud/illness" binary discussed in the previous chapter, but have not had the influence in the English-speaking world of those of Freud (very little of his extensive published work has been translated). The final part of the chapter returns to the topic of Freud's influence in considering some late twentieth-century research on self harm.

Criminology Finds the Psyche

There are three French monographs on self harm from early in the twentieth century which call into question the simplistic models of interpretation which understands self harm as a crime: Gustave David's *Des Automutilations chez les aliénés*, presented as a thesis for the degree of Doctor of Medicine at the University of Toulouse in 1899; Charles Blondel's *Les Auto-mutilators* presented for the same degree in Paris in 1906; and M. Lorthiois' *De L'auto-mutilation* (1909). These works challenge while remaining in dialogue with instrumental and criminological models of self harm.[1] Each of these writers implies that some patients who have injured themselves are not merely manipulative, but have a disturbed state of mind—which is to say, that they must be approached as requiring medical, not just moral, judgment. These works demonstrate the ongoing interests we have seen in primitivism in the work of writers like James Frazer, amplified by later scholars such as Georges Bataille, who considers the self harm of Vincent Van Gogh.

Marie Michel Edmond Joseph Lorthiois' *De L'automutilation: mutilations et suicide étranges* (1909) opens its chapter on "Definition" by declaring that self mutilation can be voluntary or involuntary, and that there are also instances in which it is impossible to answer a question about intention (11). The work is distinctive in including a chapter on self harm by animals, albeit brief (13–15).[2] In a long chapter on male genital self mutilation, Lorthiois reviews classical and early Christian stories of self castrations (at 18–21 and 21–22), including those by Arnobius of Sicca and Lucian, with historical accounts of surgery being blended into histories of religion. The main part of the chapter is a précis of reports from English, French and German sources (29–78), some receiving extended discussion. Further chapters, on self-inflicted injury of the eyes (86–100) and combustion (101–38), as well as "Diverse Kinds," likewise include reports and analysis. The cultural and historical range of cases Lorthiois manages to cover makes his book an important source for historians of self harm.

Gustave David's thesis *Des Automutilations chez les aliénés* is concerned with the psychological, pathological, medical, and legal aspects of self harm.

It makes references to theorizations of mental illness and includes a set of "observations" or brief case histories, some of which are his own and others of which come from an earlier generation of scholars, including his French colleagues Théodule-Armand Ribot (David 50–51) and Paul Garnier (78–79), as well as the author of *Psychopathia Sexualis*, Richard von Krafft-Ebing (79–81). Ribot's work is central to David's understanding of self harm: the first chapter of *Les Auto-mutilators* relies heavily on Ribot's *Psychologie de l'Attention*, published in English as *The Psychology of Attention*. Ribot's arguments in turn owe much to those of Henry Maudsley (1835–1918), a British physician well known for his emphasis on the physiological aspects of mental illness. The key premise is that the body provides a kind of foundation on which the psyche is built. That foundation is influenced by the sexual organs, the heart, the lungs and the stomach (Ribot 112), and in a sense the mind is always captive to its own "primitive ancestor," the body.

There are strong traces in this work of the evolutionary model which structured so much scholarship in the latter part of the nineteenth century. Indeed, David had been a student of Lucien Lévy-Bruhl, a philosopher and historian who later in his career became interested in "primitive thought."[3] Ribot sees attention as an effect of education or "civilization" (42), that is, he understands culture as shaping capacity in a way that blurs the lines between the physiological and the psychological. In his words, "The savage has a passion for hunting, war, and gambling for the unforeseen, the unknown, and the hazardous in all its forms; but sustained effort he ignores or contemns. Love of work is a sentiment of purely secondary formation that goes hand in hand with civilization" (Ribot 43). Making this kind of claim, taken from an apparently objective biological science—Charles Darwin and Herbert Spencer are cited—offers Ribot a scientific basis for what is essentially a claim about European cultural supremacy.

Similar interests in primitivism and religion, inflected by Christian views of suffering, are central to Bataille's reading of Vincent Van Gogh's apparent cutting off of his ear as an act of sacrifice.[4] Bataille cites a range of examples of self harm in support of his argument, although these are rather different from the case of Van Gogh. However, the bulk of his evidence comes from accounts of practices attributed to ostensibly "primitive" cultures in Africa, the Americas, Australia and the Pacific.[5] Bataille also cites what he calls "the bloody orgies of Islamic sects" (67), a point at which the patronizing interest in non–European cultures converges with the interest in religion, such that practices of other cultures are pre-packaged as "primitive." In Bataille's argument, as with Ribot's, notions of evolution and progress duel with formulations of religiosity, the latter viewed on the one hand as superstition, and on the other as a powerful device for engendering meaning through ritual.

Thus, and notwithstanding his citation of Freud's *Totem and Taboo* (72, note 16), Bataille seeks a *cultural* explanation even for actions "incontestably linked to mental disorder." In support, he turns to ancient writers:

> Even in antiquity, the insane were known to have characterized their mutila-
> tions [as sacrifice]: Areteus [in *De morborum diuturnorum et acutorum causis,*
> *signis et curatione*] writes of sick people who he saw tearing off their own
> limbs because of religious feelings and in order to pay homage to gods who
> demanded this sacrifice [67].

This rendering of Areteus is implicitly approving of actions many of Bataille's contemporaries found repugnant or threatening. This aside, Bataille's argument is notable in claiming that while mental illness might take people beyond "rational" control, it does not remove them from culture in an absolute sense. Certain forms of awareness remain. Commensurately, the meaning of symbol does not simply disintegrate; indeed, symbolic meaning takes on greater valency. Such observations make the separation of the psychotic and the non-psychotic problematic, for while we can be clear that psychosis is marked by the absence of awareness, it is much less clear what the relationship is between psychotic states and existing structures of value and meaning.

Even the idea of attention has a certain level of complexity in the theorizing of writers like Ribot and David. It can be pathological when it takes the form of the "'fixed idea'" and ecstasy (9).[6] Yet there can be nobility in obsession: Ribot asks, "what indeed is a vocation but attention" (15)? The proof of this thesis is taken from the diary of Saint Teresa of Avila (97–100), whose example Ribot distinguishes from those pathological ones in which patients characteristically display singular strength and rapid change: "a flux of words, shouts, gesticulations and impetuous movements" (102). Thus David argues that mobility itself is a sign of illness, echoing the notion of the itinerant "savage." Thus a mentally disturbed person is always in motion, always talking, crying out, singing, making faces ("Les maniaques sont sans cesse en mouvement; ils parlent, crient, chantent, grimacent, font toutes sortes des gestes" David 10). David argues that hitting, head-banging and hair-pulling are an expression of the desire for movement, and that this movement diminishes sensibility to external realities (13). No such arguments are made by Ribot, who does not consider self harm; it seems possible that David was influenced here by Janet, whose work is cited and who, in the second volume of *Névroses et idées fixes,* considers patients with physical compulsions to self harm.[7]

Charles Blondel aimed to be compendious in his dissertation on the psychological, pathological, medical, and legal aspects of self harm, *Les Auto-mutilators: étude psychopathologique et médico-légale.* Blondel makes a claim to originality on the basis of distinguishing between *individual* acts of physical injury, with which he is concerned and to which he attributes insanity. These differ from forms of self harm which occur by virtue of membership of a collective—family, political or religious sect, people or race, these having some motive sufficient to legitimate the activity, thence for contagion to occur (1). Blondel's central premise is that "voluntary" self mutilation is a manifestly abnormal reaction ("une réaction manifestement anormale," 3), and always the consequence of a psychopathology ("toujours la conséquence d'un état psychopathologique," 130). But notwithstanding this differentiation of group from individual cases, the chapter on "military self-mutilation" confounds the distinction. Blondel notes, for example, an incident in 1844 in which 14 members of the same battalion of the Foreign Legion harmed themselves in the same manner.[8] To support the latter view, Blondel notes the prevalence of forms like castration, enucleation and "voluntary combustion," all occuring in conjunction with religious delusion (130).

There is an imaginative, cross-disciplinary aspect to Blondel's work, reflected in his bringing together of philosophy, anthropology and sociology, as well as medical and legal conceptions of self harm. He was interested in the role of language, which he considers via the philosophy of Henri Bergson, and in new understandings of society offered by the sociology of Durkheim (see Blondel, *The Troubled Conscience* 26–31). Blondel is also prescient in linking civil cases of self harm to the religiosity or spiritual dilemmas of those who had injured themselves; his book is the first to bring together and to attempt to systematize the analysis of patients who had harmed themselves. However, as we have seen in discussing military medicine, the lines of inquiry opened up by these books were not really followed.

The arguments presented in the three monographs discussed above are historically significant because they show that knowledge of self harm could be the basis of academic credentialization in this period, as it was for Ballingall nearly a century before. Their existence also demonstrates a new development or possibility: taking patients with what would now be thought of as mental illness on their own terms. That is not to say that such scholarship is disconnected from the intellectual values of its time. On the contrary, the same kinds of assumptions about the relative order of cultures are evident in this writing as we might find in any other. The work of these writers, and that of a more general cultural theorist like Bataille, shows the influence of ideas about so-called "primitive cultures" popularized by works like Frazer's *Golden Bough*, and in French by Lévy-Bruhl, whom both Blondel and David acknowledge. There is a tendency to equate mental illness with "primitive thinking," a tendency also evident in some case reports discussed in chapter two. Such an argument can sometimes be read as presuming that "modern" forms of (Judao-Christian) religion accommodate rationality in ways which those of other societies do not, or, that any religious belief is merely a legacy of primitive literalism. Either claim is ultimately unhelpful for understanding self harm because the way in which belief is translated into bodily action remains unexplained.

Pierre Janet

At the same time that this research was published, the French physician Pierre Janet was transforming the understanding and treatment of mental illness. Janet has nothing like Freud's reputation in English-language scholarship, but his theorizing of the psyche offers some evocative ideas for scholars of self harm.[9] Elton Mayo, an early follower of Janet, credits him with coining

> the term dissociation, understanding there to be a splitting of the personality into primary and secondary selves, a considerable disjunction between parts of the sensory field so that there is a diminution of their mutual awareness; and, second, [that] this disjunction seems to find reflection in an equivalent lack of relation between the various systems of acquired response, these latter usually deemed in their normal synthesis to constitute what is known as personality [Mayo 30].

Writing against Freud, Janet puts the argument that not all strong emotions have "a genital origin," but can derive from traumas such as death of a loved one, violent accident, and other shocks ("Psychologic Treatment" 886–87). In a career built upon the close observation of patients, one of the more notable of Janet's arguments is that

> an idea does not persist in the mind as a simple and inert thing. Instead, it becomes an entire complex system of phantasies which continually change. Around the original idea develops, either by rationalizing or more often by association, a mixture of secondary ideas, dreams and emotions which have, in turn, their own complicated manifestations ["Psychologic Treatment" 885].

This is different from the Freudian view which understands the psyche in terms of fixed structures: the ego (roughly, the conscious sense of self), the superego (the voice of morality) and the id (which searches for pleasure). The ego balances the demand for pleasure against the demand for prohibition and control.

Janet, like Freud, sees a set of tensions between what lies within, and beyond, the horizon of conscious thought. In his view, the "system of images" which *is* the illness is itself in motion, making discernment of its logic difficult for the treating doctor. This way of understanding the relationship between the conscious and the unconscious mind—as *itself* fragmented and volatile— suggests that symbols and actions might have changing meanings even for one person, over the course of their life and illness. At the same time, that person might continue (or cease) to injure their body because they see these actions as means by which they can alter their psychological circumstances or way of feeling. Interestingly enough, this proposition was made again in 1999 by graduate researcher E. Hitchcock Scott, who asks, "what if the explanations of self-mutilation are not only divergent among individuals but within individuals?" (172; underlining in original).

Janet's "On the Pathogenesis of Some Impulsions" considers the urge "to perform certain useless, bizarre, and even dangerous acts," moving into a consideration of self mutilation under this rubric (1; 6–17). While Janet includes among these impulsions "the mania of sports," he goes on to consider patients who tear out "their hair, their eyelashes, their nails, and little pieces of skin" (5; 6). His first patient is one who he says will confound his reader's expectation that the young woman in question is "insane," having "a mystical delirium and who is anaesthetic." She has scars from burning and cutting all over her body, particularly on her hands and feet.

> [S]he is a young girl, intelligent and instructed, who is not at all delirious, at least when she is being examined, and who has preserved all her sensibilities. She hides her face and weeps when her wounds are uncovered. She says she is ashamed to let any one see the absurdities which she has committed.... Exactly like a dipsomaniac, she takes all possible oaths, but no faith can be placed in them, and she must be watched, for in a few weeks she will begin again, first causing herself a little pain, then, as the appetite grows, she will not resist the pleasure of wounding herself severely [Janet, "On the Pathogenesis" 7].

Janet claims to quote this young girl in explaining her feelings, but the material is quite unspecific, offering a description of a kind of emotional paralysis without any foray into circumstance or history. These are clarified somewhat a little later in the essay, when Janet appears to quote his patient:

> "I feel that I make an effort when I hold my hands on the stove, when I pour boiling water on my feet; it is a violent act, and it awakens me. I feel that it is done by myself and not by another.... Other people have the pleasure of doing things themselves; I desire to experience the same pleasure, and I cannot live without it. To make mental efforts alone is too difficult for me; I have to supplement them by physical efforts. I have not succeeded any other way, that is all: when I brace myself to burn myself I make my mind freer, lighter, and more active for several days. Why do you speak of my desire for mortification?" [13; ellipsis in original].

Janet contends that, while there is a relationship between asceticism and depression which is the crux of causality, in regard to *treatment*, the key to these accounts is that "These are excellent psychological observations": "Our obsessed have simply made correct psychological observations upon themselves; and have drawn inferences from them" ("On the Pathogenesis" 14). This crediting of insight—or at least, "correct ... observations"—represents a profound change within and challenge to views of medical expertise. This is unusual at any time. It is exemplified here in the resonant question which exposes and interrogates the relationship between clinical speech, and coercion: "Why do you speak of my desire for mortification?"

What drives this inquiry into self harm is not just Janet's theoretical approach, but his inclusion of the words and ideas of his patient. In attending to the woman's own account and analysis of her predilections for physical self harm, the telling of stories is taken not as a signalling device for insanity but as part of the work of diagnosis and treatment. In the sense that her own words are used to present the contours of explanation, it is the young woman herself who drives the theorizing of the self harm. The force and clarity of her assertions—her eloquent rejection of the term "mortification" and her compelling explanation of the mechanism of gratification—become central features of the academic mode, such that her own words are reconfigured as clinical observations. What is not clear, of course, is the degree to which these are transcriptions or renderings of her words (always remembering, too, that they are presented here in translation from the French). But regardless of this question of "authenticity," what *is* clear is that in being presented this way, Janet's arguments about the authority of the patient's own perspective sow the seeds for more nuanced ways of conceiving self harm proposed in the late twentieth century, not least by patients themselves.

Janet provides a condensed, evocative summary of his views: "Thought is inner language; belief becomes a special combination of language and action; memory is above all a system of recounting; emotions are regulations of action, reactions of the individual to his own actions" ("Autobiography"). This formulation can be seen as prefiguring (although not informing) modern patient advocate literature in the way it conceives the relationship between psyche, self-awareness, and self harm. For example, a 2001 report on attempted suicide and self harm among South Asian women in London claims that "Self-harm as a survival mechanism, as an important coping mechanism and potential protective factor against suicide is now a better established understanding in the (feminist) literature on self-harm" (Chantler *et al.* 69). Likewise the authors of a 1997 study of patients treated within a maximum security prison in the UK conclude that

> Self-harming helps women to attempt to regain internal control and power within an institution which removes this from them. Self-harm is a way women at Ashworth Hospital try to communicate and cope with their distress. It is the authors' view that women at Ashworth Hospital have continued to survive through their self-harming behaviours [Liebling *et al.* 20–21].

This view underpins some of the most influential studies of the past three decades.[10] To be sure, the later writers do not see those who inflict injuries on their own bodies as having "lazy minds" with "a horror of change" as Janet does ("On the Pathogenesis" 15). But his fundamental point—that self harm can be a means of managing the psyche, and a successful one at that,—underpins the late twentieth-century view.

Janet claims in his autobiography that his work has (already, in 1930) "given rise to a whole theory of neurosis and psychosis by the subconscious persistence of an emotional traumatism, and a whole method of research has been worked out to the utmost of this kind of traumatism." In setting out the terms of his fame, he is clearly keen to differentiate himself from Freud, albeit in a coded fashion, when claiming immediately after making this statement that he "had never introduced a clinical observation as a metaphysical system, and I ... never claimed that all neuropathic weaknesses were exclusively the consequence of a traumatic reminiscence" ("Autobiography"). He notes that apparently mundane things such as exhaustion, physical illness and inheritance can also play their part, further emphasizing that his arguments are clinical ones, grounded in experience not merely the generalities or aggrandizements associated with theory, or what he terms a "metaphysical system." Janet's argument is that "generally speaking, all activity conforms somewhat to reality: the simplest reflex is adapted to some fact in the real world, ... and this feeling of reality plays an important part in the operations of the will and belief" ("Autobiography").

Janet's contemporaries were wrestling with precisely these questions in attempting to understand the relationship between the conscious and the unconscious mind, specifically as it related to the conjunction between self harm and the will. In an essay on "The Association of Hysteria with Malingering" published in the *Lancet* in 1911, F. Parkes Weber, after mentioning Babinski, Freud and Janet, wondered if it were "conceivable" that

> hysterical excessive suggestibility may, on the whole, be useful rather than harmful for persons whose own will-power is pathologically deficient. Moreover, in cases in which wretched experiences have made their psychical marks or "psychical traumata" in the past, and in which the present condition is in some way gravely affected by subconscious reminiscences, "separation of consciousness" may be supposed to bring not only inconvenience and dangers, but also *a certain kind of relief* [1543; emphasis added].

However, notwithstanding the engagement, we need to be cautious in ascribing to Janet any particular sympathy for patients who had harmed themselves.

In 1929, a patient who had castrated himself was discussed by the Société Médicale Psychologie of Paris. The presenting doctors, de Massary, Leroy and Mallet, reported on their patient, a young man who, "Sans anxiété, émotion, ni excitation," without anxiety, emotion, or excitation (144) cut off his external genitalia (145). They describe the young man's background, noting in particular a complete change of character at the age of 13 (in 1915), at which time he transformed from being intelligent and hard-working to listless and disengaged (145, reiterated on 146). In the weeks leading up to his self-castration he became peripatetic and drank heavily (146). The authors devote a paragraph to sexual history, noting "masturbation fréquente" and that their patient had experienced "profound disgust" after experiencing sexual relations with a woman (146). They express some surprise at their patient's "natural" and consistent response as to why he cut off his penis, which he represents as both spontaneous, and a way of addressing the problem of having erections (146). Their conclusion is that the self mutilation "est ici le fait de l'impulsion subite, invraisemblable d'un dément précoce" (147), that it is a question of sudden impulse, unlikely to be an early [sign of] madness. They suggest instead "On y trouve un processus freudien," that one finds a Freudian process (148). The patient, more and more tormented by his erections and erotic thoughts, obeyed an impulse to relieve his suffering.[11] They propose that "Peut-être aussi, consciemment ou inconsciemment, a-t-il voulu trancher un dernier lien le rattachant à la société et à la nature humaine," perhaps also, consciously or unconsciously, he wanted to sever the last line of attachment to society and to human nature (148), a conclusion they justify on the grounds that the man expresses himself perfectly content with his situation (147).

The first two discussants queried the relevance of the Freudian apparatus, although the third, Guiraud, felt it "très probable," very probable, that investigation along psychoanalytic lines would permit the discovery of a castration complex (de Massary *et al.* 149). In response, Mallet wrestled with causality, and the even more delicate question of how much authority to grant to Freud:

> It is notable, that, at the moment, it might not indicate [alcoholism], for the act was committed without a plausible motive. This act presented, in these conditions, like an act of madness, without reason. It might be that motives, prompted by a set of illnesses, were suggested to him, at least in part, by successive questioners. For the other part, [those illnesses] might have strengthened certain tendencies which came to shape the act in question, without it being necessary to admit the presence of [Freudian] complexes, in the true sense of the word.[12]

Discussants continued to refer to this question, that is, the use of Freudian notions. Towards the end, Henri Colin argued, "Les actes des malades de cet ordre ont souvent une cause psychologique" (149), the actions of patients of this type often have a psychological cause, a remark that prompted Janet to speak for the first time:

> From the psychological point of view, there are, at bottom, two questions that are posed by this illness: (1) how did, at a precise moment, the idea to cut off

his genitals arise, and (2) how did the way to realize this idea come to him? In the matter of the clinical problem, this case does not have the appearance of a genuine dementia praecox; it seems the actions of a feeble individual, depressed, with a tendency to laziness, whom it pleased better to be in hospital than outside [149–50].[13]

In the light of such a strong endorsement of the most mundane response to self harm—to describe it as attention-seeking and self-indulgence—it was left only for Leroy to declare, against the weight of the argument thus far and perhaps in what was by now a hopeless attempt to reassert the interest of the patient, "Cette paresse est, en tout cas, singulièrement pathologique"—"this laziness is, in any case, singularly pathological" (150). Although not quite the last word, Janet's flat declaration seems to close down discussion. If this published account shows the ways in which professional rivalries might lead to a particular diagnosis, it also shows that even those doctors most interested in theorizing the psychological dimensions of self harm could revert to the criminological framework.

The same tendency is in evidence in an early essay on self harm by Carl Jung, "On Simulated Insanity" (1903). In it, Jung draws attention to the complexity which attends a diagnosis of simulation but is emphatic about the moral basis on which such patients should be judged: "it is a well-known fact that the majority of malingerers are mentally abnormal and consist in the main of degenerates of various descriptions" (160). He also observes that most are thieves (161). Working within biological models of criminality, Jung asserts that "congenital mendacity and an hysterical disposition are the beginning of simulation" (163). For even in the most severe instances of self-inflicted injury, fraud remains the model: "When, for instance, a work-shy female hysteric can burn her feet in the most atrocious way with sulphuric acid, simply in order to get a free stay in hospital ... we may expect even more refined practices in individuals who are acting from feeling-toned motivations" (163).[14] Concluding with another example of a young woman who, among other things, drove nails through her feet as part of "an enormous swindle" to pass herself off as a saint, Jung writes that "Such cases can hardly be described as simulation ... but are merely symptoms of a known mental disorder of which history affords us hundreds of examples" (186). Thus, "when an hysterical girl tortures herself in order to appear more interesting, both means and ends are the outcome of some morbid mental activity" (186).

From these discussions we can draw three conclusions. First, insight into the psyche or even professional interest by no means automatically generates sympathy for the patient. Second, therefore, theories of the psyche and the interpretation of the actions of any one patient are themselves grounded in the same kinds of cultural values which shape responses in general practice, or in military or carceral medicine. Like every other form of medical science, psychiatry and psychology operate not in an imaginary realm purged of preconception, but function not least in terms of value-based assumptions about the capacities or predilections of patients. They can also reflect agendas specific to individuals or institutional conditions. Therefore, thirdly, all theories operate in moments "small" enough for theory to be jostled by personality, perhaps even by professional rivalries or coalitions. Whether it occurs in the congenial and highly organized space of the professional seminar or the large and volatile space of the battlefield, it is impossible to predict a response to self harm.

The Unknown Ancestor: Dabrowski

The most interesting although not the most influential early work in self harm studies is Casimir [more often Kazimierz] Dabrowski's one-hundred-page essay "Psychological Bases of Self-Mutilation," published in 1937. Dabrowski (1902–1980) worked in Poland; his best-known work in English is probably *Mental Growth Through Positive Disintegration* (1970).

"Psychological Bases of Self-Mutilation" surveys and in some ways classifies forms of physical injury, but is unusual in being very careful to direct readers' attention to the limits of such a process. The frame of reference is provided by the leading European theorists of psychoanalysis, particularly Janet. The fundamental argument is that self harm is not masochistic but is connected to the desire to inflict suffering on others—an argument which prefigures Obermayer's (1955) suggestion that radical self harm represents the internalization and enactment of hostility towards another person. Repeatedly, the variety of causes and cases, the need for caution in diagnosis and consideration of etiology, and the need to be alert to psychological factors are all emphasized.

Dabrowski emphasizes the need for caution in diagnosis; for care in consideration of etiology; and being alert to psychological factors. He argues that the response (implicitly, of doctors) must be focused on "the basic disorder" and not self harm itself. While Dabrowski's arguments rest on clichéd accounts of "feminine" behavior and other stereotypes, and there is an occasional terseness about "a pathological need of arousing the interest of others" (20), his work shows a general sympathy towards and interest in "Disorders of deep sensibility" which "can be the basis of the changeable localization of self-mutilation" (20). More importantly, he points to the diversity of situations and patients in which self harm is encountered. He regards self harm as symptomatic, but not of any single condition (97). In that respect, "Psychological

Bases of Self-Mutilation," is the only synoptic study which *refuses* the logic of classification. Dabrowski concludes, "Sources of states of melancholy and depression are so diverse that presenting even a general outline concerning self-mutilation on the basis of these is impossible" (95–96).

Dabrowski wonders whether injuring one's self might act "as a compensatory substitute for psychic pain or shame" (12), as "a means of getting rid of an unbearable state of psychic tension" (13). In the light of these speculations he interrogates even those acts of self harm related to attempts to obtain compensation or escape military service, hypothesizing that "The weakening reality feeling, together with the state of anxiety, facilitates the development of obsessions" (15). Other causal factors offered include: general "excitability" (arguments which draw on Janet's case studies, [8–9]); acute "psychoneurotic conditions" (12–15); hysteria (16–21); feelings of inferiority, guilt and need for attention (22–28); general instability (29–33); sadistic and masochistic gratification (88–94); and asceticism, particularly religious asceticism (39–42), in which Dabrowski notes the coalition of and collision between ascetic practices and sexual arousal, a discussion preceded by some rather casual "anthropological" examples (34–38). Although he considers severe self harm as occasionally prefiguring suicide (43–47), in general Dabrowski does not see the two as synonymous, nor even necessarily related.

Dabrowski has a long chapter on "Michelangelo, Dostoyefsky, Weininger, Dawid, and Tolstoy," analysing possible causes for their tendencies towards self harm or actual injuries. This argument uses the lives of writers and literary characters as evidence in a general discussion of the tendencies which predispose one to, or trigger, self harm. Dabrowski pays particular attention to Dostoyevsky (52–62), whose life and work are touchstones at various points in the argument, although the definition of self harm he uses might be closer to a more generalized mental self-torture than physical injury. But they are also the foundation for Dabrowski's conclusion that a kind of will to suffering can be integral to such positive characteristics as self-sacrifice, "civic asceticism," and high achievement, a point in which he echoes Ribot on the sometimes positive outcomes of fixation. He suggests that some forms of self harm should not be the basis of concern or intervention, as they can be "a very important mechanism of self-education" (101). Thus the work is to distinguish these non-pathological forms from those "perverted practices of asceticism" that are "inconsistent with human self-respect": "the terrorization of the senses and compensation of sensual needs in a humiliating manner" (100–01). Like Janet's, this argument is historically significant not because it was influential— it was not, Garrard (1950) being one of few post-war writers to prefer Dabrowski to Menninger—but because it shows that complex models of self harm have been available for many decades.

Freud and His Followers:
Brunswick, Lewis and Greenacre

The single most influential figure in the study of the human psyche in the West is Sigmund Freud (1856–1939), a prolific author whose own voluminous scholarly writings have been supplemented by multi-volume collections of his correspondence with colleagues including Karl Abraham, Sándor Ferenczi, Wilhelm Fleiss, Ernest Jones, Carl Jung, Otto Rank, and others. This writing constitutes a monumental archive on which scholars from a wide range of medical, social science and humanities disciplines have productively drawn for more than a century. Freud's influence has spread from the specialism of "psycho-analysis," a term he coined and which is identified with his work, into the broader fields of psychiatry and medicine, as well as into popular culture. Psychoanalysis, with its focus on sexuality, the unconscious, and treatment through "talk," sits in a sometimes antagonistic relationship to those strands of psychiatry or psychology which aim to diagnose and treat all illness as physical illness, or to speak only in terms of behavior.

Freud's theories are described by one influential feminist psychoanalyst as being "built on the observation of universally present unconscious processes which [are] largely brought into being by social obstacles to the expression of human sexuality" (Mitchell 5). The most controversial of these ideas is that all human development, thence all mental illness, is a response to sexual development or impediments in it. But Freud's work is perhaps more important, in terms of the study of self harm, for consolidating belief in the existence of the unconscious, and theorizing the terms of its operation. Although Freud himself did not address the subject directly, his arguments about sexuality and the unconscious have been guiding principles for some key clinicians who have addressed self harm during the twentieth century. The significance of the unconscious lies in the commensurate assumption that it is impossible to understand the human self as a stable, single and self-controlled entity, for whom mental health is merely a matter of strength of mind. In fact, under the terms of reference set by Freud, we should understand the motives of much of what we feel and do as opaque.

Freud was singled out by Bernard Hart as "the most original and fertile thinker who has yet entered the field of abnormal psychology" (vi), although Hart also acknowledged interest in the ideas and writing of Janet, Jung, Karl Pearson and Richard von Krafft-Ebing, along with W. Trotter on "the herd instinct" (vii). In a set of essays published mainly in the late 1920s, writers like Otto Fenichel, Sándor Radó, Ruth Mack Brunswick, Nolan D.C. Lewis, Karl Menninger and Paul Schilder proposed arguments about self harm underpinned by reference to distinctively Freudian understandings of sexual and psychological development. Most of this group had direct contact with Freud: Brunswick was an intimate, and she, Fenichel and Schilder studied with him. Menninger, in turn, studied with Brunswick after she had returned to the U.S. from Europe; Lewis heard lectures from Schilder when in Vienna, meeting Freud twice (Parham 4).

One of Freud's most renowned patients was Sergius Pankejeff, often known as "the Wolf Man," whose treatment was subsequently taken over by Ruth Mack Brunswick. Although Freud's own work on Pankejeff does not deal with the subject, Brunswick's 1928 essay describes several forms of self harm. These include the patient's abrading of his body, particularly his nose, and his repeated attempts to obtain surgery and other potentially disfiguring treatments. Following Freud, Brunswick diagnoses his torment of and about his nose as "genital":

> The wound is inflicted on his nose first by himself and then by X. The patient's failure to be satisfied by his self-castration reveals a motive beyond the usual masochistic one of guilt, which, regardless of the perpetrator, would be satisfied by the act itself. The further motive is, of course, the libidinal one, the desire for castration at the hands of the father as an expression in anal-sadistic language of that father's love. In addition, there is the wish to be made into a woman for the sake of sexual satisfaction from the father. I call attention here to the patient's hallucinatory experience in early childhood, when he thought he had cut off his finger [470].

This account understands specific body parts as standing in for the genitalia, and sexual development as being organized around the negotiation of the relationship with the father. Thus both the damage inflicted on the nose, and the childhood fear/fantasy of the amputation of the finger, are seen as signposts to or confirmation of "the desire for castration" by the father. We can note the congruity between this reading, in its dependence on reference to sexual development, sexual desire and anxiety, with Bernice Engle's reading of the phallic symbolism of the still moving finger in Arnobius' version of the Attis story (see chapter one). There is a compactness and authority to such accounts, which tend towards closing down questions about self harm. The interest lies in explaining the symbolic structure and the operation of reasoning in sexual terms.

A number of writers associated with Freud, among them Sándor Ferenczi, argued that the eye was a phallic symbol, therefore that self-enucleation is symbolic of self-castration for both men and women.[15] In reply, Phyllis Greenacre's contention is that the eye has a much broader symbolic function, one which she associates with the belief that the eye can betray guilt, or that self-enucleation can be punishment for looking (557). Greenacre's 1926 essay "The Eye Motif in Delusion and Fantasy" is framed as a rejection of claims made by Karl Abraham, which rest on seeing the pupil as a female diminutive. To this hypothesis, Greenacre responds:

> In general, I cannot see any constant difference in the self-blinding complex in the two sexes, such as is implied if this always rested on the implicit symbolization of the genitals by the eyes. On the other hand, the development of the delusions of influence through the eyes in some cases certainly indicates that it is not necessarily a little maiden of the eye, but simply the guilty person—the soul, conscience or spirit which is identified with the malicious influence, especially if the eye has in its own right (vision) been the agent of guilt [559].

More obviously than most, Greenacre's argument is a refutation of—or at least an attempt to demand modification of—the Freudian view which centralizes male models of sexuality and sexual development; at the same time, it is a strong if temperate disputation of what she sees as the misogyny of male colleagues. Here, the pressure on Freudians to conform to the models and argument proposed by Freud were in tension with Greenacre's views.

Nolan D.C. Lewis, in four essays on "The Psychobiology of the Castration Reaction" (1927–28), attempts to understand male genital self harm. Lewis, clinical psychiatrist in Washington, D.C., follows Brunswick's rhetorical lead, stating his view simply and assertively:

> The symbolic transference of actual or implied mutilation whether self-inflicted[,] committed criminalistically by perverts or expressed through dream or symptomatic displacement from the genital region to other parts of the body is very commonly encountered in all phases of life, and books on medical-legal moral offenses, particularly those sections on sadistic acts, as well as those dealing with sex and with psychiatric topics are rich with instances of these symbolic self-castrations and father and society castration expressions ["Introduction" 421].

The statement is unusual in coupling pejorative views of self harm as fraud ("committed criminalistically by perverts") while understanding it *at the same time* as a symbolic or symptomatic act ("expressed through dream or symptomatic displacement"). Lewis is also unusual in representing physical self injury as one of a number of symptoms—suicide attempts, certain "mental diseases, personality reaction types"—which reflect the impulse to self castration ("Introduction" 422–23).

Lewis begins the third of his articles, "The Eshmun Complex," with the declaration that "partial or complete self-castration"—a definition which positions self harm as paradigmatically *male*—is "the only death known to the unconscious and the only death which the ego may survive" (174). Lewis's interpretations of self castration are framed by a discussion of Eshmun [the name refers to Attis], who Lewis claims castrated himself in order to escape the attentions of the mother goddess. A more-or-less orthodox account, relying on the theory of the Oedipus complex (envy of the father), frames Lewis's studies, all of his patients being said to be "frankly psychotic" (175). Lewis argues that what is distinctive about the story of Eshmun is that it leads to the death of the man who castrates himself. This is a central element of the equally unusual suggestion that self castration could represent the death of the unconscious. Echoing James Frazer's reading of the Attis stories, Lewis argues that the concern is procreation: "One who dies, dies a temporal death, while the castrate dies eternally since his germ plasm has perished" ("The Eshmun Complex" 197).

The crux of Lewis's argument is that a person who engages in forms of physical self harm, having lost the impulse of self-preservation, is "under the influence of the reproductive," "which functions here in a symbolic way" (Lewis, "The Eshmun Complex" 198). The difficulty is that in equating passivity with the female, reproductive capacity must be ignored, or perhaps we might say, be understood in terms which are quite selective. Thus Lewis is and is not distinctive. He is orthodox in echoing the hereditarian preoccupations of the day and his use of Freud's theory of the Oedipal conflict. But he is unusual in simply setting aside the female reproductive. This kind of view finds an antagonist in Karen Horney (see below), who claims that reproduction is undervalued in Freudian models of the architecture of the unconscious and the development of the self. And Lewis perhaps exemplifies Horney's complaint that the Freudian framework has a misogynist core, in the assumption that femaleness is equivalent to debilitation.

Karl Menninger and Man Against Himself

These discussions of approaches to self harm in the 1920s inspired by Freud frame Karl Menninger's essays on self-mutilation published in the 1930s, and the 1938 book *Man Against Himself*. In many respects it is the essays which make a more original contribution to the literature: "A Psychoanalytic Study of the Significance of Self-Mutilation" (1935) extends points made in "Psychoanalytic Aspects of Suicide" published two years before. Menninger considers reasons for the strengthening of "the destructive element" but, while he refers to the number of instances of self harm that has been reported ("A Psychoanalytic Study" 411), it is also evident that his thinking was influenced by the classical and Christian literature discussed in chapter one and to which his essay turns (422). In canvassing a series of broadly "literary" and "anthropological" instances of self harm, Menninger relies on sources which emphasize the ritual meaning and symbolic coherence of various practices of self harm (422–32). But the terms of his analysis can be deduced from the remark that "The savages and the psychotic have this in common, that they act without deference to the demands of a civilization which often modifies primitive tendencies almost beyond recognition" (439), claims which echo Ribot's.

Menninger offers a theory which he says holds across the array of circumstances in which he finds the practice: "self-mutilation represents the surrender or repudiation of the active rôle, accomplished through the physical removal or injury of a part of the body"; the prototypical form is self castration, having "the significance of activity generally associated with the male genital" ("A Psychoanalytic Study" 464). Active aggression is directed towards an introjected object, while "passive aggression" is directed towards "real rather than fantasied [sic] objects; the provocative behavior of nail-biting children or of malingerers, who so exasperate their friends and physicians, clearly illustrate this" (464). These processes exploit the "inherent bisexuality" of all human beings, in that erotic gratification is achieved by a shift from the active to the passive and in that respect is a manifestation of the "unconscious envy on the part of men of the female role" (464).

Here we can see the same totalizing impetus evident in the works of criminology and military medicine, but Menninger's approach differs in that he works with ideas about universal psychic structures. These function as categories just as surely as the personality types or even body parts which provide the logic for earlier classificatory systems, but they demand more subtle forms of investigation because they rely on depth not surface, the symbolic rather than the literal. The central conceptual term, repeated in the second essay, is "sacrifice." The premise is that a body part is substituted and sacrificed for the whole (408), a concept that would later be amplified as "focal suicide" (*Man Against Himself* 229). Menninger sees the symbolism so often integral to religion as operating in a similar fashion to the unconscious, in particular, by substituting a part for the whole which is then "sacrificed" to propitiate or to permit use, as, for example, in circumcision, where the foreskin is substituted for the penis ("A Psychoanalytic Study" 432).[16]

Menninger argues that the neurotic patient is able to be "more loyal to reality" ("A Psychoanalytic Study" 411) than the psychotic patient. Thus their forms of self harm are far more likely to be "[s]ubstitutive and symbolic": "neurotics frequently demand and obtain mutilation at the hands of a second party, for example in the form of surgical operations" (411; Menninger references his own 1934 essay "Polysurgery" in evidence). Given that the "nature and purpose" of neurosis is to save the personality from the "direct and serious consequences of the demands of the instincts and of the conscience," the ego, "the discriminating intelligence of the personality," makes "the best bargain possible" "if it finds itself failing" ("A Psychoanalytic Study" 411). But such bargains are the refuge of those "burdened by hate" and by conscience (413).

Against the trend of much study, Menninger also speculates that even those instances of self harm which occur during psychotic states have not literal but symbolic meaning (442). The first patient Menninger describes, a young woman who manages the "amputation" of her arm after having beaten her two-year-old child to death, can be read (as Menninger notes) as "spectacular atonement" for a terrible act, "the fruit ... of hate" ("A Psychoanalytic Study" 409).[17]

The work for which Menninger is much better known, *Man Against Himself*, is not, as it is so often characterized, a study of self harm.[18] It can better be described as a popularizing account of Freudian notions of the opposition between Eros and Thanatos. Various aspects of its presentation signal that it is not primarily a scholarly work, including this claim on the cover: "One of America's leading psychiatrists makes a brilliant and arresting diagnosis of a sickness that affects the entire world." Menninger announces that "the introduction of the psychoanalytic technique of investigation affords us an entirely new understanding of the process of [self-destructive behavior] through the elucidation of its details. It enables us to recognize how postponement of death is sometimes purchased by the life instinct at a great cost" (6). Menninger's style, which is rich with anecdote, as well as his subordination of self harm to a more generalized thesis on suicide, has made him a relatively easy target for post-war researchers able to demonstrate (as could Menninger's contemporaries) that while self harm is in some instances predictive of suicide, it is by no means either synonymous with or a substitute for taking one's own life.[19] But the terms set by *Man Against Himself*—not least its popularizing tone—offer a model for accounts which seek to sensationalize but also to "capture" the meaning of self harm by offering a universal aetiology (set of causes) and explanation.

That said, *Man Against Himself* remains a major work, in part for its *lack* of interest in "malingering." Indeed, in his brief discussion of the topic, Menninger launches a brisk attack on doctors who, he says, in their aggression towards the self harming patient are merely returning the aggression that the patient has displaced on to them: "if one reads in a detached and impassive way almost any account of malingering in the medical literature [w]hat impresses one most is the apparent irritation, hostility, even righteous indignation of the authors toward the subjects of their investigations" (287–88). Citing Jones and Llewellyn (discussed in chapter three), Menninger remarks on their untested assumption that all self-inflicted harm is malingering, and all malingering "morally reprehensible" (288). He hypothesizes that the antagonism is disproportionate because a doctor perceives, unconsciously, that feigning illness is an attack on "his" professional capacities, a desire "perhaps to overtax and ridicule his diagnostic acumen and his therapeutic efforts" (289).

Perhaps Menninger's centrality to the modern literature of self harm does not so much reflect his intellectual contribution to the debate as it does the wide availability of *Man Against Himself*: the monograph remained in view in ways that journal articles often did not, in the period when library catalogues—which used to list only books—was the main starting point for most researchers. The book was reviewed in the *British Medical Journal* in 1939, in a relatively brief but positive note ("The Ubiquity of Suicide"). A slightly longer notice appeared in the *St. Bartholomew's Hospital Journal* the same year (Rev.).[20] A more enthusiastic reader, who used a paragraph to summarize each of the book's sections, concluded by expressing reservations only about the emphasis given to Freudian thought, and the price:

> This is a most illuminating and fascinating book. The arguments for the most part carry conviction, though occasionally the author's strict Freudian upbringing intrudes itself uncomfortably. It is rich in clear clinical examples and references to fuller works, and it is easy reading. It deserves to be read widely by laymen as well as by medical men, and its style suggests that this is its purpose. If this is so, its price should be less than fifteen shillings [Rev.].

Menninger was by no means the only writer to centralize the self-destructive impulse, but he was by far the most successful in finding a popular and scholarly audience. His arguments find echoes in the work of his American colleague Edmund Bergler. In his *Principles of Self-Damage* (1959), Bergler likewise argues for the centrality of what he calls "psychic masochism," but whereas Menninger terms "a subconscious will toward self-defeat" (inside flap) pervasive in the psychic make-up, Bergler is concerned with what he terms "the lifelong fiction that [an individual] is but the innocent victim of outside malice," for "*the only pleasure one can derive from displeasure is to make displeasure into pleasure*" (6; emphasis in original). For Menninger, it is the failure to redirect outwards "the self-directed destructiveness and constructiveness with which we are—by hypothesis—born" (*Man Against Himself* 6) which leads to self harm, whereas Bergler is dedicated to proving his theory that masochism is the most pervasive, the most powerful and the most destructive of the neuroses. To make this point, both authors use the metaphor of the river, early on in their books, to emphasize the force and inevitability of self-destruction (Menninger 3; Bergler 5–6).

Freud in Practice: Case Reports

The small number of reports available which explore theoretical questions shows that psychoanalysis was not taken up to any great degree, and it was rarely deployed for thinking about self harm. The trend was to ignore or play down the potential symbolic meaning of individual acts. Mumford, writing in 1933, was heartily congratulated by his colleagues for his proposal to investigate the aetiology of self harm on the basis of "physical and racial type," adjusted for the influence of the urban environment (141; in response see Jordan; Broderick). However, in a small set of reports from the first half of the twentieth century we can see a preparedness to adopt Freudian ideas in an effort to explain or to respond effectively to a patient's self harm, and occasionally to use specific incidents to reflect on and contribute to that theorizing.

L.E. Emerson's 1933 essay "The Case of Miss A" is an early report of a woman who had injured herself, attending Massachusetts General Hospital "with a self-inflicted cut on her left arm" and a scar on her right leg forming the letter W; she said that "she had cut herself twenty-eight or thirty times" (42). Emerson reports that the patient was sexually abused from about the age of eight by her uncle. She also witnessed her father's physical abuse of her brothers, who were stripped and tied to a bedpost. After cutting herself while trying to escape a sexual assault in her kitchen, she found that a severe headache was cured: "She said she continued the cutting as a means of gaining relief from headaches, and from a '*queer feeling*' which she could not describe" (43). Later she slashed her breasts, "thinking that if she could have no babies [because of the sexual abuse] her breasts were useless" (43), and later still, inserted a knife in her vagina. The dynamics of care are an ongoing element of the "autobiography of self harm" republished in the essay: of another incident she says, "I kept them busy with that hand for about a month; they didn't seem to know why it didn't heal up" (45). One statement not explained is that "The next time Dr.— cut my arm for me I do not remember how I felt. He opened a vein" (47).

The interpretation and treatment described in the essay are in most respects orthodoxly Freudian. Emerson suggests that the young woman's presentation shows that "The psycho-sexual traumas of childhood are repressed but are also remembered" (49), "a strong component of masochism" (48) being germane. Distinguishing between the capacity to bear physical and to bear mental pain, Emerson suggests that the former is identified with the young woman's mother, who was beaten by her father, and the inflicting of suffering "satisfied her aggressive masculine impulses and identified herself with her father" (49). "To the patient, bearing pain increased her own self-respect" (49). Emerson concludes that the treatment has been more or less successful in part because of a decision *not* to do two things: to offer a complete analysis, which the doctor suggests would have been useless to someone "poor, of lowly origin, and uneducated"; and the prescription of "sexual relations or masturbation" for the woman's condition (54). While there are strict limits to the efficacy and subtlety of Emerson's framing the essay remains, as Lisa Cardyn says, "an important moment in the theorization of sexual trauma in the United States" (191). The attempt to understand the self harm stands in "stark contrast" to what other doctors regarded as sources of amusement or contempt (Cardyn 189), although some aspects of the essay suggest that the treatment itself bordered on abuse.

Margaret Brenman's 1952 study of a patient who (eventually but savagely) injures herself claims that the various forms of physical self harm the patient engaged in "were without real substance" (278), perhaps because the young woman showed a degree of control over her condition. Taking issue with several writers, including Bergler, Otto Fenichel and Freud, Brenman suggests that recent writing had tended to simplify the notion of masochism. In her view, masochism is not a single phenomenon. There

> are rather highly complex sets of configurations which issue from special varieties of infantile need and rage being pitted against a variety of mediating defense mechanisms and in interplay with the available *creative* or adaptive ego functions.... Significant redistributions of psychic energy as in a decompensation and a rebuilding bring various aspects of this complex interplay into relief [272–73].

Brenman's point is that the increasing gap between psychoanalytic theorizing and clinical observation was reducing the capacity of either mode of scholarly writing to address adequately the complexity and variability of any single patient's situation. Her own essay notes the necessary "simplification" of the case on which she reports, notwithstanding that it runs to more than twenty closely printed pages.

For some doctors, psychoanalysis was not only an option, but had proved successful as a treatment (reported in MacCormac, "Autophytic" *PRSM* 1935). But another asserted that "Those who had little character usually showed the lack in their physiognomy" (734); was wary of referral to psychoanalysis as this implied a mental problem; and cited a fifteen-year-old girl who had presented with lesions subsequently "cured" by a sensible family member. The doctor spoke to the patient and then sought help from "a married sister with whom she was living. The sister, who was both sympathetic and intelligent, went into the girl's troubles fully at home and with a completely successful result."

> Dr. Elizabeth Hunt said that she frequently met with cases of this kind in girls in their teens. She did not send all such cases to a psychiatrist; she selected them. She tried talking to the mother and securing her cooperation. Often these girls scratched themselves in their sleep and were nail-biters. When no cooperation was forthcoming she agreed it might be best to send the case to a psychiatrist. But such cases were not confined to females; the worst cases she had seen were men; one had his arm amputated [MacCormac, "Autophytic" *PRSM* 1935: 734].

One of MacCormac's colleagues took the view that self harm should in fact be kept confidential from the family, in order to protect the dignity and the welfare of the patient (Lancashire, "Dermatitis Artefacta"). The discussion seems to suggest that doctors were able to disagree about both the principle and the practice of discerning psychological issues, and commensurately, the value of referral to a specialist in psychological illnesses.

Theorizing Self Harm: Otto Fenichel

Otto Fenichel, regarded as one of the standouts of the second generation of psychoanalysts, presents an influential account of self harm in his *Psychoanalytic Theory of Neuroses* (1945). Fenichel claims that "Autocastrations have been repeatedly reported in schizophrenic cases." This implies that Fenichel does not regard self harm as an act it is meaningful to interpret. However, he suggests that there *is* a logic of the psyche underpinning self castration, that logic being associated with religiosity,

> These acts, probably, are psychologically comparable to autocastrations performed by religious fanatics who, by such radical denial of their active sexual wishes, try to regain "peaceful unity with God," that is, an extreme passive submissiveness, less of a feminine than of an early infantile "oceanic" nature [439].[21]

Fenichel speculates on self harm more generally, which he argues is "not 'beyond the pleasure principle,'" which is to say, that it can be a means of gratification. This is a crucial maneuver. While it can be taken as reinforcing the view that self harm is manipulative and instrumental, the foundation of the argument—which presumes the unconscious—diminishes the level of control that can be expected of the person who self harms.

Fenichel's reasoning hinges on his understanding of the structure and function of the ego and the superego. For him, self castration

> represents an undesired consequence of something desired. The self-destruction may subjectively have been aimed at the destruction of the object which, after introjection, is represented by the ego; and this destruction of the object may even be condensed with an ingratiation of the object. The attempt to get rid of pressure from the superego is the aim of all self-destruction.... That is what priests do who castrate themselves in order to dedicate themselves to God. Their self-castration is a means of entering into the great protecting union [439].

In making these arguments, Fenichel works from the Freudian precept that the unconscious never refuses desire, even the desire that desire be controlled. What is desired is control, but the expression of this control takes the form of passivity. Yet at the same time, that apparently universalizing logic (everyone has a superego) takes a culturally specific form, by implication, the prohibitions of a Judao-Christian god. But the gods Attis and Cybele, whom the Galli served, are associated as much with the celebration as the censure of sexual activity—indeed Apuleius accuses them of extreme licentiousness. If Attis enters into a "great protecting union" as a consequence of renouncing the male power of procreation, that union must surely be female. It is the realm of Cybele, the Great Mother.

During the process of introjection presented here, broadly one might say that (a mediated version of) the world is incorporated into the ego, for which the body itself becomes the medium of expression or a metaphor in controlling the world. The penis is the focal point, becoming a kind of universal or all powerful symbol. In this, Fenichel gives a highly masculinized account, which presumes a Judeo-Christian framework of sexual morality and the dominance of the male in procreation. Thus it cannot be clear whether removal of the penis (if that is what Fenichel is referring to by the term auto-castration) is a form of gratification which renounces, or is one that expresses, the desire for control, as well as the desire for re-enacting the merging with the mother, the "'oceanic.'" If the penis represents desire, then the destruction of the penis gratifies the superego; in regard to the priests, mentioned twice by Fenichel, the gods have a grandstand seat as the castration complex is played out. It is a view which informs Edith Weigert-Vowinkel's essay on Attis published seven years earlier (see chapter one). Both reflect the religious preoccupations and practices of their own time, projected back onto the ancient Graeco-Roman world.

In relation to theorizations of self harm, specifically destruction of the male genitalia, it matters, here, whether it is the penis or the scrotum which is being referred to. The penis is symbolic of sexual dominance whereas the scrotum is an organ associated with *reproduction*. If the penis is removed, this has a different meaning to the removal of the scrotum, not only in practical but in symbolic and psychoanalytic terms. If the scrotum is removed it is, implicitly, fatherhood which is being evaded or renounced; if the penis is removed, the cultural meanings (for Freudians) are quite different, as the phallus is the ultimate symbol of what we might call cultural power. Either might constitute a renunciation of masculinity, but neither is precisely "feminisation." The metaphors of submission and immersion associated with either act imply a dissolving of the self, which are read as a means of psychic reintegration with the mother, something the Galli might be read as seeking. But Fenichel does not mention the Galli directly, and in a sense, the great unspoken here is the status of Cybele.

This raises a further question about Fenichel's analogy between priestly self castration and the destruction of "the object" which, "after introjection, is represented by the ego." In Fenichel's formulation, the penis represents the outer world, or perhaps more aptly, the desire for control of the world as it appears to the ego. There is an overlapping or overlaying here of desire, control, the body and what lies beyond the body, all of which coalesce in the image of the male genitalia. But if Fenichel is correct in arguing for the impact of the pressure of the superego, and if Freud is correct in his theorizing of the ubiquity and meaning of the castration complex, then it is not clear why male self castration is not far more common than it is. For if the phallus—the symbol of male cultural power, identified with the penis, often implicitly or explicitly sacralized—is a means of focalizing—representing the point of view of—the desire for power, then removal of the penis constitutes the supreme expression of the desire for control. Either way—read as a desire for reintegration with the mother, or as a hyperbolic statement about the masculine capacity for domination—there is a deep psychic seduction in the removal of the penis.

In his discussion of principles of self harm, Fenichel cites Sándor Radó, whose work is the basis for Fenichel's assertion that "It may be that all real self-destruction, in the last analysis, represents remainders of the archaic reaction pattern of autonomy: a tension is overcome by abandoning the cathected organ" (365). In saying this, Fenichel signals his awareness of the shadow of the question I have just posed: why is male genital self harm not more common? Perhaps an answer is implied by Radó, whose "Developments in the Psycho-analytic Conception and Treatment of the Neuroses" (1939) Fenichel references. Radó argues that *"neurosis is ego functioning altered by faulty measures of emergency control,"* "emergency measures which reduce both the range and the efficiency of its functioning" (433). This damage can deprive the individual of control of their body (including sexual functioning), and the capacity to function as a member of the community (433–34).

Radó develops this argument into what he terms "the riddance principle" (435), by which a range of reflexes seek to rid the body of "pain-causing agents" (434). For example, sexual tension can lead an individual to want to castrate themselves, an impulse that is controlled by the intellect:

> In other cases, in psychoses or under morbid excitement, he loses his controlling insight and in a paroxysm of riddance, actually inflicts self-injury in order to end the insupportably painful tension of anticipation. In some cases, driven to end the tension, the patient brings about a situation in which he is inevitably injured by others. A refined technique of achieving this is to lure the surgeon into the performance of unnecessary operations ["Developments" 435].[22]

"Strangest of all," says Radó, "are those actions of the neurotic ego which are obviously self-injurious" (434). These self-injurious actions can be observed on three levels: the intellectual, in which the "device" is fear; the "subintellectual or affectomotor level," where the device is anxiety; and on the lowest level, "subaffect," in which the device is pain (434). Radó argues that "Control of pain is therefore directed toward eliminating the source of suffering, if necessary even by sacrifice of a part of one's own body" (434). It is a conclusion similar to that reached by Menninger in his 1935 essay "A Psychoanalytic Study of the Significance of Self-Mutilation."

Challenging Freud: Horney on Feminine Masochism

Like Phyllis Greenacre, Karen Horney was clearly motivated to respond to what she saw as her colleagues' sexism and the ways in which that sexism (mis)informed their theorizing of the function of the psyche. Horney's essay on "The Problem of Feminine Masochism" engages with the work of Helene Deutsch and Sándor Radó's essay "Fear of Castration in Women" (1933).[23] Radó himself had drawn on Karl Abraham's 1922 essay "Manifestations of the Female Castration Complex," in which Abraham declares that "Many women suffer temporarily or permanently, in childhood or in adult age, from the fact that they have been born female" (1). Also important is Freud's "Some Psychological Consequences of the Anatomical Differences between the Sexes," first published in German in 1925 and in English two years later. It is this set of papers that Horney addresses.

Karl Abraham summarily dismisses cultural arguments for women's discontent—envy of men's freedom of employment, or of sexual activity, for example—saying that these points are entirely outweighed by the "poverty in external genitals" (2). The girl is further incapacitated by her failure to recognize her inherent disadvantage, imagining herself once to have had a penis and therefore to be the victim of castration (3). The essay comments at length on penis envy, arguing that the complex is resolved at that point at which the adult woman "desires passive gratification and longs for a child" (7). Women who express their desire for masculine identity through homosexuality signify their envy through "dress, in the way of doing their hair, and in their general behaviour," as well as by having "masculine interests of an intellectual or professional character": "This type of woman is well represented in the woman's movement of today" (9). Feminism, equality and professional accomplishment—even, perhaps especially, women psychoanalysts—are designated as neurotic, their "ambition" an expression of "the phantasy of possessing the male organ" (9). The other common manifestation of a failed adjustment to the submissive role is revenge (10). The rest of the essay documents examples of patients with "maladjustment," mainly examples of women with sexual inhibition.

Sándor Radó's work is grounded in a similarly ardent Freudianism which finds the formation of all neuroses in the failure of the infant "in providing the ego with a functionally efficient genital organization" ("Fear of Castration" 474). Radó considers self-destructive urges in a subsection titled "The Choice of the Lesser Evil," which he calls "the gravest" of modes of defense, "an obscure, almost unexplored field" (468). In this state "the patient loses a modest potentiality for gratification," and as a foreseen sexual encounter looms,

> Her genital masochism is stimulated and goes into action. Wild apprehensions and terrifying fantasies occupy more and more place in the patient's living.... In this state of exalted depression, the impulsive action takes place, by means of which the woman injures herself or gets herself injured [469].

The woman experiences her injury as "a real deliverance," but it is one which "the patient *always* carries out ... while in a sort of self-stupefaction" (469). This makes the ego either blind, or able to deceive itself, as to the meaning of what is being done:

> Especially in cases that terminate in extreme self-injury, one would hesitate to ascribe to the ego any attempt at deliberative reflection. The situation can be more satisfactorily described then as an eruption of genital masochistic desires; the ego, overwhelmed, surrenders to the masochism ... [the symptoms are attributable] to the victory of genital masochism over the ego [469].

These developments can be "tempestuous" or "chronic" (469–70). Radó goes on to describe what he sees as some classic patterns in "genital masochism" (470–72).

The significance of such work lies in its structuring of female sexual experience as a desire to be injured, while the passive role congruent with proper femininity embeds the same desires into being female. In that sense, the desire to injure one's body or to be injured is built into the processes of becoming and being female. In arguing that female sexuality is intrinsically masochistic, Radó is asserting that "the woman [who] injures herself or gets herself injured," as he describes her (above), is in a specific sense, "normal." Such ideas are the platform for research into self harm by women and girls which presumes that the alliance between pleasure and pain is intrinsic to female subjectivity.

After the fifty-page essay "Fear of Castration in Women" was published in 1933, one of Radó's female colleagues moved quickly. On December 26 that year, Karen Horney delivered a critique at a meeting of the American Psychoanalytic Association. In her essay "The Problem of Feminine Masochism" she takes up the claim "that masochistic character trends of all kinds ... are much more frequent in women" (242). She notes those writers who in her view have made "the same error" of moving from "pathological" cases to generalizing about women: Richard von Krafft-Ebing and Sigmund Freud; A.W. Nemilow, [a Russian gynecologist] who "speaks of the 'bloody tragedy of women'"; and the German gynecologist Wilhelm Liepman, who, "impressed by the frequency of illnesses, accidents and pains in the female career line, assumes that vulnerability, irritability, and sensitivity are the fundamental triad of female qualities" ("The Problem" 248).[24] Slowly it emerges that the title of Horney's essay is deliberately misleading. As it goes on, we begin to realize that the "problem" Horney is actually addressing is not the behavior of women, but that of her colleagues, specifically their view that femininity is intrinsically masochistic thence that masochism is female.

Contending that the discipline has "not advanced much beyond Freud's statement that [masochism] has something to do with sexuality and with morality" (251), Horney proposes that the term is being used to describe "widely discrepant manifestations":

> The suffering may concern the physical or the mental sphere.... The gratification or relief of tension may be conscious or unconscious; sexual or non-sexual. The non-sexual functions may be very different: reassurances against fears, atonements for committed sins, permission to commit new ones, strategy in reference to goals otherwise unattainable, indirect forms of hostility [Horney, "The Problem" 252].

She calls repeatedly for evidence to support claims about female normality and female pathology, noting with evident frustration that "It seems to have become habitual in psychoanalytic thinking to assume that pain, suffering, or fear of suffering are prompted by masochistic drives, or result in masochistic gratification" ("The Problem" 251), whether because of a naïve misunderstanding or over-complication of human action, or by setting aside cultural context.

Horney contends that Radó and Deutsch "completely ignore discussion of frequency, because they maintain that the psychologic genetic factors are so forceful and ubiquitous that a consideration of frequency becomes superfluous" ("The Problem" 243). In her view, while Freud's claim that "there is no fundamental difference between pathologic and 'normal' phenomena" might provide a basis for this generalization, there are probably limits, limits which could only be demonstrated by sociological and ethnological evidence. The "refusal" of psychoanalysts to consider these factors does not, as Horney acidly remarks, "shut out their existence" (250).[25] It is the job of the psychoanalyst, she argues, to provide criteria for the anthropologist to use in determining whether the society they are examining does in fact facilitate or presume female masochism (251).

Horney's work was influenced by her engagement with the sociological and philosophical writing of Georg Simmel. Drawing on Simmel's arguments about the masculinity of what is regarded as civilized society, Horney suggests that "women have adapted themselves to the wishes of men and felt as if their adaptation was their true nature. That is, they see or saw themselves in the way that their men's wishes demanded of them" ("The Flight" 326). As she wisely observes,

> It is fairly obvious that these ideologies function not only to reconcile women to their subordinate role by presenting it as an unalterable one, but also to plant the belief that it represents a fulfilment they crave, or an ideal for which it is commendable and desirable to strive. The influence that these ideologies exert on women is materially strengthened by the fact that women presenting the specified traits are more frequently chosen by men. This implies that women's erotic possibilities depend on their conformity to the image of that which constitutes their "true nature" ["The Problem" 256].

In an essay on a similar topic, "The Flight from Womanhood," Horney concludes that for her at least, it is "impossible to judge to how great a degree the unconscious motives for the flight from womanhood are reinforced by the actual social subordination of women. One might conceive of the connection as an interaction of psychic and social factors," one which leaves men with stronger desires to be female, but better able to sublimate them because femaleness bears "the stigma of inferiority" (338).

After her criticism of the over-reliance on masochism as a catch-all category, Horney mounts a strong attack on the sexism she sees in relying on the concept to understand the formation of female subjectivity: "there may appear certain fixed ideologies concerning the 'nature' of woman; such as doctrines that woman is innately weak, emotional, enjoys dependence, is limited in capacities for independent work and autonomous thinking. One is tempted to include in this category the psychoanalytic belief that woman is masochistic by nature" ("The Problem" 256). Horney's view is that the entire profession of psychoanalysis is bound by the intellectual error of regarding masculine behavior as normatively human. Contending with this, she suggests that Freud's most basic theories of human sexual development require revision, for it is surely unlikely "that female adaptation to the male structure [of fear of castration] should take place at so early a period and in so high a degree that the specific nature of a little girl is overwhelmed by it" ("The Flight" 328). In place of Freud, then, she commends "Ferenczi's extremely brilliant genital theory" which posits that "the real incitement to coitus, its true, ultimate meaning for both sexes, is to be sought in the desire to return to the mother's womb" ("The Flight" 328).

Although referring positively to Ferenczi, Horney goes on to criticize him for misunderstanding birth as a site of potential pleasure—"surely very questionable"; her own view is that it is motherhood that offers pleasure, notably suckling and nurturing the infant. Thus, in her argument, one of the organizing principles of the psyche is not fear of castration but fear of vaginal injury; clitoral pleasure "legitimately belongs to and forms an integral part of the female genital apparatus" ("The Flight" 334). In this formulation (which is opposed to that of orthodox Freudianism), normative forms of female pleasure incorporate those of the clitoris as well as those of the vagina, and commensurately the pleasures of motherhood. Not only are these pleasures intensely felt, men are aware of and envious of them. While Ferenczi has taken the view that "the male as victor" imposes on women "the burden of motherhood" (Horney cites conversation, "The Flight" 329), Horney claims that her analyses show "a most surprising impression of the intensity of this envy of pregnancy, child-birth and motherhood, as well as of the breasts and the act of suckling" (330) among men.[26] Her views are echoed by her colleague Edith Weigert-Vowinkel's interpretation of the stories of Attis and the rites of spring, those being "like a new birth, as though man's envy of child-bearing had brought him his desired end. In the mystic union with the fruitful mother, he has given rebirth to himself" (372).

In the light of these findings from her own practice, Horney asks "whether an unconscious masculine tendency to depreciation [sic] is not expressing itself intellectually" in the hostility of Ferenczi and others towards motherhood ("The Flight" 330). Provocatively and originally, she asserts that,

> masculine envy ... certainly serves as one, if not as the essential, driving force in the setting-up of cultural values.... Is not the tremendous strength in men of the impulse to creative work in every field precisely due to their feeling of playing a relatively small part in the creation of living beings, which constantly impels them to an over-compensation in achievement? ["The Flight" 330].

The envy of motherhood produces a psychic need to denigrate women and to achieve in professional fields. Conversely, the desire to be male is not an aspect of sexual development but "a secondary formation embodying all that has miscarried in the development towards womanhood" (Horney, "The Flight" 333). In Horney's view, this leads girls to recoil from "the feminine role altogether" (333). This recoiling has *social* foundations: experiences of discrimination, which include seeing their own pleasures denigrated and being excluded from roles with power. Such experiences are not part of normal sexual and psychological development.

Horney's critique of Radó, Deutsch, Ferenczi and Freud weakens the framework of the Oedipus complex that is the foundation of Freudian thought. It also implies a need for psychiatrists to consider the ways in which the operation of their profession and its theorization of human development are embedded in and fortify sexism. Nevertheless, such work rarely finds its way into psychoanalytically-based discussions of self harm in the second half of the twentieth century. Instead, post-war theorizations of self harm have often taken for granted the validity of the Freudian approach and what Robert C. Burnham, writing in 1969, called "normal feminine masochism" (223, qtd. in Brickman 194). Indeed, Burnham himself notes that when Graff and Mallin, in one of the foundational modern studies of self harm, found a 56-year-old male dentist among their sample of 21 "he was summarily excluded from the statistics with the designation 'atypical'" (223; see Graff and Mallin 74). Amidst the prevalence and authority of this approach to self harm, Horney's views give us a different way of understanding female sexual development in Western societies, the relationship of sexual to social development, and the processes by which the self configures identity in relation to the body. In turn, they call into question the foundation of arguments made by writers like Menninger.

Reviving Feminine Masochism

The discussion of psychoanalysis reveals the contradiction between the universalist foundation of its premises and the regional and personality-based distribution of its influence. Within conventional Freudian psychoanalysis, theories about the structure and function of the psyche are understood as applying across historical periods and cultural differences, making it valid to use Greek drama of the fifth century B.C.E. (the work of Sophocles) as a way of conceptualizing and treating the neuroses of Viennese patients of the late nineteenth and early twentieth centuries. Within the regions and debates in which psychoanalysis has been prominent—in particular, the northeast of the United States, and the treatment of young women for self harm through cutting—a localized pattern of influence, conceptually distinctive, can be discerned. This is, of course, the territory of Karen Horney, who worked in New York. But it is the misogynist tradition of psychoanalysis which prevails. Dissertation writer Lisa Warren Cross seems to be speaking of the world outside the medical professions when she writes, in 1990,

> Although it is nowadays an unpopular view, I do agree with Deutsch, Kestenberg, and other traditional psychoanalytic thinkers that there is a feminine tendency towards masochism that is not totally based on internalization of a demeaned social role, and that is linked to universal feminine experiences of the body [Cross 74].

The influence of Shelley Doctors' 1979 dissertation "The Symptom of Delicate Self-cutting in Adolescent Females: A Developmental View" has generally been restricted to research students working in the New York city area, all of whom cite her unpublished thesis in their bibliography, and most of whom engage explicitly with her approach, notwithstanding a more readily available essay in the journal *Adolescent Psychiatry* which offers a précis of her findings. Perhaps surprisingly the work of Horney is more or less invisible, although a number of writers do seem to grope for feminist responses to Freudian paradigms. This would suggest either that thesis advisers were unaware of Horney's work, or that they did not regard it as authoritative.

Shelley Doctors frames her research problem as this: "'What is the relationship between the experience of disturbances in early object relations development and the sense of self, conflicts around the experience of the genitals and genital sensations, and altered states of consciousness?'" and "'How do these features relate to the behavior of cutting?'"[27] Doctors bases her PhD on an intensive study of five adolescent girls but does not quote at length from them. Since there is no mention in the discussion of methodology that Doctors has recorded her subjects' comments, it is not clear to what extent they have been mediated by the researcher. This is important when the nature of the researcher's assumptions about the authority of diagnosis is considered. Explaining her approach to interpreting these stories, Doctors asserts that

> The problem is therefore one of discovering clinical relationships between domains of experience and fitting apparently disparate phenomena into some organized and meaningful relation to cutting behavior which is consistent with general clinical knowledge [3; see also 66: "models consistent with accepted psychological knowledge"].

This is an acknowledgment of the researcher's need to fit her patients' narratives into models of medical theory, which by implication are driven by consensus. This point is emphasized in the published essay which refers to "high concordance," "striking uniformity," and patients who "virtually uniformly" "do not experience pain" (Doctors, "The Symptom" [article] 444).

The universalizing necessary to psychoanalysis is evident in the way that the thesis moves from its five-person sample to a narrative point of view in which a specific form of self harm becomes typical not only of the phenomenon itself, but of a specific group: "young women."

> Succinctly now, a review of the literature reveals several areas of striking clarity. Firstly, it is overwhelmingly a phenomena [sic] of women. Secondly, many investigators have pointed to the importance of disturbances in early object relations and the sense of self, particularly early experiences of illness and injury in the life histories of such people. Thirdly, the act seems related to conflicts around the experience of the genitals and genital sensation in an important way—it doesn't occur before the menarche, it tends to occur around the time of menstruation, and seems to occur most often in women who are said to have problems around their feelings and attitudes towards their sexual selves. Fourthly, there seems to be a considerable uniformity to the description of the experience of the act, including some shift during the course of the act

which makes the act seem discontinuous rather than continuous in time [Doctors, "The Symptom" (PhD) 1].

The mode is used in a similar thesis by another writer who, like Doctors, practiced as a therapist:

> The episode may be triggered by a disappointing in or a separating from an important person in the young woman's life. (As the behavior becomes more entrenched in her personality, then the slightest mishap may trigger it.) She begins to experience a tension growing within her, often accompanied by diffuse feelings of anger, fear, and guilt, which increase in intensity and gradually and increasingly interfere with daily functioning. Over a period of time ranging from minutes to hours, a state of tension is reached that is intolerable. It is replaced by a dissociated state of consciousness described as feeling numb, empty, unreal, wooden, trancelike. At first this feels better than the excruciating tension, but soon it feels like a terrifying isolation from people and the real world. She goes where she can be alone, and in a seemingly controlled and planful [sic] fashion that may disguise the frenzied excitement she feels, she cuts, burns or bruises herself. The act usually requires a minimum of medical attention. It may be performed in front of a mirror, or is at least experienced as if she is watching herself in a mirror or on a film screen. With the sight of the wound or startling redness of the blood comes a sense of aliveness, or connection to reality, and a great sense of relief and well-being. The sight of the blood warms and blankets her in blissful satisfaction and comfort. She feels good, capable, and whole. Now she is ready to resume her usual daily activities at a level of functioning considerably greater than that which preceded the act [Farber 5].

Sharon Farber asks useful questions about whether treatment environments might facilitate self harm. But the difficulty or the danger with this mode of writing is that, no less than the criminological literature or the literature of general medicine, the search for a template, a model, or a profile (of the self-harming girl) presupposes specific values that are not medical but social (female dysfunction). There are structural tensions here between the specificity so many writers on self harm insist on, and the impulse to generalization which drives Freudian modelling.

The same is true of other psychological modes, such as Allan Tsai's 2002 essay which aims to develop a Jungian framework through which self harm can be explained. Characterizing self harm as cutting, cutting as female, and as a 1990s epidemic unique to the United States (albeit that the signature example of a person who self harms, offered in his introduction, is Princess Diana), Tsai sets out a "profile" and description of the processes of self harm in an argument which revives the ethnological notion of primitivism:

> Modern-day cutting seems to be primarily performed as a ritual, much like the myriad of self-mutilating practices in many ancient and primitive cultures. When inner urge reaches necessity, the individual seems to go on automatic.

Similar to other forms of addictive behavior, the person unconsciously enters a self-induced trance state before, during, and after the act [Tsai 86].

There is little or no evidence to support this generalization about "forms of addictive behavior" or "self-induced trance states," but the quasi-religious framework at once elevates and estranges the behavior.

While many contemporary discussions understand self harm as a recent phenomenon, in claiming that it is almost always restricted to young women—"Girls Who Cut," as one recent article puts it (Ruberman)—in doing so they echo those nineteenth- and early twentieth-century writers who in lieu of resorting to a model based on primitivism take the high road of common sense in urging the verbal equivalent of the cold shower as the most fitting and effective response to female hysteria and male malingering. This leaves some in the thrall of such obviously misogynist ideas as those developed in Abraham's "Manifestations of the Female Castration Complex," which run parallel to the criminological models which understand self harm as moral weakness and manipulation. Thus one writer in her book *Human Rights and the Search for Community*:

> Many early psychoanalytic theorists consider self-cutting to be a manifestation of the Female Castration Complex outlined by Abraham (1922). Radó (1933) refers to self-cutting as representing a symbolic castration in order to avoid real castration. Menninger (1935) stands as one of the most influential psychoanalytic thinkers on the subject. He viewed self-mutilation as a non-fatal demonstration of the death-wish, an attack on part of the body that substitutes for the whole.... Brenman (1952), following Mahler's work on the masochistic structure of the female personality, describes self-mutilation as one manifestation of a decompensating masochistic character. Phillips and Alkan (1961) emphasize the interpersonal adaptive aspects of self-cutting. These authors, along with Brenman (1952), Freeman (1958), were the first to emphasize that the symptom can be used as emotional blackmail by the mutilator and that it appears to bring about a certain reconstitution of ego functions [Howard 29–30].

Conclusions like these rest on the proliferation of theories of self harm grounded in psychoanalytic theories, particularly in the years just preceding and then coinciding with the rise of second-wave feminism in the late 1960s and 1970s.

While we are now familiar with the idea of the emergence of the teenager as a cultural category, one grounded in consumerism, there was little or no awareness among medical writers of constituting girls as a newly formed *medical* problem. Exemplifying this trend, Stuart S. Asch writes in 1971 of "a new clinical picture that is almost rigidly consistent," of "young girls" who "complain of feeling empty or dead" and "have a proclivity for scratching or cutting their wrists, sometimes repeatedly" ("Wrist Scratching" 603). Asch argues that the cutting in *girls* produces "a relaxed, comfortable, even pleasurable passive feeling" whereas "when wrist cutting occurs in boys ... the wound is always quite painful" ("Wrist Scratching" 612). This "gendering" of self harm leads Asch to speculate, later in this essay, that this form instates the girl as aggressor while the view of the "gaping, open wound" somehow re-forms menstruation "as a helplessly and passively experienced genital mutilation" (613). The sheer weight of this kind of thinking, which grounds the predilection to self harm in the female body just as surely as any nineteenth-century writer might, misleads even overtly feminist researchers like Marie Crowe, writing in 1995, to agree that self harm is "more likely" to be done by women than men (104).

In the context of the persistence of this thinking, Meredith Braden's "The Politics of Cutting: A Feminist Analysis of Self-mutilation and Self-mutilation Research" (2003) represents an important attempt to restore an awareness of misogyny to the debate about modern medical responses to self harm, in particular among those working within the fields of psychiatry and psychology. At the same time, historical evidence allows us to challenge the assumptions in the terms that empiricist and behaviorist psychological science might be more sympathetic to. In Mayer Fisch's 1954 essay on "The Suicidal Gesture," a study of 114 patients admitted to the U.S. Navy Hospital in Philadelphia, 50 patients (all of whom were male) cut themselves, most on the wrists. This is in contrast to the 6 of 47 patients who did commit suicide (34). Fisch is not especially sympathetic to patients, most of whom he sees as having "immature and distorted personalities" (35). Yet his findings about men who self harm do not inform those discussions like Harold Graff and Richard Mallin's 1967 essay "The Syndrome of the Wrist Cutter." Graff and Mallin establish the template for the "wrist-cutter" as "an attractive young woman, age 23, usually quite intelligent (74). They do not reference Fisch. Their assertions were contested by Myrna Weissman's 1975 essay on "Wrist-Cutting," but other authors confirmed their findings. Gardner and Gardner's "Self-Mutilation, Obsessionality and Narcissism" for example uses a sample of 22 young women and confirms that self harm is the domain of those who are "exceptionally particular about their appearance" (127).[28]

Ferenczi and His Followers

The person by whom Horney is most engaged, Sándor Ferenczi was born Sándor Fränkel to Polish parents. Although Ferenczi trained in Vienna, the bulk of his writing was published in Hungarian (Ernest Jones). Four volumes of essays have been translated into English, but are not widely available. Ferenczi's first book published in English, *Contributions to Psycho-analysis* (1916), offers an indication of his standing in the professional community at the time.

There are two later collections, *Further Contributions* (1950) and *Final Contributions* (1955). The last book by Ferenczi is the fragmentary but evocative collection of notes and comments that is *The Clinical Diary of Sándor Ferenczi* (1988). For the first decades of his career, Ferenczi was at the social and intellectual centre of psychoanalysis. In a photograph of the 1911 conference which attracted the leaders of the profession, a diminutive Ferenczi stands with his head barely reaching the shoulder height of Sigmund Freud, to whom he is literally "right-hand man." Freud towers over both Ferenczi and Carl Jung, who flank him in the middle of the photograph. Jung leans forward, hands resting on the back of the chairs of the ladies seated in front. Ferenczi smiles at the camera. We might say that both look comfortably ensconced, near but not at the centre.

It is Ferenczi whose work speaks most eloquently of and to debates about self harm, not least because of his sustained, reflective and reflexive concern with the scene of psychoanalysis itself, what we can call the institutional context of the therapeutic encounter. For what differentiates Ferenczi's work from that of Freud is his insistence on two things: the specific circumstances of treatment—that is, to some extent and in some ways he rejected the self-confident universalism of psychoanalysis—and commensurately, his desire to understand and to ameliorate or negotiate the authority which the treating doctor has over the patient. It would be too much, or perhaps anachronistic, to say that Ferenczi believed in a kind of patient empowerment. And we should not sentimentalize his opinions. But it *is* clear that he believed that the institutions of psychoanalysis should themselves be the subject of constant reflection. This was a belief that his colleagues were not merely troubled but antagonized by, as they were antagonized by his insistence that the childhood sexual trauma of which his patients spoke was not a fantasy. Ferenczi's concern with the patient's experience of analysis, his constant attention to questions of the power relationship between patient and doctor, and his determination to acknowledge the prevalence and impact of early childhood sexual trauma make him an appealing figure for anyone interested in the ways in which institutions shape forms of knowledge, a subject which lies at the centre of debates about how to respond to self harm. Like Janet, Ferenczi's reputation has undergone a kind of revival in recent decades.[29] But like Janet, and notwithstanding the work of scholars like Michael Balint and Judith Dupont in biography, editing and translation, his writing has been neglected in psychoanalysis generally, and is rarely noted by scholars of self harm.

The question of the "reality," and thence of the prevalence, of childhood sexual abuse has become a fervently debated topic, particularly in North America. But in the early twentieth century this debate was conducted *within* the profession of psychoanalysis. Ironically, just as Freud had been after the publication of his *The Aetiology of Hysteria* (1896), which concluded that the cause of trauma was "premature sexual experience" (see Hermann 12), Ferenczi was left isolated and debilitated after stating his belief that sexual abuse was widespread in the middle- and upper-class families whose children sought treatment from psychoanalysts—which is to say, that such abuse was not an aberration of the ill-educated and brutalized. In a paper read at the Eleventh International Psycho-Analytical Conference held in Oxford in 1929, Ferenczi confronted his colleagues about the "really improper, unintelligent, capricious, tactless or actually cruel treatment" to which children were subjected: "Hysterical fantasies do not lie when they tell us that parents and other adults do indeed go to monstrous lengths in the passionate eroticism of their relation with children" ("Principle of Relaxation" 121). While "ameliorating" his comments by claiming the hitherto unacknowledged force and precocity of child sexual self-expression, he nevertheless suggests that "the premature forcing of genital sensations has a no less terrifying effect on children," who "really want, even in their sexual life, ... simply play and tenderness, not the violent ebullition of passion" (121).

There was a further attack in a paper read at the International Psycho-Analytical Congress in 1932. In "Confusion of Tongues between Adults and Children," an essay which Freud had insisted he not publish (see Dupont xvi–xvii) but which is now his most cited work, Ferenczi expressed his belief in the prevalence of and damage caused by "the real rape of girls ... similar sexual acts of mature women with boys, and also enforced homosexual acts" which "are more frequent occurrences than has hitherto been assumed" (161–62).[30] He was making claims not taken up until the nineteen eighties, when Freud's turn to "fantasy" in framing his understandings of infant sexuality, sexual memory and sexual development became the focus of controversy (see Masson). Ferenczi outlines the physical and psychological response to abuses or trauma in a way that resonates with modern accounts of self harm.

> *The first reaction to a shock seems to be always a transitory psychosis*, i.e., a turning away from reality ... it seems likely that a *psychotic* splitting off of a part of the personality occurs under the influence of shock. The dissociated part, however, lives on hidden, ceaselessly endeavouring to make itself felt, without finding any symptom except in neurotic symptoms ["The Principle of Relaxation" 121; emphasis in original].[31]

In another piece of writing from the same year, a fragment titled "Traumatic Self-strangulation," Ferenczi elaborates on this view in describing the psychic reaction to assault:

> The person splits into a psychic being of pure knowledge that observes the events from the outside, and a totally insensitive body. Insofar as this psychic being is still accessible to emotions, it turns its interests toward the only

attacking feelings left over from the process, that is, the feelings of the attacker. It is as though the psyche, whose sole function is to reduce emotional tensions and avoid pain, at the moment of the death of its own person automatically diverts its pain-relieving functions toward the pains, tensions, and passions of the attacker, the only person with feelings, that is, identifies itself with these [104].

These passages resonate with hundreds of accounts, whether from the point of view of the identification of self harm as a response to sexual abuse (prominent in the psychological and psychiatric literature from the 1980s onwards) or from the point of view of the dozens of reports which identify *relief* (not physical pain) as the immediate reaction to the injury (even including self amputation).

There are several difficulties with this simple analogy, however, not least that very few studies explore the patient's own response to their self harm in detail (a point raised by Cwiartka 92). The second is that Ferenczi is describing forms of assault which the victim experiences as life-threatening. In his view, only these are sufficient to force the victim to give up the will to live as a form of empowerment and survival. The third is more complex. If Ferenczi is suggesting that there is a splitting which enables the living to experience their own body as an object—a claim buttressed by Kernberg's assertion that borderline personality disorder is characterized above all by "*an intensification and pathological fixation of splitting processes*" (666)—there is little in any study of self harm which suggests that those who commit radical acts of assault on their own bodies experience their actions this way. They tend to speak *either* of indifference, or relief—severe pain can often come, sometimes quite quickly, but few accounts seem to confirm Ferenczi's speculation that the person dissociates themselves entirely regarding their own body "with interest, as if it is no longer his own self but another person who is undergoing these torments" ("Thinking with the Body" 6; see also 9). Rather than seeing self harm as *symptomatic* of borderline personality disorder, then, it might be possible to see trauma as generating and intensifying a cyclical process of re-enactment and dissolution of threats to the body, the self harm a kind of inoculation in the sense that administering a smaller and above all a *controlled* dose of a toxic substance allows the self a modicum of control.[32]

On that basis, and notwithstanding the qualifications, there is perhaps something to be taken from Ferenczi's remarks which might offer insight into patients who use extreme and repetitive forms self harm. Here one can raise the possibility that Ferenczi is correct in discerning the adopting of the perspective of the torturer, but is wrong to conclude that this hinges on a "split" from the self, or at least a split of the kind he describes. It seems possible, in fact, that inflicting injury on one's own body might be a kind of controlled re-enactment of an initial traumatic harm—*experienced* as life-threatening—in which, by taking the role of the perpetrator, the patient is (heroically) attempting a *reintegration* of the self which the original attack has split.[33] This might offer a way to explain the constant claims that the act of self harm brings peace, the experience of feeling in control, as it would also offer a theory which would underpin those various contemporary arguments that self harm is a form of therapy, that it is a way of patients attempting to respond *positively* to their own psychic fragmentation. It would also explain why experiences as apparently different as physical abuse (beating), sexual abuse (rape), and hospitalization (particularly surgery), experienced as terrifying, suffocating, confusing,—and for a child, life threatening—might be responded to in the same way: through physical self harm.[34]

Ferenczi also suggests, or speculates, that a patient is able to withdraw to a state of "manic pleasure" ("Thinking with the Body" 6) through which the tortured self achieves not only safety, but a kind of retribution. "To the extent that the assailant's motive for the aggression is sadism, the victim achieves vengeance through this newly developed insensitivity, for the sadist cannot inflict any more pain on the dead, unfeeling body, and therefore he must feel his impotence" ("Thinking with the Body" 7). If Ferenczi is correct, then the implications are profound: self harm could be understood as a psychic means by which the sadist is overcome, for the insensitivity demonstrated by the body is a victory over the damage wrought by the attack on the body. But Ferenczi quickly points out that it is difficult to modulate this kind of coping mechanism, which can operate "after even the slightest of injuries (physical or psychical)": "one no longer reacts by utilizing the alloplastic means of the nervous and mental systems, but by autoplastic, hysterical transformation" ("Thinking with the Body" 7). This argument also offers a way of also examining, narratives about self harm among those with serious disability, as well as those incarcerated, whether in prisons, mental hospitals, or institutions for the intellectual and physically handicapped.

Ferenczi's later elaborations on the psychic structures and functioning of borderline personality disorder open up ways to interpret apparently different forms of self harm, and his ideas have been taken up by a small number of writers. Imre Hermann's "Clinging—Going-in-Search," although first published in early 1935, was not translated and published in English until 1976. The essay uses Ferenczi's argument that suffering of the most intense kind can mean choosing the lesser evil. Hermann suggests that inflicting injury on one's own body effects a separation "from someone who was formerly part of the ego. Now that he has become alien, he has turned into an evil stranger, he has to be severed from the ego" (31). These actions are a "primitive form of the healing tendency" (32). If the child learns to hate "the malicious things, forming an outer world, that do not obey his will" (Ferenczi, "Introjection" 48) then some forms of self harm might be understood as acts of violence committed against those "malicious things ... that do not obey his will" (projection). Part of what is at work here is again a kind of controlled re-enactment of the trauma, with particular emphasis being on control, and thence of severance.

Hermann's reading of the unconscious motivation for deliberate self injury also takes up that recurrent and recurrently "puzzling" element of self harm: pleasure. When carrying out the harm, pain is "an incentive to carry out the final separation" and,

> at the same time, it is a sign of that liberation which may ... make itself felt in a state that can only be described as narcissistic intoxication. As such, this liberation may enter consciousness as an emotion, in an eerily pleasurable feeling [sic]. Thus, in this group of phenomena, pain arises in connection with the *separation that is striven for*, while its *successful accomplishment* brings pleasure [Hermann 32; emphasis in original].

Pleasure and re-enactment are recurrent elements of case reports and longer studies, albeit ones which are usually ignored or labelled "inexplicable." Within the framework of his argument about the centrality of the need to cling in the development of the self, Hermann suggests that masochism is "regressive intensification of ... the separation conflict, together with a healing tendency" (34). As with Ferenczi's arguments, this view is similar to those of patient advocacy groups in the UK, in seeing self harm as a coping mechanism.

Citing the work of Ferenczi, and of Freud, Hermann suggests that "the ego's striving to experience the trauma—in this case, detachment, not traumatically imposed from outside, as was the case with that prototype of all separation, the detachment of the clinging child from the mother, but as a *self-intended*, self apportioned action by a free adult" (32; emphasis in translation). Here the role of the physician is especially important: "the mystical part played in the sexual phantasy of the child by the doctor, who knows all forbidden things, who may look at and touch everything that is concealed, is an obvious factor" (Ferenczi, "Introjection" 41). This work not merely prefigures but potentially enriches modern accounts which link self harm to sexual abuse, as it also opens out potentially different ways of conceiving doctor patient relations, the iatrogenic element of self harm, and its higher incidence among those with some kind of medical training.[35] In the instance of a patient hospitalized 68 times, who had also attended outpatient facilities 600 times, the patient's "professional knowledge" made the presentation "sophisticated, and also difficult to reveal" (Castor *et al.* 231). (This was not least because of the patient's understanding of the conventions of medical record-keeping.)

Otto Kernberg's 1967 discussion of the malfunctioning of the ego in borderline personality disorder, the condition most frequently associated with self harm, argues that the differentiation of self and object is unstable in this condition. In a detailed typology of borderline personality disorder, Kernberg identifies "rage" as the signature emotion associated with physical self harm (658). In his view, Ferenczi's remarks give us two quite different ways of understanding self injury, working from the premise that they are attempts to manage the unmanageable elements of (traumatic?) experience. In particular, the "projection of aggression" and externalizing of the "bad self" are "rather unsuccessful" (669):

> This leads such patients to feel that they can still identify themselves with the object onto whom aggression has been projected, and their ongoing "empathy" with the now threatening object maintains and increases the fear of their own projected aggression. *Therefore, they have to control the object in order to prevent it from attacking them under the influence of the (projected) aggressive impulses; they have to attack and control the object before (as they fear) they themselves are attacked and destroyed* [Kernberg 669; emphasis added].

In this formulation, the attack on the body is at once therapeutic, and preemptive.

Ferenczi's interest in the psychoanalytic process is pertinent to reading accounts of self harm. Early in his work he was careful to follow Freud in arguing that it is "we physicians who deserve ... ridicule" when mocking the exaggerations of the hysterical patient, "because failing to understand the symbolism of hysterical symptoms—the language of hysteria, so to speak—we have either looked upon these symptoms as implying simulation, or fancied we had settled them by the use of abstruse physiological terms" ("Introjection" 37). This is, of course, a justification of the premise of working *with* the patient's own narratives. But Ferenczi differs from Freud in suggesting that transference—the patient's refocusing of their neurosis onto the therapist—might not necessarily be harmful ("Introjection" 57). His argument is that the neurotic "helps himself by taking into the ego as large as possible a part of the outer world, making it the object of unconscious phantasies" ("Introjection" 47). Ferenczi locates this desire for introjection, the incorporation of elements of the outer world into the self, within the "neurotic *passion for transference,*" "the most fundamental peculiarity of the neuroses" ("Introjection" 45). The difficult task of the therapist must be to work with rather than against the transference.

Ferenczi derides the sterner approach that some colleagues insist on. Early in his career, he was prepared to be critical of what he describes as a prejudice reflecting the love of asceticism inherent in a religious view which seeks to ignore the influence of "'sexual hunger'" on "the mental life of the normal and pathological" ("Introjection" 57). But as he suggests in his last major contribution to psychoanalytic theorizing, the right balance between strictness and compassion is difficult to achieve. On the one hand, "exaggerated forms and quantities of tenderness may subserve one's own, possibly unconscious libidinal tendencies"; on the other, "Nothing is easier than to use the principle of frustration in one's relations with patients and children as a cloak for indulgence in one's own unconfessed sadistic inclinations" ("Confusion of Tongues" 124). If the term "sadism" seems over-stated, we can bear in mind Marc D. Feldman's "The Challenge of Self-Mutilation," a review essay published in *Comprehensive Psychiatry* in 1988, in which he claims that in treating patients who have cut themselves, "one may be able to suture the wounds without anaesthesia" because "Pain is often absent during the cutting" (255). Louise Pembroke, who quotes Feldman, replies: "**NO** one may not. I refute this. I have yet to meet someone who does not feel the pain of suturing" ([Pembroke], "Louise Roxanne Pembroke" 48; bold in original). Elsewhere she writes, "It is common to be stitched with no or inadequate anaesthesia, not having each layer of tissue properly stitched, being used as training material or having observers present without consent" ([Pembroke] Introduction 3).

Robert Firestone takes up the matter of the self-hatred that can be created by parental anger, and its replay in the therapeutic situation. He says of his own research findings that "we learned that the expressions of intense anger against the self that had been noted in our earlier studies were not isolated occurrences. It became quite apparent that most people hated themselves with an intensity that surpassed by far anything they consciously *thought* they felt" (25). His patients "call this hostility 'the voice'" (26); the therapeutic model Firestone has developed in response to these views entails engagement with that voice of the "perfect parent and the unloved child."

> As our subjects became more aware of their inconsistencies and ambivalent attitudes, they became uneasy about the intrusion of the voice into their everyday lives. They were disconcerted and frightened to learn how deeply divided they were. Most people are very resistant to experiencing internal conflict, and desperately attempt to maintain a sense of unity, albeit false. In an effort to achieve integration and appear more consistent in their behavior and attitudes, they frequently side with the alien point of view [Firestone 67].

Another therapist inspired by Ferenczi coped with a patient who "experienced efforts to contain her reaction" in the therapy sessions "as an annihilation and repetition of the most injurious actions" she had experienced as a child from brutal and capricious parents (Perlman 330). Perlman suggests that "the unempathic aspects of the child's original experience" can be re-enacted if "the therapist asks the patient to be open and honest yet is himself distant and ambiguous" (335). The instance of therapy he describes took traumatic forms:

> She had cut herself and brought in a letter written to me in her own blood. Often she flailed around my office, tearing at my furniture, throwing herself

against the wall, pulling her hair, threatening to kill herself and quit therapy, screaming at the top of her lungs, and fleeing my office. She sometimes smashed her head with such force against my wall that I was afraid of damage to her brain [333].

More generally, as Ann C. Grief observes, "there are certain features of the analytic setting which give rise to pain and which the patient is expected to endure for the sake of the treatment" (494). In particular, this is the re-enactment of, and thence the risk of failing in, the attempt to establish a plausible and effective balance of obedience and independence in the parent relationship (Greif 494–95). Such a process places considerable demands on the therapist, not least in determining the point at which it is possible and necessary to challenge the patient's self-destruction (Greif 500).

In this context we can also reconsider the aims and methods of recent research during which pain is inflicted on or frustration induced in patients who self harm, their responses compared with a control group whose members do not harm themselves. In an experiment approved by the Ethics Committee of the University of Heidelberg and reported on in 2012, medical practitioners cut patients who had been diagnosed with borderline personality disorder (see Reitz *et al.* 607). The "subjects" were exposed to a "stress induction," which was followed by receipt of an incision in the forearm to a depth of 5 to 7 millimeters. The cutting was done by a member of the research team. The experiment was designed to explore the hypothesis that "tissue damage may play a part in disturbed stress regulation in BPD" (Retiz *et al.* 605), or more simply, to determine whether cutting the skin relieves stress (606). In the experiment itself, stress was measured in "objective" ways (heart rate) and "subjective" ones ("aversive tension"), and the finding was that patients with borderline personality disorder had elevated "baseline as well as slower return to baseline" (Reitz *et al.* 613).

Another experiment worked with pin-pricks and with capsaicin, the "active" ingredient of the chilli (Magerl *et al.*), another by the measurement of willingness to experience physical pain or emotional distress after what are termed, in the paper's abstract, "emotion-induction conditions" (Gratz *et al.*). In the latter study, reported in 2011, pain was induced by iced water and pressure to a finger-tip, inflicted after the subjects had completed a frustrating task on a computer. The researchers conclude that tolerance to pain is greater when under distress (Gratz *et al.* 71). Zanarini *et al.*'s longitudinal study of patients diagnosed with borderline personality disorder identified a cluster of "risk factors" which increased the likelihood of self harm continuing for long periods. Is it possible that experiments like those described by Reitz *et al.* and Gratz *et al.* could solidify the patient's identification with their self harm, not least when causing damage to the body is given "credence" in the sense of being a procedural element of "scientific methodology"?

As with phenomena such as homosexuality, psychoanalysis has sought to shift the terms of discussion of self harm out of criminological frameworks and into medical ones, albeit in a period in which the philosophical distinctions between the "mental" and the "moral" were much less evident than in the present. But the effects of making this shift are double-edged. By medicalizing self harm (constructing an act of self harm as evidence of illness) one might apparently diminish attention to moral questions. But to a large extent these moral frameworks remain intact. Indeed, they continue to impinge on understandings of self harm. However, the medicalizing of self harm makes those values and their effect on theorizing and the exercise of professional judgment more difficult to see. But when, for example, they underpin the interpretations of symbols and the assumptions about the contours of gender roles in sexual activity, they become embedded in the conceptual architecture of specific forms of medical and scholarly practice. They are germane to the description of the illness (and therefore seem "scientific"), rather than augmenting or informing obviously derogatory descriptions of the patient.

The tone and arguments of these chapters have suggested that self harm is demanding of interpretation. By now it should be clear, however, that self harm takes multiple forms, occurs in a range of quite different circumstances, and can be understood in a competing array of ways. The overall effect of these chapters, then, has been to demonstrate that *self harm is many things*. But the idea of self harm as *a* thing—*an illness in and of itself*—is demanded by *DSM V*. And within the behaviorist logic of the *Manual*—it describes behavior, it does not prescribe treatment—the establishing of such a template is meaningful in being potentially restrictive. The difficulty comes when, having learned of this description, readers presume that there is a template, a single illness, perhaps a single personality inclined to self harm and a single way of understanding that person.

Reflections:
Reading Self Harm

[T]he naïvety of our positivism believed that it could recognise the nature of all madness.—Foucault, *History of Madness* 122

But what form of knowledge, after all, is sufficiently singular, esoteric or regional to be given only at a single point, in a unique formulation? What learning could be so well—or so badly—understood to be known only in a single time, in a uniform manner, in a single mode of apprehension? What figure of science, however coherent or tight it might be, does not allow more or less obscure forms of practical, moral or mythological consciousness to gravitate around it?—Foucault, *History of Madness* 163

This conclusion aims to set out some key issues for conceptualizing self harm, in the light of the diversity of forms identified so far. It begins by reflecting on Foucault's claim that changes in ways of thinking reflect "a syntactical reorganisation of disease in which the limits of the visible and invisible follow a new pattern" (*Birth of the Clinic* 195, qtd. in Sheridan 39). To put this more simply, if we think of culture operating in terms of a kind of "grammar" (in which certain forms seem correct and others do not; certain forms seem persuasive and others do not), changes in social structure and value bring specific forms of illness into view whilst others fade.

Many social, economic and intellectual changes over the last five decades have affected the contours of self harm. These include the explosion of identity politics from the mid 1960s (Ferber, *Bioethics* 22), the commensurate foregrounding of the validity of personal experience, and the competitive splintering of medical specialisms. These have turned up the volume on the voices of patients, as they have turned up the volume and enlarged the scale of academic debate. Thus the number of arenas in which self harm is encountered and discussed have multiplied, and the work of advocates of non-medical interpretations of self harm have been heard in the scholarly biosphere. The new methods of the humanities and social sciences have encouraged academics in these fields to interrogate and often to recuperate practices once dismissed as different or even repulsive. To follow Foucault, what has become "visible" since the late nineteen eighties are the reparative possibilities of self harm. This approach, driven in part but not exclusively by feminism, has also entailed a revivification of ecstatic, collective, "spiritual" models of self harm associated with paganism, specifically the Galli and the cult of Cybele, and forms of self-punishment identified with Christianity, notably the re-enacting of crucifixion.

The increasing influence of this set of responses to self harm has entailed precisely that "transgression and transformation" (Sheridan 39) of institutional knowledge Foucault associates with the development and consolidation of new disciplinary and professional paradigms. Yet as Foucault's work is at such pains to demonstrate, the residues of apparently "older" or "foreign" or otherwise displaced or discredited forms of knowledge persist, whether in institutional pockets (such as specific hospitals, training institutions or bureaucracies), regions, or even entire disciplines. Thus in criminological and some medical models of self harm, or in formulations of the self which presume a congruity between a Kantian will and the responsibilities of the self, there are few signs of the critical, even celebratory, view of self harm evident in writing associated with artistic, sociological, or religious contexts. Yet taken collectively, the evidence is that those who attempt to identify patterns in the cause, nature or consequences of self harm are constantly frustrated by the complexity, the intractability, the volatility and the specificity of individual cases, and by the vast range of contexts in which self harm occurs.

In each of chapters one to four, a discipline or disciplines, a set of paradigms for self harm, and a set of scholarly genres are associated. It has been shown (in chapter two) that the case study works within the frameworks of "modern medicine" in being "particularly attuned to the individual, the abnormal event" (Sheridan 39). The criminal and military literature discussed in chapter three reflects an older model dedicated to classification: diseases, like species, "were organised and hierarchized into so many families, genera and species; their semi-autonomous existences seemed to have more to do with each other than with the body that gave them temporary shelter" (Sheridan 39). In both instances, the *genre* is structured to facilitate the application of the conceptual system: just as the monograph or thesis outlines a classificatory system for forms of self harm encountered in military and criminal contexts, so the case report identifies the new element that the reporting doctor, by virtue of observation and investigation, has been able to identify. Psychoanalytic literature, often in the form of the long article or essay collection, attempts to find a meeting point between the universality of theory and the specific psychopathology of the individual.

Reading these literatures of self harm together shows that no single perspective or approach can plausibly "explain" the phenomenon across divergent populations and instances, a point evident for at least the last quarter of a century (see Favazza, "Why"). Notwithstanding two centuries of scholarship in which the assumptions and aims of a series of writers have been to provide a "complete" picture, a workable typology for use in the education of medical professionals and treatment of patients, self harm is a phenomenon so complex and diverse that to speak of it as a single thing is inevitably and (perhaps dangerously) to simplify. There is almost no claim about self harm or those who injure themselves that cannot be contradicted by evidence from a different kind of example. Following a number of early writers (notably Dabrowski), therefore, I will argue that this variety of forms and instances, as well as the range of cultural and historical contexts in which radical physical self harm occurs, make the analytical power of typology severely limited, and the development of predictive machinery impossible. The same can be said of *responses* to self harm. While almost every contribution to the field can be read, at the same time, as a contribution to the debates within and between various areas of specialization about who has the most effective diagnostic and therapeutic tools, self harm confounds the easy positioning of participants on the basis of areas of specialization. No discipline (say, psychiatry, psychology or criminology), historical period, culture (say, American or German), theoretical stance (say, behaviorism or Freudianism) or medical field (nurse, doctor, surgeon, dermatologist, psychiatrist) is sufficient in itself to guide us in predicting how a professional will respond to self harm. Other factors kick in, notably, emotional and moral reaction.

By examining the ways in which self harm has been written about, we can call into question many of the assumptions that underpin much contemporary scholarship, understandings which have seeped into popular representations and into policy, as they have seeped into the ways of talking used by those who harm themselves, whether as "authorized" modes of speech or as beliefs to be disputed. Among these assumptions are that self harm can be categorized into different and discrete forms; that it can be understood conceptually as occurring on a "spectrum" from mild to severe; that it can (or cannot) be linked to suicidal behavior; that it is an effect of sexual abuse; that it can be identified with discrete populations; that it can be understood as a distinctively "contemporary" condition; that this modern "epidemic" (and thence the contemporary world) is historically unique; and that physical self harm in general and specific forms such as cutting the wrists are behaviors distinctive to women.[1] Above all, the analysis presented above has shown the limits of generalization and, commensurately, the fraught nature of attempting to develop predictive instruments that will allow the effective prevention and management of those who self harm. Likewise, attempts to categorize *acts* of self harm, whether by motive, by level of seriousness, or by part of the body that is attacked, seem unlikely to provide help to institutional managers or medical practitioners.

Whereas taxonomy and prediction are the least successfully realized aims of much of the literature of self harm, the few extended accounts of individual patients who have harmed themselves are often works of profound and arresting insight. Among the best of these is Susan Scheftel's doctoral dissertation "All the King's Horses and All the King's Men: A Case of Radical Self-Mutilation and Its Effects on an Entire Hospital" from 1985.[2] The Scheftel example is formidable because the thesis tracks the attempts of members of an entire hospital community to forge a *new* story, to "make sense" of events beyond the narrative and conceptual range of even the most experienced and wise. In doing so, the thesis itself forms a new kind of knowledge about self harm. As Scheftel claims (2) and demonstrates, a single case, particularly when considered in terms of the way it impacts upon those who respond to it, can be the basis of useful and original knowledge. Also useful are accounts which limit themselves to small numbers of subjects and take account of those patients' views of their situation (e.g. Machoian, among others). The implication is that certain narrative forms (particularly brief accounts, notably case reports), certain modes of knowledge (especially, behaviorist psychology, criminology, and some forms of psychiatry), certain institutional contexts (notably non-consensual ones: prison, the military and some medical institutions), and even certain forms of research and reporting, make some findings difficult either to produce or to validate.

The Impact of Self Harm

Patients and stories about them can have widely differing effects, but self harm is a powerful emotional trigger point within medical institutions. Selma Fraiberg's study of "Pathological Defenses in Infancy" refers several times to the difficulties for researchers of confronting their material: video recordings of children neglected or abused by their carers, usually their mothers, material she terms "painful to watch," "painful to read or hear" (615). Of one instance in which the treatment was not successful, she notes the ways in which aggression was turned onto the self:

> At age two and one half Betty would tear at her toenails until they bled, then regard the bloody fragments with detached interest. There was no sign she experienced pain. The simile that accompanied hostile intention at the age of sixteen months was now imbedded as a personality trait. The disorganization of personality at sixteen months took on more ominous forms at three years of age. Betty, in a play session which was recorded on videotape, represented a mother in whom the hallucinations of her own mother [who had schizophrenia] had found their way. As the voice of the persecuted and the voices of the persecutors spoke in this chilling dialogue with dolls, it was no longer possible for the observers to know when the voices spoke for the mother and when the voices spoke for the child [633–34].

Unnerved by the observations, Fraiberg, in a paper published posthumously, does not offer any further commentary on this horrific scene: a three-year-old whose "management" of her object relations sees her schooled in self harm, her own body the site of her physical aggression. The dolls with which she "replays" her relationship with her mother show the extraordinary capacity for the use of substitution (metaphor); the self harm, as Fraiberg terms it, a "simile" now "embedded as a personality trait."

There is a strong tendency in many Western cultures to be disbelieving of horror—in particular, the horrors encountered in the domestic environment (something graphically described by Bryk and Segal). Reconfigured by processes of condensation and displacement, perhaps some traumas become literally unreadable, including by the sufferer themselves, and by those trained to diagnose and to respond to them. In his discussion of this problem in *Psychosis and Power*, James M. Glass reminds us of Freud's claim that delusion is never free-floating, never plucked clean from another place. On the contrary, it "'owes its convincing power to the element of historical truth which it inserts in place of the rejected reality.'"[3] One of the more frightening consequences is that those who are mentally fragile might be particularly vulnerable not to stories per se, but to the terror of stories of destruction and self-destruction. For example,

> An epidemic of suicides by burning was reported by Ashton and Donnan during a 1-year period from 1978 to 1979, after a well-publicized self-immolation by a member of a political group. Evaluation of the 82 deaths by burning in this series found significant psychiatric histories in the majority of cases [Daniels *et al.* 144].[4]

The example demonstrates the capacity to adapt and to adopt the story of a horrific death into one's own life story. Quite what the relationship between the literal "articulation"—in the double sense of speaking, and of joining—of another's suffering to one's own is not yet well understood. Yet self harm also seems to generate the desire to speak among those who encounter it.

One survey of nurses and "mental health technicians" found that after encountering a patient who had injured him or herself deliberately, 81 percent always or frequently "talked to someone to find out more"; no respondent answered that they "never" talked about their encounter (Madden 56). Another researcher, 20 years later, found that only 25 percent (of 55) respondents said that they had received information about self harm from their course; 45 percent had developed such knowledge from their internship placement, and a rather high 69 percent said that they had learned about self harm from previous work or personal experience (Whitney 32). Although just one small sample, the finding leaves open the question of whether responses to patients who self harm are generated more through social networks and perhaps even the popular media than through formal education. Whitney's posing of this question is prefigured by Neil Kessel's 1966 essay "The Respectability of Self-Poisoning and the Fashion of Survival." Kessel notes that doctors are resistant to the view that medical fact can also be "common knowledge" (30)— in this case, that members of the public have the capacity to calculate non-lethal dosages of drugs. It is on this basis that he comes to the challenging conclusion that "Doctors are the designers of the fashion of self-poisoning" (34). It is not clear how much, if any, time is given in medical education to reflection on the emotional impact of these patients on those encountering them, and Kessel does not explore why it is that doctors might be resistant to his challenge of the overuse of "attempted suicide." Medical work can be exciting, dangerous, emotionally challenging, intellectually complex; where is the space for reflection on how to manage the emotions generated by patients whose motives or situations are complex and perhaps "untreatable" in the conventional sense?

Perhaps the frankest and among the more insightful on this subject is Scheftel, who admits of her response to her chosen subject, "I initially felt (and indulged) a temptation to bring up the topic of Mr. G in inappropriate social contexts, thereby making myself 'the life of the party'" (98). She was by no means alone: "Two of Mr. G's nurses riding a train together described how they riveted ... two complete strangers sitting opposite them by discussing Mr. G"; "I recently heard from an acquaintance that a mutual friend had kept an entire group transfixed over dinner in a restaurant" (Scheftel 98). The impulsive power of the story of self harm—giving magnetic authority to a hospital staff member among friends and strangers alike—signifies the allure. Whether the "inexplicable" character of the act is the key to the effect of these stories is not clear. Scheftel's persuasive suggestion is that the conversations, like the initial self harm, constitute a double motion of re-enactment and catharsis, attempts "to master and rework a traumatic encounter," the stories themselves constituting for that patient "another form of oral sadism" (111). Such findings are crucial, given Haughton's view that negative responses "tend to generate further self-mutilation in the more typical cutter" while skepticism leaves those whose self-damage is on the edge of lethality at much greater risk (8).

Here, the foregrounding of the "common sense" response to self harm—bewilderment and revulsion—is crucial. In many cultures we are trained to understand that threats, including threats to physical and mental health, come from "external" sources, while physical wounds and illness are regarded as matters of misfortune. There is strong reinforcement for the view that illness is a kind of intruder, an alien, best dealt with by structures that do not yield to the needs or demands of the individual. In this context, it is not hard to understand why faith in strictly defined procedures should harden when dealing with those who inflict injury on themselves. And if we note the pressure in so many institutions to develop transparent and replicable decision-making processes with provable levels of outcome, it is clear that not only nurses and doctors but teachers, prison warders, counselors and military personnel might be strongly encouraged to make and apply rules without regard to circumstances. Here, it is particularly important to note that self harm is frequently seen as something that patients themselves have some control over, even to be an expression of free will. Ironically, this view finds some support in the writing of patients' rights groups, body modification scholars and practitioners, and internet advocacy groups. But when there is a sense that patients themselves have induced or facilitated the onset of illness or injury, negative reaction is subtly sanctioned.

Leslie Young argues that "the essence of trauma is 'a threat to or a violation of body boundaries of oneself, one's family or one's community'" (qtd. in Tuttle 82). In this definition, which as Tuttle notes is an "organic" one, the integrity, the wholeness of the body and the safety provided by that wholeness are seen as foundational to wellbeing. Underpinning this view is the belief, prevalent within Western society, that the body and mind are discrete units, making each individual responsible for their own behavior, just as each individual can be separated from another in legal, medical, educational and other contexts. However, there are also arguments which see health and illness in terms not just of the individual but of the community. In an intriguing set of monographs James M. Glass, a political philosopher at the University of Maryland, has developed a set of arguments about the politics of madness which implicitly challenge the Western sense of the individual as an entity, and as solely responsible for their health. Drawing on theories of the relationship of the individual to the polity, notably the work of Aristotle (*The Politics*) and Rousseau (*The Social Contract*), Glass makes two sets of observations. Broadly, these are that those who suffer from delusion have much to teach us about the operation of "terror" in public life, second, that one of the more productive ways to respond to delusion is to think communally.

In his book *Private Terror/Public Life* Glass outlines the workings of Spring Lake Ranch, dedicated to the restoration of mental health through the operation of community. In the course of paraphrasing the views of staff at Spring Lake, Glass argues that those who work within conventional medical contexts "need [patient passivity] to confirm their own reality," particularly the value of their professional training and work (162). Commensurately, "In the hospital, sickness ties the institution's power system together, gives it identity and definition" (164), demanding of patients that they identify "with sickness rather than health" (161). In Glass's view, "the patient becomes victim-prisoner ... and projects onto professionals the qualities of superiority, intelligence, wisdom, ... benevolence and the power to banish pain" (161). Whilst bound to the institution in their search for wellness, the patient must struggle against being positioned as a person *unable* to effect their own recovery. This is a far more complicated model of patient and "treatment" than is customary in medical literature, which positions the provision of wellness as a fairly uncomplicated transaction driven by medical expertise.[5]

While often represented as a private act (contradicting stereotypes and condemnation about attention-seeking), some writers also suggest that self harm is in some ways a dialogical act, even if the interlocutor is *within*. Stuart S. Asch argues that "the *main* object relationship" in each of depression, narcissism and masochism is "with the internal object," during which the self is

> playing to an unseen, internal audience—an audience that is experienced as personification of the psychic structures derived from their early objects. These are objects from which they have never fully separated and that retain their importance *despite* the progression of the individual psychic development and despite the later appearance of new, objectively more valuable, objects ["Depression" 36; emphasis in original].

Asch argues that "careful listening usually reveals that the patient is reacting as if an internal structure is looking on approvingly, as if these constructs of psychic structures are personified and actually exist" ("Depression" 37). Perhaps significantly, he links this behavior to religious influence, suggesting that austere expressions of disapproval, for example, are "a caricature of the Protestant ethic: the praiseworthy goal has become one that demands deprivation and work foremost, with pleasure in the real world coming only secondarily, if at all" (38). Although insisting (as other writers have) that masochism is a complex formation, not a single or singular force (39), Asch also asserts that "Pain or the denial of pleasure, as a form of increasing self-esteem through control and asceticism, is ... secondary to the struggle. *The main aim is to be loved for the suffering*" (39; emphasis added). The account resonates with those in which the child goes to extraordinary lengths to impress and ingratiate themselves with parents or siblings, culminating in acute self harm (see Brenman), but also offers a way to begin thinking about the relationship between spectacle, religiosity, and self harm.

Arguments like these are by no means uncontroversial, but they are a prompt to reflection. There is not much new in the observation that the patient's "performance of illness" ideally incorporates a performance of "the desire to become well," and that this in turn, along with qualities like cheerfulness, obedience and stoicism, make "the good patient" who is likely to receive optimal care. Conversely, the patient who has palpably injured themselves—or *might* have injured themselves—has broken the medical contract. More subtly, they have asserted themselves in relation to their physical health. Concomitantly, we could expect that narratives about patients who have committed acts of self harm disrupt that "institution's power system," unsettle its sense of what is normative, and confound those assumptions which give institutions and those who work within them what Glass calls "identity and definition"—purpose and meaning. If self harm *is* perceived as being in any degree or in any way "voluntary," an act of will or choice (as most hostile responses conventionally have it), or even if it is the product or effect of precariously balanced conscious and unconscious forces, then the most efficacious "treatment" should be attempting to empower the patient, not diminish them by asserting the authority of an individual or institution who can effect a halt to the practice.

There is also the question of whether the terminology and identity adopted by some who self harm are in some sense iatrogenic. Writing in 1967, Loren H. Crabtree argues that

> The self-mutilating patient is quickly singled out by other patients, hospital personnel, and psychotherapists and is assigned the label of "slasher," "cutter," or "mutilator." Similarly, to the patient himself, the concept of *being* a "slasher," a "cutter," a "mutilator," is an important and all-pervasive aspect of his identity [91].

Podvoll, writing around the same time, similarly asserts,

> Within a hospital setting, self-mutilating patients rapidly assume an "identity" which is equated with their symptomatic acts. They become known *to both patients and staff* as "cutters," "slashers," "slicers" and "scratchers"—labels which confine the patient to the level of his symptom, yet confirm for him a distinctive and functional role in the hospital [213; emphasis added].

More specific is the possibility that the authority of the terminology of self harm is in part created and maintained by the professional cultures in which individuals who self harm are encountered. For example, Shelley Doctors echoes Podvoll in reporting that "Clinicians working in mental hospitals have seen these patients and have developed the slang terms 'scratchers,' 'slicers,' 'cutters,' or 'slashers' to refer to them" (9–10). Paul Alexander Haughton, whose

1988 thesis was completed in the American northeast, and written from the position of a researcher and medical professional, writes candidly of prison environments that

> Incidents of self-mutilation are often the first behaviors noted in a nursing report or when a patient is presented to staff. From that point on the patient carries the nickname of "cutter." With this nickname comes a series of stated or unstated assumptions which are usually to some extent supported by the patients [sic] behavior. It will be assumed by the staff that the patient is going to be manipulative, will be needy, will demand a great deal of attention, will split staff into good and bad groups, and will continue to cut at times during periods of frustration. The act itself will be seen as more manipulative than suicidal, viewed as a way of seeking attention or transferring certain feelings onto the staff [2].

What these writers suggest is that the term "cutter" is as much in circulation in medical cultures as in communities of those who self-harm. In the years before the net, and before patient activism, it was less likely that patients were able to share information in sufficient numbers or with sufficient authority to spread this term into the medical literature and into general parlance. The colloquial term may even have been generated within the medical professions, helping to give those who engage in self harm an identity that has a coherence and legibility, even beyond hospital settings, it might otherwise not have had. In respect of the relationship between contagion and medical authority, we might then ask whether some forms of research, such as studies which ask subjects to develop "an imaged self-mutilative act" (Haines *et al.*), potentially induce self harm.

While there are dangers in asserting that physical self harm is "often ... a contagious response to an institutional environment" (Greig 13; see also Scheftel 44), Greig's subsequent references give statistics for self harm which suggest it is no higher there than in the general population.[6] Scheftel suggests that what she identifies as intra-institutional contagion "seems to be related to the intensity of counter-transference reactions elicited in staff members" (44, for which she cites Offer and Barglow, who reflect on contagion and the effect of self harm on hospital staff). Suggestion or contagion plays a part not only in military and criminal contexts (where it is well documented) but also in "private" instances of self harm, where (in particular) religious injunctions and spiritual experience are seen as playing a primary role. We might speak, here, of a kind of narrative contagion, or contagion by narrative: the proliferation of stories which through their form (in particular, their provision of motives, of character roles, of endings) seduce not only those who carry out self harm but those who respond to it. For just as there is a narrative contagion in relation to the treatment of self harm, so too (as Chandler *et al.* argue, using different terminology), is there an observable narrative contagion in *research* about self harm, in which specific kinds of characters, identities and even research questions become conventional and therefore authoritative. More original, more challenging studies occasionally rise from the flat surface of convention, but something like an intellectual meniscus seems to pull the surface back into its conventional shape. It is not surprising, then, that some of the most valuable work comes not from research by established academics—which, while always needing to promote originality must also work within strict narrative and conceptual conventions to be accepted *as* research—but by graduate students, often with direct experience of self harm, with sufficient intellectual courage to present their own, dissident, findings.

However, the use of fixed categories and procedures for responses to self harm, constantly sought by some kinds of researchers and by institutions like prisons or schools, simplifies decision-making. For example, "borderline personality" is a now common diagnosis which is used to characterize those who injure themselves. The proliferation of a particular diagnostic term such as "borderline" means that if patients are described as having certain personal failings, such as being "difficult," then it is possible that those who encounter them will presume the patient *is* "borderline," regardless of the diagnosis. There is a certain tautology here: if one self harms then one is likely to be thought to be suffering from "borderline personality disorder"; if one is thought to be suffering from "borderline personality disorder" there is an expectation of self harm, but each of these two things can become not merely categories but subtle inducements. Considering this effect of labelling, one Australian nursing educator noted Rosenhan's study from the 1970s which embedded "sane" patients into psychiatric hospitals across the United States. The "patients" took between 17 and 52 days to convince doctors that they should be discharged. "The pseudo-patients were recognized as such *by real patients*, but apparently not by nurses and doctors" (Horsfall 426). Such a finding suggests that structures which seem to provide professional certainty can come to seem not reassuring at all, but arbitrary.

Jerome L. Kroll's 1978 essay "Self-Destructive Behavior on an Inpatient Ward" is a rare example of a study of the effects of hospital atmosphere on patients, noting two earlier studies of the same mental hospital which found "organizational instability and lowered staff morale" coinciding with "a sharp increase in patient suicides" (430). Kroll studied a women-only psychiatric ward for 18 months, finding that the number of incidents of self harm first nearly doubled, and then dropped from 41 to 12, as the atmosphere (controlled to a large degree by resident physicians) changed (433). Commenting on "atmosphere," Marie Crowe notes, "Nurses often feel frustrated and disappointed that their interventions have been thwarted, interpreting cutting behaviours as deterioration or lack of improvement" (109). She cites D.G. Barstow's

1995 essay "Self-injury and Self-mutilation: Nursing Approaches" which describes "Disparaging or hostile comments, painful restraints, suturing without anaesthesia, rough handling of the injured part, deliberate delay in treatment and withholding pain medication [as] frequently employed covert ways of 'punishing the client'" (qtd. in Crowe 109).

The trauma caused to those who witness self harm and its aftermath runs through some two hundred years of writing. A fascination with self harm is evident in much of this work. The person who tells the story often confounds assumptions about the lack of coherence, composure or rationalization for their actions: in fact, it can be the person who has injured themselves who has the more complete and more convincing account of their actions. The customary shapes of medical narratives are often confounded by self harm—not only does the patient sometimes "compete" with the professional for authority, so too do medical professionals compete for ownership of or distance from the patient. Often logistics shapes responses: as a simple example, self harm in institutions is often encountered first by staff tasked with the oversight of incarceration—prison guards. These contexts, like emergency wards, are not conducive to careful investigation or long-running treatments of the patient who has injured themselves deliberately.

While the aim of developing predictive measures reflects chronic defensiveness in the administration of hospitals, prisons, and the military, it also meets a need within most forms of academic inquiry, particularly social and medical sciences, in which empirical methods vie to seem just that—scientific. Indeed, formal hierarchies of evidence, for example, for research grant applications, put the case study at the bottom and the synoptic survey at the top, thereby prioritizing homogeneity and synthesis over depth and complication (e.g. NHMRC). This need for prediction shapes early psychiatry and even early psychoanalysis in distinctive ways. Only rarely is such pressure acknowledged, but Bernard Hart, author of a primer of psychoanalysis widely read before, during and after the First World War, argues that just like astronomy and physics, psychiatry is grounded in belief in "the method of science," a method which "must explain the facts which we actually find, and it must enable us to predict the occurrence of future facts" (16). The messiness of psychological processes and the fact that "causal" factors do not lead human beings with similar backgrounds to respond in the same way have necessitated the development of the notion of "predisposition." But while there are literally hundreds of theses and studies which, on the basis of beliefs similar to those outlined by Hart in 1916, set out to develop instruments for the prediction of self harm, not a single one manages to do so. Just as it is not useful to think of self harm as a single phenomenon, commensurately, it is not especially productive to use methods of inquiry which presume that it is.

In following this foundational behaviorist goal, researchers continue to ignore the work of writers like Kuehn, Offer and Barglow, Oscroft, Podvoll, and Scheftel, who encourage or even demand reflection on the ways in which medical approaches to knowledge might structure unhelpful forms of interaction with patients. This argument is being taken up by nurses, but not by other sections of the medical professions (Clarke and Whittaker; French; Madden). The demand for prediction reflects the desires of large institutions, whose leaders are keen to know who is likely to injure themselves, as well as the premises of positivist inquiry which claims to observe the world as it is. In some instances, a kind of statistical hysteria envelops the reporting of the research, as endless refinements of category and causality produce less and less effective results. More sophisticated researchers reflect on the imperative itself. For example, two scholars were approached by the administrators of a prison "to develop a screening tool which could be used to identify, at the time of intake, inmates who would present self-destructive behavior while remanded" to enable prison authorities to distinguish between "genuine" attempts at suicide and "manipulative" forms of self harm that could be dismissed as "attention-seeking" (Holley and Arboleda-Florez 167).[7] The differentiation presumes not only that motive can be discerned by lay people (guards), but that such discernment offers an adequate indication of the likely outcome (i.e. that no serious injury would be inflicted by anyone not "really" intent on taking their own life). These researchers however seem to have subverted their brief—indeed, in their last sentence they conclude that "punitive responses to these inmates may increase the likelihood that more serious and dramatic self-destructive behaviors will ensue" (177).

Behaviorism

As has been hinted at in the discussion so far, the dominant paradigm through which self harm has been responded to in North America over the last fifty years is behaviorism, a set of psychological beliefs associated with the work of B.F. Skinner, which sets the prediction and control of behavior as a major goal of research.[8] Such modes are almost *de rigeur* in reporting patients whose self harm is understood as an (inevitable) expression of an organic disease, notably Lesch-Nyhan disease and Cornelia de Lange syndrome. The perceptual framework used to diagnose and treat the patient—which is essentially mechanistic—does not allow for the consideration of the patient's background, nor does it permit more complex emotional elements of causes of self harm to be factored in.

Studies of individual or groups of patients with these conditions usually ignore other factors known to be associated with self harm—for example, sexual abuse, or incarceration, or serious medical interventions in early childhood.[9] Instead, for followers of Skinner, self harm is "a major behavioral disorder" albeit one that "terrorizes both the afflicted individual and observers who are alarmed and helpless" (Bruhl *et al.* 191). The existence of repetitive forms of self harm among animals is taken as sufficient evidence of the validity of Skinner's assertion that self harm is a form of gratification, or a way of ensuring that less desirable "stimuli" are avoided (Skinner paraphrased in Bruhl *et al.* 193). As this example reveals, what underpins behaviorism is a strong belief in the literal and the logical, the tight packaging of cause and effect. Behaviorists necessarily reject Freudian notions of displacement and condensation; they reject the claim that the ways in which the self understands its experiences and expresses its desires can be metaphorical. The authors of one recent article, members of an ophthalmology unit, are blunt on the whole idea of symbolism: "Forget Freud and Oedipus: It's all about Untreated Psychosis" (Large and Nelson). They echo writers like Fras and Coughlin, who in 1971 (citing eight other studies) assert bluntly that in instances of feigned illness "The achievement of insight should not be the goal of treatment" (117).

Another instance of this tendency is shown by William H. Goeckerman, writing in 1930 when Freud was still alive, who explicitly rejects the need for "a freudian [sic] type of psychoanalysis" (645). He speculates, "The ordinary emotions such as anger, fear, worry, and ambition when dominating mental life for a considerable period are probably sufficient to produce gross anatomic changes" (645). Going on to describe a patient who did not respond to "the normal treatment" of "roentgen ray [X-ray], arsenic, and mercury" (646), Goeckerman expounds a theory of the relationship between body and mind which radically simplifies their interaction:

> It is an accepted fact that the emotions transmit their somatic and visceral impulses by way of the autonomic nervous system. The close functional relationship of this system with the endocrine organs will permit the visualization of organic changes in tissue as the result of emotional impulses. The significance of the emotions as factors in producing disease conditions is further emphasized by the fact that they have many of the characteristics of reflexes and are, therefore, not entirely under conscious control [648].

Goeckerman acknowledges that there might be a relationship between the emotions and organic disease, and the attentive physician will factor an understanding of this relationship into treatment, but suggests consideration of the unconscious is a kind of perversion or unnecessarily elaborate complicating of a relatively simple organic process.

Such approaches, which sideline the psyche, mean that much of the literature of self harm, particularly the archive constituted by case reports, under-reports or simply ignores key elements of "cause," including those related to trauma. Yet there seems little reason to assume that patients with serious developmental illnesses have *not* had experiences which are associated with the emergence of self-harming behavior. These might include, for example, sexual abuse, incarceration, the application of strict physical restraints, and/or exposure to invasive or life-threatening medical procedures. Indeed, the latter three would seem likely to coincide with institutionalization. We might also conjecture that the more limited psychic resources available to this group (Grossman 46) might mean that other forms of trauma compound the problem. Even one study of prisoners (a group who had been removed to a unit for those who was violent towards others) found that the subgroup of those who harmed themselves was far more likely than others to have witnessed violence and themselves to have been injured during childhood, although these researchers then posit the consequences to be "a genetic or a developmental defect" (Bach-y-Rita and Veno 1016). They go on to suggest that the "environmental deprivation" has parallels in studies of monkeys (1017; see Tinklepaugh), implying a stimulus-response model or, to be more precise, a lack of stimulus and compensatory response. But in terms of the consideration of environment, even Bruhl and colleagues note Green's claim that "self-injurious behavior" (SIB) might "occur as a 'response to a reduction of environmental stimulation associated with institutionalization and isolation'" (194).[10]

These authors offer accounts of individuals which suggest that this hypothesis might be plausible. A couple of pages after noting Green's comment, they describe an 18-year-old woman who had been admitted to formal care at the age of six "for being extremely hyperactive and noisy, and in the habit of pulling her hair and eating it":

> At the age of 18, she was still very disturbed day and night and did not tolerate any garment on her upper torso. She ripped them to pieces and responded with fierce SIB when unable to tear them off. Medication with various tranquilizers over extended periods and three different programs of behavior modification had been tried without success. Because of persistent skin lacerations and ecchymoses of both eye regions, electric skin shock (ESS) treatment with a specially designed jacket was proposed. While this proposal was under consideration, the resident was transferred to another dormitory ... with the surprising result that her tearing of garments and SIB disappeared within a few weeks without any special steps being taken. No satisfactory explanation could be found [Bruhl *et al.* 196–97].

One could argue that the "stimulus-response" model used by these researchers made it impossible for them to identify the kinds of "causes" which might be suspected here. And indeed the researchers comment on their own refusal to explore "any psychodynamic interpretation" on the grounds that it could only be "speculative": "When S.M. unfailingly reacted to her mother's voice with

SIB, it could have signified the desire to get attention or ... to express hate against the mother or desire to get even with her, or it could have been just irritation by the voice" (266). But the example of a patient who ceased her self harm after moving wards suggests that even in severe and long-running instances such as this, there is a possibility that self harm can cease *without* intervention of any kind, confounding those who argue that it is intractable.

In their report on their 30-month study of the efficacy of electric shock, whilst claiming a high success rate in extinguishing self harm (72.7 percent), these authors note a dozen case reports from the second half of the 1960s and 1970s by therapists who used "painful but harmless electric skin shock" using the "Hot Shot Prod," a tool that proved "entirely harmless and without hazard" even when used by two mothers at home (200). Bruhl and colleagues note that "the method most widely used to deliver aversive stimulation by ESS has been the cattle-prod" (248). Indeed, they note that although the establishment of their research unit and the ensuing study were held up by factors such as a hiring freeze (the project ultimately entailed the creation of nine new positions, with total planned staffing of 24 [208–09]), it was "especially, the manufacture of a remote-controlled electric shock device" which delayed the commencement of their research (205–06).[11] But this method is not one that can be consigned to a less knowing past: beyond debates about surgery, behaviorist responses (mainly aversive treatments) and drug regimes, the re-emergence of ECT in the new millennium is a signal development in recent forms of response to self harm.

ECT, colloquially known as "shock treatment," was the common and perhaps even predominant treatment of self harm in institutional contexts in the early 1970s (see Ruckman 13, summarizing current research in 1977; Bruhl *et al.*, esp. 199–203). In that respect, the work of Bruhl and colleagues on a project initially scheduled to commence in 1971 is exemplary. Johnson and Baumeister's review of more than 60 published essays on treatment for self-injurious behavior, published in 1978, found that the most frequently reported treatment was by electric shock. Then as now, it was used especially for children. For example, Jones, Simmons and Frankel report in 1974 on a case of the successful treatment of self harm in a nine-year-old patient diagnosed with autism, for whom courses of aversive shock administered when she was five years old and after had proven ineffective, leaving her entirely captive to physical restraints and fed by tube (243–44).[12] Consoli *et al.* in 2013 found decreased levels of self harm in four of the seven adolescents (aged 12–14) who had received electroconvulsive therapy. In a 2011 report, the treatment was used on an 11-year-old boy who had been diagnosed with autism and bipolar disorder, and for whom neither behavioral therapy nor drugs had proved efficacious (Wachtel *et al.*; see also Siegel *et al.*).

One might ask, why do such things matter? They matter because modern medicine is a contestation between various forms of specialization for claims to efficacy. One "wild card" here is ambition: some and perhaps many researchers dream of a "breakthrough," something that will become identified with their name and give powerful impetus to their career. The pressure for newness is fierce, and all academic knowledge is structured, in a sense, by the tensions between innovation and substantiation. In respect of emotion, this plays out as a struggle between ambition and the tempering of methods and interpretation of results by what can be called judiciousness, which psychiatrists might understand as the mature formation of the ego which refuses a splitting of good and bad. "Fashion" is often referred to pejoratively, but in research, innovation is acclaimed—the drive to be first. But it is very difficult to be completely new and at the same time to have research work carefully substantiated. More often, good scholarship works on a model of accretion; Kuhn's famous "paradigm shift" is extremely rare, albeit often sought. The relationship of the new research to the old is often strictly prescribed. Graduate students, in particular, are required to make "an original contribution to knowledge" but also to substantiate their findings with a painstaking survey of the relevant theoretical literature and precisely designed research which follows strictly established protocols. If particular writers or paradigms become unfashionable, those who continue to espouse their value are easily dismissed as intellectually and socially out of touch: resistant to new ideas perhaps, or "provincial."

Commensurately, the role of history in academic reflection is crucial: without a sense of the historical context of debates about self harm, each medical professional responds alone; even specialists might respond *ab initio*. At the same time, the drive to do "new things" can constitute a pressure against reflection and an incentive to remain silent. One rare example of methodological contestation is provided by Charles E. Dean's letter in the *Journal of Clinical Psychiatry*, which queried a report by Price *et al.* on the use of "limbic leucotomy"—surgical lesions in the brain—as a treatment for self harm. Dean suggests that

> it seems worthwhile to note that despite some improvement in 4 of the 5 cases, all patients required many months of continuing inpatient care, and in several it appears that hospitalization continues ... with case D remaining in a locked unit and allowed to bang her head for 5 minutes out of every hour after her rituals and head-banging returned within 6 months of surgery....
>
> In addition, the authors might have commented more fully on the legal issues involved in consent. They did mention that consent of the parents or guardians was obtained, but the case histories suggest considerable doubt about the competency of any patient to give informed consent [Dean, "Limbic Leucotomy"; the authors' response follows this contribution].

Dean also raises the question of the "staggering" financial burden created by the surgery and its aftermath, elsewhere noting his own success with ECT and prescription drugs which proves, he says, "both life saving and highly economical" ("Repeated").

In comparison to the five operations protested by Dean, Dossetor *et al.* report that a program of twice daily massage, incorporating a level of reciprocity—the patient was permitted to massage their carer, and to control the terms of related physical play—saw "six months of steady improvement" which meant "she was on no medication for the first time in ten years; she wore no splints or helmets; and her injuries had all healed, so she required no dressings" (638). Equally, Wallenstein and Nock report success—again in a single patient—with a program of physical exercise. A meta-study by Denis *et al.* reinforced the efficacy of "non-aversive, non-intrusive" forms of treatment. The terms of these claims are essentially disputational: they signal that a position is being taken against those who argue for the purely organic bases of self harm, and they have an eye to institutional conditions, contesting the view that it is impossible to institute intensive, individualized, non-pharmaceutical regimes on a mass scale. Thus Dossetor *et al.* argue that their form of treatment *saved* time: "L.H.'s improvement has meant that she copes better with group activities ... and ... in outings" (639). But there were other obstacles: "Only some of the younger staff were able to allow themselves to be drawn into this massage and imitation play routine. Others found the childishness of copying L.H.'s games too embarrassing" (638–39).

But direct challenge to the methods detailed in case reports is rare: much more commonly, writers in medical fields simply assert the efficacy of their approach, their focus being on precedent not alternatives. The conventions of citation and of narrative structure—a survey of reports on earlier, similar patients—also work towards the maintenance of conformity. A readership in sympathy with the methodology is often presumed or promoted by the placement in a journal specific to that field. If the "competition for results" is mentioned, it is in terms of respective outcomes of different methods; this is much more common than mention of the contest for resources and authority that takes place within the research and clinical arenas.

Speculations on Siblings, Speech and Controlled Re-Enactment

> The patient was a healthy well-developed intelligent child. Past history revealed that she had been admitted to hospital at the age of 5, suffering from traumatic asphyxia after being knocked down by a lorry. She slept with a younger sister aged 4.—Burton-Brown

> This may be a unique example of an autophytic eruption in twins; I have only once before observed mimicry in a contact but in that case the lesions occurred in cousins, school girls who were associated

together and in whom the lesions were in effect a childish prank, which
nevertheless deceived their elders for some considerable time.—Mac-
Cormac, "Self-inflicted lesions"

Having challenged the legitimacy of the search for patterns in terms of
diagnosis, treatment, and predicting actual cases of self harm, I would like
nevertheless to offer a set of observations about patterns in narratives about
self harm. This has a caveat: these comments are highly speculative, not least
because they condense elements I began to notice in many documents about
self harm. In almost every medical source I read, two of three things seemed
to be present in the patient's background: trauma, religion, or siblings. The
mention of religion is conventional but what is not generally observed is the
way in which references to religion link ancient cultures, patients, and actual
practices. It is clear that self harm is authorized, proliferated and given meaning
by religion, by representations of religious figures, and by positive responses
to acts of devotion which entail self-inflicted physical suffering. No writer has
focused on this nexus at sufficient length to offer meaningful hypotheses about
these relationships.

The reference to trauma is newly conventional, by which I mean that it
is present in much of the literature generated in the fields of psychology and
psychiatry over the last forty years. The general focus, though, tends to be
Freudian in referring mainly to sexual events, especially those experienced in
childhood or youth. By "trauma," though, I do not mean always or only sexual
abuse (although this is present in numerous accounts) but, very often, severe
medical trauma, often experienced in early childhood, entailing a period of
hospitalization and major surgery, or experiences such as war, extreme violence
in the home, displacement or incarceration.[13] The difficulty in further exploring this pattern lies in the fact that references to traumatic experiences are
often only made in passing in case reports, and that literature covering war
and prison tends implicitly to normalize these environments. Thus some of
the most powerful evidence for this line of association between trauma and
self harm remains fragmented or fleeting, not explored by the writers who
note it.

It is perhaps the third of these terms, "siblings," that will surprise those
familiar with the literature of self harm. Part of this suggestion entails querying the centrality given to parents and parenting in psychoanalytic frameworks
for explaining the development of the self. For example, Didier Anzieu suggests that the primal source of masochistic fantasy is that the child shares the
skin of the mother. One might ask: what if it were also or instead the skin of
the sibling? Read any text in the field of psychiatry and the word "sibling"
will be coupled with the word "rivalry." This is limiting, not least in that it

blinds us to the ways in which siblings might function as sources of comparison which prompt a *range* of responses, not necessarily hostile. It does not necessarily capture the subtlety or intensity of love, even of sexual attraction, that might charge sibling relationships, or the ways in which the existence of siblings can shape the reception of the child into the family.[14] Above all, it is blind to the longevity and power of sibling relationships, and the centrality of siblings to the formation of one's social world and one's relationship to it. As Juliet Mitchell notes (of social sciences, although perhaps more accurately of psychiatry itself), "the general tendency ... has been to privilege over all else the vertical relationship of child-to-parent" (x).

Suggesting a possible set of associations does not mean that an only child is inoculated against the possibility of self harm. But in some as yet ill-defined way, the presence of siblings, usually only mentioned in passing, recurs in many case reports in particular. It is a persistent detail in discussions which otherwise tend to foreground parental interaction, that interaction often entwined with or being the source of traumatic experience. Mitchell's speculations on the force of sibling relationships resonate with debates about psychological and physical destruction:

> I believe we have minimized or overlooked entirely the threat to our existence as small children that is posed by the new baby who stands in our place or the older sibling who was there before we existed. There follows from this an identification with *the very trauma of this sense of non-existence* that will be "resolved" by power struggles: being psychically annihilated creates the conditions of a wish to destroy the one responsible for the apparent annihilation [xv; emphasis added].

In Mitchell's formulation, siblings have been overlooked, being associated with fear of annihilation, fear of castration, narcissism, the desire "to be the object, not subject, of love" (3–4; 4). Surely siblings are significant agents in shaping interpretations of parents' behavior—rationalizations or challenges—ventriloquizing, undermining, or inflecting the parents' voices? Mitchell's argument for the significance of siblings is bound up in her (feminist) arguments about the privileging of masculinity as normative. Most important, though, is her observation about the presence of siblings and the experience of non-existence, the latter a recurrent theme in accounts from those who self harm about why they do so: to restore belief in their emotional existence. For Mitchell, the sibling is the focus of a fundamental conflict: "the ecstasy of loving one who is like oneself is experienced at the same time as the trauma of being annihilated by the one who stands in one's place" (10).

In a long discussion of the case of "Mrs. X" (89–96), Mitchell sets out a story of conditions which would fit the paradigmatic circumstances for self harm, including early hospitalization and traumatic, sexualized relations with a sibling. Mitchell notes her fear that this patient had a death drive, "a compulsion ... towards a deadly stasis" (92) which unsettled her analyst. Because Mitchell's focus is on advancing her argument in relation to siblings and gender, there is perhaps a tendency to "read over" certain forms of violence against the self in her report of this case. She does not read Mrs. X's "many marital infidelities," sexual encounters which are preceded by beatings from her intended partners, as a form of self harm, but as "perversions" and "hysteria." They could, however, be interpreted as a means of managing either and perhaps *both* the desire for punishment for an early abortion, and the desire to kill the child that she has been trying to conceive and is now carrying.

To make such a speculation might be seen as pushing too far the definition of self harm offered in the introduction: does being beaten by a sexual partner meet the criteria of self-inflicted injury? Does it meet the criteria of physical damage sufficient to demand medical treatment? On the face of it, in this specific instance the answer to such questions must be "no," although treatment by the psychoanalyst is certainly medical treatment (here, implicitly, for the response to traumatic experience). On the other hand, it is possible that pushing the definition of self harm to include those instances in which members of the medical profession themselves are positioned to offer "treatment" that is potentially damaging not of the body but of the *psyche*—here, the abortion of a fetus which Mrs. X has convinced herself, without any evidence, is horribly deformed. In this reading, treatment itself can be seen as a form of "management" through controlled damage of the kind proposed by those who argue that self harm can be an effective prophylactic against more serious forms of damage (including suicide). This line of thinking leads me to include this discussion by Mitchell, not as "proof" of the value of these speculations, but as a means of testing the boundaries of definitions of self harm.

The Language of Self Harm: Speech and Controlled Re-Enactment

One of the propositions raised in graduate theses is that self harm can be understood as metaphor and self-expression (see for example McLane; Tuttle; Scott). In this respect, one could posit that self harm, in some complex and volatile sense, functions psychologically as a kind of controlled re-enactment of traumatic experience, a possibility that is raised by Oscroft. Following Judith Lewis Herman, Tuttle similarly contends, "'The trauma is not expressed in memories, but in somatosensory re-living, behavioral re-enactments and repeated self-harm by others or self-inflicted'" (qtd. in Tuttle

91). There is a possibility that harming one's self, in certain modes and contexts, might be neither symptomatic nor expressive, so much as it is a mode through which responses to an originary trauma can be renegotiated and re-formed. What I am suggesting here is that self harm might in some circumstances be an effective somatosensory mode by which individuals come to terms with horrifying events—violence on themselves or others, sexual abuse, even a serious illness or major medical procedure—which they were not, at the time, able to control.

This distils the assertion by patient activists that their actions constitute a valuable choice, a form of treatment, a way of controlling and dissipating feeling—and reclaiming feeling.[15] In such claims, self harm is seen as proof of the capacity of the individual, through a form of re-enactment, to reshape memory by living through a process that is not merely metaphoric of, but structurally (somatically) a literal, embodied, *reconstitution* of, that memory. It is precisely the *control* of the wounding, and the ensuing control of response, which effect a literal but re-formed "incorporation" of that past into the body. In making such an argument, the conceptualizing of self harm demands a reconfiguring of common-sense understandings of self and other, specifically as they are organized on the basis of assumptions about a more or less inevitable relationship of proximity and benignity between the feelings and the body—that those who are close by will help us; those who are distant will do us harm. That is not to say that such feelings would always reflect a consensual reality, but it is to speculate that what is at stake in understanding self harm in terms set by advocates is insight into the patterns of rationalization—a significant emotional and conceptual challenge.

Janice McLane's essay "The Voice on the Skin," published in the highly regarded North American feminist philosophy journal *Hypatia*, argues that self harm is a mode of expression, and in that way, a kind of language, used by women who have experienced sexual abuse. McLane's essay has been particularly influential in the fields of cultural studies and sociology. A similar argument to that she proposes had been made a year earlier by a psychiatric nurse working in Auckland (New Zealand), although it is possible that the siting of this essay in an antipodean journal of mental health nursing made it less visible to North American scholars in humanities and social sciences. In that essay, author Marie Crowe is careful to emphasize that not all women who are abused cut themselves, nor have all women who cut themselves been abused. Working in dialogue with philosophy and cultural studies, she argues as McLane does that the body is a surface which becomes "a means of signification" for women who have been abused (104). She suggests that "the act of 'cutting up' is a signifier of an experience or feeling for which the woman has no other means of signification," and is a vehicle "for the woman to reintegrate herself as a subject" (106). Crucially, though, the meanings which women attribute to their own actions differ.

In rather more poetic language, McLane argues that injuring one's self functions to re-enact trauma in containable ways, that it is a mechanism which "reinstates the boundary between the existence and the non-existence of self" (112): "a beating heart, which looks like any other heart, becomes an injury-circulating mechanism. Sometimes it's a vulva which goes from simply sensed body-part to the dimly remembered site of cruelty" (110). As such, injuring one's body is a form of agency, a way of confirming one's emotional existence. The genius of the mode is that self injury "allows the rest of life to stand in temporary contrast as that which does *not* have wounds or pain" (112; emphasis in original). The trauma is "simultaneously expressed and controlled" (112). McLane's view is supported by Miller and Bashkin's report of a patient about whom they concluded that "he preserved in the flesh, in a dramatic and conspicuous manner, the history of events he could not integrate into the fabric of his personality" (647).

McLane asserts that "injuring herself shows the self-mutilator that she can care for herself. She does so insofar as self-mutilation allows her to finally create and express feeling ... that is, to connect with the self is to care for the self, even if the connection is made through self-attack" (McLane 112). The body itself becomes a continuous narrative, one which the conscious mind is not capable of remembering or producing (Miller and Bashkin 646–47). The basis is the inability to establish or to maintain connection which is why, McLane argues, "Contrary to many medical and lay opinions, self-mutilators seldom seek to exhibit their wounds or behavior in public, or to manipulate others through self-wounding. Rather, they protectively hide what they do, keeping the act and its meaning strongly private" (115). This analysis of the foundations of self harm—crudely, as a means to treat the problem of silence or unspeakability—leads McLane to assert that as a reclaiming of self it is speech for which victims of damage must strive. Although the Miller and Bashkin case is different—they comment on the patient's pride in his injuries (640)—the two sources have in common an argument for the use of self harm as a form of self expression and of self control.

The question is whether we can go so far as to argue that self harm represents a form of "magical thinking" which does not differentiate between the physical and the symbolic (Gregory and Mustata). For Gregory and Mustata, who analyzed 66 autobiographical accounts of self harm posted on the web, the argument is that the metaphorical potential of the release of blood is (mis)taken as catharsis. I prefer to think of self harm as a form of communication, a view which incorporates McLane's hypothesis without necessarily concurring with the approving stance that characterizes similar work in cultural studies. The view that self harm is a way of speaking is summed up in a letter to the *British Medical Journal* published in 2002, which discusses a poem given to hospital staff by a patient who had harmed themselves:

> The poem illustrates how self harm can be an attempt to deal with chaotic feelings in a person's mind. These feelings will often include anger and hatred, which the self harmer may be trying to communicate to one or more others who have let them down, abandoned them, or abused them. The self harmer may be unable to express these feelings in words or may feel that verbal expression is too dangerous. The language of the body is used as an alternative means of communication [Clark].

But as the letter writer notes, the difficulty is not only with speaking, but with hearing and understanding that speech.

> Staff who care for victims of self harm often do not have the time or skills required to translate this language. Instead they are often overwhelmed with concerns about risk management. Thus the concern about whether a patient intended to die and whether he or she is still at risk over-rides the key question: "what is this person trying to communicate to me or to others through the language of self harm?" [Clark].

If self harm *is* a language, then our question becomes, how to read it. For in acceding to these ways of conceiving self harm, we are yet left with the question of how to deal with terrors and traumas so great that, when metabolized or manifested, those closest to the person are traumatized. At the same time, then, we need to be cautious in attributing efficacy to such modes of what can be called coping or treatment—that is, there is a risk of accentuating the expressive element of self harm at the cost of acknowledging its punitive function and/or effects. (This is something that McLane is careful to consider, although this aspect of her argument is sometimes overlooked.) Perhaps the philosopher Slavoj Žižek does this when he writes, that acts of self harm "guarantee the subject's inclusion in the (virtual) symbolic order" (Žižek). In his view, "Far from being suicidal, far from signaling a desire for self-annihilation, cutting is a radical attempt to (re)gain a stronghold in reality, or (another aspect of the same phenomenon) to firmly ground our ego in our bodily reality, against the unbearable anxiety of perceiving oneself as non-existing" (Žižek).

The specific danger in regarding self harm as simply and effectively therapeutic is that the way of speaking itself begins to assume a fixed shape, one that brings relief rather than resolution. In Alfred Hitchcock's film *Vertigo* the protagonist, traumatized by his own near-death and his part in the "fall" and deaths of first a colleague, and then a woman he is being paid to protect, becomes obsessed by the belief that if he can re-enact his trauma he will be able to recover from it. But the lesson provided by the film's ending is that "replays" *necessarily* end in the same way: even if the characters are different, the psychological template is too powerful to break free from. Guilt and death, both symbolized in the film by the eye and the spiral, act as a kind of narrative vortex which drives the protagonist to "the same ending" each time (death by falling), just as surely as our replay of the film itself must always "end the same way." If *Vertigo* constitutes a lesson in film—the ending never changes—it also seems to want to function as a pedagogy of trauma, one which teaches that endings cannot be changed merely by efforts of will, however well-intentioned. In the same terrible way, the child Betty described by Selma Fraiberg seems psychologically confined in a horrifying replay of her mother's delusions which the child re-enacts with dolls, a three-year-old caught in the narrative trap of her own mother's replay of trauma through story (Fraiberg 634).

The great struggle for those caught in a cycle of repeated self harm is to "change the ending." In his chapter on "Julia," whom he terms a borderline patient, James M. Glass repeatedly emphasizes the patient's estrangement from communal reality, indeed insists on this aspect of the "borderline" as being on the borderline of community. Julia carves the words "Dear Mom, I love you all" on her leg, using a kitchen knife, after which it takes her mother "several minutes to notice her daughter's bleeding" (*Private Terror* 108). Glass argues that "there is a strong reality-based component to the self's sense of its estrangement from a common humanity" and observes of this patient that "people close to her, particularly her parents and sisters, had in fact not acknowledged her pain" (*Private Terror* 108). In a world that she experienced as one of "enmity, malevolence and evil" the only possible response was to become "cold, brutal, cruel, and manipulative" (*Private Terror* 109), a description which resonates with accounts of coping in prison environments and indeed the traumas that can be experienced in hospitalization or therapy. At the same time, in crisis, Julia experiences her body/her self as radically, impossibly, fragmented, in her own words "beyond pain ... dissolved into something else" (*Private Terror* 109). She says, "I feel condemned to some shadowy border-life, always hurting underneath" (110). Describing Julia's situation, Glass suggests that she experienced life as cruelly unloving because it failed to see her hurt; because she could not be loved *as wounded* she therefore found herself living in a world she experienced as tempestuous and sadistic. Using McLane's formulation, we can say that her body has become her medium.

Glass argues that Julia had a public, compliant self that meshed with the image of a "highly successful and talented family," and a "hidden self" which allowed play to her badness. It was this hidden self which "registered itself on the physical boundaries of body: to be real was to scratch the flesh with razor blades, to draw blood," or to eat (*Private Terror* 111). What is uncertain, here, is what role self-injury plays in this schema, as it is outlined by Glass. Does the self harm occur because the self is a *participant* in the punishment, the body an object; or does it occur as a way of reintegrating the body *with* that bad self, a bringing of that self into being through the restoration of feeling? Glass's own conclusion, developed through political philosophy, along with the writing of Winnicott as well as Jacques Lacan's and Freud's readings of the tragedy of Oedipus, is that the self harm is suicidal. For this patient, "as for Oedipus, the driving force was the desire of death" (*Private Terror* 113). But is injuring one's self, in this context, quite the same thing as suicide? Glass seems not to think so, even though the argument tends to blur the lines between masochism and death. He suggests that for Julia, masochism "filled out the context of her being; it structured her language, her sense of self-description. It impelled her use of razor blades *as a statement about life and 'healing'*" (*Private Terror* 113; emphasis added).

If we are to accept Julia's accounts of her feelings, it might be that this is an instance in which self harm—here, coupled with drastic variations in food intake, and commensurately drastic losses and gains of weight—served a powerful therapeutic function. Glass goes on to point this out, as he analyzes the meaning of the razor.

> By cutting, Julia knew herself to be alive, and the knowledge that she bled relieved tension. Anger (and disillusionment) revealed itself in the etched surfaces of the body-as-text, as a series of marks that stood out as signs, stigmata of the self's utter alienation.... Not only did she have the power to control the pace of her dying through the release of blood and mutilation of tissue; she also possessed control over the sense of well-being accompanying the knowledge that she had the power to harm herself.... At some point in her treatment [the razor] became significant as a symbolic presence that reminded Julia of her will-to-be [*Private Terror* 115].

The phrase "stigmata of the self's utter alienation" is a compelling one, brilliant in its evocation of a religious tradition of suffering and redemption, and its coupling of that tradition with a statement of brute despair which nevertheless conceives of a therapeutic potential in self harm. But the crediting of the therapeutic relation between Julia and Glass himself as revealing the therapeutic *function* of the cutting might be a little too neat, or too optimistic about the effect of that institutional authority which Glass elsewhere so astutely observes. What I am suggesting here is that such an interpretation risks reading the self harm a bit too literally—that by Julia, for example, as a cry for help. That said, carving messages to one's mother/family in one's skin seems to demand precisely this approach.

Glass makes similar moves in a later work, *Psychosis and Power*, which likewise contains a chapter on a borderline patient who harms herself. Like Julia, Maureen is depicted as having "two selves," an abominable private self and a compliant public one. It is the hidden self "that cut into her body, carving the message of the self-hating fantasies that possessed her. Maureen saw her own body as a psychotic object, on the border between the civil world and the finality of death," and by harming it she preserved her existence (Glass, *Psychosis and Power* 98). "When razor blades were no longer available, laxatives served their purpose, and when laxatives were discovered, daily purging and head banging replaced them" (93). This is a rare instance in which a patient who is termed highly self-conscious about her situation resorts to the form of self harm associated with mental disability, namely, head-banging. But the patient's own sense of her actions associates them with pleasure: "Maureen described to me how she enjoyed watching her blood flow. Making the cuts excited her.... And she found peace—'a balance of power' inside herself, a truce in the endless war of self-defilement—only when contemplating death, cutting, and the mutilation of her genitals" (Glass, *Psychosis and Power* 99).

In a long "quote" from Maureen—although the source material is not given and therefore we do not know whether this is direct speech, reported speech, transcribed speech or the patient's own writing—she says,

> I don't know why such acts give me pleasure, but they do. I like to rub my wrists to irritate the scars; I like that they're there.... They give me a great deal of comfort and it makes me feel good to know I can touch them if I want to.... Of course I'm concerned that I hurt myself, who wouldn't be? But it's something I have to do; it's something I like to do. Oh, I control it; I'm not suicidal; I'm not going to cut so deep I'll sever an artery or do something crazy like that; ... it's just that I like the pleasure of cutting [all ellipses in original] [Glass, *Psychosis and Power* 100].

What is perhaps notable here is the way in which Maureen uses a touchstone of normative behavior: who would not be concerned about harming themselves? She will not do something "crazy" like severing an artery. Within that framework her words might be interpreted by unsympathetic readers as clear evidence of manipulation, indicated by the claim to "control it."

In several key respects, notably those just mentioned, this unsettles Glass's explanation of this patient. And there is something else unsettling, two other "asides" which might in other circumstances or for another writer have become foundational. One of the unusual aspects of Glass's writing about psychosis is his lack of interest in aetiology. Late in this chapter there is a paragraph on Maureen's childhood, a rarity in his work. It begins with the claim that "There were concrete, historical reasons why Maureen experienced sexuality as a fragmented form of violence. When she was eight or nine, she and her fifteen-year-old half-brother began an incestuous relationship that lasted for a number of years until it was discovered by her father" (Glass, *Psychosis and Power* 99). The comments tell us several things; among them is that Maureen and her brother had the same mother, but different fathers. One of the precipitating factors in the breakdown which led her to hospital—we get the impression that prior to that time, her self harm, whether "under control" or the means of that control, or both, was not known to family or friends, and not sufficient to cause her to seek medical treatment of any kind—was the birth of her second child. At this point Maureen became traumatized by the idea of parenting: she asked the nurses to take her child, telling them she could not look after her (Glass, *Psychosis and Power* 92). In the lack of interest in background, and specifically in sexual assault and maternity, does Glass miss the opportunity to extend his analysis?

Researching Self Harm

It might be thought that disciplines and their related institutions—criminology and prisons, for example, psychiatry and private practice, nursing and hospitals (or nursing and prisons) shape responses to self harm, and they do. Much of the literature of self harm is grounded in assumptions about the pervasiveness of fraud and criminality, as well as the triviality of hysteria, assumptions which mean that there can be pressure to redirect patients who are seen as having deliberately injured themselves from the medical to the judicial realm. This can include not merely neglect but incitement, at least according to one prison inmate who offered this account of being taunted by a guard:

> MHDM 10: I had a cat there tell me, he said, "Why didn't you cut your jugular vein? All you got to do is cut it over there." And I said, "That's a joke; I don't know what side it's on." He said, "No, it's on this side. What you should do is cut down this way. This way, if you cut the vein, they can't stitch it up." He says, "Tell them other people down there that." I told him, "I'll do you one better. You put it down in writing and I'll bring it down there." He said, "Ah, no, that wouldn't be right." I said, "No, it wouldn't be right, and you wouldn't have that badge, either" [Toch 315].

Likewise patients who would have been of concern for those working in psychiatry have often been seen as having "merely" physical injuries, or being criminal, just as doctors working outside of psychiatry and psychology have acknowledged their inability to treat traumatic self-injury.

The difficulty here is not just intellectual but logistical. A 1998 masters dissertation submitted in the School of Social Work at the University of California asserts that "without a clear understanding of the causes and functions of self-mutilation, it will be difficult for social workers to treat these clients and even more difficult for them to engage their clients in therapeutic dialogue about the issue" (Whitney 2). Whitney's study is essentially a piece of advocacy for increasing the attention given to self harm in the curriculum of the degree she was completing at the time of writing. In one sense this is unremarkable: a statement by a graduate student about the value of the knowledge they are developing in their thesis. On the other hand, if what I have said so far is true, then we have a problem: how can students in any single medical or associated degree—whether criminology, social work, psychology or education—engage intellectually with, let alone develop an effective therapeutic apparatus for, "self harm" in terms other than as a single phenomenon with a clearly defined set of causes and an equally clear-cut set of responses, self harm perhaps being a briefly considered subtopic in a larger field? Here, the competition for authority between forms of knowledge does researchers no service: as that competition intensifies, we are increasingly pressured to provide "hard"—i.e. *quantitative*—evidence to support increasingly specialized claims (against which some writers call for the value of multi-disciplinarity and teamwork in responding to self harm).[16]

A great deal of academic research is highly specialized and, in a specific way, single-minded, marching down a path of what might be called micro-specialization, addressing and influencing only a small group. Put another way, there is a certain intellectual cost to methodological certainty, that can be measured in the restriction of the parameters of the outcomes. Ultimately, in the case of self harm for example, such research is justified in terms of identifying a "cause" as the basis for the future development of a "cure," reflecting the coalition of bureaucratic and medical regimes which centralize diagnosis and prognosis in the exchange between patient and doctor. There is often an expectation from patient and from institution about what one writer calls "a collusion of bad faith": "finding a diagnosis that will make a patient eligible for the care he [sic] has come to expect, that we think he should have, and that our managers want us to be able to provide" (Eisold). Medical bureaucracy, patient interaction, and research agendas work in coalition to diminish complication, variation or difference. Charles Rosenberg brilliantly encapsulates the situation in regard to what he terms "the tyranny of diagnosis," with its attendant promise of prognosis and recovery:

> Diagnosis is central to the definition and management of the social phenomenon that we call disease. It constitutes an indispensable point of articulation between the general and the particular, between agreed-upon knowledge and its application. It is a ritual that has always linked physician and patient, the emotional and the cognitive, and, in doing so, has legitimated physicians' and the medical system's authority while facilitating particular clinical decisions and providing culturally agreed-upon meanings for individual experience. Not only a ritual, diagnosis is also a mode of communication and thus, necessarily, a mechanism structuring bureaucratic interactions. Although diagnosis has always been important in the history of clinical medicine, it became particu-

larly significant in the late twentieth century with the proliferation of chemical, imaging, and cytological techniques and the parallel conflation of diagnosis, prognosis, and treatment protocols. Diagnosis labels, defines, and predicts,
and, in doing so, helps constitute and legitimate the reality that it discerns [16].

As Rosenberg notes, the removal of social and individual factors leaves illness
framed by funding categories and disaggregated by research specializations.

In terms of research design in relation to self harm, there is a consistent
difficulty in that researchers who focus on a single physiological, social, or psychological element do not address the question of whether that factor is causal,
co-incidental, or consequent on the self harm.[17] What Rosenberg describes as
the nineteenth-century displacement of fluid categories of illness defined by
progression or flux by "stable disease entities that could be—and were—imag-
ined outside their embodiment in particular individuals" has not served the
investigation of self harm well (18). In this sense, what Rosenberg terms "the
iatrogenesis of nosology"—the concept that belief in a particular category of
disease might play a part in its "discernment" and description by doctors, and
in its induction and persistence by the patient—is significant (Ferber, *Demonic*
10).

In the light of this *resistance* to the structures and the assumptions underpinning dominant forms of scholarly inquiry and publishing, as well as the
provision of medical treatment where specialists might work in isolation or
competition, what makes responses to and analyses of self harm so fascinating
is the way in which competing paradigms jostle against each other within different times and places. For example, notwithstanding the mesmerizing and/or
alienating effect of stories about a patient who has severed their penis, it is
also possible for writers whose interests lie elsewhere to note without attending
to complex elements of instances of patients who self harm.[18] Although it is
the patient, the subject group, or the theoretical problem which is usually fore-
grounded, it is overwhelmingly clear that these institutional structures might
themselves be contributing to the proliferation of self harm in some quite
specific ways: that is, that as a phenomenon that is not widely understood by
specialists but *is* widely talked about in the community, as well as in films, literature, television and the internet, self harm might in some sense be iatrogenic. We can note the proliferation of representations of self harm in films
and novels and on the internet (see Potera; Messina and Iwasaki; Adler and
Adler, "The Cyber Worlds"), although the internet can also be used for programs of treatment and amelioration (see Flessner *et al.*; Mitchell and Ybarra).

Assertions that self harm has reached "epidemic" proportions stand in
contrast to attempts by doctors and others to filter knowledge of self-inflicted
injuries among troops out of the public sphere during periods of war. This
might in part represent changed media values, as it might also reflect changes

in the profile of the "typical" practitioner, from traumatized male soldier to adolescent girl. But we can see, somewhat unexpectedly, that in the course of the twentieth century, the paradigmatic patient shifted from being male to female, while the causes of "hysteria" have shifted from physical combat to sexual abuse. What is new is the assumption that intellectual and cultural shifts variously labelled postmodernity or poststructuralism have broken down prejudice. Such faith has left one researcher declaring, in 1998, that "The distinction traditionally drawn between fashionable, transgressive and pathological ways of turning toward the body no longer hold" (Rose). This assertion works without reference to a history in which religious, military and medical contexts responded to serious self harm in ways that, if they might themselves be pathologically violent, could also indicate the profound ambiguity of actions which might make one action able to be read as all three of these things at once—"fashionable, transgressive, and pathological."

This lack of attention to history has left scholars working with the assumption that they are dealing with a "modern problem" that is (by inference) explicable in terms exclusive to the present. The second is that the vast majority of writers on self harm have wrestled with problems of classification and precedent, attempting to establish a lineage or rationale for quite different cases— without, one must note, attending to that history which I have just mentioned. Again and again, investigators remark on the peculiarity of the case(s) under investigation while attempting to establish what might be typical. And again and again, researchers and doctors attempt to establish patterns and classifications for causality and types of self harm, only to be frustrated by the sheer complexity of individual patients. These problems have been further exacerbated by those who have presumed the intellectual self-sufficiency and efficacy of their own "discipline." The most sought after goal is the identification of "causes" that would lead, ultimately, to the development of effective programs for prediction and prevention. There are many recent examples of these studies, in which the "holy grail" is either prediction (see for example Armey *et al.*; Perry *et al.*; Holley and Arboleda-Flórez) or, less often perhaps, "cure." Specific studies attempting to identify causality have proposed experiential factors ranging from complications at birth (Young *et al.*) to bankruptcy (Kidger *et al.*) and biochemical signatures from dopaminergic insufficiency which might affect brain function (Devine) to reduced secretion of the hormone cortisol (Kaess *et al.*). The pattern is to identify a factor which appears to be higher in the sample of those who self harm than in the control group, then call for further research and/or better service provision to ameliorate self harm.

As an example of the ways self harm resists encapsulation, we can consider a single page of the UK weekly *Nursing Times*, which in 2001 carried three stories on self harm on a single page. It is the gaps and collisions between these stories that show the intensity, responsibility and complexity of the experience of nurses in responding to patients who self harm. All three related to self harm in the context of imprisonment. "Call to Double Nurse Numbers" cites the report *Prison Medicine: A Crisis Waiting to Happen*, which claims that some 90 percent of prisoners in Britain had "mental health or substance misuse problems," which are implicitly related to self harm. From a similar perspective, "Prison Checks Must Be More Rigorous" notes the outcome of an inquiry into the death of a prisoner and the recommendation that nurses ask prisoners not just whether they have a "recent" history of suicide attempt or self harm, but whether they have *any* history of self harm or suicidal thoughts. And under the headline "Damages for 'gothic horror,'" is the following:

> A prison nurse won a claim for damages against the prison service after she had to rescue an inmate who had disembowelled himself with shards of glass.
> Pauline Stewart had post traumatic stress disorder after being exposed to what a judge described as a "gothic horror" at High Down Prison, Surrey....
> In spite of a history of self-mutilation, Mr. Holden, who had Munchausen's syndrome, was able to buy the glass coffee jar from the prison shop. He later cut himself from the pubis to the breastbone with a large piece of glass.
> Mr. Holden later committed suicide.
> Ms. Stewart, who was the only nurse on duty, described the scene as like a "butcher's shop." The cell was splattered with blood and faeces.

All three stories implicitly buttress the profession's claims about understaffing in prisons. The only mentions of the prisoner himself in the account of nurse Pauline Stewart's ordeal are in the material quoted above—the blunt diagnosis, and the equally blunt note that he subsequently killed himself which is implicitly linked to the fact that Stewart was "the only nurse on duty." Implicitly the trauma is exacerbated by Stewart's isolation, the prison setting, and by the knowledge that the wound had been self-inflicted.

Taken together these three stories are a cruel but correct marker of the diverse ways in which self harm can be represented, even in a single publication, at a single moment, in relation to a single strand of the medical professions. For the nurses, responding to a patient whose injury is self-inflicted is at once an industrial issue (in the main story, "Call to Double Nurse Numbers"), a source of trauma (in "Damages for Gothic Horror"), and something that they must do *more* about (in "Prison Suicide Checks Must Be More Rigorous"). But if "doing more" means also knowing more, when is time to be made, and resources provided, for that acquisition of knowledge? Sympathy for those who are responding to the demands of the prison workplace is given priority (logical in a publication directed towards nurses). The substitution of the words "nurses" for "medicine" in the boxed text is indicative of this: it is nurses, not patients, whose conditions constitute the crisis, notwithstanding the two prisoner suicides reported. For one group of nursing staff, the role might almost be one of carer/mentor, certainly one of education; for Pauline Stewart, responding to a single act of violence was, according to this report, the cause of her career ending. And implicitly in all three stories we see the complex and coercive ways in which institutional conditions shape and limit possibilities in responding to self harm.

Chapter Notes

Preface

1. See for example Joel Kahan and E. Mansell Pattison, "Proposal for a Distinctive Diagnosis: The Deliberate Self-Harm Syndrome (DSH)," *Suicide and Life-Threatening Behavior* 14.1 (1984): 17–35, which is addressed to *DSM III* and focuses on the separation of self harm from suicide.

2. While male self castration can often precede suicide, it is unusual for amputation of the penis to prove fatal, e.g. "A Case of Self Amputation" by Mohd Kaleem Khan, Mohammad Amir Usmani and Shaukat A. Hanif, "A Case of Self Amputation of Penis by Cannabis Induced Psychosis," *Journal of Forensic and Legal Medicine* 19.6 (Aug. 2012): 355–57. Almost any case report of a severed penis might have been chosen to illustrate this point. For an exception see Galt, although in that case, the throat was slashed in addition to the genitals.

3. This makes a multidisciplinary collection especially welcome: see Matthew K. Nock, ed. *Understanding Nonsuicidal Self-injury: Origins, Assessment, and Treatment* (Washington, D.C.: American Psychological Association, 2009).

4. For researchers who regard Menninger as inaugurating the field, explicitly or implicitly, see for example Elizabeth Eden Lloyd, "Self-mutilation in a community sample of adolescents," PhD Diss., Louisiana State University and Agricultural & Mechanical College, 1997 (1); Sandra Vallin Heinsz, "Self-Mutilation in Child and Adolescent Group Home Populations," PhD Diss., Walden University, 1999 (3), and Joan S. Kimball, "Self-Mutilation as an Affect Regulation Strategy: The Role of Attachment and Childhood Sexual Abuse," PhD Diss., Seattle Pacific University, 2003 (1). It is important to note, here, that research resources available during the twentieth century did not allow for easy location of journal articles from the pre-war period.

Introduction

1. While a great deal of intellectual effort has been put into differentiating self harm from suicide, the new terminology has also been criticised as self harm can precede suicide, particularly if it has been repeated. See Daniel Lewis Zahl and Keith Hawton, "Repetition of Deliberate Self Harm and Subsequent Suicide Risk: Long Term Follow-up Study of 11583 Patients," *British Journal of Psychiatry* 185.1 (2004): 70–75. For other critiques of terminology see Chandler *et al.* 99, and Y. Solomon and J. Farand, "'Why Don't You Do It Properly': Young Women Who Self-injure," *Journal of Adolescence* 19 (1996): 111–19.

2. This claim is made by Gratz *et al.* (63); two of the four publications cited in evidence are by the lead author.

3. These authors cite four articles. Aviva Laye-Gindhu and Kimberly A. Schonert-Reichl's "Nonsuicidal Self-harm Among Community Adolescents: Understanding the 'Whats' and 'Whys' of Self-harm," *Journal of Youth and Adolescence* 34.5 (Oct. 2005): 447–57, uses a sample of 424, finds a rate of 15 percent, but cites rates as high as 39 percent; Jennifer J. Muehlenkamp & Peter M. Gutierrez, "An Investigation of Differences between Self-injurious Behavior and Suicide Attempts in a Sample of Adolescents," *Suicide and Life Threatening Behavior* 34.1 (Spring 2004): 12–23 uses a sample of 390, finds a rate of 15.9

percent, but cites rates as high as 40 percent; the same authors' "Risk for Suicide Attempts Among Adolescents Who Engage in Non-suicidal Self-injury," *Archives of Suicide Research* 11.1 (Feb. 2007): 69–82 uses a sample of 540, finds a rate of 23.2 percent and cites rates as high as 40 percent; Shana Ross and Nancy Heath, "A Study of the Frequency of Self-mutilation in a Community Sample of Adolescents," *Journal of Youth and Adolescence* 31.1 (Feb. 2002): 67–77 finds a rate of 13.9 percent in a sample of 61 students in two high schools, and offers a careful survey of the literature.

4. For the useful charting of which see Adler and Adler, "The Demedicalization," esp. 556; 560–61.

5. See McHale and Felton for a recent overview of material on this topic and Saunders *et al.* for a synoptic study; Bierdrager provides case studies of eight clinical psychologists, Scheftel or a hospital; also Law *et al.* In a forum in the *Hastings Center Bulletin*, commentators reacted against suggestions that a patient—in this case, herself a medical professional—be tricked or coerced into disclosing self harm. See "Case Studies: When Patients Harm Themselve," *Hastings Center Report* 14.2 (April 1984): 22–23, with contributions by Nathan Selleck (22), Joy Curtis (22–23) and Arthur L. Caplan (23).

6. For a very different account of the responses and responsibilities of nursing staff in the case of a patient who had tried to suicide by immolation, in which sexuality and gender identity were not ostensibly at issue, see Kuehn.

7. See for example Shelley R. Doctors, "Further Thoughts on Self-Cutting," Symposium: The Treatment Resistant Patient: Erotic and Aggressive Aspects of Self-Mutilation, *Psychoanalytic Review* 86.5 (Oct. 1999): 733–44 and in the same issue, Jane G. Tillman, "Erotized Transference and Self-mutilation," 709–19.

8. The unusually capacious definition of self-injury—"elopement" is included in the list of "incident factors," for example—reduces the value of the finding.

Chapter 1

1. It is by no means the case that invoking classical literature is limited to the literature of self harm—see for example Andreas Sputteka and Thomas H. Eiermann, "The Art of Compromise in Transfusion/Transplantation Medicine (and Some Parallels in Classical Litera-

ture)" in *Transfusion Medicine and Hemotherapy* 40.3 (2013): http://www.karger.com/Article/FullText/351879)—but the reasons for doing so are beyond the scope of this book.

2. Freud's interest in the dream contrasts with the views of a near contemporary, a psychologist who found the "absurdity" of his own dreams "revolting" (Ribot 107) and therefore to be ignored.

3. Frazer's discussion of Attis in the first two editions of *The Golden Bough* is relatively brief (1894: 296–301; 1900: 130–37). Hepding's 1903 doctoral thesis *Attis: seine Mythen und sein Kult* lays out the classical sources on Attis at length; after the publication of this work, and Graillot's, Frazer extended his discussion for the third edition of *The Golden Bough* to more than fifty pages, referencing Hepding. Another useful overview of sources is Will Roscoe's heavily footnoted essay on Attis (see esp. 196 note 2; 198–203), while Weigert-Vowinkel provides a more compressed account (356–57). There are two principal sources: brief accounts by authors in Greek and Latin, and artefacts such as statues or stones (Roller 64–65).

4. The confusion continues in medical writing: "founding documents" in the literature of self-castration, such as Blacker and Wong's 1963 survey and report of four cases, make no distinction between instances in which either or both of penis and testicles are removed. Daniel Stroch's "Self-Castration" is quite rare in offering a brief account of a patient who had removed his entire scrotum, by which means he hoped to address the problem of persistent pain in his back and testicles: *Journal of the American Medical Association* 36.4 (26 Jan. 1901): 270.

5. Pliny's comment about "avoiding dangerous results" comes in a discussion of pottery, in which it is said that "if we accept the account of Marcus Celius" the castration is always effected with "a piece of Samian pottery" (vol. 9: 383 [Book 35, Section 46]). In the context it is the use of Samian pottery that seems to be being questioned. Another mention (in this chapter on art) is made in the story that the emperor Tiberius coveted a painting by Parrhasius of a priest of Cybele (Vol. 9: 313 [Book 35, Section 36]; elsewhere, *Natural History* mentions the Galli in a discussion of the sexual organs of animals (including humans) (Vol. 3: 597 [Book 11, Section 109]).

6. Against this convention, we could note the defence of the East and of academic interest in its cultures by scholars like Herbert

Strong and John Garstang, writing about "The Syrian Goddess" early in the twentieth century, as translator and commentator respectively.

7. The latter essay has not been widely available to English speakers as it was not included in the standard English language translation of the works of Lucian by Fowler and Fowler.

8. Hence some scholars believe that Attis was understood in Phrygia as a name which referred to a human priest. Philippe Borgeaud contends that "this 'realistic' Attis, from the end of the third century until Catullus (c.84– c.54 B.C.E.), almost eclipses the mythological character for two centuries, while maintaining a near identification with this character" (38).

9. Also called Dionysus of Miletus, a Greek city on the west coast of Anatolia. For this information about a little-known ancient figure, Borgeaud references 32 F 7 of Felix Jacoby's *Die Fragmente der Griechischen Historica* (147).

10. This is close to Peter Levy's translation (see Pausanias, *Guide to Greece* 271–72), but Frazer is preferred here because of the influence of his study of Pausanias, and his further scholarship on Attis.

11. I thank Ika Willis for this observation.

12. Roberts and Donaldson's 1882 translation is preferred as a more temperate work than McKracken's of 1949: see note 14.

13. Both longer versions of the Attis story are proccupied with autochthony and legitimacy. The fertilisation "holds a very different meaning, depending upon whether one considers it in the Athenian context, where Erichthonios is a human ancestor, or in the Pessinontian context, where Agdistis, before being stopped, is a cosmic monster who threatens the gods" (Borgeaud 46).

14. These views of Attis are perpetuated by scholars including the mid twentieth-century translator of Arnobius, McCracken, who in a frankly partisan work takes Arnobius' disaste for the "wretched stories" at face value. See Arnobius of Sicca, *The Case Against the Pagans*, trans. George E. McCracken, vol. 2, Books 4– 7 (Ancient Christian Writers, no. 8, Westminster, Maryland: Newman Press; London: Longmans, Green and Co., 1949) 373–659.

15. Ronan footnotes *Titus Andronicus* V.iii.73–76; *King John* V.vii.114; and *Richard III* V.v.23–26. A more deliberate and obvious example of self harm in Shakespeare's work is Portia's action in slicing her thigh in *Julius Caesar* (II.i.327–30) to demonstrate to her husband her capacity to keep her secrets.

16. Michie's translation says that Attis,

"moved by madness, bemused in his mind / Lopped off the load of his loins with a sharp flint" (125, poem 63); Guy Lee renders these lines "by raving madness goaded, his wits astray / He tore off with a sharp flint the burden of his groin" (75, poem 63).

17. Green and others call into question the poem's feminisation of Attis' speaking position (Catullus, 2005: 239), although it is not quite clear whether the discomfort arises from the representation of the self castration, or from the shift to the feminine voice after that event.

18. This is a slightly different view from that put by Roller, but it complements rather than contradicts it: Roller claims that the "Graeco-Roman god Attis ... had no counterpart in Phrygia" (114).

19. The Latin word for "man," is associated with virtue and virility. We can read the integrity of the body back over the integrity of character and the capacity for sexual expression. I am indebted to Tim Chandler for this point.

20. Engle confirms conversation with Menninger on this topic (364; see also note, 372).

21. In this Engle is supported by John Garstang's commentary on "The Syrian Goddess," but she does not cite this essay.

22. The less afflicted find substitutes, that is, they use "less serious and painful mutilations" (364) to purge themselves of religious guilt.

23. Favazza has earlier given a slightly longer account of the story but there is little sense of competing versions, something which is evident in the sources that are cited. These include Frazer's *Golden Bough* and the essay by Engle discussed above.

24. Other biblical stories, less often cited, are of the man "cutting himself with stones" (Mark 5:5), whom Jesus relieves by exorcising, and I Kings 18:28, in which the priests of Ba'al gash themselves with knives "til the blood gushed out among them" (noted in Menninger, "A Psychoanalytic Study" 424).

25. In another version, cactus is tied to the Penitente's back and chest; he carries a rosary, then moves across the cactus on his knees (Henderson 16–17). In Forrest's version, the Penitente walks across cactus (200).

26. In a 1916 essay Herbert Bolton asserts that "in the Spanish system ... the essence of the mission was the *discipline*, religious, moral, social, and industrial, which it afforded" (59). Bolton is by no means disinterested in analysing what he calls "Spain's frontiering genius" (65), but the implication of his argument is that the rites of the Penitentes are contiguous with

Spanish understandings of religiosity. It is a view Michael P. Carroll, a leading modern scholar of the movement, contests. See Herbert Eugene Bolton, "The Mission as a Frontier Institution in the Spanish American Colonies," *New Spain's Far Northern Frontier: Essays on Spain in the American West, 1540–1821*, ed. David J. Weber (Albuquerque: University of New Mexico Press, 1979) 49–65.

27. Interestingly one reviewer of Benn's *Burning for the Buddha* draws attention to the problem of reading, noting his "striking and provocative claim, that whereas Indian readers would have easily recognized the hyperbole and rhetorical movements of the *Lotus* [story of self-immolation], Chinese readers were conditioned by their own traditions of reading to take the scripture quite literally." Ryan Overbey, Rev. of *Burning for the Buddha* by James A. Benn, http://www.h-net.org/reviews/showrev.php?id=24572 On the Indian case, see Catherine Weinberger-Thomas, *Ashes of Immortality: Widow-Burning in India*, trans. Jeffrey Mehlman and David Gordon White (Chicago and London: University of Chicago Press, 1999).

28. On 5 April 1873 W.W.B. of Edinburgh asked readers of *Notes and Queries* for information (279), to which J. Manuel replied on 14 Nov. 1874, quoting the *Second Report of the Commission on Historical Manuscripts* (London: 1871, p. 208): "In the Legends of the Scottish Church St. Triduana is represented as one of the Companions of St. Kegulus in his mission, leading an eremitical life at Roscoby in Angus, and dying at Restalrig, near Edinburgh, where she was held in reverence down to the Reformation." John Foster's "The Legend and Shrine of Saint Triduana" in the *British Journal of Opthalmology* 37.12 (763–65) pleads the case for a "local" patron saint to rival St. Lucia. This essay, which admits to only three sources (one of which is the local vicar), is the main source for later writers. The saint's name is also given as Triduan, Triduana and Tridun.

29. In Los Angeles, see the section "Legendary Background of Autoenucleation at 181–82 of Howard R. Krauss, Robert D. Yee, and Robert Y. Foos, "Autoenucleation," *Survey of Opthalmology* 29.3 (Nov.-Dec. 1984): 179–87; in Liverpool, Brown *et al.*; in Singapore, see Tin Aung, E.Y. Yap, H.B. Fam, and N.M. Law, "Oedipalism," *Australian and New Zealand Journal of Opthalmology* 24.2 (May 1996): 153–57 at 154; in Spain, A. Arruga, "La Mutilació Deliberada de los Ojos" [Deliberate Mutilation of the Eyes], *Archivos de la Sociedad*

Española de Oftalmología 78.6 (June 2003): 339–40 at 339. Most of these sources mention most of the following: Oedipus, Odin, Saint Lucia, St. Triduana, a beggar encountered by Marco Polo, and the gospel of Matthew.

30. The paper notes that "Mr. Bishop being absent, the paper was read by Mr. G.R. Pendrill," with the further note that "The following is an extended summary of the paper."

31. Reading a draft of this chapter my colleague Ika Willis, a classicist by training, was aghast at the use of this version of the story. She points out that "a woman with no vagina is not a man" and notes that the transgendering of Caenis is an invention of Ovid (in the *Metamorphoses*), Caenis having also appeared in Homer and other sources where his gender is not at issue. The transformed Caenis is a symbol of cultural impenetrability—he is invulnerable to weapons; contrastingly, as many instances in classical literature show, being male does not save one from rape. In these ways, the "version" used by the doctors seems to misunderstand the story.

32. As part of this larger essay "On Virtue" (Chapter 29 of his *Essays*), Montaigne introduced another story of self castration, this time claiming personal knowledge: "About seven or eight years since, a husbandman yet living, but two leagues from my house, having long been tormented with his wife's jealousy, coming home one day from his work, and she welcoming him with her accustomed railing, entered into so great fury that with a sickle he had yet in his hand, he totally cut off all those parts that she was jealous of and threw them in her face." Bataille ignores this first case from Montaigne, although it is not irrelevant to his argument.

33. The terms for such an association were confirmed by the publication of Freud's *Totem and Taboo: Resemblances Between the Psychic Lives of Savages and Neurotics*, trans. A.A. Brill (London: Routledge, 1919), which first appeared in essay form just before World War I.

34. Of the three men covered by case reports, two were diagnosed with borderline personality disorder and one with schizophrenia, although the authors also note that as far as prison authorities were concerned the self mutilation itself was proof of mental illness (Alroe and Gunda 511).

35. http://pages.zdnet.com/AsiaBill/id11. html (as part of an advertisement for a guesthouse), accessed 22 May 2004. The same text was also at http://www.geocities.com/pilipin oinjapan/holy_week.html; accessed 22 May

2004 and still available in 2014. A less sensationalised account, one which seems to confirm that the practices are found more than acceptable to at least some clergy of the Catholic church (in claiming that some are participants), is at http://www.newsflash.org/2000/04/tl/tl001049.htm, accessed 22 May 2004 and still available in 2014.

36. The relationship between "popular and biomedical discourses" in discussions of self harm is noted also by Brickman (94), who cites Paula Treichler but does not otherwise offer an explanation for the phenomenon.

Chapter 2

1. See Charles E. Rosenberg's chapter "The Tyranny of Diagnosis" 13–37; for an example of the conceptual and practical effects of this pressure, see Grant L. Hutchinson, *Disorders of Simulation: Malingering, Factitious Disorders, and Compensation Neurosis* (Madison, Connecticut: Psychosocial Press, 2001).

2. Nicholas P. Jones notes that of four patients on whom he offers a report, three related their actions to a desire to remove an "evil eye" (573); see also cases reported by Dr. G.H. Bergmann, "Ein Fall von religiöser Monomanie, die eine unerhörte Selbstverletzung veranlasste," *Allgemeine Zeitschrift für Psychiatrie und Psychisch-gerichtliche Medizin* [Berlin, Leipzig] 3 (1846): 365–80, and by Dr. Ideler, the latter of a woman in her forties who "in an attack of religious mania" (717) removed both her eyeballs: "Fall von Selbstverstümmlung bei einer Geisteskranken," *Allgemeine Zeitschrift für Psychiatrie und psychisch-gerichtliche Medizin* [Berlin; Leipzig] 27 (1871): 717–21. Both cases reported by Jambur Ananth, Harriet S. Kaplan and Keh-Ming Lin are of patients with religous delusions: "Self-Inflicted Enucleation of an Eye: Two Case Reporsts," *Canadian Journal of Psychiatry* 29.2 (March 1984): 145–46. Favazza (1987) includes in his bibliography several early accounts of cases involving self-enucleation and self harm, as does Menninger ("A Psychoanalytic Study" 452). Favazza cites von Carion C. Stellwag's "Extirpation des Bulbus" (1858), C. Lafon's "Les Auto-mutilations oculaires" (1907), A. Terson's "L'auto-enucleation des deux yeax [sic] dans la mélancholie avec délire religieux" (1911), Georges Crouigneau's "Arrachement traumatique du muscle droit inférieur de l'œil gauche et arrachement simultané du globe oculaire droit dans un cas d'au-

tomutilations répétées chez une mélancolique" (*Bulletins et mémoires de la société et journal de médecine de Paris* 27 Nov. 1887), and A[dolf] Franceschetti's *Beitrag zur Kenntnis der Evulsio Nervi Optici* (Contributions to knowledge on the evulsion of optical nerves; 1923) which offers a bibliography before presenting 53 cases, including two of his own, of which he says that there is "great aetiological variation" (22). He divides the injuries into three types: those caused by foreign bodies; by shooting; and by trauma. Menninger's cases include J. Allen Smith, "Voluntary Propulsion of Both Eyeballs," *Journal of the American Medical Association* 98 (30 Jan. 1932): 398, although this article describes a patient with a temporary, voluntary and painless condition, only dubiously termed self-mutilation; Harries, "Zwei weitere Fälle schwerer Selbstverletsungen der Augen" (Two cases of self-inflicted eye injuries by insane persons), *Psychiatrisch-nuerologische Wochenschrift* 27 (6 July 1929): 342–43; and Goodhart and Savitsky (1933). See also T. Axenfeld, "Über Luxation, Zerstörung und Herausreissung des Augapfels als Selbstuerstummelung bei Geisteskranken" (On dislocation, destruction and the tearing out of eyeballs as self-harm among the mentally ill) *Zeitschrift für Augenheilkunde* 1 (1899): 128–51. A relatively recent case is documented by O. Grandmontagne, C. Faruch, P. Blasquez and J. Delpech in "Une automutilation spectaculaire," *Annales médico-psychologiques* 143.10 (Dec. 1985): 940–46.

3. An overview of cases is provided by Bruce E. Keogh, Celia M. Oakley and Kenneth M. Taylor's "Chronic Constrictive Pericarditis Caused by Self-mutilation with Sewing Needles: A Case Report and Review of Published Reports," *British Heart Journal* 59.1 (Jan. 1988): 77–80 at heart.bmj.com

4. If transference can be very generally understood as the redirection of other relationships into the therapy situation (so that the analyst becomes the object of a kind of "reply," and that reply itself the subject of investigation in therapy), countertransference is the technical term used to describe the feelings of the physician for the patient, which Freud suggests arises from the patient's influence on the unconscious. The complexities of the term are discussed in Douglass W. Orr, "Transference and Countertransference: A Historical Survey," *Essential Papers on Countertransference*, ed. Benjamin Wolstein (New York: New York University Press, 1988) 91–110.

5. The cases which Lopez cites are M. Silvy, *Memoires de la Société Médicale* (Année 5me p. 181) [at p. 6 of Lopez]; Heckholdt and Otto, "Copenhagen Needle Case," *Medico-Chirologi-cal Review* 7.22 (Oct 1925): 559 which describes a young woman who discharged more than 400 needles over the period from August 1807 to December 1823 [at 77–78]; and Dupuytren, no reference given, although this author is quoted: "I have seen at the Hôtel Dieu, a great number of women and children, who *had been affected with the strange mania of swallowing pins and needles*" [italics in Lopez; at 81].

6. A 2001 report from India describes a Hindu man who did not have any psychiatric illness, nor any sexual preoccupations, but said that he had severed his genitals in order to remove any obstacle to salvation: M.S. Bhatia and S. Arora, "Penile Self-mutilation," *British Journal of Psychiatry* [*The Journal of Mental Science*] 178.1 (Jan 2001): 87–88.

7. Menninger ("A Psychoanalytic Study" 445) notes ten accounts of self-castration, among which are Nolan D.C. Lewis (1927–28), Charles Blondel (1906), and de Massary, Leroy and Mallet (1929). Favazza's cases not discussed here (with slightly corrected references in some instances) are Conrado O. Ferrer, "Auto-mutilaciones en un alcoholista hipocondriaco" ("Self-mutilation of hypochondriac alcoholic patient"), *Semana Medica* [Buenos Aires] Jan. 9, 1930; И. Б. Галант, "Мастурбация и автокастрация в картине шизофренически-параноидного заболевания" (I.B. Galant, "Masturbation and autocastration in cases of paranoid forms of schizophrenia"), *Zhurnal Nevropatologi i psikhiatrii imeni* 21 (1928): 385–92; (n.b. Menninger, "A Psychoanalytic Study" 445 translates schizophrenia as "dementia praecox"); [Staatsanwalt Eckert in München.] XVIII. "Zur Frage der Selbstentmannung," *Archiv fuer Kriminal-Anthropologie und Krim-inalistik* 46 (1912): 277–88; J. Ingegnieros, 'Un Case de auto-castration en un degenerado hereditario con neurasthenia y sifilofobia,' *Se-mana Medica* [Buenos Aires] 8 (1901) [this essay cannot be traced for this source and date]; "Über Selbstentmannung" [About self-castration], *Archiv fur Kriminal-Anthropologie und Kriminalistik mit einer Anzahl von Fach-männern*, ed. Hans Gross (Leipzig: F.C.W. Vogel, 1903), 263–65; and Dr. Schmidt-Petersen, "Ueber Selbst-Kastration," *Zeitschrift für Medizinalbeamte* [Berlin] 15 (1902): 735–37. Case 97 in Richard von Krafft-Ebing's *Psy-*

chopathia Sexualis: With Special Reference to the Antipathetic Sexual Instinct: A Medico-forensic Study (12th ed., trans. F.J. Rebman. New York: Physicians and Surgeons Book Company, 1922) describes a man who fanta-sised about eating the skin of a young woman; after unsuccessful pursuit of potential victims, he "would cut a piece of skin from his own arm, thigh or abdomen and eat it" (239).

8. It is notable that the patient's work de-manded skill in cutting, that he had had a tes-ticle removed (i.e. had experience of surgery), and that his personal life was such that he had a motive to reduce his sexual desire.

9. Butler regards "neurasthenia" as a grab-bag term which was clarified by Janet, by Freud, and by English psychiatrists (1943: 98).

10. See E.H. Jones, *The Road to En-dor: Being an Account of How Two Prisoners of War at Yozgad in Turkey Won Their Way to Freedom*. 7th ed. London: John Lane, the Bodley Head; New York: John Lane, 1920. The self injuries they inflicted included hanging themselves (204–05).

11. The case in question was Parsons, "Psy-chology of Traumatic Amblyphobia," *Proceed-ings of the Royal Society of Medicine, Neurological Section* 8 (1915). The example is interesting be-cause Buzzard went on to write *An Outline of Neurology and Its Outlook* (1921). In terms of specialism, we might expect him to be reasonably inured to this kind of argument, although the tone of his Foreword to Yealland implies sup-port for Yealland's robustly intolerant approach to the treatment of mental illness in wartime.

12. In responding to a paper which in-cluded this material, medical historian Sally Wilde remarked that "all responses are emo-tional." I understand her to mean that all de-cisions about treatment do, in some way, reflect the nature and degree of sympathy the patient has been able to evoke.

13. For an earlier reading of this account, see Menninger, "A Psychoanalytic Study" 454–56.

14. This case was drawn to my attention by Cynthia Anne Simpson's Dissertation (see 9).

15. Other works of this "anthropological" kind include D.I. Bachmayer's "Tooth Muti-latingh Practices Among the Barakwena and Vassakela Bushhmen in West Caprivi and the Peoples of Kavango," *Journal of the Dental As-sociation of South Africa* 37 (March 1982): 173–77; Sture Lagercrantz's essay on self-mutilation of fingers in Africa, "Fingervers-tummelungen und ihre Ausbreitung in Afrika: Zur Verbreitung der Monorchie," *Zeitschrift*

für Ethnologie 70 (1938): 199–208; J. Imbelloni's *Intorno ai crani "incredibili" degli indiani Natchez: nuove orientazioni critiche e tassinomiche sulla deformazione artificiale* ("incredible skulls of the Natchez Indians"; Estratto da Atti del XXII Congresso internaz. degli Americanisti. Roma—Settembre 1926. Roma: Ricardo Garroni, 1928), and his jointly authored *Deformaciones intencionales del cuerpo humano de character étnico* (with Adolfo Dembo) (San Juan, Buenos Aires: José Anesi, 1938).

16. Two foreign workers are said to have injured themselves so that they would "not have to work"; contrastingly, "The behaviour of the other 17 patients is much less comprehensible," not least because every single patient, including two children, "went on ... to even more severe automutilation" (328).

17. For a recent overview see Uwe Gieler, Sylvie G. Consoli, Lucia Tomás-Aragones, Dennis M. Linder, Gregor B.E. Jemec, Françoise Poot, Jacek C. Szepietowski, John De Korte, Klaus-Michael Taube, Andrey Lvov and Silla M. Consoli, "Self-Inflicted Lesions in Dermatology: Terminology and Classification: A Position Paper from the European Society for Dermatology and Psychiatry," *Acta Dermato-Venereologica* 93.1 (Jan. 2013): 4–12, in which the following terms are considered: "malingering; factitious disorders; Münchausen's syndrome; simulation; pathomimicry; skin picking syndrome and related skin damaging disorders; compulsive and impulsive skin picking; impulse control disorders; obsessive compulsive spectrum disorders; trichotillomania; dermatitis artefacta; factitial dermatitis; acne excoriée; and neurotic and psychogenic excoriations."

18. C. Hawkins, writing in the *British Journal of Rheumatology* in 1989 of a case of self-induced arthritis, encouraged colleagues to be "sympathetic rather than triumphant," "supportive instead of punitive," dealing with the patient in private and *not* referring him or her to a psychiatrist. See "Clinical Conundrum," *BJR* 28.1 (1989): 69.

19. See Thomas P. Beresford, "The Dyanmics of Aggression in an Amputee," *General Hospital Psychiatry* 3 (1980): 219–25 which describes a young man who engineered an amputation of his lower leg, after shooting himself in the foot.

20. Obermayer (4) queries this genealogy, arguing that Sydenham (in 1681) drew attention to the skin in considering "'hysteric diseases'" and Turner (in 1726) "attributed rosacea

in a woman to grief over her husband's death"; he goes on to note several other early cases and contributors, including Damon's *Neuroses of the Skin* (4–5). Other writers sought to identify patterns, Raffaele Rivalte offering "Notes on One Hundred Cases of Cutaneous Malingering" (*Giorn. Ital. d. Mal. Ven. e delle Pelle* 4 [1916]: 415. Press clipping pasted into offprint of "Two Cases for Comment." Weber, [Papers] 163: Box 84, Folder 2) while Pernet presented "Two Cases of Dermatitis Artefacta" in 1915. See also S. Duret-Cosyns, "Introduction: A La Dermatologie Psychosomatique," *Archives Belges de dermatologie et de syphiligraphie* T. 27.2 (1971): 281–88.

21. Georges Dieulafoy argued for the coining of the term "disinterested pathomimia," that is, as the term for describing those instances in which no material advantage was obtained by the injury to the skin that had been inflicted by the patient (Ulnik 205, citing Garzón and Consigli).

22. For a 1975 example see I. Sneddon and J. Sneddon, "Self-inflicted Injury: A Follow-up Study of 43 Patients," *British Medical Journal* 30 Aug. 1975: 527–30.

23. Obermayer's bibliography (431–71) is an extraordinary piece of work, if occasionally misleading, while his early chapters present his own perspective on this literature (see esp. Chapter one, "Historical Considerations" [3–8] and Chapter 4, "Theories of Mechanisms and Methods of Study" [34–92]). His work is discussed because it offers a compendium of writing about self-harm and dermatology in the first half of the twentieth century.

24. (Obermayer 123). The sources are Michelson; Carroll Spaulding Wright, "Psychosomatic Aspects of Dermatoses," *Clinics* 3.4 (Dec. 1944): 711–27 and Carroll S. Wright, "Psychosomatic Factors in Dermatology," *Southern Medical Journal* 42.11 (1949): 951–58; the quotation from Wright comes from the 1944 essay, but Wright's own wording hints at a more qualified view that is borne out in the discussion of his cases: "The majority but not all of the cases diagnosed as 'neurotic excoriations' [i.e. self harm] are probably true psychoses" (716). Wright's 1949 essay usefully offers a set of references on discussions of the significance of psychiatry for dermatology published in English and in German in the first half of the twentieth century (see 951).

25. Obermayer reports his failure to develop a model which sought to correlate skin disorders with models of personality (38).

26. James Glass says of the patient Julia and her relationship to the razor blade, "Having control over the possibility of her own annihilation led Julia to disavow annihilation altogether" (*Private Terror* 18).

27. For a brief critique of the idea of the contract see Anthony Harrison, "A Harmful Procedure," *Nursing Times* 94.27 (8 July 1998): 38–39.

Chapter 3

1. For an overview of "shell-shock" and attitudes to mental illness in the First World War, which positions several of the key writers discussed here, see Peter Leese, *Shell Shock: Traumatic Neurosis and the British Soldiers of the First World War* (Houndmills: Palgrave Macmillan, 2002).

2. Such views are still being expressed: Fiona Reid acknowledges conflicting perspectives, but signals her own sentiments in remarking that "It was not possible consistently to take a sympathetic view of cowardice and desertion. After all, many men were pushed beyond reasonable limits" (100). Reid links "malingering" to "self-inflicted injury" and attributes both to "a loss of nerve" (58). *Broken Men: Shell Shock, Treatment and Recovery in Britain 1914–30* (2010. London and New York: Continuum, 2011).

3. I am indebted to Sam Allender for this insight regarding the capaciousness of categories of illness.

4. Research into women who self harm in prison contexts is a relatively new phenomenon. See for example Cassandra Kenning, Jayne Cooper, Vicky Short, Jenny Shaw, Kathryn Able and Carolyn Chew-Graham, "Prison Staff and Women Prisoners' Views on Self-harm: Their Implications for Service Delivery and Development: A Qualitative Study," *Criminal Behaviour and Mental Health* 20.4 (Oct. 2010): 274–84; Lisa Marzano, Karen Ciclitira and Joanna Adler, "The Impact of Prison Staff Responses on Self-harming Behaviours: Prisoners' Perspectives," *British Journal of Clinical Psychology* 51.1 (March 2012): 4–18; and Lisa Marzano, Keith Hawton, Adrienne Rivlin and Seena Fazel, "Psychosocial Influences on Prisoner Suicide: A Case-control Study of Near-lethal Self-harm in Women Prisoners," *Social Science and Medicine* 72.6 (March 2011): 874–83.

5. Unlike many scholarly works published in this period and after, Gavin includes complete documentation of his sources and there-fore offers perhaps the most useful bibliographical resource for this period. See also Ballingall's *Outlines of Military Surgery* (1855: 603–16).

6. The exception he notes is Cesare Biondi (Salinari 1), whose numerous articles are included in his bibliography.

7. John Money's account of what he calls "The Skoptic Syndrome" is based on a letter he received from a correspondent, reprinted at 115–26 of the article; the correspondent subsequently also sent pictures of his genitals.

8. This is in contrast to, for example, psychoanalytic approaches, which see a symbolic significance (if displaced or condensed) in the site and mechanisms of self harm (e.g. Scheftel 90–94).

9. Only late in the book does McCurdy lay his cards on the table in relation to mental illness, declaring that "It is only the physician who constantly maintains the psychological standpoint ... who will be consistently successful in treating the war neuroses" (128). R. Gregory Lande's recent history *Madness, Malingering and Malfeasance: The Transformation of Psychiatry and the Law in the Civil War Era* (Dulles, Virginia: Brassey's, 2003) notes that the United States' *Articles of War* of 1775 have a subtle condemnation of malingering (151), a view Lande shares.

10. It is no coincidence that it was Collie who edited André Léri's *Shell Shock: Commotional and Emotional Aspects* (1919) for the London University Press's "Military Medical Manual" series. The book is implicitly a reply to G. Roussy and J. L'Hermitte's *The Psychoneuroses of War* (ed. William Aldren Turner, trans. Wilfred B. Christopherson, London: London University Press, 1918) in the same series.

11. Interestingly Collie cites the first but not the much more substantial second edition of Hector Gavin's work on self harm (1843), his book thereby appearing more original than it might otherwise have seemed.

12. See also "An Epitome of Current Medical Literature. War Number. Medicine. 47. Simulation of Disease," *British Medical Journal* 19 May 1917: 1 and "An Epitome of Current Medical Literature. Simulation of Disease," *British Medical Journal* 28 July 1917: 1–4. Clippings, Folder 2. Concern about "Insincerity in Cases of War Injury" continued to be expressed in the *Lancet*, and interest was maintained after war's end: see "Malingering and the Simulation of Disease," *Lancet* 20 Dec. 1919: 1158, Folder 2.

13. W.G. Eckert, in "The Pathology of Self-Mutilation and Destructive Acts: A Forensic Study and Review," *Journal of Forensic Sciences*

22.1 (1977): 242–50, calls these two works "Excellent treatises ... as seen by experienced investigators" (247).

14. One recent study of more than 40,000 soldiers has found (self-reported) rates of depression and self harm inverse to rank: see Mark S. Riddle, John W. Sanders, James J. Jones and Schuyler C. Webb, "Self-reported Combat Stress Indicators Among Troops Deployed to Iraq and Afghanistan," *Comprehensive Psychiatry* 49.4 (2008): 340–45.

15. On Germany, see also W. Mayer, "Über Simulation und Hysterie (During the War)," *Zeitschrift für die gesamte Neurologie und Psychiatrie* [Berlin] 39 (1928) 315–28.

16. The first day of the invasion is commemorated in Australia and New Zealand as "Anzac day," a solemn national holiday marked by dawn memorial services followed by parades of former and current members of the armed forces and their descendants. Tens of thousands of people from these countries go to Turkey to attend a ceremony *in situ*. So high is demand for places at the centenary commemoration in 2015 that a national ballot was held to allot them.

17. We can assume that in referring to the *frequency* of what he regards as misdiagnosis of malingering, Butler is speaking of punishments administered by other armies, for the Australian one "managed to get through the war without the introduction of a death penalty for most offences so punishable in other armies" (74).

18. The fact that the Australian army did not allow the death penalty is mentioned by Herbert (207).

19. This might have been a reflection of the belief that American "social psychology" was dominated by the behaviorism espoused by J.B. Watson (Butler, vol. 3, 59). Behaviorism remains the dominant paradigm in treatment and research for self harm in North America, notwithstanding the contributions made in psychoanalysis, criminology (especially in the 1970s) and, more recently, sociology.

20. Weber, [Papers] Box 84, Folder 1, which contains the Blondel doctorate.

21. The initial story is 2 Aug. 1917 (3). The doctor and an accomplice were sentenced to 12 months in prison: see "Sentences in Heart Pills Case: Judge and the Employment of Decoys," *Times* 20 Oct. 1917: 3. Both this clipping and the earlier one are preserved in the Weber Papers, Box 84, Folder 2.

22. That the case was an appealing one is suggested by the fact that it was recalled later by Judson S. Bury, who gave a paraphrase of

Buzzard in his own piece in the *Lancet* in 1920. Bury concludes that "True malingering—that is, conscious simulation—is rare. It is, however, often combined with true hysteria, or unconscious simulation, and it is such combinations that I think lend themselves most readily to dramatic cures" (68).

23. In their footnote for this information, referenced to *Casualties and Medical Statistics* (London: HMSO, 1972): 206, Copp and McAndrew note that the official figures for self-inflicted wounds were .21 per thousand among British troops, 2.4 among Canadian and .1 among New Zealanders.

24. The notes are written onto A.F. Hurst and E.A. Peters, "A Report on the Pathology, Diagnosis, and Treatment of Absolute Hysterical Deafness in Soldiers," *Lancet* 6 Oct. 1917: 517–19. Clipping pasted into "Otological Section," Weber, [Papers] Folder 2. Weber references Arthur F. Hurst, "The Causes, Diagnoses, and Treatment of Hysterical Deafness, with Notes on the Auditory-Motor Reflex and the Psychology of Hearing," *Seale Hayne Neurological Studies* 1.5 (1919): 279–90, an essay which contains passing reference to "malingering." The "operations," which were "completely successful in several cases" (288) are considered at 287–89.

25. See also Michelson (247), for a case in which a placebo was recommended by the treating psychiatrist. In informal discussion I have been told of the continuing use of placebo treatments, but the risk lies in forms of structuring payment which potentially make such treatment itself a kind of fraud.

Chapter 4

1. Both Blondel and Lorthiois are cited as authorities on self harm by Georges Bataille, writing in France in the late 1920s (see Bataille 71, note 6; note 7); Blondel is also cited in some French reports, e.g. M. Bourgeois, "L'automutilation génitale," *Contraception-fertilité-sexualité* 12.4 (April 1984): 597–601 at 600 and M. Bourgeois, J.-F. Daubech and A.-M. Lemerle, "Enquête sur l'automutilation chez l'adulte en milieu psychiatrique: A propos de 90 cas," *Annales médico-psychologique* 142.10 (1984): 1287–95 at 1287.

2. Although there is no consistent or synoptic literature, case studies from psychological or veterinary science indicate that those animals which do self harm tend to be incarcerated (see for example T.V. Joe Layng, Paul Thomas An-

dronis and Israel Goldiamond, "Animal Models of Psychopathology: The Establishment, Maintenance, Attenuation, and Persistence of Head-banging by Pigeons," *Journal of Behavior Therapy and Experimental Psychology* 30.1 (March 1999): 45–61 and Babette M. Fontenot, Mandi N. Wilkes and Cheryl S. Lynch, "Effects of Outdoor Housing on Self-Injurious and Stereotypic Behaviour in Adult Male Rhesus Macaques," *Journal of the American Association of Laboratory Animal Science* 45.5 (Sep. 2006): 35–45. This resonates with those studies of self harm which identify it as an expressive mode, particularly for those who are unable to find speech or another form of communication which can gain traction in the social world (see Reflections), although significantly, Fraiberg notes Harlow and Harlow's observations of self harm in their 1965 study of monkeys deprived of nurturing and socialisation (Fraiberg 632); the work of Harlow and of Tinklepaugh is often cited, and has been followed by John P. Gluck, Michael W. Otto and Alan J. Beauchamp who used electric shocks to induce self harm: see their "Respondent Conditioning of Self-injurious Behavior in Early Socially Deprived Rhesus Monkeys," *Journal of Abnormal Psychology* 94.2 (May 1985): 222–26.

3. A contemporary and correspondent of James Frazer, Lévy-Bruhl's works in ethnology include *Les fonctions mentales dans les sociétés inférieures* (Paris, 1910; *How Natives Think*, London: Allen and Unwin, 1926) and *La mentalité primitive* (Paris, 1922; *Primitive Mentality*, trans. Lilian A. Clare, London: Allen and Unwin; New York: Macmillan, 1923).

4. Much has been made of Van Gogh's actions, not least by psychiatrists and biographers—see for example Albert J. Lubin's "Vincent Van Gogh's Ear," *Psychoanalytic Quarterly* 30 (1961): 351–84 or Harold P. Blum's "Van Gogh's Fantasies," *Journal of the American Psychoanalytic Association* 57.6 (2009): 1311–26. However, aspects of the event are unusual, which is to say, uncharacteristic of cases of self harm. Two historians have proposed that Van Gogh's ear was in fact cut off by Gauguin but the two artists made a pact to keep Gauguin's involvement secret: see Hans Kaufmann and Rita Wildegans, *Van Goghs Ohr: Paul Gauguin und der Pakt des Schweigens* (*Van Gogh's Ear: Paul Gauguin and the Pact of Silence*) (Berlin: Osburg, 2008).

5. While one is a young artist who bit off his finger (Claude, Borel and Robin), another is a young woman who tore her eyes (a case which Bataille takes from Lorthiois 94).

6. Ribot cites a set of German and Italian authors on the notion of the "fixed idea" (84), although Janet's *Névroses et idées fixes* had been published in 1898.

7. Janet considers two patients: a ten-year-old child whose face and hands were covered with wounds and scabs (389), another with trichotillomania, or pulling out hair (390–91). The term "trichotillomania" seems to have been coined by François Hallopeau in a brief case report, "III. Alopécie par grattage (trichomanie ou trichotillomanie)," *Annales de dermatologie et de syphiligraphie: Bulletin de la Société Française de Dermatologie et Syphiligraphie* 10 (1889): 440–41.

8. "Au mois de février 1844, 350 hommes du 3ᵉ battalion du 1ʳᵉ régiment de la Légion étrangère étaiant campés à Sidi-Bel-Abbès dans la province d'Oran. Un soldat s'étant mutilé en se tirant volontairement un coup de fusil dans le poignet, 13 autres se mutilèrent de la même manière dans l'espace de 20 jours" (124). Sourced to *Annales médico-psychologique* 1re série 12 (1848): Variétiés 436.

9. Mark S. Micale says that the work of Janet has undergone a kind of revival "among mental health professionals concerned with the psychology of trauma" (*Approaching Hysteria* 9; see also "Jean-Martin Charcot" 130). Interest has been facilitated by the republication of Janet's major works by L'Harmattan (although they have not been translated into English). William James, in his *Principles of Psychology* (1890), makes frequent reference to Janet's work, particularly his case studies of "Lucie" and "Léonie." He mentions correspondence in note 10 of his chapter "The Emotions" and there he, like Mayo, credits Janet in regard to the term "dissociation."

10. Notably Favazza's *Bodies under Siege*, Marilee Strong's *A Bright Red Scream*, and in the UK, a series of publications by the Bristol Basement Project: see various publications led by Lois Arnold or Louise Pembroke. Less accommodating of this view are Conterio *et al.*, who, working from the same feminist principles as the Basement Project writers, see potential damage in facilitation.

11. In this respect, these authors see their case as a "more complex one" than that reported by Guiraud and Cailleux: see "Le meutre immotivé, réaction libératrice de la maladie chez les hébéphréniques," *Société Médicale Psychologie* 25 Oct. 1928: 148.

12. "Il est à noter, de plus, que, sur le moment, il ne pouvait indiquer, pour l'acte accom-

pli, aucun motif plausible. Cet acte se présentait, dans ces conditions, comme un acte démentiel, sans explication. Il se peut que les motifs, invoqués par la suite par le malade, lui aient été suggérés, en partie du moins, par les interrogatoires successifs. D'autre part, il se peut fort bien que certaines tendances viennent déterminer l'acte en question, sans que pour cela il soit nécessaire d'admettre la présence de complexes, au sens vrai du mot" (de Massary *et al.* 149).

13. "Du point de vue psychologique, il y a, au fond, deux questions qui se posent à propos de ce malade: (1) comment a surgi à un moment précis l'idée de se couper les parties, et (2) comment cette idée amène-t-elle, de suite, sa réalisation? En ce qui concerne le côté clinique de problème, le malade n'a pas l'aspect d'un vrai dément précoce; il semble s'agir d'un individu faible, déprimé, avec tendance à la paresse, ce qui fait qu'il se plaît mieux à l'hôpital que dehors" (de Massary *et al.* 149–50).

14. Jung cites, here, A.E. Hoche's *Handbuch der gerichtlichen Psychiatrie* (Berlin: Hirschwald, 1901, 1909).

15. Greenacre, "The Eye Motif" 556–57, who references, for men, S[ándor] Ferenczi, *Contributions to Psycho-Analysis*, trans. Ernest Jones (London: Stanley Phillips, 1916: 228–32; see also 223), and for women, Oskar Pfister, *The Psychoanalytic Method*, trans. Charles Rockwell Payne (New York: Moffat, Yard, 1917), 160.

16. In developing this theory of substitution, Menninger cites Franz Alexander (in *The Psychoanalysis of the Total Personality: The Application of Freud's Theory of the Ego to the Neuroses*), Otto Rank (in "Zur Genese des Kastrationskomplexes," *International Zeitschrift für Psychiatrie*, both 1930), and Sándor Radó's "Fear of Castration in Women."

17. Menninger cites recent reports of self-inflicted injury in the context of psychosis: Jacob Conn's, discussed above, which does not fit this paradigm; MacKenna's, in which the author says bluntly that since the patient is a yokel who "did not possess the gift of being able to express himself clearly ... it was very hard to determine the nature of the eruption from which he had suffered" ("A Case of Extensive Self-Mutilation" 314); and H.R. Sharma, whose account is too brief to admit of any diagnosis, and in which psychosis is not mentioned. Only C.I. Urechia's "Autophagie des doigts chez un paralytique en rapport avec une pachyméningite cervicale" ["Autophagia of fingers by patient with general paralysis and cervical pachymeningitis"], *Société de Neurologie de Paris* (March 1931):

350–52, mentions psychosis. The case of the woman Menninger describes recalls that of John Jay Chapman, who inflicted burns to his hand which resulted in amputation after Chapman had punched a man whom he believed was being too friendly to Chapman's then girlfriend, later wife. See Melvin H. Bernstein, *John Jay Chapman* (New York: Twayne, 1964), 27; John E. Mullen, "The Enigma of John Jay Chapman," PhD Diss., Graduate College, University of Iowa, 1980, 127–29.

18. There is a chapter on "self-mutilations" which runs to 55 pages, about ten per cent of the work. The latter two thirds of this chapter discuss religion (248–61), then offer a formulaic discussion of self harm in organic diseases, psychosis, and customary forms as they are encountered by doctors (261–83).

19. For a rare and early attempt to problematise terminology around self harm and suicide see Kessel.

20. F. Parkes Weber has written "very good" on the review, but it is not clear whether he is referring to the review, or the book.

21. Both references which Fenichel gives for these claims are from Menninger; he also cites A.A. Brill's "The Concept of Psychic Suicide," *International Journal of Psycho-Analysis* 20 (1939): 246–51, although this essay deals with the capacity to die at will (in non-violent ways). At least one writer argues that Fenichel was "clearly influenced by Menninger" (Scheftel 16); this might be true of his thinking on self harm, but other theorists play a more central role in his *Psychoanalytic Theory of Neurosis*, a book in which he deals with self harm to a limited extent.

22. Radó cites here not Menninger, but page 16 of his own essay "The Psychoanalysis of Pharmacothymia (Drug Addiction)," *Psychoanalytic Quarterly* 2 (1933): 1–23 (rpt in *Journal of Substance Abuse Treatment* 1.1 1984: 59–68). This identification of a kind of "self harm by proxy"—specifically, inducing doctors to perform surgery, particularly amputations, is evident in several case reports discussed in chapter two (Dieulafoy; Heidingsfeld; Prosser Thomas). More opaque still are those cases of amputation undertaken knowingly by a surgeon to address what is sometimes termed body dysmorphia or apotemnophilia, in which the patient is convinced that one of their limbs is extraneous (reported in the media by Dyer).

23. That said, Horney deals with Deutsch mainly by ignoring her work.

24. Horney's preparedness to engage with her

colleagues, and to publish criticisms even of Freud (see esp. 255, note 8), is unusual: she is called "the most outspoken of Freud's critics" by the authors of *Freud's Women* (Appignanesi and Forrester 433), who discuss the debates about female sexuality in some detail (see 430–54).

25. Pursuing this line of thinking, studies of self harm in its social context suggest that patterns can be correlated with circumstances, including social disadvantage (see Corcoran *et al.*). One study concludes that the correlation between self harm and employment status is closer than that between self harm and either class or gender: Robert Young, Michael Van Beinum, Helen Sweeting and Patrick West, "Young People Who Self-harm," *British Journal of Psychiatry* 191.1 (July 2007): 44–49.

26. Garrard describes a case of male self-mutilation of the breast (99), in the context of anxiety and desire about fatherhood, and heterosexual sexual acts.

27. This is part of that "rash of theorizing" that Haughton observes on women and self harm (22). Doctors' response to this question as laid out in the thesis has been declared "elegant, comprehensive and concise" by Cross (68), who, like Doctors, essentialises and generalises a "feminine" sensibility, albeit positively instead of negatively.

28. Gardner and Gardner note with obvious reservation Graff and Mallin's "treatment" of holding the patient's hand and embracing them, something the British writers gloss as "cuddling" (131).

29. See for example Adrienne Harris and Lewis Aaron, eds, *The Legacy of Sándor Ferenczi* (Hillsdale, New Jersey and London: Analytic Press, 1993); André Haynal, *Disappearing and Reviving: Sándor Ferenczi in the History of Psychoanalysis* (London: Karnac Books, 2002); Peter L. Rudnytsky, Antal Bokay and Patrizia Giampieri-Deutsch, eds, *Ferenczi's Turn in Psychoanalysis* (New York and London: New York University Press, 1996); and Arnold W. Rachman, *Sàndor Ferenczi: The Psychotherapist of Tenderness and Passion* (Northvale, N.J.: J. Aronson, 1997).

30. Gail S. Greenspan and Steven E. Samuel in their essay "Self-Cutting after Rape" in the *American Journal of Psychiatry* 146.6 (June 1989): 789–90 present three women who begin self harming after being raped; Mary de Young's "Self-Injurious Behavior in Incest Victims: A Research Note" *Child Welfare* 61.8 (1982): 577–84 likewise associated self harm with the aftermath of sexual assault, finding

an astonishing 57.7 percent of her sample of 45 female patients—all of whom had been sexually assaulted by their father or stepfather—had engaged in self harm for at least three months, their acts including "cutting and slashing, bruising, scratching, and burning, to deliberate attempts to break bones and, in one case, self poisoning" (579).

31. Ferenczi goes on, "For this notion I am partly indebted to discoveries made by our colleague [his patient], Elisabeth [sic] Severn, which she personally communicated to me." On this complex and troubling relationship see Christopher Fortune, "The Case of 'R.N.': Sándor Ferenczi's Radical Experiment in Psychoanalysis," *The Legacy of Sándor Ferenczi*, ed. Adrienne Harris and Lewis Aaron (Hillsdale, New Jersey, and London: Analytic Press, 1993), 101–20, esp. 108. The two papers referred to here are "The Principle of Relaxation and Neocatharsis," (German original) *International Zeitschrift für Psychiatrie*, English translation *International Journal of Psycho-Analysis* in 1930 (121), and "Confusion of Tongues between Adults and the Child" (German original) *International Zeitschrift für Psychiatrie* 1933; English translation published as "Confusion of Tongues between the Adult and the Child (The Language of Tenderness and of Passion)" *International Journal of Psycho-Analysis* 30 (1949): 225–30. Both papers were read at the International Psycho-analytical Congress.

32. Needless to say such an argument is at odds with the now-conventional arguments about trauma and unspeakability proposed by Cathy Caruth—see for example "Traumatic Departures: Survival and History in Freud," *Trauma and Self*, ed. Charles B. Strozier and Michael Flyn (Rowman and Littlefield, 1996): 29–43 and, in particular, Cathy Caruth, *Unclaimed Experience: Trauma, Narrative and History* (Baltimore: Johns Hopkins University Press, 1997). While Caruth concurs on the point of what she terms "determined repetition" ("Traumatic Departures 33), her argument or claim is that the trauma is at some level literally unspeakable, but this repetition is understood as "flashback" and made complex by the inexplicability or ungraspability of survival.

33. On the horrors and dangers of re-enactment during therapy, see Perlman (338–39). The concept of re-enactment is discussed in graduate dissertations by Katharine Elizabeth Oscroft (1988) and Gordon E. Tuttle (1997).

34. The picture is further complicated by those instances in which self harm is used as a

means to *escape* trauma—Robert Johnson's interviews with more than 300 prisoners who had self harmed disclosed several cases in which young men seem to have chosen self-inflicted injury as a means of avoiding rape or sexual assault (475–76).

35. In what is presented as the first account by an adult survivor of Münchausen by proxy—a horrific case in which damage to the limbs extended over many years, inflicted by thrice-weekly hammering among other things—it was noted that the abusive parent was a nurse, her handwriting evident on *"nursing notes, medication sheets, and intake and output records"* (Bryk and Segal 2, emphasis in original). The case later developed into one of self harm (5). Other writers note the over-representation of those in "caring professions"—"17 nurses, one nun, two medical technicians and voluntary psychiatric social worker" among their sample of 42 patients with Münchausen syndrome, and that more than half of the 42 "had also mutilated themselves in some way" (59): see M.W.P. Carney and J.P. Brown, "Clinical Features and Motives among 42 Artifactual Illness Patients," *British Journal of Medical Psychology* 56.1 (March 1983): 57–66.

Reflections

1. There are innumerable articles, especially from the last quarter of the twentieth century, which claim that self harm is distinctive to women or girls, some of which will be discussed below. One very thorough study which collected data over a two-year period, albeit on a broad spectrum of behavior called self harm, argues that when figures are sourced from hospitals and doctors the ratio of women to men is about 2:1, but when this is supplemented by figures from prisons, rates of self harm are fairly even for men and women (309): see F. Gordon Johnson, B. Gail Frankel, Roberta G. Ferrence, George K. Jarvis and Paul C. Whitehead, "Self-Injury in London, Canada: A Prospective Study," *Canadian Journal of Public Health* 66.4 (July-Aug. 1975): 307–16. These authors also speculate that there is under-reporting of self harm when the patient is seen by physicians or the self harm occurrs in gaols (309).

2. A synopsis of the case is presented in a jointly-written article, of which Scheftel is lead author, in the *Bulletin of the Menninger Clinic* 50.6 (Nov. 1986): 525–40. I found Scheftel's thesis the most difficult to read of any source discussed in this book. Following the injunction of Christos Tsiolkas, I have tried to turn towards, rather than away from, this material. But as medical professionals would be quick to point out, I think, my encounter only entails reading, not dealing with a patient in situ, as so many writers describe themselves as doing.

3. Freud's essay "Constructions in Analysis" is in *Moses and Monotheism: Three Essays*, trans. James Strachey, ed. James Strachey with Anna Freud, assisted by Alix Strachey and Alan Tyson, The Standard Edition of the Complete Psychological Works of Sigmund Freud, Vol. 23 (London: Hogarth, and the Institute of Psycho-Analysis) 255–70. The quote above is at 268.

4. These authors reference J.R. Ashton and S. Donnan, "Suicide by Burning as an Epidemic Phenomenon: An Analysis of 82 Deaths and Inquests in England and Wales in 1978–9." *Psychological Medicine* 11 (1981): 735–39.

5. Glass's approach finds an echo in Helen Gremillion's *Feeding Anorexia: Gender and Power at a Treatment Center*, Body, Commodity, Text (Durham: Duke University Press, 2004).

6. The statistics are unreliable because they collapse self harm and attempted suicide, although this would tend to indicate over- not under-reporting (Greig 13).

7. In the 1970s, some states in the U.S. implicitly required prison or medical staff to make a judgment on whether or not the self harm was "genuine" or "manipulative" in order to determine the appropriate response: see Research and Reporting Unit, Division of Program Development and Evaluation, [Virginia] Department of Corrections, *Self-Mutilation at the Penitentiary and Powhatan*, Report no. 7821 and Supplement, Sept. 1978, 33.

8. There are numerous studies of individuals or small numbers. Much larger in scale is Bruhel *et al.* which presents the results of a 30-month study of 18 patients. The appeal of behaviorist methods, as they are outlined in multiple studies, is that they can be used by non-specialist staff, and can be implemented on a larger scale than other therapies.

9. There are numerous examples in the Anglophone literature, but interestingly the same is characteristic of case reports from non–English-speaking countries. See for example Yoshihiko Hoshino, Motohisa Kaneko, Yuko Yashima and Hisashi Kumashiro, "Self-Mutilative Behavior and Its Treatment in Autistic Children," *Fukushima Journal of Medical Science* 29.3–4 (1983): 133–40.

10. Their source is Arther H. Green, "Self-

Mutilation in Schizophrenic Children," *Archives of General Psychiatry* 17.2 (Aug. 1967): 114–21.

11. In this study a cattle prod was used "only in exceptional conditions," and "as back-up for the remote-control unit whenever it was out of order, or in distant localities" (248). The tool was generally unwieldy, "requiring the assistance of several staff members to hold the resident for the shock to be delivered" (249). The investment of resources in this project also shows that behaviorist methods are not of themselves cheaper.

12. The essay reveals signs that the researchers found the "shock program" "very distressing" (Jones, Simmons and Frankel 243), not least because the self harm increased and the patient's condition deteriorated. The essay reports that a program of limited periods of social isolation and careful reintegration into the social activities of the ward, including meals, was successful.

13. Hansi Kennedy and George S. Moran's "The Development Roots of Self-Injury and Response to Pain in a 4-Year-Old Boy," *Psychoanalytic Study of the Child* 39 (1984): 195–212, seeks to confirm Selma Fraiberg's argument (in "Pathological Defenses in Infancy") that distortions in object relations in early childhood can "lead to a modification of the threshold for physical pain" (212). This, in turn, amplifies the self harm that can ensue during disruption of development, as in this case study. The authors argue of their patient that "hurting himself was a compromise between the wish to hurt [his new sibling], the desire to retain his mother's love, and the condemnation of his own aggression in the form of self-punishment" (205). Grossman concurs in his findings that "from early infancy on, there is a capacity to respond to traumatic treatment with destructive and self-destructive behavior" (28). He references in support J.M. Herzog, "A Neonatal Intensive Care Syndrome: A Pain Complex Involving Neuroplasticity and Psychic Trauma," *Frontiers of Infant Psychiatry*, ed. J.D. Call *et al.* (New York: Basic Books, 1983), 291–300.

14. On which see Sándor Ferenczi, "The Adaptation of the Family," and "The Unwelcome Child." In this context, it may be significant that David Finkelhor's survey of nearly 800 students at six New England institutions found that 15 percent of women and 10 percent of men reported some sexual experience involving a sib-

ling (171), the prevalence peaking from ages seven to 12 (175). See "Sex Among Siblings: A Survey on Prevalence, Variety, and Effects," *Archives of Sexual Behavior* 9.3 (1980): 171–94.

15. Contrastingly, when faced with a selection of responses to a hypothetical patient who had chewed off his thumb and finger, nurses rejected the notion of "choice" for the patient, which were seen as being outweighed by the professional responsibility to provide care and the apparently diminished judgment of the patient (27). See Susan Hunn Garritson, "Ethical Decision Making Patterns," *Journal of Psychosocial Nursing and Mental Health Services* 26.4 (April 1988): 22–29.

16. Jolly and Galanos, for example, set out several reasons why a dermatologist should "not relinquish the patient [thought to be a neurotic excoriator] to a mental health professional," advocating collaboration over serial treatment by those working in different specialisations. They describe a case in which such collaboration has only just begun to occur, and the outcomes of which are not yet known: P.A. Jolly and A.N. Galanos, "Neurotic Excoriators: Advantages of an Interdisciplinary Treatment Approach," *Alabama Journal of Medical Sciences* 20.2 (Apr. 1983): 180–81.

17. Perhaps more importantly, time and money are directed away from research into the social and psychological factors already known to bear on self harm. It is not surprising that sociologists should find that most medical studies of self harm fail to consider adequately questions of context and advocate the discussion of the meanings of the practice(s), while problematizing the stereotyping of those who self harm (see Chandler *et al.*; Temple and Harris).

18. For example Roland M. Kohr, publishing in the *American Journal of Forensic Medicine and Pathology* 11.4 (1990): 324–28, notes but does not comment on "multiple contusions ... of varying ages" (325) in the genital area of a research chemist who had slashed his penis and wrists before poisoning himself with chloroform. His interests in the essay, "Suicide by Chloroform Ingestion Following Self-Mutilation," lie in alerting colleagues in forensic medicine to the use of a "usual substance of method" of suicide (328) and only the barest details of the patient's background— age, gender, race and occupation—are given.

Bibliography

Aboseif, Sherif, Reynaldo Gomez and Jack W. McAninch. "Genital Self-Mutilation." *Journal of Urology* 150 (Oct. 1993): 1143–46.

Abraham, Karl. "Manifestations of the Female Castration Complex." *International Journal of Psycho-analysis* 3 (1920): 1–29.

Ackerman, A. Bernard, Don T. Mosher and Harry A. Schwamm. "Factitial Weber-Christian Syndrome." *Journal of the American Medical Association* 198.7 (14 Nov. 1966): 731–36.

Adam, James. "Cases of Self-Mutilation by the Insane." *Journal of Mental Science* 29 (1883): 213–19.

Adamson, R.O. "A Case of Dermatitis Artefacta, and its Sequel." *British Medical Journal* 2 July 1910: 15.

Adler, Patricia, and Peter A. Adler. "The Cyber Worlds of Self-Injurers: Deviant Communities, Relationships, and Selves." *Symbolic Interaction* 31.1 (2008): 33–56.

_____. "The Demedicalization of Self-Injury: From Psychopathology to Sociological Deviance." *Journal of Contemporary Ethnography* 36 (2007): 537–70.

Adler, Peter, and Patricia A. Adler. *The Tender Cut: Inside the Hidden World of Self-injury.* New York: New York University Press, 2011.

Agris, Joseph, and C. Wilton Simmons, Jr. "Factitious (Self-Inflicted) Skin Wounds." *Plastic and Reconstructive Surgery: Journal of the American Society of Plastic Surgeons* 62.5 (Nov. 1978): 686–92.

Alao, Adekola O., Jennifer C. Yolles and Wendy Huslander. "Female Genital Self Mutilation." *Psychiatric Services* 50.7 (1 July 1999): 971.

Al-Qattan, M.M. "Factitious Disorders of the per Limb in Saudi Arabia." *Journal of Hand Surgery* (British and European Volume) 26B.5 (2001): 414–21.

Alroe, Christopher John, and Venkat Gunda. "Self-amputation of the Ear: Three Men Amputate Four Ears within Five Months." *Australian and New Zealand Journal of Psychiatry* 29.3 (1995): 508–12.

"Amputation of the Whole of the External Genitals During Delirium Tremens, Under the Care of Messrs. Francis and Grant, Market Harborough." *British Medical Journal* 5 Feb. 1870: 130.

Anderson, Donald Lee, and Godfrey Trygve Anderson. "Nostalgia and Malingering in the Military during the Civil War." *Perspectives in Biology and Medicine* 28.1 (Autumn 1984): 156–66.

Andrews, Judson B. "Case of Excessive Hypodermic Use of Morphia. Three Hundred Needles Removed from the Body of an Insane Woman." *American Journal of Insanity* 29.1 (July 1872): 13–19.

Andrews, T.C., D.L. Cull, J.J. Pelton, S.O. Massey, Jr., and J.M. Bostwick. "Self-mutilation and Malingering among Cuban Migrants Detained at Guantanamo Bay." *New England Journal of Medicine* 24 Apr. 1997: 1251–53.

Anzieu, Didier. "Skin Ego." *Psychoanalysis in France.* Ed. Serge Lebovici and Daniel Widlöcher. New York: International Universities Press, 1980. 17–32. Rpt. and trans.

from *Nouvelle Review de Psychanalyse* 9 (1970): 195–208.

Appignanesi, Lisa, and John Forrester. *Freud's Women.* London: Weidenfeld and Nicholson, 1992.

Apuleius. *The Metamorphosis [or Golden Ass] of Apuleius.* Trans. Thomas Taylor. 1822. Birmingham: Cosby, 1893. archive.org/stream/cu31924074297007#page/n7/mode/1up Accessed 17 Sep. 2013.

Aretaeus. *The Extant Works of Aretaeus, the Cappadocian.* Ed. and trans. Francis Adams. Boston: Milford House, 1856. Digital Hippocrates Collection. www.chlt.org/sandbox/dh/aretaeusEnglish/page.59.a.php?size=240x320

Armey, Michael F., Janis H. Crowther and Ivan W. Miller. "Changes in Ecological Momentary Assessment Reported Affect Associated with Episodes of Non-suicidal Self-injury." *Behavior Therapy* 42.4 (Dec. 2011): 579–88.

Army. *Report of the War Office Committee of Enquiry into "Shell-Shock."* Presented to Parliament by Command of his Majesty. 1922. London: Imperial War Museum, 2004.

Arnobius. *The Seven Books of Arnobius Adversus Gentes.* Ed. Alexander Roberts and James Donaldson. Trans. Hamilton Bryce and Hugh Campbell. Ante-Nicene Christian Library. Translations of the Writings of the Fathers down to A.D. 325. Vol. 19. Edinburgh: Clark, 1871.

Arnold, Lois, and Anne Magill. *The Self-harm Help Book.* Bristol: Basement Project, 1998.

———. *Working with Self-injury: A Practical Guide.* Bristol: Basement Project, 1996.

Arons, B.S. "Self-Mutilation: Clinical Examples and Reflection." *American Journal of Psychotherapy* 35.4 (1981): 550–58.

Asch, Stuart S. "Depression, Masochism, and Biology." *Hillside Journal of Clinical Psychiatry* 7.1 (1985): 34–53.

———. "Wrist Scratching as a Symptom of Anhedonia: A Predepressive State." *Psychoanalytic Quarterly* 40.4 (1971): 603–17.

Askill, John, and Martyn Sharpe. *Angel of Death.* London: Michael O'Mara, 1993.

Bach-y-Rita, George, and Arthur Veno. "Habitual Violence: A Profile of 62 Men."

American Journal of Psychiatry 131.9 (Sep. 1974): 1015–17.

Badano, Luigi P., Elisabetta Daleffe, Daniela Miani and Ugolino Livi. "Multiple Intracardiac Sewing Needles in a Schizophrenic Woman with Self-Injurious Behaviour." *Journal of the American College of Cardiology* 55.18 (2010): 1997.

Baker, Nicholas H. "Modern Day Crucifixion in the Philippines." http://www.wildcat.co.uk/text/crucifixion_txt.htm Accessed 22 May 2004; no longer available.

Ballingall, Sir George. *Outlines of Military Surgery.* 2nd ed. Edinburgh: Adam and Charles Black, 1838.

———. *Outlines of Military Surgery.* 5th ed. Edinburgh: Adam and Charles Black; London: Longman and Co., 1855. At https://archive.org/details/outlinesofmilita1855ball

Barker, J.C., and S. Lucas. "An Investigation of a Case of Munchausen Syndrome (Hospital Addiction) under Deep Hypnosis: Report of a Clinical Conference." *American Journal of Clinical Hypnosis* 8.2 (Oct. 1965): 128–38.

Bartholow, Roberts. *A Manual of Instructions for Enlisting and Discharging Soldiers, with Special Reference to the Medical Examination of Recruits, and the Detection of Disqualifying and Feigned Diseases.* Philadelphia: Lippincott, 1864.

Bataille, Georges. "Sacrificial Mutilation and the Severed Ear of Vincent Van Gogh." *Visions of Excess: Selected Writings, 1927–1939.* Ed. Allan Stoekl. Trans. Allan Stoekl, with Carl R. Lovitt and Donald M. Leslie, Jr. Theory and History of Literature, Vol. 14. Minneapolis: University of Minnesota Press, 1985. 61–72.

Battle, R.J.V., and J.D. Pollitt. "Self-Inflicted Injuries." *British Journal of Plastic Surgery* 17 (Oct. 1964): 400–12.

Beck, Warren A. "The Penitentes." *New Mexico, Past and Present: A Historical Reader.* Ed. Richard N. Ellis. Albuquerque: University of New Mexico Press, 1971. 171–83.

Beilin, Leon M., and Julius Grueneberg. "Genital Self Mutilations by Mental Patients." *Journal of Urology* 59 (1948): 635–41.

Belbenoît, René, Prisoner No. 46635. *Dry*

Guillotine: Fifteen Years among the Living Dead. Trans. Preston Rambo. New York: E.P. Dutton, 1938.

Benn, James A. *Burning for the Buddha: Self-Immolation in Chinese Buddhism.* Honolulu: University of Hawai'i Press, 2007.

Bennum, I. "Psychological Models of Self-Mutilation." *Suicide and Life-Threatening Behavior* 14.3 (Fall 1984): 166–85.

Bergler, Edmund. *Principles of Self-Damage.* 1959. Madison, Connecticut: International Universities Press, 1992.

Beto, Dan Richard, and James L. Claghorn. "Factors Associated with Self Mutilation Within the Texas Department of Corrections." *American Journal of Corrections* 30 (Jan.-Feb. 1968): 25–27.

Bharath, Srikala, Mehendra Neupane and Somnath Chatterjee. "Terminator: An Unusual Form of Self-Mutilation." *Psychopathology* 32.4 (July-Aug. 1999): 184–86.

Biach, Robert M. "The Psychiatric Aspects of Malingering." *Handbook of Correctional Psychology.* Eds. Robert M. Lindner and Robert V. Seliger. New York: Philosophical Library, 1947. 321–32.

Bick, Esther. "The Experience of the Skin in Early Object-Relations." *International Journal of Psycho-Analysis* 49 (1968): 484–86.

Bierdrager, Christine Noriko. "The Experience of Providing Psychotherapy to the Self-mutilating Patient: A Phenomenological Investigation." PhD Diss., California School of Professional Psychology, Fresno Campus, 1996.

Bishop, W.J. "Some Historical Cases of Autosurgery." *Report of Proceedings (Scottish Society of the History of Medicine) 1960–61*: 23–32.

Blacker, K.H., and Normund Wong. "Four Cases of Autocastration." *Archives of General Psychiatry* 8.2 (Feb. 1963): 169–76.

Bland, Michael. *Arnobius of Sicca: Religious Conflict and Competition in the Age of Diocletian.* Oxford Early Christian Studies. Oxford: Clarendon, 1995.

Blaszczynski, Alex. Foreword. *Scarred for Life: The True Story of a Self-harmer.* Balmain, NSW: Limelight, 2002. x-xii.

Blondel, Charles. *Les Auto-mutilators: étude psychopathologique et médico-légale.* Thèse

pour le doctorat in médecine. Présentée ou soutenue le Mercredi 27 Juin 1906, à 1 heure. Paris: Rousset, 1906.

_____. *The Troubled Conscience and the Insane Mind.* Psyche Series. London: Kegan Paul, 1928.

Bode, Katherine. *In/visibility: Women Looking at Men's Bodies in and through Contemporary Australian Women's Fiction.* PhD Diss., University of Queensland, 2005.

Böhni, Fritz. *Richtlinien für die Beurteilung von Fingerverletzungen beim Holzspalten.* Basel, Med. Diss. (Aus: Zeitschrift fur Unfallmedizin u. Berufskrankheiten, 1949.

Boisseau, Edmond. *Considérations sur les maladies simulées, dans l'armée en particulier.* Extrait des *Annales d'hygiène publique et de médecine légale.* 2e série, 1868, T. XXXI. Paris J.-B. Baillière et fils, 1869.

_____. *Des maladies simulées et des moyens de les reconnaître [Texte imprimé]: leçons professées au Val-de-Grâce.* Paris: J.-B. Baillière et fils, 1870.

Bollas, Christopher. *Being a Character: Psychoanalysis and Self Experience.* New York: Hill and Wang, 1992. London: Routledge, 1993.

Bonte, Wolfgang. "Self-Mutilation and Private Accident Insurance." *Journal of Forensic Sciences* 28.1 (Jan. 1983): 70–82.

Borgeaud Philippe. *Mother of the Gods: From Cybele to the Virgin Mary.* Trans. Lysa Hochroth. Baltimore and London: Johns Hopkins University Press, 2004.

Borrell, Antonio Macià. *La persona humana: derechos sobre su proprio cuerpo vivo y muerto; derechos sobre el cuerpo vivo y muerto de otros homres.* Barcelona: Bosch, 1954.

Braden, Meredith K. "The Politics of Cutting: A Feminist Analysis of Self-mutilation and Self-mutilation Research." DPsych Diss., California School of Professional Psychology, San Francisco Bay Area Campus, 2003.

Bradley, John M. "A Case of a Self Made Eunuch." *Weekly Bulletin of the St. Louis Medical Society* 28.10 (17 Nov. 1933): 133–34.

Brenman, Margaret. "On Teasing and Being Teased: And the Problem of 'Moral Masochism.'" *Psychoanalytic Study of the Child* 7 (1952): 264–85.

Brickman, Barbara Jane. "'Delicate' Cutters: Gendered Self-mutilation and Attractive Flesh in Medical Discourse." *Body & Society* 10.4 (Dec. 2004): 87–111.

Brill, A.A. "The Concept of Psychic Suicide." *International Journal of Psychoanalysis* 20 (1939): 246–51.

Broderick, F.W. "Acne Vulgaris." *British Medical Journal* 11 Feb. 1933: 248–49.

Brown, A., M.A. al–Bachari, and K.K. Kambhampati. "Self-inflicted Eye Injuries." *British Journal of Opthalmology* 75.8 (Aug. 1991): 496–98.

Bruhl, H.H., L. Fielding, M. Joyce, W. Peters and N. Wieseler. "Thirty-Month Demonstration Project for Treatment of Self-Injurious Behavior in Severely Retarded Individuals." *Life-Threatening Behavior: Analysis and Intervention. Monograph of the American Association of Mental Deficiency* 5 (1982): 191–275.

Brunswick, Ruth Mack. "A Supplement to Freud's 'From the History of an Infantile Neurosis.'" *International Journal of Psychoanalysis* 9 (1928): 439–76.

Bryk, Mary, and Patricia T. Segal. "My Mother Caused my Illness: The Story of a Survivor of Münchausen by Proxy Syndrome." *Pediatrics* 100.1 (July 1997): 1–7.

Budny, P.G., P.J. Regan, P. Riley, and A.H. Roberts. "Ritual Burns: The Buddhist Tradition." *Burns: Journal of the International Society for Burn Injuries* 17.4 (Aug. 1991): 335–37.

Burnham, Robert C. [Contribution to] Symposium on Impulsive Self-mutilation: Discussion." *British Journal of Medical Psychology* 42 (1969): 223–27.

Burton-Brown, Jean. "Traumatic Enlargement of Clitoris." *British Medical Forum* 25 Feb 1950: 408–09. Weber, [Papers] Box 84, Folder 1.

Bury, Judson S. "The Physical Element in the Psycho-Neurosis." *Lancet* 10 July 1920: 66–68. Torn out article, Weber, [Papers] Box 84, Folder 2.

Butler, A.W. *The Official History of the Australian Army Medical Services in the War of 1914–18. Volume II: The Western Front.* Canberra: Australian War Memorial, 1940.
_____. *The Official History of the Australian Army Medical Services in the War of 1914–18. Volume III: Special Problems and Services.* Canberra: Australian War Memorial, 1943.

Buzzard, Farquhar. [Comment on Parsons, "Psychology of Traumatic Amblyphobia."] *Proceedings of the Royal Society of Medicine* (Neurological Section) 8 (1915): 66.
_____. Foreword. *Hysterical Disorders of Warfare.* By Lewis R. Yealland. London: Macmillan, 1918. v-viii. At http://archive.org/details/hystericaldisord00yealuoft

"Call to Double Nurse Numbers." *Nursing Times* 97.17 (26 April–2 May 2001): 8.

Calof, David L. "Chronic Self-Injury in Adult Survivors of Childhood Abuse." *Treating Abuse Today* 5.3 (May-June 1995): 11–17.

Caner, Daniel F. "The Practice and Prohibition of Self-Castration in Early Christianity." *Vigilae Christianae* 51 (1997): 396–415.

[Caplin, Rosalind.] "Rosalind Caplin." *Self-Harm: Perspectives from Personal Experience.* Ed. Louise Roxanne Pembroke. 27–29.

Cardyn, Lisa. "The Construction of Female Sexual Trauma in Turn-of-the-Century American Mental Medicine." *Traumatic Pasts: History, Psychiatry, and Trauma in the Modern Age, 1870–1930.* Ed. Mark Micale and Paul Lerner. Cambridge Studies in the History of Medicine. Cambridge: Cambridge University Press, 2001. 172–201.

Carr, Edward G. "The Motivation of Self-Injurious Behavior: A Review of Some Hypotheses." *Psychological Bulletin* 84.4 (1977): 800–16.

Carroll, Michael P. *The Penitente Brotherhood: Patriarchy and Hispano-Catholicism in New Mexico.* Baltimore and London: Johns Hopkins University Press, 2002.

Castor, Birgitta, Jan Ursing, Magnus Åberg, and Niklas Pålsson. "Infected Wounds and Repeated Septicemia in a Case of Factitious Illness." *Scandinavian Journal of Infectious Diseases* 22.2 (1990): 227–32.

Catalano, G., M. Morejon, M. Alberts and V.A. Catalano. "Report of a Case of Male Genital Self-Mutilation and Review of the Literature, with Special Emphasis on the Effects of the Media." *Journal of Sex and Marital Therapy* 22.1 (1996): 35–46.

Catullus. *The Poems of Catullus.* Trans. Guy Lee. Oxford: Clarendon Press, 1990.

_____. *The Poems of Catullus: A Bilingual Edition.* Trans. James Michie. New York: Random House, 1969.

_____. *The Poems of Catullus: A Bilingual Edition.* Trans. Peter Green. Berkeley, Los Angeles and London: University of California Press, 2005.

Chaikhouni, Amer. "Self-inflicted Transanal Stripping of the Colorectal Mucosa." *Diseases of the Colon and Rectum* 25.3 (April 1982): 245–48.

Chandler, Amy, Fiona Myers and Stephen Platt. "The Construction of Self-injury in the Clinical Literature: A Sociological Exploration." *Suicide and Life-Threatening Behavior* 41.1 (2011): 98–109.

Channing, Walter. "Case of Helen Miller: Self-Mutilation: Tracheotomy." *American Journal of Insanity* 34.3 (Jan. 1878): 368–78. Also at https://archive.org/details/americanjournalo3418amer

Chantler, Khatidja, Erica Burman, Janet Batsleer and Colsom Bashir. *Attempted Suicide and Self-harm (South Asian Women): Project Report, March 2001.* Manchester: Women's Studies Research Centre, Manchester Metropolitan University, Elizabeth Gaskell Campus, 2001.

Clark, Andrew. [Letter.] "The Language of Self Harm Is Somatic and Needs to Be Learnt." *British Medical Journal* 30 Mar. 2002: 788–89.

Clarke, Liam, and Margaret Whittaker. "Self-mutilation: Culture, Contexts and Nursing Responses." *Journal of Clinical Nursing* 7.2 (1998): 129–37.

Claude, H., A. Borel, and G. Robin. "Une automutilation révélatrice d'un état schizomanique." *Annales médico-psychologiques* 82.1 (1924): 331–39.

Cohen, Earl. "Self-Assault in Psychiatric Evaluation: A Proposed Clinical Classification." *Archives of General Psychiatry* 21.1 (July 1969): 64–67.

Collie, John. *Fraud in Medico-Legal Practice.* London: Edward Arnold, 1932. See also "Doctor and Malingerer."

_____. Prefatory Note. *Shell Shock: Commotional and Emotional Aspects.* By André Léri. Trans. Anon. Ed. John Collie. Medical Manual Series. London: London University's Press, 1919. xiii–xvii.

_____, and Arthur H. Spicer. *Malingering and Feigned Sickness.* [London:] John Collie, 1913.

_____, with Arthur H. Spicer [and Christine Murrell]. *Malingering and Feigned Sickness: with Notes on the Workingmen's Compensation Act, 1906, and Compensation for Injury, Including the Leading Cases thereon.* 2nd ed. London: Edward Arnold, 1917.

Conn, Jacob H. "A Case of Marked Self-mutilation Presenting a Dorsal Root Syndrome." *Journal of Mental Disease* 75.3 (March 1932): 251–62.

Consoli, Angele, Johan Cohen, Nicolas Bodeau, Vincent Guinchat, Lee Wachtel and David Cohen. "Electroconvulsive Therapy in Adolescents with Intellectual Disability and Severe Self-injurious Behavior and Aggression: A Retrospective Study." *European Child and Adolescent Psychiatry* 22.1 (Jan. 2013): 55–62.

Conterio, Karen, and Wendy Lader, with Jennifer Kingson Bloom. *Bodily Harm: The Breakthrough Treatment for Self-injurers.* New York: Hyperion, 1998.

Coons, Philip M. "Self-amputation of the Female Breast." *Psychosomatics* 27.9 (Sep. 1986): 667–78.

Cooper, William White. *On Wounds and Injuries of the Eye.* London: John Churchill, 1859. https://archive.org/stream/onwoundsandinju00coopgoog#page/n4/mode/2up

Copp, Terry, and Bill McAndrew. *Battle Exhaustion: Soldiers and Psychiatrists in the Canadian Army, 1939–1945.* Montreal and Kingston: McGill-Queens University Press, 1990.

Corcoran, Paul, Ella Arensman, and Ivan J. Perry. "The Area-level Association between Hospital-treated Deliberate Self Harm, Deprivation and Social Fragmentation in Ireland." *Journal of Epidemiology and Community Health* 61.12 (2007): 1050–55.

Cormia, F.E. "Basic Concepts in the Production and Management of the Psychosomatic Dermoses: I." *British Journal of Dermatology* 63.3 (March 1951): 83–92.

_____. "Basic Concepts in the Production and Management of the Psychosomatic Dermoses: II." *British Journal of Dermatology* 63.4 (April 1951): 129–51.

_____, and David Slight. "Psychogenic Factors in Dermatoses." *Canadian Medical Association Journal* 33.5 (Nov. 1935): 527.

Cortyl, E., and L. Martinenq. "Automutilations répétés chez une mélancolique." *Annales médico-psychologiques* 12 (1884): 425–36.

Covington, Dennis. *Salvation on Sand Mountain: Snake Handling and Redemption in Southern Appalacia.* Reading, Massachusetts: Addison Wesley, 1995.

Crabtree, Loren H. "A Psychotherapeutic Encounter with a Self-Mutilating Patient." *Psychiatry* 30.1 (Feb. 1967): 91–100.

Crayton, John W., and Daniel X. Freedman. "Psychotropic Drugs in Dermatological Practice." *International Journal of Dermatology* 16.6 (July 1977): 512–19.

Cross, Lisa Warren. "Body and Self in Feminine Psychology: As Illustrated by Delicate Self-mutilation and the Eating Disorders." PhD Diss., Graduate Faculty in Psychology, City University of New York, 1990.

Crowe, Marie. "Cutting Up: Signifying the Unspeakable." *Australian and New Zealand Journal of Mental Health Nursing* 5 (1995): 103–11.

Culliford, Larry. "Autocastration and Biblical Delusions in Schizophrenia." [Letter.] *British Journal of Psychiatry* 150 (1987): 407.

"Cut Up Kids." http://www.smh.com.au/tv/Documentary/Cut-Up-Kids-4310452.html

Cutting the Risk: Self Harm Minimisation in Perspective. DVD and Manual. www.dur.ac.uk/resources/sass/NSMG_manual2.pdf Accessed 13 Sep. 2013.

Cwiartka, Monika. "A Sense of Self: Reconceptualizing Autoimmunity." MA Thesis, English, McMaster University, Hamilton, Ontario, 2002.

Dabrowski, Casimir [Kazimierz]. "Psychological Bases of Self-Mutilation." Trans. William Thau. *Genetic Psychology Monographs* 19.1 (Feb. 1937): 5–104. Also published separately: Provincetown, Massachusetts: Journal Press, 1937.

_____, with Andrzej Kawczak and Michael M. Piechowski. *Mental Growth Through Positive Disintegration.* London: Gryf, 1970.

Dale, Leigh. "In Good Faith? Self Harm in *The Jesus Man* and *The Glade Within the Grove.*" *Indian Journal of World Literature and Culture* 9–10 (2013): 119–34.

_____. "Rev. of *The Glade within the Grove* and *The Ballad of Erinungarah,* by David Foster." *Journal of Australian Studies* 56 (1998): 189–92.

"Damages for 'Gothic Horror.'" *Nursing Times* 97.17 (26 April–2 May 2001): 8.

Damon, Howard F. *The Neuroses of the Skin: Their Pathology and Treatment.* Philadelphia: J.B. Lippincott, 1868. http://books.google.com.au/books?id=evJpWhQlJfYC&pg=PR9&source=gbs_selected_pages&cad=3#v=onepage&q&f=false

Daniels, Stephanie M., John D. Fenley, Pauline S. Powers and C. Wayne Cruse. "Self-inflicted Burns: A Ten-Year, Retrospective Study." *Journal of Burn Care & Rehabilitation: Official Journal of the American Burn Care Association* 12.2 (Mar-Apr. 1991): 144–47.

David, Gustave. *Des Automutilations chez les aliénés.* Thèse pour le Doctorat en Médecine, Faculté mixte de Médecine et de Pharmacie, Université de Toulouse, 1899. Toulouse: Imprimerie Saint-Cyprien, 1899.

Davidson, D.C. "Amputation of the Penis." *Lancet* 16 Feb. 1884: 293.

Davies, Nick. *Murder on Ward Four: The Story of Bev Allitt and the Most Terrifying Crime Since the Moors Murders.* London: Chatto and Windus, 1993.

Davies, Susan, Diana Bell, Fiona Irvine and Richard Tranter. "Self-administered Acupuncture as an Alternative to Deliberate Self-harm: A Feasibility Study." *Journal of Personality Disorders* 25.6 (2011): 741–54.

Davis, Haldin D. "Dermatitis Artefacta." *Clinical Journal* 30 April 1924: 211–16.

Dean, Charles E. "Limbic Leucotomy in Self-Mutilation." *Journal of Clinical Psychiatry* 63.12 (Dec. 2002): 1181.

_____. "Repeated Self-mutilation and ECT." *American Journal of Psychiatry* 158.8 (Aug. 2001): 1331.

de Massary, Leroy, and Mallet. "Auto-mutilation sexuelle chez un schizophrène. *Annales médico-psychologique* 87.2 (1929): 144–50.

Denis, Jo, Wim Van den Noortgate, and Bea Maes. "Self-injurious Behaviour in People with Profound Intellectual Disabilities: A Meta-Analysis of Single Case Studies." *Research in Developmental Disabilities* 32.3 (2011): 911–23.

Derblich, W. *Die simulirton Krankheiten der Wehrpflichtigen.* Wien: Urban & Schwarzenberg, 1878.

Devine, Darragh P. "Animal Models of Self-injurious Behaviour: An Overview." *Methods in Molecular Biology* 829 (2012): 68–85.

Diagnostic and Statistical Manual of Mental Disorders: V [DSM V]. 5th ed. Arlington: American Psychiatric Association, 2013.

Dible, J. Henry. *Napoleon's Surgeon.* London: William Heinemann Medical Books, 1970.

Dieulafoy, Georges. "Escarres multiples et récidivantes depuis deuz ans et demi aux deux bras et au pied. Amputation du bras gauche. Discussion sur la nature de ces escarres. Pathomimie." *Presse Médicale* 16.47 (10 June 1908): 369–72.

Diodorus Siculus. *Diodorus of Sicily: With an English Translation.* 12 volumes. London: Heinemann, 1933–67.

"Doctor and Malingerer." Rev. of *Fraud in Medico-Legal Practice*, by John Collie. *Times Literary Supplement* 30 June 1932: 478.

Doctors, Shelley. "The Symptom of Delicate Self-cutting in Adolescent Females: A Developmental View." *Adolescent Psychiatry* 9 (1981): 443–60.

_____. "The Symptom of Delicate Self-cutting in Adolescent Females: A Developmental View." PhD Diss., Ferkhauf Graduate School of Humanities and Social Sciences, [Albert Einstein College of Medicine, Jack and Pearl Resnick Campus,] Yeshiva University, [New York,] 1979.

Doran, Allen R., Alec Roy, and Owen M. Wolkowitz. "Self-Destructive Dermatoses." *Psychiatric Clinics of North America* 8.2 (June 1985): 291–98.

Dossetor, D.R., S. Couryer, and A.R. Nicol. "Massage for Very Severe Self-injurious Behaviour in a Girl with Cornelia de Lange Syndrome." *Developmental Medi-cine and Child Neurology* 33.7 (July 1991): 636–44.

Dundes, Alan. *Bloody Mary in the Mirror: Essays in Psychoanalytic Folkloristics.* Jackson: University Press of Mississippi, 2002.

Dupont, Judith. Introduction. *The Clinical Diary of Sándor Ferenczi.* xi-xxvii.

Dyer, Clare. "Surgeon Amputated Healthy Legs." *British Medical Journal, Clinical Research ed.* 5 Feb. 2000: 332.

Edinburgh Medico-Chirurgical Society. "Malingering." [*Lancet* 14 Dec. 1912: 1653–54.] Weber, [Papers] Box 84, Folder 2.

Editorial. "Simulation of Disease." [*British Medical Journal* 28 July 1917: 25]. Clipping, pasted onto the back of anonymous review of Jones and Llewellyn, headed "Malingering." Weber, [Papers] Box 84, Folder 2.

Edwards, Stephen D., and Jeanette Hewitt. "Can Supervising Self-harm Be Part of Ethical Nursing Practice?" *Nursing Ethics* 18.1 (Jan. 2011): 79–87.

Eisenberg, Leon. "The Sleep of Reason Produces Monsters: Human Costs of Economic Sanctions." Editorial. *New England Journal of Medicine* 336 (24 April 1997): 1247–50.

Eisold, Kenneth. "The Erosion of Our Profession." *Psychoanalytic Psychology* 24.1 (2007): 1–9.

Emerson, Ernest B. "Mental States Responsible for Malingering." *Medical Press* [155,] 5 Dec. 1917: 433–36. Reprinted from *Boston Medical and Surgical Journal* 24 May 1917. Article offprint. Weber, [Papers] Box 84, Folder 2.

Emerson, L.E. "The Case of Miss A: A Preliminary Report of a Psychoanalytic Study and Treatment of a Case of Self-mutilation." *Psychoanalytic Review* 1 (1933): 41–54.

Engelstein, Laura. *Castration and the Heavenly Kingdom: A Russian Folktale.* London and Ithaca: Cornell University Press, 1999.

Engle, Bernice S. "Attis: A Study of Castration." *Psychoanalytic Review* 23 (1936): 363–72.

Estefan, Andrew, Margaret McAllister and Jennifer Rowe. "Difference, Dialogue,

Dialectics: A Study of Caring and Self-Harm." *Many Voices: Toward Caring Culture in Healthcare and Healing.* Ed. Kathryn Hopkins Kavanagh and Virginia Knowlden. Madison: University of Wisconsin Press, 2004. 21–61.

Evenson, Richard C., Ivan W. Sletten, Harold Altman and Marjorie L. Brown. "Disturbing Behavior: A Study of Incident Reports." *Psychiatric Quarterly* 48.2 (1974): 266–75.

Faller-Marquardt, M. "Self-inflicted Injuries with Negative Political Overtones." *Forensic Science International* 159.2–3 (June 2006): 226–29.

Farber, Sharon Klayman. "A Psychoanalytically Informed Understanding of the Association Between Binge-Purge Behavior and Self-Mutilating Behavior: A Study Comparing Binge-Purgers Who Self-Mutilate Severely with Binge-Purgers Who Self-Mutilate Mildly or Not at All." PhD Diss., School of Social Work, New York University, 1995.

_____. *When the Body Is the Target: Self-harm, Pain, and Traumatic Attachments.* Northvale: Jason Aronson, 2000.

Favazza, Armando R. *Bodies Under Siege: Self-mutilation and Body Modification in Culture and Psychiatry.* 2nd ed. Baltimore: Johns Hopkins University Press, 1996.

_____. *Bodies Under Siege: Self-mutilation, Nonsuicidal Self-injury, and Body Modification in Culture and Psychiatry.* 3rd ed. Baltimore: Johns Hopkins University Press, 2011.

_____. "Why Patients Mutilate Themselves." *Hospital and Community Psychiatry* 40.2 (Feb. 1989): 137–45.

_____, and Karen Conterio. "Female Habitual Self-Mutilators." *Acta Psychiatrica Scandinavica* 79 (1989): 283–89.

_____, and Richard J. Rosenthal. "Diagnostic Issues in Self-Mutilation." *Hospital and Community Psychiatry* 44.2 (Feb. 1993): 134–40.

_____, with Barbara Favazza. *Bodies under Siege: Self-Mutilation in Culture and Psychiatry.* Baltimore: Johns Hopkins University Press, 1987.

Feinsod, M. "The Surgeon and the Emperor: A Humanitarian on the Battle-field." *Harefuah* 135.9 (1 Nov. 1998): 340–43; 408 [English abstract].

Feldman, Marc D. "The Challenge of Self-Mutilation: A Review." *Comprehensive Psychiatry* 29.3 (May-June 1988): 252–69.

_____. *Playing Sick? Untangling the Web of Munchausen Syndrome, Munchausen by Proxy, Malingering, and Factitious Disorder.* New York: Brunner Routledge, 2004.

Fenichel, Otto. *Psychoanalytic Theory of Neurosis.* 1945. London: Routledge and Kegan Paul, 1946.

Fennig, Silvana, Gabrielle Carlson and Shmuel Fennig. "Contagious Self-Mutilation." Letter. *American Academy of Child and Adolescent Psychiatry* 34.4 (April 1995): 402–03.

Ferber, Sarah. *Bioethics in Historical Perspective.* London: Palgrave Macmillan, 2013.

_____. *Demonic Possession and Exorcism in Early Modern France.* London and New York: Routledge, 2006.

Ferenczi, Sándor. "The Adaptation of the Family to the Child." 1927. *Final Contributions to the Problems & Methods of Psycho-analysis.* 61–76.

_____. "The Analytic Interpretation and Treatment of Psychosexual Impotence." 1908 [German]. *First Contributions to Psycho-analysis.* 11–34.

_____. *The Clinical Diary of Sándor Ferenczi.* Ed. Judith Dupont. Trans. Michael Balint and Nicola Zarday Jackson. Cambridge and London: Harvard University Press, 1988.

_____. "Confusion of Tongues between Adults and the Child." 1933 [German]; 1949 [English]. Paper read at the Twelfth International Psycho-Analytical Congress in Wiesbaden in September 1932. *Final Contributions to the Problems & Methods of Psycho-analysis.* 156–67.

_____. *Final Contributions to the Problems & Methods of Psycho-analysis.* Ed. Michael Balint. Trans. Eric Mosbacher and others. International Psycho-Analytical Library, no. 48. London: Hogarth Press, and the Institute of Psycho-Analysis, 1955; New York: Basic Books, 1955.

_____. *First Contributions to Psycho-analysis.* First published as *Contributions to Psycho-analysis*, trans. Ernest Jones

(London: Stanley Phillips, 1916); subsequently published in the U.S. as *Sex in Psycho-analysis*. Trans. Ernest Jones. Brunner/Mazel Classics in Psychoanalysis, 6. New York: Brunner/Mazel, 1952.

_____. *Further Contributions to the Theory and Technique of Psycho-analysis*. 2nd ed. Comp. John Rickman. Trans. Jane Isabel Suttie. International Psychoanalytical Library no. 11. 1926. London: Hogarth Press, 1950.

_____. "Introjection and Transference." 1909 [German]. *First Contributions to Psycho-Analysis*. 35–93.

_____. "The Principle of Relaxation and Neocatharsis." 1930 [German and English]. Paper delivered at the Eleventh International Psycho-Analytical Congress in Oxford in August 1929. *Final Contributions to the Problems & Methods of Psycho-analysis*. 108–25.

_____. "Symbolism: I. The Symbolic Representation of the Pleasure and the Reality Principles in the Œdipus Myth." *First Contributions to Psycho-Analysis*. 253–69.

_____. "Thinking with the Body Equals Hysteria." 1932. *The Clinical Diary of Sándor Ferenczi*. 4–8.

_____. "Traumatic Self-strangulation." 1932. *The Clinical Diary of Sándor Ferenczi*. 102–06.

_____. "The Unwelcome Child and His Death Instinct." 1929. *Final Contributions to the Problems & Methods of Psycho-analysis*. 102–07.

_____, Karl Abraham, Ernst Simmel and Ernest Jones. *Psycho-analysis and the War Neuroses*. International Psychoanalytic Library, no. 2. London, Vienna, New York: International Psycho-analytical Press, 1921.

Fidler, R.F. "A Psychiatric Review of Fifty Cases of Gunshot Wounds Self-Inflicted." *Journal of Mental Science* 94 (July 1948): 565–74.

Firestone, Robert W. *Voice Therapy: A Psychotherapeutic Approach to Self-Destructive Behavior*. New York: Human Sciences, 1988.

Fisch, Mayer. "The Suicidal Gesture: A Study of 114 Military Patients Hospitalized Because of Abortive Suicide Attempts." *American Journal of Psychiatry* 111.1 (July 1954): 33–36.

Flessner, Christopher A., Suzanne Moudon-Odum, Allison Stocker and Nancy J. Keuthen. "StopPicking.com: Internet-based Treatment for Self-Injurious Skin Picking." *Dermatology* 13.4 (2007): 3.

Forrest, Earle R. *Missions and Pueblos of the Old Southwest: Their Myths, Legends, Fiestas, and Ceremonies, with Some Accounts of the Indian Tribes and Their Dances; and of the Penitentes*. Cleveland: Arthur H. Clarke Company, 1929.

Forsyth, David. "The Place of Psychology in the Medical Curriculum." Reprinted from *Proceedings of the Royal Society of Medicine* Section of Psychiatry 25.8 (June 1932): 30–42, also paginated 1200–1212. London: John Bale, Sons and Danielson, 1932. Weber, [Papers] Box 84, Folder 3. Also at http://www.ncbi.nlm.nih.gov/pmc/articles/PMC2184138/pdf/procrsmed00799–0052.pdf

Foss, Tara D. "Editorial: National Inquiry into Self-harm Breaks Down Taboos." *British Journal of Nursing* 15.7 (2006): 353.

Foster, David. *The Glade within the Grove*. 1996. Sydney: Vintage, 1997.

Foster, Jonathan. "Mother Tells of Baby's Death at Hospital: The Ward 4 Murder Trial." *Independent* 23 Mar. 1993. At www.independent.co.uk/news/uk/mother-tells-of-babys-death-at-hospital-the-ward-4-murder-trial-14999307.html Accessed 13 Sep. 2013.

Foucault, Michel. *The Birth of the Clinic: An Archaeology of Medical Perception*. Trans. A.M. Sheridan Smith. 1973. World of Man: A Library of Research in the Human Sciences. Ed. R.D. Laing. New York: Vintage, 1975.

_____. *History of Madness*. [*Histoire de la Folie à l'âge classique*. 1972.] Ed. Jean Khalfa. Trans. Jonathan Murphy and Jean Khalfa. 2006. London and New York: Routledge, 2009.

Fraiberg, Selma. "Pathological Defenses in Infancy." *Psychoanalytic Quarterly* 51 (1982): 612–35.

Fras, Ivan, and Bonnie E. Coughlin. "The Treatment of Factitial Disease." *Psychosomatics* 12.2 (March 1971): 117–22.

Frazer, J.G. "Attis." Book Second of *Adonis Attis Osiris. Studies in the History of Orien-*

tal Religion. [*The Golden Bough: A Study in Magic and Religion.*] 3rd ed, revised and enlarged. London: Macmillan, 1914. Vol. 6 [also called Part 4, vol. 1, Book 2]. 261–317. At archive.org/details/goldenboughstudy 06frazuoft Accessed 1 Sep. 2013.

_____. "Attis." *The Golden Bough: A Study in Magic and Religion.* 2nd ed, revised and enlarged. London: Macmillan and Co., 1900. Vol. 2. 130–37. At archive.org/ details/goldenboughstud02frazuoft Accessed 1 Sep. 2013.

_____. "Attis." *The Golden Bough: A Study in Comparative Religion.* Vol. 1. London: Macmillan, 1894. 296–301. At archive. org/details/goldenboughstudy01fraz Accessed 1 Sep. 2013

French, Susan. "A Portfolio of Academic, Therapeutic Practice & Research Work, Including an Exploration of the Differences in Beliefs, Attitudes and Behavioural Intentions of Two Nursing Staff Groups Towards Clients Who Deliberately Self-harm, Working with an Accident and Emergency Department or a Community Mental Health Team." Psych Diss., University of Surrey, 2001.

Freud, Sigmund. "The Case of the Wolf Man." *The Wolf Man and Sigmund Freud.* Ed. Muriel Garnder. 1972. Harmondsworth: Penguin, 1973. 171–285.

_____. "The Dream-Work." *The Interpretation of Dreams.* [Chapter six.] Trans. A.A. Brill. Psychclassics.yorku.ca/Freud/Dre ams/dreams.pdf

_____. "Some Psychical Consequences of the Anatomical Differences between the Sexes." 1925. *The Ego and the Id and Other Works.* Ed. James Strachey with Anna Freud, assisted by Alix Strachey and Alan Tyson. The Standard Edition of the Complete Psychological Works of Sigmund Freud. Vol. 19 (1923–1925). London: Hogarth, and the Institute of Psycho-analysis, 1950. 248–60.

_____, and Sándor Ferenczi. *The Correspondence of Sigmund Freud and Sándor Ferenczi.* Vol. 1., 1908–1914. Ed. Eva Brabant, Ernst Falzeder, and Patrizia Giampieri-Deutsch. Transcribed by Ingeborg Meyer-Palmedo. Trans. Peter T. Hoffer. Cambridge and London: Belknap Press of Harvard University Press, 1993.

Frith, Maxine. "Children Self-harm Aged Nine, Warn Nurses." *Independent* [UK] 26 April 2006: 20.

Frost, Miranda J. *Self-harm and the Social Work Relationship.* Social Work Monographs, 134. Norwich[: University of East Anglia], 1995. [Abridged version of dissertation, MSW, University of Sussex.]

Galt, John. "Suicidal Amputation of the Penis." *Medical Herald* [Louisville, Kentucky] 6.5 (Sep. 1884): 225–28.

Gandevia, Bryan. "Malingering in the Penal Era: Its Epidemiological and Social Implications, with Contemporary Observations." *Festschrift for Kenneth Fitzpatrick Russell, M.B. M.S. D.Litt F.R.A.C.S., F.R.A.C.P.: Proceedings of a Symposium Arranged by the Section of Medical History, A.M.A. (Victorian Branch) 25 February 1977.* Carlton, Victoria: Queensbury Hill, 1978. 59–89.

Gardner, A.R., and A.J. Gardner. "Self-Mutilation, Obsessionality and Narcissism." *British Journal of Psychiatry* 127 (1927): 127–32.

Garrard, Robert L. *Self-Mutilation.* Edgewood Medical Monographs 1 (1950): 90–101.

Garstang, John. "Introduction: The Syrian Goddess in History and Art." Lucian, *The Syrian Goddess.* Trans. Herbert A. Strong. London: Constable and Co., 1913. At www.sacred-texts.com/cla/luc/tsg/tsg04. htm Accessed 18 July 2013.

Garzón, R., and C.A. Consigli. "Result of Narcoanalysis in a Case of Pathomimia." *Revista de la Facultad de Ciencias Médicas* (Córdoba) 10.3–5 (May-Oct. 1952): 547–56.

Gasparro, Giulia Sfameni. *Soteriology and Mystic Aspects in the Cult of Cybele and Attis.* Leiden: E.J. Brill, 1985.

Gavin, Hector. *On Feigned and Factitious Diseases, Chiefly of Soldiers and Seamen, on the Means Used to Simulate or Produce Them, and on the Best Modes of Discovering Impostors; Being the Prize Essay in the Class of Military Surgery, in the University of Edinburgh, Session, 1835–6, with Additions.* London: Churchill, 1843. This document is part of The Nineteenth Century, Chadwick Healy Microfiche set, at N.1.1.2340.

_____. *A Probationary Essay on the Feigned and Factitious Diseases, Chiefly of Soldiers and Seamen: Submitted ... to the Examination of the Royal College of Surgeons of Edinburgh When Candidate for Admission*. Edinburgh: Printed at the University Press, 1838.

Gerard, Andrew, Gregory de Moore, Olav Nielssen and Matthew Large. "Survivors of Self-Inflicted Stab Wounds." *Australasian Psychiatry* 20.1 (Feb. 2012): 44–48.

Gibbs, John Joseph. *Stress and Self-injury in Jail*. PhD Diss., School of Criminal Justice, State University of New York at Albany, 1978.

Gilman, Sandor L. "How New is Self-harm?" *Journal of Nervous and Mental Diseases* 200.12 (2012): 1008–16.

Glass, James M. *Private Terror/Public Life: Psychosis and the Politics of Community*. Ithaca and London: Cornell University Press, 1989.

_____. *Psychosis and Power: Threats to Democracy in the Self and the Group*. Ithaca and London: Cornell University Press, 1995.

Goeckerman, William M. "The Relationship of the Emotions and Cutaneous Lesions." *Medical Clinics of North America* 14 (1930): 645–49.

Goldenberg, Edward, and Lindbergh S. Sata. "Religious Delusions and Self-mutilation." *Current Concepts in Psychiatry* 4.5 (1978): 2–5.

Goldney, Robert D., and Ian G. Simpson. "Female Genital Self-mutilation, Dysorexia and the Hysterical Personality: The Caenis Syndrome." *Canadian Psychiatric Association Journal* 20.6 (Oct. 1975): 435–41.

Goldsmith, W.N. "Pitfalls in Diagnosis: [First Series—Section 1] Lesions of the Skin; Article no. V. Dermatosis Artefacta." *Medical Press and Circular* 6 Jan. 1937: 7–10.

Golla, F.L. "Croonian Lectures on the Objective Study of Neurosis. Delivered before the Royal College of Physicians of London on June 9th. Lecture I." *Lancet* 16 July 1921: 115–22.

_____. "Croonian Lectures on the Objective Study of Neurosis. Delivered on June 14th before the Royal College of Physicians of London. Lecture II." *Lancet* 30 July 1921: 215–21.

_____. "Croonian Lectures on the Objective Study of Neurosis. Delivered on June 16th before the Royal College of Physicians of London. Lecture III." *Lancet* 6 Aug. 1921: 265–70.

_____. "Croonian Lectures on the Objective Study of Neurosis. Delivered on June 21st before the Royal College of Physicians of London. Lecture IV." *Lancet* 198.5112 20 August 1921: 373–79. Torn out article. Weber, [Papers] Box 84, Folder 2.

Goodhart, S.P., and Nathan Savitsky. "Self-Mutilation in Chronic Encephalitis. Avulsion of Both Eyeballs and Extraction of Teeth." *American Journal of Medical Science* 185 (1933): 674–84.

Graff, Harold, and Richard Mallin. "The Syndrome of the Wrist Cutter." *American Journal of Psychiatry* 124.1 (July 1967): 36–42.

Graillot, Henri. *Le Culte de Cybèle, mère des dieux, à Rome et dans l'Empire romain*. 1912. Paris: Fontemoing, 2012.

Grant, Jon E., Brian L. Adlaug, Samuel R. Chamberlain, Nancy J. Keuthen, Christine Lochner, and Dan J. Stein. "Skin Picking Disorder." *American Journal of Psychiatry* 169.11 (Nov. 2012): 1143–49.

Gratz, Kim L., Claire Hepworth, Matthew T. Tull, Autumn Paulson, Sue Clarke, Bob Remington and C.W. Lejuez. "An Experimental Investigation of Emotional Willingness and Physical Pain Tolerance in Deliberate Self-harm: The Moderating Role of Interpersonal Distress." *Comprehensive Psychiatry* 52.1 (Jan. 2011): 63–74.

Great Britain. Department of Health. *The Allitt Inquiry: Independent Inquiry Relating to Deaths and Injuries on the Children's War at Grantham and Kesteven General Hospital During the Period February to April 1991*. London: Her Majesty's Stationery Office (HMSO), 1994.

Greenacre, Phyllis. "The Eye Motif in Delusion and Fantasy." *American Journal of Psychiatry* 82.4 (April 1926): 553–79.

Gregory, Robert J., and Georgian T. Mustata. "Magical Thinking in Narratives of

Adolescent Cutters." *Journal of Adoles-
cence* 35.4 (2012): 1045–51.
Greif, Ann C. "Masochism in the Thera-
pist." *Psychoanalytic Review* 72.3 (Fall
1985): 491–501.
Greig, Deirdre N. *Neither Bad Nor Mad:
The Competing Discourses of Psychiatry,
Law and Politics.* Forensic Focus 20.
Philadelphia and London: Jessica Kings-
ley, 2002.
Greilsheimer, H., and J.E. Groves. "Male
Genital Self-mutilation." *Archives of General Psychiatry* 36.4 (Apr. 1979): 441–46.
Grisolia, Andres, Kenneth L. Graham and
Richard S. McKee. "Self-inflicted Division of the Achilles Tendon: Experience
with 70 Patients." *Clinical Orthopaedics
and Related Research* 87 (1972): 206–08.
Grognard, C. "Tatouage, Piercing: décora-
tion? Décorporation? Dénaturation du
corps ou retour au primitif?"/"Tattoos,
Piercing, Body Art? Body Damage? Debasement of the Body or Return to a
Primitive Way of Life?" *Gynécologie, ob-
stétrique & fertilité* 34.1 (Jan. 2006): 41–
43. doi: 10.1016/j.gyobfe.2005.11.006
Grossman, William I. "Pain, Aggression, Fantasy, and Concepts of Sadomasochism."
Psychoanalytic Quartely 60.1 (1991): 22–
52.
Gupta, Madhulika A. "Emotional Regula-
tion, Dissociation, and the Self-induced
Dermatoses: Clinical Features and Impli-
cations for Treatment with Mood Stabi-
lizers." *Clinics in Dermatology* 31.1 (Jan.-
Feb. 2013): 110–17.
_____, Aditya K. Gupta and Herbert
F. Haberman. "The Self-Inflicted Der-
matoses: A Critical Review." *General Hos-
pital Psychiatry* 9.1 (Jan. 1987): 45–52.
Hahn Rafter, Nicole. *Creating Born Crimi-
nals.* Urbana and Chicago: University of
Illinois Press, 1997.
Haines, Janet, Christopher L. Williams,
Kerryn L. Brain and George V. Wilson.
"The Psychophysiology of Self-Mutila-
tion." *Journal of Abnormal Psychology*
104.3 (1995): 471–89.
[Harrison, Diane.] "Diane Harrison." *Self-
Harm: Perspectives from Personal Experi-
ence.* Ed. Louise Roxanne Pembroke. 5–
12.
Hart, Bernard. *The Psychology of Insanity.*

Cambridge Manuals of Science and Literature. 1912. 3rd ed. Cambridge: Cambridge University Press, 1919.
Haughton, Paul Alexander. "Cutting: Repetitive Self-mutilation in Adult Populations."
PsychD Diss., Graduate School, Hahne-
mann University, Philadelphia, 1988.
Haxthausen, Holger. "The Pathogenesis of
Hysterical Skin-Affections." [*British Journal of Dermatology and Syphilis* 48.11
(Nov. 1936): 563–67.]
Heidingsfeld, M.L. "Factitious Dermatitis,
with Report of an Unusual Case." *Uro-
logical and Cutaneous Review* [St. Louis]
Technical Supplement (1915): 311–14 + 5
plates between 312 and 313.
[Helen.] "Helen." *Self-Harm: Perspectives
from Personal Experience.* Ed. Louise Rox-
anne Pembroke. 23–24.
Heller, E. *Simulationen und ihre Behand-
lung: für Militair-, Gerichts- und Anstalts-
Ärzte bearbeitet.* Fürstenwalde: Geelhaar,
1882.
Hendershot, Edna, Alverd C. Stutson and
Thomas W. Adair. "A Case of Extreme
Sexual Self-mutilation." *Journal of Foren-
sic Sciences* 55.1 (2010): 245–47.
Henderson, Alice Corbin. *Brothers of Light:
The Penitentes of the Southwest.* 1937. Las
Cruces, New Mexico: Yucca Tree, 1998.
Henderson, Antony, Aruna Wijewardena,
Jeff Streimer and John Vandervord. "Self-
inflicted Burns: A Case Series." *Burns:
Journal of the International Society for
Burn Injuries* 39.2 (March 2013): 335–40.
Hepding, Hugo. *Attis: seine Mythen und sein
Kult. Religionsgeschichtliche Versuche und
Vorarbeiten.* Geiszen: J. Richer'sche Ver-
lagsbuchhandlung (Alfred Töpelmann),
1903. At archive.org/details/attisseine-
mythe01hepdgoog
Herbert, A.P. *The Secret Battle.* London:
Methuen, 1919.
Hermann, Imre. "Clinging—Going-in-
Search: A Contrasting Pair of Instincts
and Their Relation to Sadism and
Masochism." *Psychoanalytic Quarterly*
45.1 (1976): 5–36.
Hill, Kerry, and Rudi Dallos. "Young Peo-
ple's Stories of Self-harm: A Narrative
Study." *Clinical Child Psychology and Psy-
chiatry* 17.3 (2012): 459–76.
Holden, Ward A. "Self-mutilation of the

Eyes: By an Ancient Saint and a Modern Sinner." *Proceedings of the Charaka Club* 2 (1906): 55–57.

Holley, Heather, and J.E. Arboleda-Flórez. "Hypernomia and Self-Destructiveness in Penal Settings." *International Journal of Law and Psychiatry* 11 (1988): 167–78.

Hopkins, Clare. "'But What About the Really Ill, Poorly People?' (An Ethnographic Study into What It Means to Nurses on Medical Admissions Units to Have People Who Have Harmed Themselves as Their Patients)." *Journal of Psychiatric and Mental Health Nursing* 9.2 (2002): 147–54.

Horney, Karen. "The Flight from Womanhood: The Masculinity-Complex in Women, as Viewed by Men and by Women." *International Journal of Psychoanalysis* 7 (1924): 324–39. Rpt in Karen Horney, *Feminine Psychology*, 1967. New York: Norton 1993. 54–70.

_____. "The Problem of Feminine Masochism." *Psychoanalytic Review: An American Journal of Psychoanalysis* 22.3 (July 1935): 241–57. Rpt in Karen Horney, *Feminine Psychology*, 1967. New York: Norton 1993. 214–34.

Horsfall, Jan. "Towards Understanding Some Complex Borderline Behaviours." *Journal of Psychiatric Mental Health Nursing* 6.6 (Dec. 1999): 425–32.

Hovell, T. Mark. "Discussion on Functional and Simulated Affections of the Auditory Apparatus." [*Royal Society of Medicine*] Otological Section [*Proceedings*] 18 April 1913: 73–86. Partial Offprint. Weber, [Papers] Box 84, Folder 2.

Howard, Rhoda E. *Human Rights and the Search for Community*. Boulder: Westview, 1995.

Howden, James C. "Notes of a Case: Mania Followed by Hyperæsthesia and Osteomalacia. Singular Family Tendency to Excessive Constipation and Self-mutilation." *Journal of Mental Science* 28 (April 1882): 49–53.

Huguet, J. *Recherches sur les maladies simulées et mutilations volontaires: observées de 1859 à 1896 chez les jeunes gens, conscrits ou militaires en activité de service envoyés à la 2. Compagnie de pionniers jusqu'en 1875 et, depuis cette époque, à la 4. Com-*

pagnie de discipline. Paris: H. Charles-Lavauzelle[, 1900].

"Hun Cruelty to Hun." [*Daily Mail* 31 May 1914: 3.] Clipping, in Weber [Papers] Box 84, Folder 2.

Hutre, A. *Les maladies provoquées au pénitencier de la Nouvelle-Calédonie*. M.D., Université de Montpellier, 1886. Montpellier: Gustave Firmin, imprimeur-éditeur de l'Association Générale des étudiants Des Chroniques de Languedoc de la *Revue Populaire de Médecine et de Pharmacie,* 1888.

Ingram, John T. "The Personality of the Skin." *Lancet* 22 April 1933: 899–92.

"Insincerity in Cases of War Injury." *Lancet* 6 Oct. 1917: 541. Press clipping pasted into offprint of "Two Cases for Comment." Weber, [Papers] Box 84, Folder 2.

James, A.H., and T.G. Allen-Mersh. "Recognition and Management of Patients Who Repeatedly Swallow Foreign Bodies." *Journal of the Royal Society of Medicine* 75.2 (Feb. 1982): 107–10.

James, William. *The Principles of Psychology*. London: Macmillan, 1890. ebooks.adelaide.edu.au/j/james/william/principles/complete.html Accessed 16 August 2013.

Jamieson, R.A. "Self-mutilation in China." *British Medical Journal* 18 Mar. 1882: 397–98.

Janet, Pierre. "Autobiography of Pierre Janet." *History of Psychology in Autobiography*. Vol. 1. Ed. Carl Murchison. Worcester: Clark University Press, 1930. 123–33. http://psychclassics.yorku.ca/Janet/murchison.htm

_____. *Les Névroses*. Paris: Ernest Flammarion, 1910.

_____. *Névroses et idées fixes*. Vol 1: *Études Expérimentales sur les troubles de la volonté, de l'attention, de la mémoire, sur les émotions, les idées obsédantes et leur treatment*. Travaux du laboratoire de Psychologie de la clinique à la Salpêtrière. Première Série. Paris: Félix Alcan, 1898.

_____. "On the Pathogenesis of Some Impulsions." *Journal of Abnormal Psychology* 1.1 (April 1906): 1–17. [Boston: Old Corner Book Store.] Weber, [Papers] Folder 4.

_____. "Psychologic Treatment of Hysteria: Importance of L'Idée fixe," from *Traité de*

Thérapeutic Appliquée (ed. Albert Robin, Paris: J. Rueff, 1899). Trans. Charles E. Goshen. *Documentary History of Psychiatry: A Source Book on Historical Principles*. Ed. Charles E. Goshen. London: Vision, 1967. 883–88.

Jiménez-Cruz, J.F. "Microsurgical Penis Replantation after Self-mutilation." *European Urology* 27.3 (1995): 246–48.

Johnson, Elmer H., with Benjamin Britt. "Felon Self-Mutilation: Correlate of Stress in Prison." 1969. Bound t.s. John Jay College of Criminal Justice Library, City University of New York.

Johnson, Robert. "Youth in Crisis: Dimensions of Self-Destructive Conduct Among Adolescent Prisoners." *Adolescence* 13.51 (Fall 1978): 461–82.

Johnson, S.A. "Tics, Delusions and Phobias." *Medical Times* 101.3 (March 1973): 141–48.

Johnson, Willard L., and Alfred A. Baumeister. "Self-injurious Behavior: A Review and Analysis of Methodological Detail of Published Studies." *Behavior Modification* 2.4 (Oct. 1978): 465–87.

Jonas, Stanislaw P. "Transsexualism and Social Attitudes. A Case Report." *Psychiatrica Clinica* [Basel] 9.1 (1976): 14–20.

Jones, Ernest. Translator's Preface. *First Contributions to Psycho-analysis*, by Sándor Ferenczi. n.p.

Jones, Fredric H., James Q. Simmons and Frederick Frankel. "An Extinction Procedure for Eliminating Self-Destructive Behavior in a 9-Year-Old Autistic Girl." *Journal of Autism and Childhood Schizophrenia* 4.3 (1974): 241–50.

Jones, G.M. "Provincial Hospital Reports: Jersey Hospital: Extraordinary Self-Mutilation." *Lancet* 25 July 1857: 88–89.

Jones, Nicholas P. "Self-enucleation and Psychosis." *British Journal of Opthalmology* 74.9 (Sep. 1990): 571–73.

Jordan, Alfred C. "Acne Vulgaris." *British Medical Journal* 11 Feb. 1933: 248.

Jung, C.G. "On Simulated Insanity." 1903. *Psychiatric Studies*. 1940. Trans. R.F.C. Hull. The Collected Works of C.J. Jung, vol. 1. London: Routledge and Kegan Paul, 1957. 159–87.

Kaess, Michael, Markus Hille, Peter Parzer, Christiane Maser-Gluth, Franz Resch, and Romuald Brunner. "Alterations in the Neuroendocrinological Stress Response to Acute Psychosocial Stress in Adolescents Engaging in Non-suicidal Self-injury." *Psychoneuroendocrinology* 37.1 (2012): 157–61.

Kalin, Ned H. "Genital and Abdominal Self-surgery." *Journal of the American Medical Association* 18 May 1979: 2188–89.

Karpinski, Patricia Anne. "External and Internal Correlates of Self-mutilating Behaviors in Severely Disturbed Adults." PsychD Diss., Spalding University, 2003.

Katō, Bunnō, Yoshirō Tamura and Kōjirō Miyasaka, trans. "The Story of the Bodhisattva Medicine King." *The Three Fold Lotus Sutra*. With revisions by W.E. Soothill, Wilhelm Schiffer and Pier P. Del Campana. New York and Tokyo: Weatherhill/Kosei, 1975. 303–11.

Katz, Ian. "The Verdicts: Beverley Allitt." *Guardian* 18 May 1993.

Kellock, Thomas H. "A Form of Self-mutilation of the Penis in Young Boys." *British Journal of Children's Diseases* 12 (July 1915): 209–12. Reprint. Weber, [Papers] Box 84, Folder 2.

Kernberg, Otto. "Borderline Personality Organization." *Journal of the American Psychoanalytic Association* 15.3 (1967): 641–85.

Kerr, Douglas J.A. "A Case of Self-Mutilation." *British Medical Journal* 12 Feb 1927: 278. Clipping pasted into the title pages of Charles Blondel. Weber, [Papers] Box 84.

Kessel, Neil. "The Respectability of Self-poisoning and the Fashion of Survival." *Journal of Psychosomatic Research* 10 (1966): 29–36.

Khan, Jemshed A., Lucinda Buescher, Carl H. Ide and Ben Pettigrove. "Medical Management of Self-Enucleation." *Archives of Opthalmology* 103.3 (March 1985): 386–89.

Khouzam, Hani Raoul, and Nancy Jane Donnelly. "Remission of Self-Mutilation in a Patient with Borderline Personality during Risperidone Treatment." *Journal of Nervous and Mental Diseases* 185.5 (May 1997): 348–49.

Kidger, Judi, David Gunnell, Jeffrey G.

Jarvik, Karen A. Overstreet, and William Hollingworth. "The Association Between Bankruptcy and Hospital-presenting Attempted Suicide: A Record Linkage Study." *Suicide and Life-Threatening Behavior* 41.6 (2011): 676–84.

Kimber, Veronica, and Saxby Pridmore. "Self-enucleation of One Eye." Correspondence. *Australian and New Zealand Journal of Psychiatry* 43.11 (Nov. 2009): 1084.

Kirman, Brian. "Self Injury and Mental Handicap." *British Medical Journal* 31 Oct. 1987: 1085–86.

Klonsky, E. David, Thomas F. Oltmanns and Eric Turkheimer. "Deliberate Self-harm in a Non-clinical Population: Prevalence and Psychological Correlates." *American Journal of Psychiatry* 160.8 (Aug. 2003): 1501–08.

Kloocke, Ruth, Heinz-Peter Schmiedebach and Stefan Priebe. "Psychological Injury in the Two World Wars: Changing Concepts and Terms in German Psychiatry." *History of Psychiatry* 16.1 (2005): 43–60.

Kok-Van Alphen, C.C., H.J.M. Völker-Dieben, L.J. Blanksma and R. Vecht-Van Den Bergh. "Automutilation of the Cornea: I. Ophthalmological Aspects." *Documenta Ophthalmologica* 52.2 (1982): 327–31.

Kraft, David P., and Haroutun M. Babigian. "Somatic Delusion or Self-Mutilation in a Schizophrenic Woman: A Psychiatric Emergency Room Case Report." *American Journal of Psychiatry* 128.7 (Jan. 1972): 127–29.

Kroll, Jerome L. "Self-Destructive Behavior on an Inpatient Ward." *Journal of Nervous and Mental Disease* 166.6 (1978): 429–34.

Kuehn, Candyce N. "Management of a Self-Immolation Victim." Case Studies in Critical Care. *Critical Care Nursing Clinics of North America* 6.4 (Dec. 1994): 863–72.

Laignel-Lavastine, M.M., and Paul Courbon. "La simulation de l'aliéné devant la guerre." *Paris médical* 27: 20 April 1918. See Web http://www2.biusante.parisdescartes.fr/livanc/?cote=111502x1918x27&do=pdf (nos. 305–08): 1 Notion de la guerre, de ses dangers et de ses obligations; 2 Notion de l'exemption des obligations militaires conférée par la maladie ou la folie; 3 Possibilité de créer des troubles objectifs ou subjectifs capables de donner l'illusion de la maladie; 4 Possibilité du choix entre la folie et la maladie pour simuler; 5 Caractères de la simulation de l'aliéné. Also published as *La simulation de l'aliéné devant la guerre.* Paris: Ballière, 1918.

Lancashire, G.H. "Dermatitis Artefacta." Letter. *British Medical Journal* 3 Sep. 1910: 659.

_____. "Dermatitis Artefacta." *British Medical Journal* 22 July 1922: 504.

Lang, Colleen M., and Komal Sharma-Patel. "The Relation Between Childhood Maltreatment and Self-Injury: A Review of the Literature on Conceptualization and Intervention." *Trauma, Violence and Abuse* 12.1 (Jan. 2011): 23–37.

Large, Matthew Michael, and Olav B. Nelson. "Forget Freud and Oedipus: It's all about Untreated Psychosis." *British Journal of Ophthalmology* 96.8 (Aug. 2013): 1056–57.

Lash of the Penitentes. Dir. Harry J. Revier. 1937.

Law, G. Urquhart, H. Rostill-Brookes and D. Goodman. "Public Stigma in Health and Non-healthcare Students: Attributions, Emotions and Willingness to Help with Adolescent Self-harm." *International Journal of Nursing Studies* 46.1 (2009): 107.

Lelewer, Georg. *Die strafbaren Verletzungen der Wehrpflicht in rechtsvergleichender und rechtspolitischer Darstellung.* Wien, Liepzig: Kaiserl. und königl. Hof-Buchdruckerei und Hof-Verlags-Buchhandlung Carl Fromme, 1907.

Léri, André. *Shell Shock: Commotional and Emotional Aspects.* Trans. Anon. Ed. John Collie. Medical Manual Series. London: London University's Press, 1919.

Lewis, Nolan D.C. "The Psychobiology of the Castration Reaction." [Introduction; Biophysiology of Castration; Historical Considerations.] *Psychoanalytic Review* 14 (1927): 420–46.

_____. "The Psychobiology of the Castration Reaction." [The Castration Complex and Its Symbolic Expressions.] *Psychoanalytic Review* 15 (1928): 53–84.

_____. "The Psychobiology of the Castration Reaction." [The Eshmun Complex: Overt Castration (Self-Castration) and Substitutive Mutilation.] *Psychoanalytic Review* 15 (1928): 174–209.

_____. "The Psychobiology of the Castration Reaction: Fundamentals and Classifications; Bibliography." *Psychoanalytic Review* 15 (1928): 304–23.

Liebling, Helen, Hazel Chipchase and Rebecca Velangi. "Why Do Women Self-harm at Ashworth Maximum Security Hospital." *Dangerous, Disordered and Doubly Deviant: Selected Papers from the Special Hospital Psychology Advisory Group (SHPAG) Annual Conference 1994.* Ed. Nashater Deu and Lona Roberts. Issues in Criminological and Legal Psychology, no. 27. Leicester: British Psychological Society for the Division of Criminological and Legal Psychology, 1997. 10–22.

Livy. *The History of Rome.* Vol. 4. Trans. Canon Roberts. Ed. Ernest Rhys. Everyman's Library. London: J.M. Dent, 1905. At mcadams.posc.mu.edu

[Lloyd.] "Religious Monomania; Self-Mutilation. (Under the care of Mr. Lloyd.)" *Lancet* 15 Nov. 1851: 456.

Lopez, A. "Spiders Discharged from the Eye: Hysterical Monomania." *American Journal of Mental Science* 6.11 (July 1843): 74–81. http://journals.lww.com/amjmedsci/Citation/1843/07000/Spiders_discharged_from_the_Eye_Hysteric.7.aspx

Lorthiois, M[arie Michel Edmond Joseph]. *De l'Automutilation: mutilations et suicide étranges.* Paris: Vigot Frères, 1909.

Lucian. *The Syrian Goddess.* Trans. Herbert A. Strong. London: Constable and Co., 1913. Accessed 18 July 2013. http://www.sacred-texts.com/cla/luc/tsg/tsg07.htm

_____. *The Works of Lucian of Samosata: Complete with Exceptions Specified in the Preface.* Trans. H.W. and F.G. Fowler. Oxford: Clarendon, 1905.

Lucretius [Titus Lucretius Carus]. *On the Nature of Things [De Rerum Natura].* Trans. William Ellery Leonard. At ebooks.adelaide.edu.au/l/Lucretius/l94o/ Accessed 18 July 2013.

MacCormac, H. "Autophytic Dermatitis." *British Medical Journal* 11 Dec. 1937: 1153–55.

_____. "Autophytic Dermatitis." [*Proceedings of the Royal Society of Medicine (Dermatology)* 27 (1935): 734–36.]

_____. "Self-inflicted Hysterical Lesions of the Skin, with Special Reference to the After-History." *British Journal of Dermatology and Syphilis* 38.10 (Oct. 1926): 371–75.

_____. "Self-inflicted Lesions in Twins." Royal Soc. Med., Derm. Section, 15 May 1947. *British Journal of Dermatology* 60.3 (March 1948): 1065.

Machin, Rosana. "Neither Ill, Nor Victim: The Self-injury in the Emergency Care." *Ciência & saúde coletiva* 15.4 (Nov.-Dec. 2009): 1741–50.

Machoian, Lisa. "The Possibility of Love: A Psychological Study of Adolescent Girls' Suicidal Acts and Self-mutilation." EdD Diss., Harvard University, 1998.

MacKee, George M. "Neurotic Excoriations." *Archives of Dermatology and Syphilis* 1 (1920): 256–69.

MacKenna, R.M.B. "A Case of Extensive Self-Mutilation of the Scalp, Presumably Following a Tricophytic Infection." *British Journal of Dermatology and Syphilis* 42.7 (July 1930): 313–19.

Madden, Nancy E. "Coping Processes Used by Front-Line Nursing Staff in Response to Clients' Self-mutilation." MSc Diss., Graduate School, Rutgers University, Newark, 1984.

Madge, Nicola, Ella Arensman, Keith Hawton, Elaine M. McMahon, Paul Corcoran, Diego De Leo, Erik Jan de Wilde, Sandor Fekete, Kees van Heeringen and Mette Ystgaard. "Psychological Characteristics, Stressful Life Events and Deliberate Self-harm: Findings from the Child & Adolescent Self-harm in Europe (CASE) Study." *European Child & Adolescent Psychiatry* 20.10 (Oct. 2011): 499–508.

Magerl, Walter, Daniela Burkart, Andres Fernandez, Lutz G. Schmidt and Rolf-Detlef Treede. "Persistent Antinociception through Repeated Self-injury in Patients with Borderline Personality Disorder." *Pain* 153.3 (2012): 575–84.

Mahon, Alyce. "Staging Desire." *Surrealism: Desire Unbound.* Ed. Jennifer Mundy. London: Tate Publishing, 2001. 277–91; notes 324–25.

Maio, Paula, Raquel Santos and Jorge Cardoso. "Letter: Factitial Dermatitis: An Unusual Presentation in an Old Woman." *Dermatology Online Journal* 18.4 (2012): 10-. escholarship.org/uc/item/48v806gp

"Malingering." [*Medical Echo* 16 (Oct. 1938): 54–58.] Offprint with handwritten reference, probably by F. Parkes Weber. Weber, [Papers] Box 84, Folder 2.

"Malingering and Self-maiming: Tricks to Evade Service." [*Times* 14 Sep. 1916: 3.] Weber, [Papers] Box 84, Folder 2.

"Malingering and the Simulation of Disease." *Lancet* 20 Dec. 1919: 1158.

Mario, A.I., and M. Tare. "Deliberate Self harm with Mercury Injection in Forearm." *Journal of Hand Surgery, European Volume* 35.5 (2010): 426–27.

Marshall, Paul. *Scarred for Life: The True Story of a Self-harmer*. Balmain, NSW: Limelight, 2002.

Martin, Graham, Sarah V. Swannell, Phillip L. Hazell, James E. Harrison and Anne W. Taylor. "Self-injury in Australia: A Community Survey." *Medical Journal of Australia* 1 Nov. 2010: 506–10.

Masson, Jeffrey Moussaief. *The Assault on Truth: Freud's Suppression of the Seduction Theory*. New York: Farrar, Straus and Giroux, 1984.

Mayo, Elton. *The Psychology of Pierre Janet*. London: Routledge and Kegan Paul, 1951 [printed 1952].

McCurdy, John T. *War Neuroses*. Cambridge: University Press, 1918.

McHale, J., and A. Felton. "Self-harm: What's the Problem? A Literature Review of the Factors Affecting Attitudes towards Self-harm." *Journal of Psychiatric and Mental Health Nursing* 17.8 (2010): 732–40.

McLane, Janice. "The Voice on the Skin: Self-Mutilation and Merleau-Ponty's Theory of Language." *Hypatia* 11.4 (Fall 1996): 107–18.

McMahon, C.E. "Nervous Diseases and Malingering: The Status of Psychosomatic Concepts in Nineteenth Century Medicine." *International Journal of Psychosomatics* 31.3 (1984): 15–19.

Meachen, G. Norman. "Case for Diagnosis; (?) Dermatitis Artefacta. [*Proceedings of the Royal Society of Medicine, Dermatological Section* 7 (19 March 1914): 159].

Clipping. Weber, [Papers] Box 84, Folder 5.

Meléndez, A. Gabriel. *Hidden Chicano Cinema: Film Dramas on the Borderland*. Latinidad: Transnational Cultures in the United States. New Brunswick: Rutgers University Press, 2013.

Menninger, Karl A. *Man Against Himself*. London: Hart-Davis, 1938.

_____. "Polysurgery and Polysurgical Addiction." *Psychoanalytic Quarterly* 3 (1934): 173–99.

_____. "Psychoanalytic Aspects of Suicide." *International Journal of Psycho-Analysis* 14 (1933): 376–90. Rpt. in *Essential Papers on Suicide*. Ed. John T. Maltsberger and Mark J. Goldblatt. Essential Papers in Psychoanalysis. New York: New York University Press, 1996. 20–35.

_____. "A Psychoanalytic Study of the Significance of Self-Mutilations." *Psychoanalytic Quarterly* 4 (1935): 408–66.

Merenova, Elena V. "A Comparison of Early Childhood Recollections of Repetitive Self-mutilators and Non-self-mutilators in a State Prison Population." PhD Diss., Indiana State University, 2001.

Mesirow, Tanya Roman. "Self-mutilation: Analysis of a Psychiatric Forensic Population." PsychD Diss., California School of Professional Psychology—Berkeley/ Alameda, 1999.

Messina, Emily, S., and Yoshitaka Iwasaki. "Internet Use and Self-injurious Behaviors Among Adolescents and Young Adults: An Interdisciplinary Literature Review and Implications for Health Professionals." *Cyberpsychology, Behavior and Social Networking* 14.3 (2011): 161–68.

Micale, Mark S. "Jean-Martin Charcot and *les névroses traumatiques*: From Medicine to Culture in French Trauma Theory of the Late Nineteenth Century." *Traumatic Pasts: History, Psychiatry, and Trauma in the Modern Age, 1870–1930*. Ed. Mark Micale and Paul Lerner. Cambridge Studies in the History of Medicine. Cambridge: Cambridge University Press, 2001. 115–39.

_____. *Approaching Hysteria: Disease and its Interpretations*. Princeton: Princeton University Press, 1995.

Michelson, Henry E. "Psychosomatic Studies in Dermatology. A. The Motivation of Self-induced Eruptions." *Archives of Dermatology and Syphilis* 51 (1945): 245–50.

Millard, Chris. [Review.] "Reinventing Intention: 'Self-harm' and 'the Cry for Help' in Postwar Britain." *Current Opinion in Psychiatry* 25.6 (Nov. 2012): 504–07.

Miller, Emanuel, A.T.M. Wilson and Eric Wittkower. "Clinical Case Studies and Their Relationships, Including the Psychosomatic Disorders." *The Neuroses in War*. Ed. Emanuel Miller. London: Macmillan and Co., 1940. 55–84.

Miller, Frank, and Edmund A. Bashkin. "Depersonalization and Self-Mutilation." *Psychoanalytic Quarterly* 43 (1974): 638–49.

Milne, Charles. "An Unusual Case of Self-Mutilation." *Lancet* 18 April 1914: 1149–50.

Mitchell, Juliet. *Siblings: Sex and Violence*. London: Polity, 2003.

Mitchell, Kimberley J., and Michele L. Ybarra. "Online Behaviour of Youth Who Engage in Self-harm Provides Clues for Preventive Intervention." *Preventive Medicine* 45.5 (2007): 392–96.

Moffaert, Myriam van. "The Spectrum of Dermatological Self-Mutilation and Self-Destruction Including Dermatitis Artefacta and Neurotic Excoriations." "Body Dysmorphic Disorder." *Psychocutaneous Medicine*. Eds. John Y.M. Koo and Chai Sue Lee. New York: Marcel Dekker, 2003. 169–89.

Monasterio, Erik, and Craig Prince. "Self-cannibalism in the Absence of Psychosis and Substance Abuse." *Australasian Psychiatry: Bulletin of the Royal Australian and New Zealand College of Psychiatrists* 19.2 (2011): 170–72.

Money, John. "The Skoptic Syndrome: Castration and Genital Self-Mutilation as an Example of Sexual Body-Image Pathology." *Journal of Psychology and Human Sexuality* 1.1 (1988): 113–28.

Montaigne, Michel de. "On Virtue." *Essays of Michel de Montaigne*. Ed. William Carew Hazlitt. Trans. Charles Cotton. 1877. Project Gutenberg. www.gutenberg. org/files/3600/3600-h/3600-h.htm Chapter four.

Moodie, Roy L. "The Amputation of Fin-

gers Among Ancient and Modern Primitive Peoples and Other Voluntary Mutilations Indicating Some Knowledge of Surgery." *Surgical Clinics of Chicago* 4 (1920): 1299–1306.

Moon, Mi Hyoung, Keon Hyun Jo, Hyun Song, and Hwan Wook Kim. "Self-inflicted Intracardiac Sewing Needle." *European Journal of Cardio-Thoracic Surgery: Official Journal of the European Association for Cardiothoracic Surgery* 43.2 (2013): 439–40.

Moran, Paul, Carolyn Coffey, Helena Romaniuk, Craig Olsson, Rohan Borschmann, John B. Carlin, and George C. Patton. "The Natural History of Self-harm from Adolescence to Young Adulthood: A Population-based Cohort Study." *Lancet* 21 Jan. 2012: 236–43.

Mourgue, R. Rev. of M.M. Laignel-Lavastine and P. Courbon, *La simulation de l'aliéné devant la guerre* (*Paris médical*, 1918, 20 April). Clipping. Weber, [Papers] Box 84, Folder 2.

Mumford, P.B. "Acne Vulgaris: A Symptom, Not a Disease." *British Medical Journal* 28 Jan. 1933: 141–42.

Musafar, Fakir. Epilogue. Body Play: State of Grace or Sickness? In Armando Favazza, *Bodies under Siege*, 1996 ed. 325–34.

Myers, C.S. *Shell Shock in France, 1914–18*. Cambridge: Cambridge University Press, 1940.

Newman, Shana Jemeela. "Self-mutilating Survivors of Childhood Sexual Abuse: A Treatment Program." PsychD Diss., Miami Institute of Psychology, Caribbean Center for Advanced Studies, 1998.

NHMRC. "NHMRC Additional Levels of Evidence and Grades for Recommendations for Developers of Guidelines, Stage 2 Consultation, Early 2008—end June 2009." [Canberra:] Australian Government/National Health and Medical Research Council, 2009. At http://www.nhmrc.gov.au/_files_nhmrc/file/guidelines/stage_2_consultation_levels_and_grades.pdf Accessed 4 Jan. 2014.

Nicoll. "Remarkable Case of Persistent Ingestion of Needles." *Lancet* 14 March 1908: 772–77.

Novak, Teodora Gregurek, Tomislav Duvančić and Majda Vučić. "Dermatitis Artefacta: Case Report." *Acta Clinica Croatica* 52 (2013): 247–50.

Obermayer, Maximilian E. *Psychocutaneous Medicine.* American lecture series, 239. Springfield, Ill.: Charles C. Thomas, 1955.

Oddie, Geoffrey A. *Popular Religion, Elites, and Reforms: Hook-swinging and Its Prohibition in Colonial India, 1800–1894.* New Delhi: Manohar, 1995.

O'Donovan, W.J. *Dermatological Neuroses.* Psych Miniatures, No. 5. London: Routledge and Kegan Paul, 1927.

_____. "The Psychological Factor in Dermatitis." *British Journal of Dermatology and Syphilis* 39.2 (Feb.1927): 49–54; plates between 50–51.

Offer, Daniel, and Peter Barglow. "Adolescent and Young Adult Self-Mutilation Incidents in a General Psychiatric Hospital." *Archives of General Psychiatry* 3.2 (Aug. 1960): 194–204.

Oldershaw, Anne, Clair Richards, Mima Simic and Ulrike Schmidt. "Parents' Perspectives on Adolescent Self-harm: Qualitative Study." *British Journal of Psychiatry: The Journal of Mental Science* 193.2 (2008): 140–44.

Omidvar, Targol, and Vandad Sharifi. "Amphetamine Psychosis and Eye Autoenucleation." Letter. *Australian and New Zealand Journal of Psychiatry* 46.1 (Jan. 2012): 71.

Oscroft, Katharine Elizabeth. "Self-mutilation: A Hermeneutical Case Study." MEd Thesis in Counselling Psychology, Faculty of Graduate Studies and Research, Department of Educational Psychology, University of Alberta, 1988.

Ovid. *Fasti.* Trans. James George Frazer. 2nd ed. Rev. G.P. Goold. Cambridge: Harvard University Press; London: Heinemann, 1989.

Parham, William. "Nolan D.C. Lewis: A Register of His Papers in the Sigmund Freud Collection in the Library of Congress." Rev. Margaret McAleer, with Brian McGuire. lcweb2.loc.gov/service/mss/ead xmimss/eadpdfmss/2008/ms008011.pdf

Pasini, Mario. *L'autolesionismo nel diritto penale italiano.* Diss., Genova, 1936.

Pausanias. *Guide to Greece. Volume 1: Central Greece.* Trans. Peter Levi. 1971. Harmondsworth: Penguin, 1985.

_____. *Pausanias's Description of Greece.* Trans. J.G. Frazer. 1897. 6 vols. New York: Biblo and Tannen, 1965.

[Pembroke, Louise R.] Introduction. *Self-Harm: Perspectives from Personal Experience.* Ed. Louise Roxanne Pembroke. 1996. 1–4.

[Pembroke, Louise Roxanne.] "Louise Roxanne Pembroke." *Self-Harm: Perspectives from Personal Experience.* Ed. Louise Roxanne Pembroke. 31–60.

Pembroke, Louise Roxanne, ed. *Self-Harm: Perspectives from Personal Experience.* 1994. Rev. ed. London: Survivors Speak Out, 1996.

Pérez de Villagrá, Gaspar. *History of New Mexico.* 1610. Trans. Gilberto Espinosa. Los Angeles: Quuivira Society, 1933.

Perlman, Stuart D. "I Do This for Your Own Good: A Story of Shrieking, Disaster and Recovery." *American Journal of Psychoanalysis* 69.4 (2009): 330–47.

Pernet, George. "Two Cases of Dermatitis Artefacta." *Royal Society of Medicine* 18 Feb. 1915: 89–91.

Perry, Amanda E., Rania Marandos, Simon Coulton and Mathew Johnson. "Screening Tools Assessing Risk of Suicide and Self-harm in Adult Offenders: A Systematic Review." *International Journal of Offender Therapy and Comparative Criminology* 54.5 (Oct. 2010): 803–28.

Pliny, the Elder. *Natural History in Ten Volumes.* Trans H. Rackham (vols. 1–5, 9); W.H. Jones (vols 6–8); D.E. Eichholz (vol. 10). Loeb Classical Library. Cambridge: Harvard University Press; London: William Heinemann, 1939–1986.

Podvoll, Edward M. "Self-mutilation within a Hospital Setting: A Study of Identity and Social Compliance." *British Journal of Medical Psychology* 42.3 (Sep. 1969): 213–21.

Potera, Carol. "YouTube Self-Harm Videos Under Scrutiny." *American Journal of Nursing* 111.6 (June 2011): 20. journals. lww.com/ajnonline/Fulltext/2011/060 00/Youtube_Self_HarmVideos_Under_ Scrutiny.17.aspx

Poynter, Brittany A., Jon J. Hunter, John H. Coverdale and Cheryl A. Kempinsky. "Hard to Swallow: A Systematic Review of Deliberate Foreign Body Ingestion."

General Hospital Psychiatry 33.5 (2011): 518–24.

Price, Bruce H., G. Rees Cosgrove, Scott L. Rauch, Michael A. Jenike, Edwin H. Cassem and Isin Baral. Reply [to Charles E. Dean]. *Journal of Clinical Psychiatry* 63.12 (Dec. 2002): 1181–82.

Price, Bruce H., Isin Baral, G. Rees Cosgrove, Scott L. Rauch, Andrew A. Nierenberg, Michael A. Jenike and Edwin H. Cassem. "Improvement in Severe Self-Mutilation Following Limbic Leucotomy: A Series of 5 Consecutive Cases." *Journal of Clinical Psychiatry* 62.12 (Dec. 2001): 925–32.

"Prison Suicide Checks Must Be More Rigorous." *Nursing Times* 97.17 (26 April–2 May 2001): 8.

Prosser Thomas, E.W. "Dermatitis Artefacta: A Note on an Unusual Case." *British Medical Journal* 17 April 1937: 804–06.

Pulido, Alberto López. *The Sacred World of the Penitentes*. Washington and London: Smithsonian Institution, 2000.

Pusey, William Allen, and Francis E. Sennear. "Neurotic Excoriations with Report of Cases." *Archives of Dermatology and Syphilology* 1 (1920): 270–78.

Radó, Sándor. "Developments in the Psychoanalytic Conception and Treatment of the Neuroses." *Psychoanalytic Quarterly* 8 (1939): 427–37.

_____. "Fear of Castration in Women." *Psychoanalytic Quarterly* 2 (1933): 425–75.

Rashid, Mohammed, and Ishaan Gosai. "The Girl Who Swallows Knives: Uncontrollable Deliberate Self-harm in a Teenage Girl with Borderline Personality Disorder." *BMJ Case Reports* 2011. DOI 10.1136/bcr.07.2010.3136

Rebman, Renée C. *Addictions and Risky Behaviors: Cutting, Bingeing, Snorting, and Other Dangers*. Issues in Focus Today. Berkeley Heights NJ and Aldershot: Enslow, 2006.

Reitz, Sarah, Annegret Krause-Utz, Esther Pogatzki-Zahn, Ulrich Ebner-Priemer, Martin Bohus and Christian Schmahl. "Stress Regulation and Incision in Borderline Personality Disorder: A Pilot Study Modeling Cutting Behaviour." *Journal of Personality Disorders* 26.4 (Aug. 2012): 605–15.

Rev. of *Malingering, or the Simulation of Disease*, by A. Bassett Jones and Llewellyn J. Llewellyn, with W.M. Beaumont, and John Collie, *Malingering and Feigned Sickness, with Notes on the Workman's Compensation Act, 1906, and Compensation for Injury, Including the Leading Cases Thereon*. *British Medical Journal* 28 July 1917: 117–18.

Rev. of *Malingering, or the Simulation of Disease*, by A. Bassett Jones and Llewellyn J. Llewellyn, with W.M. Beaumont. *Lancet* 4 Aug. 1917: 163. Clipping, Weber, [Papers] Box 84, Folder 2.

Rev. of *Man Against Himself*, by Karl A. Menninger. *St. Bartholomew's Hospital Journal* April 1939. Weber, [Papers] Box 84, Folder 4.

Ribot, Théodule-Armand. *The Psychology of Attention*. Chicago: Open Court, 1890.

Richardson, Robert G. *Larrey: Surgeon to Napoleon's Imperial Guard*. London: John Murray, 1974.

Rivers, William H.R. "The 'Complex.'" Chapter 11 of *Instinct and the Unconscious: A Contribution to a Biological Theory of the Psycho-Neuroses*. 1920. At psychclassics.asu.edu/Rivers/chap11.htm

Rives, J.B. "Phrygian Tales." *Greek, Roman, and Byzantine Studies* 45.3 (2005): 223–44.

Robinson, Jo, Alison R. Yung, Hok Pan Yuen, Cathy Martin, Ally Hughes, Gennady N. Baksheev, Simon Dodd, Swagata Bapat, Wayne Schwass and Patrick McGorry. "Does Screening High School Students for Psychological Distress, Deliberate Self-Harm, or Suicidal Ideation Cause Distress—And Is It Acceptable?" *Crisis: The Journal of Crisis Intervention and Suicide Prevention* 32.5 (2011): 254–63.

Rogers, Richard, ed. *Clinical Assessment of Malingering and Deception*. 2nd ed. New York and London: Guilford, 1997.

Roller, Lynn E. *In Search of God the Mother: The Cult of Anatolian Cybele*. Berkeley, Los Angeles and London: University of California Press, 1999.

Ronan, Clifford J. "Lucan and the Self-Incised Voids of *Julius Caesar*." *Comparative Drama* 22.3 (Fall 1988): 215–26.

Roscoe, Will. "Priests of the Goddess: Gender Transgression in Ancient Religion."

History of Religions 35.3 (Feb. 1996): 195–230.

Rose, Gitte Braut. "'Skin-deep' Impressions: Somatic Sense in an Age of Simulated Significance (Kerstin Ekman)." PhD Diss., McGill University, 1998.

Rosenberg, Charles E. *Our Present Complaint: American Medicine, Then and Now.* Baltimore: Johns Hopkins University Press, 2007.

[Ross, Maggy.] "Maggy Ross." *Self-Harm: Perspectives from Personal Experience.* Ed. Louise Roxanne Pembroke. 13–15.

Ruberman, Louise. "Girls Who Cut: Treatment in an Outpatient Psychodynamic Psychotherapy Practice with Adolescent Girls and Young Adult Women." *American Journal of Psychotherapy* 65.2 (2011): 117–32.

Ruckman, Alice McGee. *Self-abuse in Deaf-blind Children: A Case Study.* Thesis presented to the Faculty of the Graduate School of the University of Texas at Austin in partial fulfillment of the Requirements for the Degree of Master of Arts, 1977.

Rusche, Georg, and Otto Kirchheimer. *Punishment and Social Structure.* 1939. New York: Russell and Russell, 1968.

Rutkowski, Krzysztof, and Edyta Dembińska. "Research and Treatment of War Neuroses at the Clinic for Nervous and Mental Diseases at the Jagiellonian University in Krakow before World War II in the Context of Psychiatry in Europe." *Psychiatria Polska* 48.2 (2014): 383–93.

Said, Edward W. *Orientalism.* 1978. Harmondsworth: Penguin, 1985.

Salinari, Salvatore. *L'autolesionismo nelle sue varie forme e nei suoi esiti. Memoria onorata del premio Riberi per il 1924.* Collana Medico-Militare; Publicata dal Ministero della Guera—Direzione Centrale di Sanità Militare, Vol. XIII. Roma: Libreria dello stato, 1926.

Sanislow, Charles A., Katherine L. Marcus and Elizabeth M. Reagan. "Long-term Outcomes in Borderline Psychopathology: Old Assumptions, Current Findings and New Directions." *Current Psychiatry Reports* 14.1 (2012): 54–61.

Sarkar, Siddarth, and Yatal Pal Singh Balhara. "Needles in Legs: A Response to Command Hallucinations." *Journal of Neuropsychiatry and Clinical Neurosciences* 24.2 (2012): E10–E12.

Saunders, Kate E.A., Keith Hawton, Sarah Fortune and Suhanthini Farrell. "Attitudes and Knowledge of Clinical Staff Regarding People Who Self-harm: A Systematic Review." *Journal of Affective Disorders* 139.3 (2012): 205–16.

Scheftel, Susan. "All the King's Horses and All the King's Men: A Case of Radical Self-Mutilation and Its Effects on an Entire Hospital." PhD Diss., Graduate Faculty in Psychology, City University of New York, 1985.

Schilder, Paul. "Remarks on the Psychophysiology of the Skin." *Psychoanalytic Review* 23 (1936): 274–85.

Schmieder, Linda Marie. "Neuropsychological Characteristics of Self-mutilating and Other Subgroups of Borderline Women." PhD Diss., Fielding Institute, 1997.

Schoppmann, S., R. Schröck, W. Schnepp and A. Büscher. "'Then I just showed her my arms....' Bodily Sensations in Moments of Alienation Related to Self-injurious Behaviour: A Hermeneutic Phenomenological Study." *Journal of Psychiatric and Mental Health Nursing* 14.6 (Sep. 2007): 587–97.

Scott, E. Hitchcock. "The Body as Testament: A Phenomenological Study of Chronic Self-mutilation by Women Who Are Dissociative." PhD, The Union Institute, 1999.

Scott, Forbes, and Marshall. "Feigned Diseases." *The Cyclopædia of Practical Medicine: Comprising Treatises on the Nature and Treatment of Diseases, Materia Medica and Therapuetics, Medical Jurisprudence, etc., etc.* Ed. John Forbes, Alexander Tweedie and John Connolly. Vol. 2 EME-ISC. London: Sherwood, Gilbert, and Piper, and Baldwin and Cradock; Whittaker, Treacher, & Co, 1833. 133–57. At: https://archive.org/details/cyclopaedi-aprac00dunggoog

"Self-mutilation by Soldiers." *British Medical Journal* 22 May 1915: 899–900.

Seuse, Heinrich. *The Life of Blessed Henry Suso by Himself.* Christian Classics Ethereal Library. http://www.ccel.org/ccel/suso/susolife.pdf Accessed 3 Jan. 2014.

Seymour, Dr. "St. George's Hospital. Clinical Lecture." *Lancet* 5 May 1832: 134–36.
_____. "Looking Back." *Lancet* 7 May 1910: 1279.

Shank, Theodore. "Ron Athey: Self Mutilation as Religious Experience." *Beyond the Boundaries: American Alternative Theatre.* New and enlarged edition of *American Alternative Theatre.* 1982. New ed. Ann Arbor: University of Michigan Press, 2002. 221–24.

Sharma, H.R. "A Mirror of Hospital Practice. An Extraordinary Case of Self-Mutilation." *Indian Medical Gazette* 65 (June 1930): 327–28.

Sheridan, Alan. *Michel Foucault: The Will to Truth.* 1980. London and New York: Routledge, 1990.

Shimizu, A., and I. Mizuta. "Male Genital Self-mutilation: A Case Report." *British Journal of Medical Psychology* 68.2 (June 1995): 187–89.

Siegel, Matthew, Briana Milligan, Douglas Robbins and Glenn Prentice. "Electroconvulsive Therapy in an Adolescent with Autism and Bipolar I Disorder." *Journal of ECT* 28.4 (2012): 252.

Simpson, C. Augustus. "Darmatitis [sic] Factitia and Neurotic Gangræne." *Journal of Cutaneous Diseases* 35.6 (Aug. 1917): 493–97.

Simpson, Cynthia Anne. "An Exploratory Study of Self-Mutilation." PhD Diss., University of Kansas, 1981.

Sinani, Fatos, Gentian Vyshka and Besim Ymaj. "Self-infliction of Faked Gunshot Wounds in Absence of Overt Psychopathology." *Forensic Science International* 206.1–3 (2011): e1-e4.

[Smith, Andy.] "Andy Smith." *Self-Harm: Perspectives from Personal Experience.* Ed. Louise Roxanne Pembroke. 17–19.

Sneddon, I.B. "Dermatitis artefacta." *Proceedings of the Royal Society of Medicine* 70.11 (Nov. 1977): 754–55.

Soliman Ben Said. Poster. Weber, [Papers] Box 84, Folder 4.

Stadelmann, Hermann. *Die strafbaren Fälle der Selbstverletzung nach schweitzerischem Recht.* Zürich: J. Rüegg Söhne, 1932. Dissertation, Zürich, 1932.

Stokes, John H. "The Effect on the Skin of Emotional and Nervous States. II. Masochism and Other Sex Complexes in the Background of Neurogenous Dermatitis." *Archives of Dermatology and Syphilis* 22 (1930): 803–10.

Strabo. *The Geography of Strabo.* Loeb Classical Library 1928. At penelope.uchicago. edu/Thayer/E/Roman/Texts/Strabo/ 12H*.html Accessed 19 July 2013.

Stroch, Daniel. "Self-castration." *Journal of the American Medical Association* 36.4 (1901): 270.

Strong, Marilee. *A Bright Red Scream: Self-Mutilation and the Language of Pain.* New York: Viking, 1998.

Sullivan, Nikki. *Tattooed Bodies: Subjectivity, Textuality, Ethics, Pleasure.* Connecticut and London: Praeger, 2001.

Sutton, Richard F. "Trichotillomania." *Journal of the American Medical Association* 63.24 (1914): 2126–28.

Taylor, Gary. *Castration: An Abbreviated History of Western Manhood.* London, New York: Routledge, 2000.

Temple, Bogusia, and Jennifer Harris. "The Devil in the Detail: Producing an Account of Self-Harm." *Qualitative Report* 5.1–2 (May 2000): http://www.nova. edu/ssss/QR/QR5-1/temple.html

Thompson, Mark. *American Character: The Curious Life of Charles Fletcher Lummis and the Rediscovery of the Southwest.* New York: Arcade Publishing, 2001.

Tinklepaugh, Otto Leif. "The Self-mutilation of a Male Macacus Rhesus Monkey." *Journal of Mammalogy* 9.4 (Nov. 1928): 293–300.

Toch, Hans. *Men in Crisis: Human Breakdowns in Prison.* With contributions by John J. Gibbs, Robert Johnson and James G. Fox. Chicago: Aldine, 1975.

Triggle, Nick. "Nurses Back Supervised Self-harm." *BBC News* 25 April 2006. News. bbc.co.uk/2/hi/health/9492834.stm Accessed 13 Sep. 2013.

Troisier, S. "Aspects actuels de la pathologie carcéral en France." Special issue, "Pathologie Résultant de la Privation de la Liberté." Société de Médecine de Charleroi et Fédération Nationale des Anciens Prisonniers de Guerre, Charleroi, 12 Sep. 1982. *Revue Médicale de Liège* 38.20 (15 Oct. 1983): 765–71.

Tsai, Allan. "Sacred Cuttings: Self-Mutilation

and the Soul." *Psychological Perspectives: A Quarterly Journal of Jungian Thought* 43.1 (2002): 82–91.

Tsiolkas, Christos. *The Jesus Man.* Sydney: Random House Australia, 1999.

Tuttle, Gordon E., Jr. "Sexual Orientation, Caretaker Abuse and Borderline Personality Disorder." PhD Diss., Boston University, 1997.

"The Ubiquity of Suicide." Review of *Man against Himself,* by Karl A. Menninger. *British Medical Journal* 11 Feb. 1939: 273. Clipping, pasted onto article "Moral Imbecility" by A.F. Tredgold. Weber, [Papers] Box 84, Folder 4.

Ulnik, Jorge. *Skin in Psychoanalysis.* London: Karnac, 2007.

"United Services Medical Society; Malingering." Clipping, *Lancet* 26 Nov. 1910: 1554. Weber, [Papers] Box 84, Folder 2.

Van Dyke, Paul. *An Investigation of Self-mutilation at the Texas Prison System in Terms of the Minnesota Multiphasic Personality Inventory and Other Measures.* Thesis presented to the Faculty of the Graduate School of the University of Texas in Partial Fulfillment of the Requirements for the Degree of Master of Arts, University of Texas, 1953.

Vertigo. Dir. Alfred Hitchcock. Paramount Pictures, 1958.

Wachtel, Lee E., Richard Jaffe and Charles H. Kellner. "Electroconvulsive Therapy for Psychotropic-refractory Bipolar Affective Disorder and Severe Self-injury and Aggression in an 11-Year-Old Autistic Boy." *European Child & Adolescent Psychiatry* 20.3 (March 2011): 147–52.

Walker, Norman. "A Lecture on Dermatitis Artefacta." *British Medical Journal* 18 June 1910: 1481–83.

_____. *An Introduction to Dermatology.* 1899. 7th Edition. Edinburgh: W. Green & Son, 1922.

Wallenstein, Matthew B. and Matthew K. Nock. "Physical Exercise as a Treatment for Non-suicidal Self-injury: Evidence from a Single-case Study." *American Journal of Psychiatry* 164.2 (Feb. 2007): 350–51.

Waller, Kevin. Preface. *Scarred for Life: The True Story of a Self-harmer.* Balmain, NSW: Limelight, 2002. viii–ix.

Wan, S.P., D.W. Soderdahl and E.M. Blight, Jr. "Nonpsychotic Genital Self-mutilation." *Urology* 26.3 (Sep. 1985): 286–87.

Waugaman, Richard M. "Genital Self-mutilation." Letter. *Psychiatric Services* 50.10 (Oct. 1999): 1362.

Weber, F. Parkes. "The Association of Hysteria with Malingering: The Phylogenetic Aspect of Hysteria as Pathological Exaggeration (or Disorder) of Tertiary (Nervous) Sex Characters." *Lancet* 2 Dec. 1911: 1542–43.

_____. [Papers.] Self-mutilations for various purposes, needle-swallowing etc. Hysterical malingering and simulation or aggravation of symptoms without hysteria. Some "shell-shock" cases. 1901–1954. Request Arch. & MSS PP/FPW/B.163. Wellcome Library, London.

_____. "Possible Pitfalls in Life Assurance Examination and Remarks on Malingering." Offprint from *British Medical Journal* 9 Feb. 1918: 167–69; also London: C.E. Gray, 1918.

Weigert-Vowinkel, Edith. "The Cult and Mythology of the Magna Mater from the Standpoint of Psychoanalysis." Trans. Frances M. von Wimmersperg. *Psychiatry: The Journal of the Biology and the Pathology of Interpersonal Relations* 1 (Aug. 1938): 347–78.

Weissman, Myrna M. "Wrist Cutting: Relationship Between Clinical Observations and Epidemiological Findings." *Archives of General Psychiatry* 32.9 (Sep. 1975): 1166–71.

Wetsman, Howard C. "Borderline Personality Disorder Afloat." *Navy Medicine* 81.2 (Mar.-Apr. 1990): 20–23. At https://archive.org/details/NavyMedicineVol.81 No.2March-april1990 Accessed 30 Dec. 2013.

Whiting, Marcus. "Self-castration: A Case." *Peoria Medical Monthly: A Practitioner's Journal* 5.5 (Sep. 1884): 297–300.

Whitney, Lynnette Erin. "Social Work Students' Knowledge About Issues Related to Self-mutilation." MSW Diss., California State University, Long Beach, 2004.

Whittle, Louise, and The National Self-Harm Network. *The Clothier Report: Implications for People Who Self-harm.* Brochure. National Self-Harm Network: Campaigning for the Rights and Understanding of People Who Self-harm. In National Self Harm Network. *Self-injury: Resources and Information for People Who Self-injure, Health and Mental Health Professionals, Relatives and Advocates.* [London: Self-Harm Network, 1998.] British Library.

Winnicott, D.W. "Transitional Objects and Transitional Phenomena: A Study of the First Not-me Possessions." *International Journal of Psycho-analysis* 34 (1953): 89–97.

Yealland, Lewis R. *Hysterical Disorders of Warfare.* London: Macmillan, 1918.

Young, Robert, Vincent Riordan, and Cameron Stark. "Perinatal and Psychosocial Circumstances Associated with Risk of Attempted Suicide, Non-suicidal Self-injury and Psychiatric Service Use: A Longitudinal Study of Young People." *BMC Public Health* 11 (2011): 875. At http://www.biomedcentral.com/1471–2458/11/875 Accessed 24 June 2014

Zanarini, Mary C., Corina S. Laudate, Frances R. Frankenburg, D. Bradford Reich and Garrett Fitzmaurice. "Predictors of Self-Mutilation in Patients with Borderline Personality Disorder: A 10-Year Follow-up." *Journal of Psychiatric Research* 45.6 (June 2011): 823–28.

Žižek, Slavoj. *Welcome to the Desert of the Real.* www.lacan.com/desertsym.htm Accessed 14 Sep. 2013.

Zuppinger, Werner, Dr. *Der Schutz gegen sich selbst im Polizeirecht.* Dissertation. Winterthur: P.G. Keller, 1956.

Index